The Best Mexican and Central American Travel Tips

The Best Mexican and Central American Travel Tips

John Whitman

HarperPerennial
A Division of HarperCollinsPublishers

**To Donna,
my wife and traveling partner,
who has experienced the roller coaster ride of
Central America and Mexico with me.**

HarperCollins books may be purchased for educational, business, or sales promotional use. For information, please write to: Special Markets Department, HarperCollinsPublishers, Inc., 10 East 53rd Street, New York, New York 10022.

Map: Donna Whitman of Creative Designs

FIRST EDITION

Library of Congress Cataloging-in-Publication Data
Whitman, John.
    The best Mexican and Central American travel tips / John Whitman. — 1st ed.
        p.   cm.
    Includes index.
    ISBN 0-06-273268-4
    1. Mexico—Guidebooks. 2. Central America—Guidebooks.
I. Whitman, John. II. Title.
F1209.W44 1994   94-25950
917.204'835—dc20

94 95 96 97 98 ◆/RRD 10 9 8 7 6 5 4 3 2 1

Contents

Foreword

Things should be made as simple as possible, but not simpler.

—Albert Einstein

There's an old saying: "There's my truth, your truth, and the truth." This book is about my truth regarding travel to Central America and Mexico. And, my truth is based on keeping things simple. For the purposes of this guide Central America includes Belize, Costa Rica, Guatemala, and Honduras. Not covered are El Salvador, Nicaragua, and Panama. While people do travel through these three areas, it is often at considerable risk. In being truthful my main concerns are your safety and satisfaction. However, you will be quite safe if you follow the tips included throughout the guide. Central America and Mexico offer an extraordinary range of memorable experiences, some highly enjoyable, others equally annoying. Extensive travel throughout this region is like a roller coaster ride with the highs very high and the lows right at the bottom. This guide tells it like it is. In that way, you're going to save lots of money ($100 at a minimum), time, and trouble. You'll also find it simple to read, enjoyable, and straight to the point. It's filled with specific information to make the very most of your trip and avoid most of the common mistakes made by the typical traveler (including me). It tells you what you really need to know to get what you want. If you disagree with some of my comments or tips, write in. If any of the recommended companies exceed or don't match your expectations, let me know. If you'd like to add a few tips to the guide, I'd appreciate it very much. Put your seat belts on (as if that were always possible) and enjoy the ride!

John Whitman
P.O. Box 202
Long Lake, MN 55356

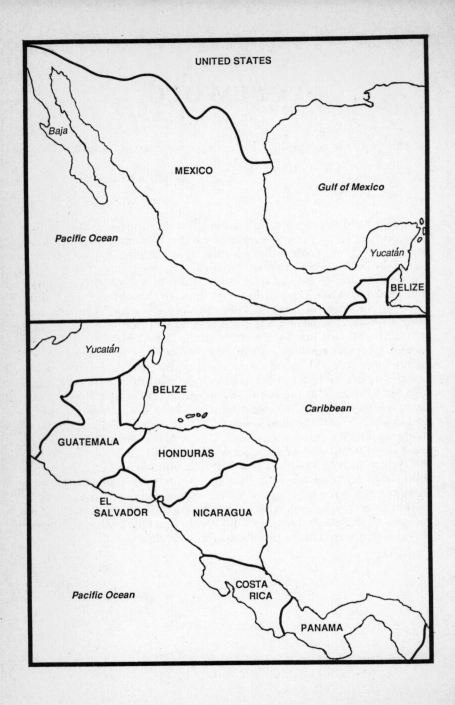

Travel Documents

You'll need certain documents to travel freely through Central America and Mexico.

Passports

Passports are required in Central America, but not in Mexico. Still, get one because it's the best form of identification and most useful in cashing traveler's checks. If you already have one, verify that it will be valid for the entire length of your trip. Otherwise, apply for a new one.

Kinds of Passports
- Ask for the special 48-page passport when you apply. It provides added space for the visas you may need (see p. 3).
- The new passport contains inks, graphics, and a kinegram (like a credit-card hologram) to stem the growing tide of forgeries.

When to Apply for a Passport
- Apply for a passport as far in advance as possible.
- If you need visas, apply months in advance (see p. 3).
- Passports are issued on the basis of the beginning day of your intended trip. If you will be leaving shortly, emphasize this.
- You can pay extra for quick turnaround (usually 14 days).
- It is possible to get a passport in as little as a day in emergencies.
- The following agencies specialize in handling quick turnarounds of both passports and visas for a fee (quite expensive):

Travisa
2122 P Street NW
Washington, DC 20037
Tel: (800) 222-2589
(202) 463-6166

Washington Passport and
Visa Service
2318 18th Street NW, Suite 200
Washington, DC 20009
Tel: (800) 272-7776
(202) 234-7667

Applying for a First Passport
- To get your first passport, apply in person. Younger children (under 12) need not apply in person.

- The passport agency is in your telephone directory under U.S. Government Offices. The service may be handled by a federal, state, or probate courthouse or at a designated post office.
- Call for hours. Ask about the least busy days and hours. This saves you hours of waiting.
- Passport Application: You will need to fill out a passport application in person. Your social security number is critical. So is proof of your identity and U.S. citizenship. Ask about this when calling.
- Two Passport Photos: You'll need 2 passport photos, taken within the last 6 months.
- Many agencies issuing passports now offer a passport photo service as well. Ask what the fee will be and the cost of *extra* prints. Then call several passport photo studios as well as the local branch of the American Automobile Association (AAA) for cost comparison. A separate trip might save you money.
- Get 2 spares for emergencies and additional photos for visas (see p. 3).

Passport Fees

- You pay passport and execution fees. Call ahead to see what the total charges will be.
- When you call, ask how the payment should be made. Some offices accept credit cards, although at an additional fee.

Applying if You Have Had a Passport Before

- If you have had a passport during the last 8 years and appeared in person for your first passport, you can apply for your new passport by mail..
- Call the nearest passport agency for Passport Office Form DSP-82, "Application for Passport by Mail." Fill it out, sign, and date it. Attach your old passport, 2 up-to-date passport photos, and the required payment.
- If your name has changed, include a certified copy of your marriage certificate, or of the change-of-name papers.
- Send the passport by registered mail and keep the receipt.
- The following center (set up for mail-in applications) will usually get your passport back to you within 14 days:

Passport Center
P.O. Box 371971
Pittsburgh, PA 15250-07971

Checking and Protecting Your Passport

- When your passport arrives in the mail, check it. If there is an error, return the passport to have it corrected. Never write in, alter, or mutilate any portion of a passport, as this would make it invalid.
- Make 2 photocopies of the information contained in your passport. File one of the photocopies in a safe place and take the other with you. Don't carry it with your passport! Once abroad you can put the passport in a hotel safe and carry the photocopy with you as identification.

If You Lose Your Passport in the United States or Canada

- If your passport is lost or stolen in the United States, contact the Passport Office, Department of State, Washington, DC 20524 *immediately*.
- Canadian citizens should report lost or stolen passports to the closest Canadian passport office (one in each province).

Visas

Visas are special notations and stamps, added to your passport by officials of foreign countries, which allow you to enter and leave these countries. The countries in this guide do not require citizens of the United States to have visas except for study, long-term stays, and for business travel. Canadians may have to get visas for some countries. Regulations change frequently, so ask to be sure.

- Business travelers should get visas well in advance. If you can carry on your business discreetly, skip them. If you're obviously on business or make repeated trips to an area for business, get visas.
- Although a visa is required for foreign study, get one only if you intend to stay longer than entry documents allow.
- If you plan to travel to South America, get a leaflet entitled Visa Requirements of Foreign Governments (Passport Office Publication M-264) from the passport agency. Write the embassy or consulate of the foreign country to get a visa application form with information on fees and procedure.
- Canadians should contact a travel agency or passport office. Information is in the Travel Information Manual, which agents should have.

Special Tips on Getting Visas

- Use registered mail and keep the receipt.
- Include a check for the visa as well as enough money to cover *return postage* by registered mail.

- Always apply for visas at the foreign consulate or embassy in the city nearest you. You'll find the addresses in the Congressional Directory, found in most major libraries.
- In Canada refer to the Travel Information Manual previously mentioned.
- Allow an extra 3 to 6 weeks for *each* necessary visa.

Entry Documents

Each country has its own entry requirements. Some stamp your passport, others require you to carry a stamped paper. In Mexico the paper is known as a tourist card (*tarjeta de turista*). Always carry your stamped passport (or a photocopy) and any stamped document (or a photocopy) with you. If you do not have the documents, you can be arrested. If you intend to stay for long periods of time or plan on frequently traveling to and from a specific country, contact the tourist office for up-to-date regulations regarding such visits. Some may require visas. The National Tourist Offices are listed on p. 25.

- Don't alter or mutilate these documents in any way.
- Avoid getting them wet. Officials resent faded documents.
- Don't lose the documents. If photocopied, you'll have an easier time replacing them.
- You must have the document to leave the country.

Travel with Minors

Any parent who wants to take a minor into Central America or Mexico must have one of two affidavits notarized ("Affidavit of Sole Custody" or "Affidavit of Parental Consent"). Contact appropriate tourist offices for affidavits).

- Officials often don't ask for this form, but they can. Without it, you may be denied entry.

Minors Traveling Alone

If you're under 18 and want to travel without your parents, have 2 copies of a notarized letter signed by both parents stating that this is okay.

International Student and Youth ID Cards

If you're a full-time student or young person, get an International Student Identification or Youth Card.

• The following organizations specialize in both youth and student travel. Contact them for current regulations. Many universities have branch offices:

Council on International
  Educational Exchange
  (CIEE)
205 East 42nd Street
New York, NY 10017
Tel: (212) 661-1450

STA
6560 North Scottsdale Road,
  Suite F-100
Scottsdale, AZ 85253

Tel: (800) 777-0112
  (602) 596-5151

Travel Cuts
187 College Street
Toronto, ON M5T 1P7
Canada
Tel: (416) 979-2406

International Youth Hostel Cards

You'll find most hostels in Mexico and a few in Costa Rica. If you plan to use them, get a card in advance

American Youth Hostels
1108 K Street NW
Washington, DC 20005
Tel: (202) 783-4943

All mail should be sent to:

American Youth Hostels
P.O. Box 28607
Central Station
Washington, DC 20038

Canadian Hostelling
  Association
18 Byward Market
Ottawa, Ontario K1N 7A1
Tel: (613) 241-1400

Bring a sleeping sack (like a sheet), which you can make yourself or pick up from:

The Metropolitan New York
  Council
75 Spring Street
New York, NY 10012
Tel: (212) 431-7100

International Camping Carnet

If you plan to camp out, it may help to have an International Camping Carnet (see pp. 158–162). The card is available from:

National Campers and Hikers Association
4804 Transit Road
Building 2
Depew, NY 14043
Tel: (716) 668-6242

Insurance

If you carry any insurance at all, it will probably cover part of your trip. Exceptions to this general rule, and additional information on the subject, are detailed below.

Accident Insurance
- Check to see whether your policy is valid abroad.
- Many auto and travel clubs offer free accident insurance.

Baggage Insurance
- Avoid the need for this insurance by traveling with carryon luggage and by leaving valuables at home (this includes engagement rings and wedding bands).
- If you can't, ask about a *personal articles floater.* It is most useful for expensive camera equipment.

Car Insurance
- Drive your own car only in Belize and Mexico. If you don't have 4-wheel drive, skip Belize. See pp. 95–96.

Evacuation Insurance
- If you're seriously injured while abroad, you may require surgery or blood transfusions. If possible, get back to Canada or the United States. (see p. 24).
- If you have a serious illness, take out this insurance. Study the fine print to make sure it covers *pre-existing* conditions.

Health Insurance
- Medicare and Medicaid don't cover you for travel abroad. Buy temporary health insurance as necessary.

- Most health policies cover you, but ask. You'll pay for expenses abroad to be reimbursed later.
- Carry your insurance card and a credit card. These help you get care quickly and could save your life.
- Costs for medical treatment abroad are low.

Home Insurance

- Your home may not be covered if you are away for more than 30 days. Check with your agent for advice.

Life Insurance

- Flight insurance is basically a ripoff. Flying is—statistically—incredibly safe. The exceptions are the small commuter lines (not up to FAA standards).
- Travel and auto clubs often provide life and accident insurance to members.
- Many credit card companies now offer *free* flight insurance if you charge the flight to the card.
- Some travel agencies offer *free* insurance to customers.

Trip Cancellation Insurance

- Some airline tickets (charter and special fares) have a rigid and steep penalty for cancellation. For these consider trip cancellation insurance.
- Good insurance covers *pre-existing* conditions (an illness already known about or treated for).
- It should cover all activities, such as biking, hiking, parasailing, riding horses, riding motorbikes, scuba diving, snorkeling, white water rafting, and so on. Many policies exclude any kind of strenuous, outdoor activity. These policies are worthless.
- You can get trip cancellation insurance from travel agencies or directly from the following companies (*read the fine print*):

International Travelers
   Assistance Association
P.O. Box 10623
Baltimore, MD 21285
Tel: (800) 732-5309

Tele-Trip Company, Inc.
(Mutual of Omaha)
3201 Farnam Street
P.O. Box 31685
Omaha, NE 68131
Tel: (800) 228-9792

The Travelers Companies
1 Tower Square
Hartford, CT 06183
Tel: (800) 243-3174

Travel Guard International
1145 Clark Street
Stevens Point, WI 54481

Tel: (800) 782-5151
Travel Insurance Services
P.O. Box 299
Walnut Creek, CA 94596
Tel: (800) 937-1387

Documents for a Trusted Friend

Following is a list of things you should leave with a trusted friend or relative. Although your trip may go without a hitch, this simple precaution could save you an incredible amount of trouble and time.

Itinerary: Come as close to places and dates as possible. If you know the name, telephone, and fax numbers of hotels include them.

List of traveler's check numbers: Carry a list of these numbers, and leave a duplicate list at home—just in case you lose everything, including the list of traveler's check numbers.

Numbers of credit cards: Photocopy all your credit cards. Leave one copy with a friend.

Number, date, and place of issue of passport: Photocopy this information and leave it with a friend. Carry a reduced photocopy with you.

Airline ticket numbers, date and place of issue: If you want to get reimbursed for lost or stolen airline tickets, have these numbers readily available—it will really help. Carry a copy with you.

Money

Your trip will cost whatever you're willing to spend. You may want to travel for a few months on next to nothing. Or, you may want to splurge on a once-in-a-lifetime experience which only lasts a week. There's an old saying, "If you don't open your eyes, you'll open your purse." Hopefully, with the tips in this guide your eyes will be wide open so that your purse only opens as far as you want it to. This section is only a small part of that eye-opening experience (the other chapters contain hundreds of cost-cutting ideas).

How Much Will A Trip Cost?

You probably have a certain amount of money to spend. Following are a few things to keep in mind:

Normal Trip Expenses

How much you spend will depend on how willing you are to trade time and energy to save money. If you're wily and willing, you can save a lot. However, a bare-bones budget will include the following:
- Medicines and medical preparation.
- Basic travel gear which you don't already have.
- The expense of getting to your destination.
- Entry and exit fees from each country.
- Travel within the region.
- Places to stay.
- Food.
- Entry fees to places of interest.
- Purchases of any kind.
- Costs for any special interest activity.
- Reserve money for emergencies.

Typical Costs by Country

BELIZE

Small entry and exit fees. Bus travel is extremely inexpensive. Plane travel is reasonable. Car rental is exorbitant. Getting to atolls and isolated cayes (islands) by boat is expensive. Places to stay range in price from next to nothing (wooden huts in isolated areas) to $200 dollars. Jungle lodges are extremely expensive. There are very *few* hotels in the moderate range ($40-$50), and this is a real problem. A local will pay several dollars for a basic, hearty meal. More expensive restaurants vary in value for your money. Food in stores tends to be expensive and limited. The amount you pay in markets varies with your bargaining skill. Variety of available food is a problem, especially on islands. Entry fees to local sites (very few) are reasonable. Overall assessment: The best of Belize is expensive, although many areas on the mainland can be seen at modest prices. Special interest activities are expensive.

COSTA RICA

Small entry and exit fees. Bus travel is extremely inexpensive. Plane travel is reasonable with prices rising rapidly. Car rental is exorbitant. Getting to Isla del Coco (Coco Island) is very expensive, but few people go there. Places to stay range in price from several dollars to $200 or more. Fishing and jungle lodges are extremely expensive. There are *many* hotels in the moderate range, often discounted in the off season. A local will pay several dollars for a good, hearty meal. Food in stores tends to be expensive and limited. Markets have lots of fresh food at reasonable prices. Fresh fruit (over 200 hundred varieties) is exceptional. Entry fees to local sites are low. Tip: Don't pay to get into the National Theater (have a fresh juice in the restaurant, ask for a token for the bathroom, and see the theater for nothing). Overall assessment: You can see the best of Costa Rica on a moderate budget. Special interest activities are expensive.

GUATEMALA

Entry and exit fees moderate. Bus travel extraordinarily inexpensive. Mini-bus and taxis also reasonable, even for long-distance legs. Plane travel reasonable, but expensive by local standards. Hotels are an excellent value, many falling into the budget to moderate range. A local will pay several dollars for a so-so meal. Since meals are reasonably priced in more expensive hotels and restaurants, they are a good value. Food in stores tends to be reasonably priced but limited. Food in markets is plentiful and inexpensive. Entry fees to local sites are generally low with the exception of Tikal. Overall assessment: You can see the best of Guatemala on a low to moderate budget. Special interest activities are presently limited.

HONDURAS

Entry and exit fees moderate. Bus travel is extremely inexpensive. Mini-bus and taxis are reasonable. Plane travel is reasonable. Hotels fall into all categories. Don't let anyone tell you that there are nothing but expensive hotels on Roatan. There are many budget and moderate hotels there as well. *Price and quality are not necessarily related.*

Meals are reasonably priced but vary in quality. Food in stores is reasonably priced but limited. Entry fees are low. Overall assessment: You can see much of the country on a low to moderate budget. Special interest activities are moderate (rafting) to expensive (diving).

MEXICO
Entry and exit fees are low. Train travel is a steal. Bus travel is inexpensive. Car rental is very expensive. Toll roads are outrageously priced. Taxis vary from moderate to expensive. The metro in Mexico City is the best travel bargain in the world. There are many budget and moderate hotels in areas appealing to Mexicans. Prices in many touristic areas are inflated, but bargaining hard is expected in off-peak periods. Small, intimate inns and finer resorts are extremely expensive. You can find excellent, filling meals for a few dollars. More expensive meals in finer restaurants are generally a good value. Food in stores is reasonably priced and plentiful in larger towns, less so in smaller ones. Food in markets is inexpensive. Entry fees vary from reasonable to overpriced. Price is usually related to whether a spectacle or site would appeal as much to Mexicans as to foreigners. If so, the price drops. Special interest activities are extremely varied and range from moderate to expensive.

Carrying Money

Once you've decided where you want to go and how much you plan to spend, how you carry your money becomes the next decision.

Traveler's Checks
Each year, more than a million travelers lose cash due to theft and negligence. For this reason, rely on traveler's checks.
- Traveler's checks are available from many banks. There is suspicion about lesser-known traveler's checks. American Express and Bank of America checks remain the easiest to cash—and even they can be hard to cash in rural or remote areas.

Fee-Free Traveler's Checks
Normally, you pay a 1 percent service fee when buying traveler's checks. However, if you'll look around, you'll find traveler's checks that you can buy without paying this fee.
- Many travel clubs and banks offer fee-free traveler's checks to members or preferred customers.

When You Buy Traveler's Checks

- Count them. Occasionally a check is missing. Sign them as instructed.
- Each traveler should carry individual checks. This divides the responsibility and allows each person freedom in using them.
- Get checks in varying value. Sometimes it's hard to cash large denomination checks. At other times you want to convert just enough money to get by for a short time.
- When traveling in Mexico, get some checks from American Express and some from Bank of America. Some banks will only cash one or the other. It sounds absurd, but that's the way it is. In Central America the American Express checks are most easily recognized and cashed.
- Keep a record of all checks used. The simplest way: write all the numbers down and strike the number off the list as it is cashed. This will be essential information if you lose remaining checks.
- Don't carry this record in the same place as your checks. If your checks get ripped off or lost, you'll lose the record as well.

Credit Cards

Carrying two credit cards makes sense for travel in this region.

Credit Card Basics

Most major hotels and restaurants now accept credit cards, although a few will only take a specific company's card, often adding a surcharge to the bill. Credit cards are essential for renting cars and paying for plane flights.

- The best credit cards are American Express and Visa.

Advantages of Credit Cards

- Credit cards are safer than cash, because if lost or stolen, you have limited liability.
- You don't need to carry large amounts of cash .
- Thieves are less interested in credit cards than cash. Still, they will steal them so protect them like cash.
- If you plan to rent a car, you need a credit card or a large amount of cash for the deposit.
- Some credit cards cover the deductible on car rentals abroad. This is very important if you plan to rent a car in Central America or Mexico (see pp. 95–96).
- Credit card companies allow you to use their money on a float— you may not have to pay the bill for a month or two.

- Companies convert all charges to dollars at the rate of exchange prevailing at the time the charges are submitted. You avoid the currency exchange hassle by using the card.
- *Disadvantage*: Some hotels, restaurants, and shops add a surcharge to the bill for their use. Ask in advance if any surcharge will be added. You may decide to pay the bill in cash (*efectivo*) instead. Surcharges are most common in Costa Rica.

How to Bring Money Into the Region

The following tips will help you avoid common pitfalls in carrying money, giving you peace of mind and an edge on the market.

- Carry fifty to one hundred $1 bills depending upon your length of stay. Use small bills for everything from paying a departure tax to a cab ride. Although they are not legal tender, you'd never know it by the way they're snapped up throughout the region.
- The bulk is a nuisance outweighed by usefulness.
- Carry as much U.S. currency as you can afford to lose. Best are smaller notes—five, ten, and twenties.
- *Note that $100-dollar bills are impossible to cash, because counterfeit notes in this denomination have flooded the area.*
- Canadians should convert their money into U.S. currency, because Canadian currency is a hassle to use and exchange.
- U.S. currency (hard currency) is worth more in a bank than traveler's checks and even more when dealing on the black market.
- Carry this money in different places on your body as outlined in the section on Protecting Property (see pp. 173–177).

Medical Preparations

Over 60 percent of travelers get sick during a trip abroad. Even the most scrupulous traveler following *all* the standard travel advice can get sick. *When you travel to developing countries, especially to inland and remote areas, you run a risk of illness which is much greater than you'd run in more developed countries.* The hints in this chapter can help you prevent major health problems.

Preparing for the Trip

Before traveling, do several things. See a doctor and get prescriptions for appropriate medications, update or get vaccinations as recommended, have a dental checkup, and take out any appropriate insurance. If you are pregnant or have a chronic health problem, follow the tips outlined below. After reading this chapter, also read the section on Staying Healthy Once Abroad (see p. 219). Reading this additional chapter before traveling abroad is important, because it will help you decide what medications to buy in advance. Read it before you see a doctor so that you can get up-to-date advice on specific questions you may have.

Seeing A Doctor

Go to a public travel clinic or see a doctor specializing in tropical medicine. Travel clinics are in constant contact with the Centers for Disease Control in Atlanta. Any doctor specializing in tropical medicine will be equally well informed. If you have any problems after your trip, this is the person you're going to want to go to. If you have trouble locating such a doctor, send an 8 1/2 x 11, stamped (presently 98 cents), self-addressed envelope to the following address:

Traveler's Health and Immunization Services
148 Highland Avenue
Newton, MA 02165
Tel: (617) 527-4003

- Special tip: know your blood type. This could save your life.

Inoculations

Get vaccinations in Canada or the United States before traveling abroad. Doctors sometimes disagree on what vaccinations and medications are appropriate. The longer you travel and the more remote your destination, the more you need protection. The vaccinations suggested in this chapter help prevent the most serious illnesses, but they are not foolproof. If you behave like a fool, you can still end up getting the very diseases you've tried to prevent.

- Many vaccinations are free or inexpensive at public clinics. Call around to save as much as $50 to $100 on shots.
- Start immunizations well ahead of your trip.
- Some have side effects which could affect your trip.
- Keep a complete record of your inoculations.

Cholera

Cholera occurs sporadically in all countries covered in this guide, but most often in Guatemala and Mexico. It is caused by bacteria. The main symptom is acute diarrhea. The disease is quite dangerous, especially in children.

- Do not get inoculations for cholera. The reliability of these shots is questionable. Side effects are common.
- Journalists traveling to Honduras must be vaccinated against this disease. Avoid revealing your occupation.
- A new oral vaccine is being developed and has been 90 percent effective in tests. Ask about it.

Diptheria (see Tetanus)

Hepatitis

Hepatitis is a viral disease resulting in inflammation of the liver. Hepatitis is spread by contaminated food and drink, contaminated blood, as well as sexual contact with an infected person. There are several types of hepatitis. New serums have and are being developed. Ask about the latest improvements to make an informed decision. If you get hepatitis, a good diet and rest is the only cure. Some forms of the disease can be fatal. Take prevention seriously.

- Gamma (immune) globulin can be fairly effective in preventing hepatitis A (infectious hepatitis), but not 100 percent. Dosage relates to trip duration.
- Since the shot provides only short-term protection, get it only if you'll be traveling to more remote areas with poor sanitation. Get shots about 14 days ahead of your trip.
- Two new vaccines, Havrix and Vaqta, may be approved by the FDA by the time you read this. These should be more reliable and longer lasting (with boosters) than gamma globulin.
- Gamma (immune) globulin interferes with inoculations for measles, mumps, and rubella. Allow time to space vaccinations appropriately.

- Hepatitis B (serum hepatitis) is becoming more common, although only 5 to 10 percent of the population in the U.S. has been exposed to it. In other countries the rate is much higher. Unfortunately, only about half of the people who have this disease show symptoms and become unknowing carriers.
- Hepatitis B serum is roughly 96 percent effective against hepatitis B, which can be debilitating at best, deadly at worst.
- Hepatitis B serum is given in three doses over a 6-month period. Shots are very expensive. A new oral vaccine (more expensive) has been developed and is given over a shorter period of time. Ask about it.
- If you plan to travel extensively in developing countries, get vaccinated no matter what the cost. It is doubly important to be immunized if you have frequent sexual contact or can in any way come in contact with someone else's blood—almost all health professionals now get vaccinated against this disease.
- Some doctors recommend a blood test before giving you the serum. If the cost of the test is low, have it. However, if the test is expensive, skip it.
- If pregnant, have the test to rule out any chance of giving the disease to your child.
- All children should be vaccinated as soon after birth as possible (ideally, within 12 hours).
- Booster shots are controversial. Most doctors do not recommend them.
- Hepatitis C is a third, rare strain. There is not yet any protection against it, although it can be extremely serious.
- Hepatitis E, a fourth strain, is serious if you're pregnant. Otherwise, it tends to run its course without permanent damage. As with hepatitis C, there is no prevention yet.

Malaria

Malaria is a serious disease, yet nearly 90 percent of people traveling to malarial areas do not take preventive measures. This is an equivalent to Russian roulette with your health. In Mexico alone there are 40,000 or more cases a year in one state alone. Symptoms include aching muscles, chills, fever, and sweats. The chance of getting malaria in major tourist areas is remote, but not absent. In rural areas, the chance increases. If traveling during the wet season to any jungle area, malaria is a true threat. Prolonged stays in areas with malaria require prevention.

- Tropical or wet areas of Belize, Costa Rica, Guatemala, and Honduras are potientally dangerous.

- Following are Mexican states noted for malaria: Campeche, Chiapas, Chihuahua (May to October), Colima, Durango, Guerrero, Jalisco (May to October), Michoacán, Morelos (May to October), Nayarit, Oaxaca, Puebla (May to October), Quintana Roo, Sinaloa (May to October), Sonora (May to October), Tabasco, Veracruz, and the Yucatán.
- In theory, the simplest way to protect yourself from malaria is to protect yourself from mosquitoes (see p. 236).
- Since that's not quite as simple as it sounds, your necessary backup is *Chloroquine phosphate* (commonly sold as Aralen). These pills are usually effective against the strain of malaria found in all countries covered in this guide, but are not reliable against other strains found in other areas.
- You take one pill a week, starting the treatment 2 weeks before the trip and continuing it for 4 to 6 weeks after.
- Diarrhea and headache are possible side effects. A positive side effect is reduction of pain from arthritis.
- If you stay in a malaria-prone area for more than a year, talk to your doctor about treatment with Primaquine.
- If you travel to Panama or South America, you will need a second medication. It has many more side effects. Get to a travel clinic before going to these areas.
- **Special note**: Even if you take Chloroquine phosphate as directed, there is a slight chance of getting malaria anyway. If you develop any signs of the disease, always see a doctor specializing in tropical diseases and mention where you've been traveling. Malaria is easiest to treat in its earliest stages.

Measles
This viral disease is highly contagious. You're familiar with its red spots. Anyone who has not had measles should be immunized against it, even if you've already been vaccinated once. Most children today are routinely vaccinated, but check to be sure.

Polio (Poliomyelitis)
This highly infectious viral disease causes fever, paralysis, and permanent deformities. All doctors agree that a vaccination against this disease is essential. You may need a booster every 5 years.

Rabies
Rabies is an extremely dangerous viral disease, generally caused by a bite from an infected animal. Rabies is present in Central America

and Mexico. Few doctors recommend vaccinations against it, unless you're going to be exploring caves or are bitten by an animal abroad.

Sun Protection (see p. 241)

Tetanus/Diphtheria

Tetanus is a bacterial disease, generally caused by a wound. It's death rate is 30 percent. Diphtheria is also a bacterial disease. The death rate is roughly 10 percent. Doctors agree that all travelers should be inoculated against these diseases (covered in one shot). You may be due for a booster every 5 years.

Tuberculosis

This bacterial disease is quite common. However, your chances of getting it are remote. You get it from someone coughing on you or from unpasteurized milk. Vaccinations are recommended, especially for children.

Typhoid

Typhoid is a serious illness caused by a bacteria. Symptoms include high fever, coughing, diarrhea, fatigue, headache, and intestinal pain. It's transmitted through contaminated water or food.

- Typhoid shots are somewhat controversial. Their value can only be related to risk. If you'll be traveling to remote areas, it may well be worth the cost of this "insurance." If you are pregnant or sick with anything more serious than a cold, you should not be immunized.
- Initially, you'll get two typhoid shots one month apart. After that, boosters are effective. Boosters are recommended every 3 years. You can get three shots in one month, but this is not as effective as two shots one month apart.
- Some people have a reaction, but most have soreness only. Have shots far ahead of your trip.
- An oral vaccine (more expensive) now exists and is taken in 3 doses 2 days apart.
- Since typhoid shots are not 100 percent reliable in preventing the disease, follow tips for the prevention of diarrhea (see p. 226).

Yellow Fever

This is an acute viral disease caused by mosquito bites. Symptoms are extreme fatigue, high fever, and yellowish skin. Shots are not required except in Honduras for journalists (don't tell officials). If you intend to travel into Panama or into South America, get yellow fever shots.

Getting Health Information

Information regarding vaccinations and health precautions is continually being updated and refined. In Canada the Travel Information Offices of Health and Welfare can give you current information and health bulletins . For useful, current bulletins in the U.S. contact the Centers for Disease Control or order "Health Information for International Travel" from the Government Printing Office:

The Centers for Disease
  Control
Atlanta, GA 30333
Tel: (404) 332-4555 or
332-4559 (hotline), or
639-2888 (front desk for
  after hours emergencies).

Superintendent of Documents
U.S. Government Printing
  Office
Washington, DC 20402
Tel: (202) 783-3238

Tips on Medications

- Bring fresh drugs with you. If you're not sure about the value of older medications, call your pharmacist.
- Certain medications are affected by heat. Ask about this when you buy yours. If they will deteriorate rapidly in the Tropics, keep them as cool as possible with common-sense measures.
- Carry enough of any prescription to last a week or two beyond your expected stay.
- Keep all prescription drugs in the original containers. Some of these containers are huge, so ask the pharmacist to divide the amount into two smaller containers, both clearly labeled. Throw empty containers away as drugs are used up.
- If your drugs contain narcotics or controlled substances, then carry your doctor's prescription with you. Just photocopy this before having the prescription filled.
- Get the generic name of any drug you're using. Many drugs are available over the counter in Central America and Mexico at extremely low prices.
- Never put drugs into luggage that will be checked on a plane. Always carry them with you.

- Bring a spare pair of glasses with you in a hard case. A lens can be duplicated from the pieces of broken glasses.

First-Aid Kit

Carrying a first-aid kit makes a lot of sense, especially for longer trips. Items to pack are alcohol (rubbing in small, plastic bottle), adhesive tape, antibiotic ointment, antiseptic solution, aspirin (or similar pain killer), baking soda, bandaids, gauze, iodine, insect repellent, imodium, needle, sunscreen, and tweezers.

Special Medical Conditions

Following are a few tips on special problems which affect some people who should take special precautions while traveling.

If You're Pregnant

If you're pregnant, get suggestions from your doctor before traveling abroad. Usually, you can't have immunizations or take certain medications. Malaria pills are an exception. During early pregnancy stay out of heat, as in saunas and hot tubs. The heat is associated with birth defects. Airlines vary in their regulations as to whether or not you'll be allowed on board after a certain month in your pregnancy (usually the eighth month). Ask about such policies. If late in pregnancy, get a letter from your doctor stating the due date.

Pacemakers

It is generally safe to travel with pacemakers as long as you follow a few tips:
- Carry a multi-lingual card with you proving you have a pacemaker.
- Ask to be manually inspected at airports. Show the staff your card. You will set off the buzzer going through a security check.
- Never go into a power plant. The stuff written about microwaves is nonsense (you'd have to get into one for it to be a problem). But, power plants could kill you.

Heart or Respiratory Problems
- If your problem is severe, schedule a series of short flights. This allows you to get fresh air for awhile at each stopover.
- Fly first class where the ventilation is superior.
- In tourist class ask for a seat as far from the smoking section as possible. Turn on the ventilation above you immediately.

- Carry an inhaler. Use it as necessary.
- Use antihistamines exactly as directed. A number cannot be combined with antibiotic or antifungal medications.
- On some international flights planes are sprayed with pyrethrin or sumithrin (synthetic pyrethrin) insecticides. If you hear an announcement for this, ask to be given a moist cloth. Cover your nose and mouth with this until the spray has settled.
- Mexico City has smog. Its high altitude compounds the problem. Panachel on Lake Atitlán in Guatemala suffers from temperature inversions which trap smoke in the valley. San José in Costa Rica is also in a valley and prone to smog. Stay in Santa Catarina on Lake Atitlán or in one of the hillside areas outside San José (for example, La Posada de la Montaña in San Isidro de Heredia).
- The following company specializes in producing protective masks for people with severe allergies or respiratory problems (write for a free catalog):

Boboli Imports, Inc.
9936 77th Avenue
Edmonton, Alberta T6E 1M5
Canada
Tel: (403) 448-0393

Diabetics

- Consider signing up with one of the organizations in this chapter providing medical identification and help in emergencies.
- Carry urine-testing equipment, regular and long-lasting insulin, oral drugs or syringes, extra carbohydrates (your schedule will get fouled up), and a doctor's note stating that you are a diabetic. This note helps you explain syringes when you cross borders.
- Becton-Dickinson distributes syringes abroad.
- Consider subscribing to:

Diabetic Traveler
P.O. Box 8223 RW
Stamford, CT 06905
Tel: (203) 327-5832

Traveling with a Disability

Central America and Mexico are simply not yet set up for disabled travelers. However, the following information should be helpful.

Newsletter

Aimed at people who are disabled but want to travel:

Travelin' Talk
P.O. Box 3534
Clarksville, TN 37043
Tel: (615) 552-6670

Disabled Travelers

Travel to Central America and Mexico is quite difficult for disabled travelers, although some progress is being made. Only a few hotels are accessible. Transportation for the disabled is hard to find or non-existant. Still, several organizations offer limited trips to this region, some on an individual basis, some with groups. A few organizations offer health professionals to accompany travelers:

Accessible Journeys
35 West Sellers Avenue
Ridley Park, PA 19078
Tel: (800) 846-4537
    (610) 521-0339

Directions Unlimited
720 North Bedford Road
Bedford Hills, NY 10507
Tel: (800) 533-5343
    (914) 241-1700

Evergreen Travel Service
4114 198th Street SW
Lynnwood, WA 98036
Tel: (206) 776-1184

Flying Wheels Travel
143 West Bridge Street
Owatonna, MN 55060
Tel: (800) 535-6790
    (507) 451-5005

Handicapped Scuba
    Association
7172 West Stanford Avenue
Littleton, CO 80123

Tel: (303) 933-4864
    (805) 648-6740

Linli Travel, Inc.
    (Nautilus Tours)
19510 Ventura Boulevard,
    Suite 107
Tarzana, CA 91356
Tel: (818) 344-3640

MedEscort International
ABE International Airport
P.O. Box 8766
Allentown, PA 18105
Tel: (800) 255-7182
    (610) 791-3111

Mobility International USA
P.O. Box 10767
Eugene, OR 97440
Tel: (503) 343-1284

New Directions
5276 Hollister Avenue,
    Suite 207
Santa Barbara, CA 93111
Tel: (805) 967-2841

Sundial Special Vacations
600 Broadway
Seaside, OR 97138
Tel: (800) 547-9198
   (503) 738-3324

Wilderness Inquiry
1313 Fifth Street Southeast
P.O. Box 84
Minneapolis, MN 55414
Tel: (612) 379-3858

Traveling Nurses' Network
P.O. Box 129
Vancouver, WA 98666
Tel: (206) 694-2462

Useful Medical Organizations

If you have a chronic illness or medical problem, contact the following organizations for information on their services, which include everything from lists of English-speaking doctors to insurance. Medic Alert is noted for its engraved bracelets giving information on medical conditions and allergies to drugs. TravMed includes a free copy of *International Travel Health Guide* with its insurance. Compare the offerings of all companies before deciding which one best matches your needs:

Access America
P.O. Box 90315
Richmond, VA 23286
Tel: (800) 284-8300

International Association of
   Medical Assistance to
   Travelers (IAMAT)
417 Center Street
Lewiston, NY 14092
Tel: (716) 754-4883

Assist-Card International
1001 South Bayshore Drive,
   Suite 2302
Miami, FL 33131
Tel: (305) 381-9959

International SOS Assistance,
   Inc. (mailing address)
P.O. Box 11568
Philadelphia, PA 19116
Tel: (800) 523-8930
   (215) 244-1500

Carefree
P.O. Box 310
120 Mineola Boulevard
Mineola, NY 11501
Tel: (800) 645-2424

International SOS Assistance,
   Inc.
8 Neshaminy Interplex,
   Suite 207
Trevose, PA 19053
Tel: (800) 523-8930
   (215) 244-1500

Healthcare Abroad
107 West Federal Street
P.O. Box 480
Middleburg, VA 22117
Tel: (800) 237-6615

Medic Alert Foundation
P.O. Box 1009
Turlock, CA 95381
Tel: (800) 344-3226

Travel Assistance International
1133 15th Street, N.W.,
    Suite 400
Washington, DC 20005
Tel: (800) 821-2828
    (202) 331-1609

TravMed
P.O. Box 10623
Baltimore, MD 21285
Tel: (800) 732-5309
    (410) 296-5225

Worldwide Assistance Services
1133 15th Street N.W.
Washington, DC 20005
Tel: (800) 821-2828

Medical Evacuation

If you'll be doing high-risk activities or have a serious health condition, take out medical evacuation insurance. If you have a serious illness or accident requiring surgery or blood transfusions and have the time to get back to Canada or the United States, do it.

Air Evac International, Inc.
4320 Viewridge Avenue,
    Suite D
San Diego, CA 92123
Tel: (800) 854-2569
    (619) 292-5557
Belize, Costa Rica, Guatemala,
Honduras, Mexico.

Critical Air Medicine, Inc.
4141 Kearney Villa Road
San Diego, CA 92123
Tel: (800) 247-8326
    (619) 571-0482
Belize, Costa Rica, Guatemala,
Honduras, Mexico.

Life Flight
1203 Ross Sterling
Herman Hospital,
    Texas Medical Center
Houston, TX 77030
Tel: (800) 231-4357

(800) 392-4357 (TX)
(713) 797-3590
Belize, Costa Rica, Guatemala,
Honduras, Mexico.

NEAR (Nationwide Emergency
    Ambulance Return)
P.O. Box 1339
Calumet City, IL 60409
Tel: (800) 654-6700
    (708) 868-6700
Belize, Costa Rica, Guatemala,
Honduras, Mexico.

Schaefer's Ambulance, Inc.
4627 Beverly Boulevard
Los Angeles, CA 90004
Tel: (800) 229-4727
    (213) 469-1473
Mexico.

Getting Information

This book outlines the very best of what to see and do in Central America and Mexico. Still, it's missing maps, which you can get for free; specific listings of hotels and restaurants; and detailed information on sights or destinations, also free if you know where to ask. By using the resources mentioned in this chapter, you'll get exactly what you want for your upcoming trip. For information related to driving in Mexico see pp. 90–98, 194–205.

National Tourist Offices

Tourist offices usually offer free maps. Every person in your party should have a map appropriate to the kind of travel you're doing. Free maps vary in quality, but are generally good enough for trip planning. The National Tourist Offices can give you general information. Some have excellent pamphlets. Others are poorly organized. The more specific your question, the more unlikely it will get answered. These offices shy away from any kind of comparison.

- Write the office nearest you well ahead of your planned departure (preferably several months in advance) to allow as much time as possible for a reply. Ask for a free map.

Belize

Belize Tourist Board
Port Executive Building
8 Haven Avenue
Port Washington, NY 11050
Tel: (800) 624-0686
 (516) 944-8554

Belize Tourist Board
P.O. Box 325
83 North Front Street
Belize City, Belize
Central America
Tel: 011 (501) 27 72 13

Costa Rica

Costa Rican Tourist Board
(Instituto Costarricense
 de Turismo)
P.O. Box 672712
Marietta, GA 30067
Tel: (800) 327-7033

Costa Rican Tourist Board
(Instituto Costarricense
 de Turismo)
Apartado Postal 777-1000
Avenida 4, Calles 5/7,
 12th Floor
San José, Costa Rica
Central America
Tel: 011 (506) 23 84 23

Guatemala

Guatemala Tourist
  Commission
299 Alhambra Circle,
  Suite 510
Coral Gables, FL 33134
Tel: (800) 742-4529
  (305) 442-0651

Instituto Guatemalteco
  de Turismo (INGUAT)
7a. Avenida 1-17, Zona 4
Centro Civico
Guatemala City, Guatemala
Central America
Tel: 011 (502) (2) 31 13 33

Honduras

Honduras Tourist Bureau
(Instituto Hondureno de Turismo)
Apartado 32601
Colonia San Carlos
Edificio Europa
Tegucigalpa, D.C.
Honduras
Central America
Tel: 011 (504) 22 21 24

Mexico

Mexico has a toll-free information line to answer basic questions on travel to Mexico (Tel: (800) 446-3942). In Mexico the 24-hour number is (91-800-90392) and in Mexico City (250-0123).

Mexican Government
  Tourist Office
70 East Lake Street,
  Suite 1413
Chicago, IL 60601
Tel: (312) 565-2778

Mexican Government
  Tourist Office
10100 Santa Monica
  Boulevard, Suite 224
Los Angeles, CA 90067
Tel: (213) 203-8191

Mexican Government
  Tourist Office
128 Aragon Avenue
Coral Gables, FL 33134
Tel: (305) 443-9160

Mexican Government
  Tourist Office
One Place Ville Marie,
  Suite 1526
Montreal, P.Q. H3B 2B5
Tel: (514) 871-1052

Mexican Government
  Tourist Office
2707 North Loop West,
  Suite 450
Houston, TX 77008
Tel: (713) 880-5153

Mexican Government
  Tourist Office
405 Park Avenue, Suite 1402
New York, NY 10022
Tel: (212) 755-7261

Mexican Government
  Tourist Office
Avenue of the Stars
Epcot Center
Mexico World Showcase
Lake Buena Vista, FL 32830
Tel: (407) 827-5315

Mexican Government
  Tourist Office
2 Bloor Street West,
  Suite 1801
Toronto, Ontario M4W 3E2
Tel: (416) 925-1876

Mexican Government
  Tourist Office
999 West Hastings,
  Suite 1610
Vancouver, BC V6C 1M3
Tel: (604) 669-2845

Mexican Government Tourist
  Office (Embassy)
1911 Pennsylvania Avenue NW
Washington, DC 20006
Tel: (202) 728-1750

For information on the Baja Peninsula and hotel reservations there contact:

IMPA Mexican Information
7860 Mission Center Court, Suite 202
San Diego, CA 92108
Tel.: (800) 225-2786
        (619) 298-4105

Agents and Agencies

Travel agents can be excellent resources, especially those specializing in travel to Central America and Mexico. Always ask for an agent who has traveled to the area you plan to visit. You might have to call several agencies to find such a person. Specific agencies or tour operators have been mentioned for special interest activities in the chapter on Doing Things (see pp. 258–338).

Good Agents Should Give You Good Information
- A good agent will save you lots of time and aggravation by outlining options.
- A good agent may come up with an airfare lower than one quoted to you by an airline.
- A good agent compares car rental rates quickly and makes reservations.
- Few agents deal with ground transportation other than car rental and tours. It's best to get this kind of information locally.
- Good agents will give you access to specialized books: *Official Airline Guide, Official Hotel and Resort Guide, STAR (Sloane*

Travel Agency Reports), and *World Travel Directory*. These all contain helpful, if dry, information. You'll quickly learn to read between the lines.

- A good agent has traveled in an area or has the resources to find out exactly which hotel will match your personality and pocket book. Note, however, that Central America is changing so rapidly that many agents and travel books have no idea about gems, which may have just opened. Superb agents know how to ferret these out.
- In many instances agents make hotel reservations free of charge. In some instances, you will be charged for faxes or telephone calls. Always ask about any potential charges upfront. Charges are most common for reservations in small hotels, which do not pay commissions to agents.
- If you want to take a cruise or a tour, definitely go to a travel agent. This is the very heart of their business.
- If you're going on a special interest tour, compare what a local agent has to offer with one of the companies listed in the chapter on Doing Things (pp. 258–338).
- A good agent places you on a cruise or tour which matches your personality. You pay nothing extra for this service. Tours and cruises are popular because travel in these areas requires a great deal of expertise.
- Many agencies also have a library of offbeat or unusual travel books, which you can look through to help you make decisions. These books are often not available in local librairies, are out of print, or would take you weeks to order from the publisher.

Picking an Agency

- Larger agencies tend to have more clout than smaller ones. Find out whether the agency has representatives abroad, just in case something does go wrong.
- Ask the agency what travel it specializes in. If it doesn't match your travel plans, ask the agency to refer you to another one.
- In special cases, you may want to work with agents in other cities. If the best agency for a special-interest tour is in Los Angeles, carry on your business through the mail. Always ask for a toll-free number to avoid long-distance phone bills.

Recognizing a Good Agent

A good travel agent is one who has your best interest in mind. A good agent will find you the best possible price for any type of travel, even though commissions are based on cost. A good agent gets back to you quickly and carries through with all promises. An excellent agent does the above but also knows the area in which you'll be traveling and has personal experience with places being recommended. Reward such an agent with all of your business. A letter of praise to a supervisor is recommended.

- Most travel agents are members of the American Society of Travel Agents (ASTA), so be wary of those who are not. ASTA maintains a file of complaints. You can write or call them:

  ASTA
  1100 King Street
  Alexandria, VA 22314
  Tel: (703) 739-2782

- Look for the initials CTC—for Certified Travel Consultant—after an agent's name. This designation signifies that the person has a good reputation and has been through a specialized course.

Other Sources of Information

Following are commonly used and not so commonly known sources of information on Central America and Mexico.

Travel Books

By looking at the different types of guides available, you'll soon find the kind which suits your personality. Each of the guides is written for a specific type of traveler. Some are obviously aimed at backpackers and penny pinchers while others are more upscale. There are also many guides to Central American countries and Mexico which are not as well-known. These are often sold in the individual countries, through mail order catalogs, or in specialty stores (there are now 70 stores selling only travel books). Frankly, the information contained in this guide is good enough for travel in Belize, Guatemala, and Honduras. You can pick up additional free information on these areas once there. However, if you're planning extensive travel to Costa Rica or Mexico, buying a guide with detailed hotel listings would be helpful. This would be especially true for travelers heading into remote or relatively unexplored areas. In these two countries you can do this kind of travel quite safely as long as you use common sense and follow the locals lead (see pp. 178–186).

- Read thoroughly at least one guide which matches your budget and personality.
- The more you know, the better you'll plan; the better you plan, the more likely you are to get what you want.
- Few guides are current on hotels and restaurants. It's impossible for them to be. Central America and Mexico are changing so

rapidly that no one can keep up. However, if you're on a tight schedule, the hotel recommendations in good guides are a good start. If the same hotel is highly recommended in three or four guides, it's probably a good bet and hard to get into without advance reservations during peak periods. Do your reading far in advance. Quoted prices may be obsolete.

- If you have the stamina, read as many guides as you can. Many of them are available at librairies. Buy the one which suits your personality and style of travel. Rip out the pages which apply to the areas you'll be visiting. Carry with you only materials needed. Or, simply take good notes along. Unless you're traveling for weeks, carrying an entire book doesn't make sense.

Travel Magazines

Read the following magazines for good travel information: *Conde Nast*, *Gourmet*, *National Geographic Traveler*, *Travel Holiday*, and *Travel and Leisure*. A good librarian can also show you how to look up information by specific destinations. Following is a magazine specializing in travel to Mexico only:

Mexico Events
P.O. Box 188037
5838 Edison Place, Suite 10092008
Carlsbad, CA 92009
Tel: (619) 929-0707

Airline Magazines

Airline magazines, distributed for free on flights, are quite expensive to order on a subscription basis. However, they often give valuable insights into the region you'll be visiting.

Aboard
North South Net
100 Almeria Avenue, Suite 220
Coral Gables, FL 33134
Tel: (305) 441-9744

This magazine is used by Aviateca (the Guatemalan airline) and Sahsa (the Honduran airline).

Caminos del Aire
Internacional de Revistas,
  CA de CV
Torcuato Tasso 231
Colonia Polanco
Mexico, DF, CP 11560
Tel: 254-2933

This is the in-flight magazine of Mexicana.

Lacsa's World
E.R. Publishing, Inc.
The Centre at Palm & Stirling
9900 Stirling Road, Suite 244
Cooper City, FL 33024
Tel: (305) 431-0161

This magazine is used by Lacsa, the Costa Rican national airline.

Tour Companies

The brochures of tour companies are often highly informative. If you read them carefully, they can give specific details which are most useful in planning a trip. By comparing the information from a number of companies, you may decide that a tour is a fine option. Or, you may decide to travel independently but see many of the sites or do many of the things suggested in the tour brochures themselves (see pp. 258–338).

Travel Reports and Newsletters

Travel reports can help with trip planning. Travel clubs (mentioned later) have their own newsletters. To find out which of these reports suits your personality, write to each one asking for a sample copy. Note that INT offers a networking service to its readers who can write in asking other readers for information on a specific area in Central America (responses generally take several months).

Consumer Reports Travel Letter
P.O. Box 53629
Boulder, CO 80322
Tel: (800) 999-7959
    (303) 666-7000

Entree Travel
P.O. Box 5148
Santa Barbara, CA 93150
Tel: (805) 969-5948

Great Expectations
P.O. Box 18036
Raleigh, NC 27619
Tel: (919) 846-3600

A magazine which offers networking and travel advice for a fee.

International Living
824 East Baltimore Street
Baltimore, MD 21298
Tel: (410) 234-0691

International Travel News (ITN)
2120 28th Street
Sacramento, CA 95818
Tel: (916) 457-3643
    (800) 366-9192
    (to subscribe)

Tico Times (Newspaper)
Apartado 4632
Avenida 9, Calle 15
1000 San Jose, Costa Rica
Central America, or

Tico Times
Dept. 717
P.O. Box 025216
Miami, FL 33102

Travel Smart
Communications House
40 Beechdale Road
Dobbs Ferry, NY 10522
Tel: (800) 327-3633
       (914) 693-8300

TravelMex
Apartado 31-750
45050
Guadalajara, Jalisco
Mexico

Covers Mexico only.

Auto Clubs

The auto clubs are listed on p. 81. Most of the auto clubs deal primarily with Mexico. The AAA has books on Mexico as well as camping information. When joining a club, ask about available information which can be useful whether you're driving or not.

Travel Clubs

Travel clubs not only provide information but often can get you special discounts on hotels, insurance, and other assorted services. Always check into what these have to offer before traveling abroad.

CLUB MEX
3450 Bonita Road, Suite 101
Chula Vista, CA 91910
Tel: (619) 585-3033

A Mexican travel club with newsletter, auto and health insurance, and information on fishing (and boats).

The Good Sam Club
Customer Service
P.O. Box 500
Agoura, CA 91301
Tel: (800) 423-5061

Oriented toward anyone with an RV—invaluable if you have one.

South American Explorers Club
126 Indian Creek Road
Ithaca, NY 14850
Tel: (607) 277-0488

Not only excellent for information on Central America and Mexico, but also for networking and setting up special interest trips.

Camping Information

If you're a member of the American Automobile Association (AAA) you can get good camping information on Mexico. Other organizations worth contacting:

KOA, Inc. (Two campgrounds in Mexico)
P.O. Box 30558
Billings, MT 59114
Tel: (406) 248-7444

Sanborn's Mexican Insurance Service
P.O. Box 1210
McAllen, TX 78502
Tel: (512) 682-3402

Getting Detailed Maps

Detailed maps are expensive, but essential for long-term or off-road travel. Following are several companies offering excellent maps to Central America and Mexico as well as numerous publications covering the area. Write each for a catalog with prices.

International Travel
   Map Productions
P.O. Box 2290
Vancouver, BC V6B 3W5
Canada
Tel: (604) 687-3320

Map Link
25 East Mason Street
Santa Barbara, CA 93101
Tel: (805) 965-4402

Professor Antonio E. Rosales
Roatan
Bay Islands, Honduras
Central America
Tel: 011 (504) 45 15 59

Offers an extremely detailed map of Roatan (Mapa Guia Turistico de Roatan). If you can get it ahead of time it will help you picture the island and know exact locations of everything.

San Diego Map Center
2611 University Avenue
San Diego, CA 92104
Tel: (619) 291-3830

South American Explorers
   Club
126 Indian Creek Road
Ithaca, NY 14850
Tel: (607) 277-0488

World Aeronautical Charts
U.S. Department of Commerce
National Oceanic &
   Atmospheric Administration
6501 Lafayette Avenue
Riverdale, MD 20840
Tel: (301) 436-6990

Getting Information Abroad

Once in Central America or Mexico, you can get information in a wide variety of ways.

Local Tourist Offices

In all major cities you'll find tourist offices either in airports or in city centers with tons of free information on travel within the country. Any hotel you stay in can give you directions on how to get to the tourist information office. The trip is always worthwhile.

Networking with Other Travelers

I mention networking several times because it's so important. Keep asking other travelers about their finds, the things they found most interesting or dull, the hotels which may have just been built and are still great buys, restaurants which really met their expectations or didn't, contacts who were most helpful, local tours which turned out to deliver everything they promised—ask, ask, ask. Judge the recommendations by the person you're talking to. If somone has just spent several months traveling through Costa Rica and only mentions one or two hotels, one special experience, and one restaurant, wouldn't you give those special attention? While traveling, I get more useful, up-to-date information from other people than from any other source.

Local Telephone Books

Strangely enough local telephone books sometimes have interesting tidbits of information on local tours and sights. Some do, some don't. Leaf through them quickly to see whether they do.

Local Hotel Publications

Finer hotels almost always have some sort of local publication in the room. Some of these are free, others are meant to stay in the room. These are often interesting with quite detailed information on local attractions. Some even offer special discount coupons. If nothing is in your room, ask about local publications at the front desk.

Local Tour Operators and Travel Agencies

Go into several of these and ask them for free brochures on available sightseeing trips or tours. Some of these might interest you. You can either go with the tour or make independent arrangements. In any event, the maps and information provided are often highly detailed and excellent.

Hightly Detailed Maps in Mexico

DETENAL produces highly detailed maps geared to off-road travel. The organization has offices in Durango, Hermosillo, Mérida, Mexico City (booth at airport), Monterrey, Napoles, Oaxaca, Puebla, San Luis Potosí, Toluca, and Zapopan. Look up the address in local phone books. At present, it has maps of the following states: Aguascalientes, Baja California, Coahuila, Colima, Guanajuato, Jalisco, México, Morelos, Nayarit, Nuevo León, Tamaulipas, Tlaxcala, and Zacatecas.

Itineraries

This chapter provides information on trip planning. Decide where to go by reading it and the section on Doing Things (pp. 258–338). Have a map in front of you as you plan.

Where Do You Want to Go?

You have the perfect vacation mapped out in your personality—try to match your destination with what you want most. You may just want warm weather, a nice beach, a good view, and a chance to relax. Or, to travel extensively and know as much about a country as you can in the time available. Perhaps, you're focused on special interest activities. Naturally, if a trip is long enough, you can combine a wide variety of goals. But, on short trips this can be quite difficult. Define your goals ahead of time so that your expectations meet reality.

The major questions are: How much time do you have? How much money? How much energy? And, what do you really like to do? Following are a few general comments about individual countries:

BELIZE

Belize, formerly British Honduras, has gotten a lot of press in recent years. The country is quite small. You get around it by boat, bus, 4-wheel drive, plane, and taxi. Its main claim to fame is the barrier reef and the many islands or cayes (keys) along it. The islands vary greatly. Some are bare coral, some coral with sand, and others surrounded by mangroves. There are also three magnificent atolls or islands surrounded by coral reefs. Inland, is mostly hilly terrain covered in many parts with dense jungle. There are a few minor archaeological sites and many ruins still covered with vegetation. Many of the people speak English, although a basic knowledge of Spanish is becoming increasingly important with immigration from nearby countries. You can sample quite a bit of what the country has to offer in a trip of 10 to 14 days. The chapter on Doing Things covers the following special interest categories which may apply to some of the areas listed below: Archaeology, Birding, Diving, Fishing, Kayaking (sea), Photography, Sun, and Wildlife

Altun Ha: A minor, but popular archaeological site, just north of the international airport in Belize City.

Ambergris Caye: This is the most popular island for relaxation. The small airport is right next to the school in town. The island is cut in two by a channel. The more northerly resorts are isolated and must be reached by boat, which is seen by some as an advantage, by others as a disadvantage. Many of the resorts on the north are serviced by generators. A few are geared primarily to fishing. The island is north of Belize City just off Mexico's Yucatán peninsula.

Baboon Sanctuary: Really a misnomer, the area protects the Howler Monkey (see p. 336). You will see howler monkeys (*saraguato*). West of the international airport at Belize City.

Belize City: If traveling by plane, you'll arrive at the Belize Airport. If possible, continue on from there. Skip Belize City. It has little to offer and is quite dangerous, especially at night. Your hotel will be surrounded by heavily armed guards. This is not a pleasant place.

Belize Zoo: Not very far from the airport. Some love it, others don't. Since many animals are hard to see in the wild, this gives you an idea of what you would see if you were extraordinarily lucky.

The Blue Hole: There are two blue holes in Belize, one inland (south of Belmopan), one in the center of an atoll (Lighthouse Reef) offshore. The latter is a spectacular dive site (see p. 305). The other is a popular touristic attraction as well (never leave anything in your car here).

Caracol: An extremely large Mayan city in the process of being excavated. Becoming more accessible. Best go in the dry season from January to May. South of Benque Viejo in the southwestern part of the country.

Caye Caulker: A smaller island than Ambergris and popular with backpacker types. Prices are lower, partially because the island is noted for its sand flies and no-see-ums. South of Ambergris Caye.

Cockscombe Jaguar Preserve: Highly unlikely that you'll see any jaguars, but birding and trekking are popular here. Many local tours to this area are available. South of Dangriga in the southern part of the country.

Crooked Tree Sanctuary: This is a favorite area of birders. I would only go here if that's your major interest (see p. 266). It's northeast of the international airport.

Glover's Reef: Another of the atolls. Great for diving and fishing (see the appropriate sections under Doing Things). If you can afford to get to and stay here, do it. Well off Dangriga in the south central region.

Jungle Lodges: Contact your travel agent for the names of the most popular jungle lodges. The country has some of the finest in Central America. They are quite expensive, sometimes difficult to get to, but often surrounded by large tracts ideal for birding and hiking. An example would be Chan Chich Lodge in northwestern Belize with its own 130,000 acre reserve. A newer, lesser-known spot is Chau Hiix (Chow Heech). Both are in or near Mayan ruins.

Lamanai: One of the prettiest, if minor, archaeological sites. Half the fun is getting there. In the northwestern part of the country close to the Crooked Tree Wildlife Preserve.

Lighthouse Reef: Location of the dive site known as the Blue Hole. One of the most memorable areas in the country, this atoll is worth the cost to visit. Lies well off the coast to the east of Belize City.

Panti Maya Medicine Trail: Popular among people interested in tropical plants and their medicinal value. This is becoming an increasingly important issue with the destruction of rain forests throughout the entire region. On the Ixchel Farm near San Ignacio. Call in advance. Tel: 011 (501) 823180.

Placencia: A strange little town with a long curving beach reputed to be the finest in the country. The beach is okay at best. The resorts here vary from nice to dismal. In town are a number of tiny huts, noisy and cheap. The smell of grass permeates the air and may explain why a number of people claim this is paradise and have taken up residence here. The lodges cater primarily to divers and fishermen. Permit fishing is excellent. Bonefishing and tarpon are also possible. The run to diving and fishing is quite long. The peninsula is in the southern part of the country.

Mountain Pine Ridge Area: One of the loveliest areas in the country. Wonderful for birding and hiking. Best to go with someone who really knows the terrain. Usually included on local tours. Right in the center of the country, west of Dangriga.

Turneffe: One of the atolls. Lovely and famous for snorkeling, diving, and fishing (especially bonefish). All the atolls are worth a special effort to visit. Off Belize City en route to Lighthouse Reef.

Xunantunich: Getting to this minor archaeological ruin (pronounced "shoonahntookneetch") is fun. It's the location and trip which really count. The ruin is outside San Ignacio towards Benque Viejo. Right on the border of Guatemala in the center of the country. Many tourists visit it on the overland route to Tikal (about 85 miles into Guatemala).

COSTA RICA

Everybody who's anybody is going to Costa Rica. It's the hot spot of Central America. You get around it by boat, bus, 4-wheel drive, plane, and taxi. The fact that this is a small country is deceptive. To get to know this country takes months. If you were to flatten out all its mountains, Costa Rica would be immense. It's got so many things you'll love. The exception is that the roads are absolutely horrendous (this will change in the coming years). It is a safe country in which to travel, but thievery is a way of life. You'll only scratch the surface of this amazing country in a trip of 3 weeks. Give yourself lots and lots of time, certainly no less than 10 to 14 days at the very minimum.

The chapter on Doing Things covers the following special interest activities, many of which are related to places mentioned below: Beaches, Birding, Boating, Butterflies, Diving, Fishing, Gardens, Golfing, Kayaking (Inland and Sea), Museums, Music, Photography, Riding, Snorkeling, Sun, Surfing, Turtle watching, Volcanoes, White water rafting, and Windsurfing.

Arenal: See Fortuna.

Cahuita: In theory, this is one of the prime areas for snorkeling on the southern Caribbean. No one there seemed to know what time of year this would actually be possible. When I went, the sea was rough and filled with silt. I was given nothing but contradictory information about when to come. Under no circumstances would I make the long trip here without calling ahead about water conditions.

Carara Biological Reserve: This is one of the most accessible and reliable areas for birding. If possible, come with a guide. Southwest of San José.

CATIE (The Tropical Agriculture Research and Training Center): Often suggested as a tourist destination, I'd skip it. Near Turrialba east of San José.

Fortuna: This is a small town with quite a few hotels because it's the base for excursions (generally at night) to see Arenal. The latter is an active volcano. Seeing the red glow of the cone is only possible on clear nights. The best time is during the dry season from December to early summer. You will only view the crater from a long distance. Do not expect to get close. In the central northern part of the country.

Golfito: This southern Pacific port was described by a resident as "funky." I'd call it foul. People were extremely unpleasant. The port is jammed on weekends with Costa Ricans who come into a giant facility where they can buy goods at duty-free prices. Note that there is a ferry crossing from Golfito to the Osa Peninsula, which makes that area more accessible in the rainy season. There is a fabulous park (Corcovado) on the peninsula (see p. 291).

Irazú: This volcano is not as popular as Poás, but is accessible up a steep, winding, but well-paved road. Much of the mountain is farmed forming a photogenic checkerboard of colors and textures. The area is often covered with clouds. You'll be right on the edge of the crater. Short excursion to northeast of San José.

Lankester Gardens: Popular and accessible tourist attraction from San José. Most people enjoy a short visit to see the flowers. Orchids are its specialty. The gardens are close to Cartago (see p. 282), to the southeast of San José.

Lake Arenal: Much of the property around Lake Arenal is now for sale, since locals have learned its value to foreigners who are choosing this area for retirement. The lake is pretty enough and popular with wind surfers. Located in the central northern part of the country.

Liberia: Included not because of the town, but for its proximity to one of the lesser visited but interesting national parks, Rincón de la Vieja. For an incredible horse ride go to the Rancho Buena Vista north of Liberia (getting into the ranch is an experience by itself). In the far northwestern area of the country.

Monteverde: The name of a little mountain town and a reserve protecting birds. The area is reached up a steep, difficult road. It's in a cloud forest, so bring an umbrella. The town has a wide variety of accommodations. Since 30,000 people come to the reserve each year, birding is not as easy as one might think. Hire a local guide. If you're not in good shape, forget it. Northeast of Puntarenas.

Special tip: Some of the more expensive hotels have their own little birding areas where only customers are allowed in.

Nancite and **Naranjo Beaches** (*Playas*): These beaches on the Northern Pacific coast are spawning grounds for up to 75,000 turtles from late August to early December. October is often the best month.

National Parks: You can get tons of information on National Parks from the tourist office in downtown San José. Brochures list facilities, attractions, and best time of year to go. The system is extensive. Some of these parks are easy to get to and visit, others require no less than a week to see. There is practically no access to a few, which really would be viewed as expeditions. Costa Rica is having a hard time protecting these parks. Despite what you've heard, only 3 percent of the country's rain forest has been preserved. The destruction continues at a rate of 130,000 acres per year. See pp. 290–293 for information on individual parks.

Nicoya Peninsula: A fabulous part of the country with so many lovely beaches you could spend months traveling up and down the coast. The roads here are still unbelievably bad. This may some day be one of the hottest touristic areas in Central America. A couple of its beaches are prime spots for turtle watching. In the northwest.

Ostional: This refuge is noted for turtle watching in early fall (see p. 330). On the Pacific coast to the southwest of the small town of Nicoya on the Nicoya Peninsula.

Pavones Beach (*Playa*): Costa Ricans claim that Pavones is the location of the longest wave in the world. There are dozens of surfing areas along both coasts. Surfers take note (see p. 326). South of Golfito near Panama.

Poás: This is an active volcano, varying from 1/2 mile to 1 mile wide depending upon your source. It's easily accessible with a good road. It is different from Arenal in that you can look into the crater. It's one of the most visited areas in the country. Short excursion to northwest of San José.

Puerto Limón: This is a dangerous port on the southern Caribbean. The crack traffic is heavy. There is no reason to go here whatsoever.

Puntarenas: This port offers passenger and car ferry service to two points on the Nicoya Peninsula. Many locals insist that the Tempisque-Puerto Moreno ferry farther north is much easier to use with far fewer delays. I agree. The port is west of San José on the Gulf of Nicoya.

Quepos: The area is a hilly peninsula with lots of hotels and restaurants to serve Manuel Antonio, a park noted for its lovely beaches. A violent storm came through in 1993 and did a lot of damage to the trees around the park. The beaches are still attractive. South of San José on the Pacific coast.

San José: The sprawling, noisy, congested capital is located in the center of the country. Eat in the dining room of the National Theater (ask for a pass to the bathroom which will allow you to see the theater without paying an entry fee). Both the Gold and Jade Museums are worth seeing, if you're interested in museums. As soon as possible, get out of the capital. It's infamous for thievery.

Sarapiquí River: You can either take short or extended trips on this jungle river. More extended trips can take you into Nicaragua. Locals insist that this is completely safe, but I'd be wary. Incidents along borders are quite common (see p. 268). In the northwest close to Nicaragua.

Talamanca: This is the southern region of the Caribbean coast, where great banana plantations flourish. Coastal beaches often have fine, black sand. The area appeals mainly to budget travelers and surfers. The water is often rough and dirty, which makes snorkeling, even in prime coral areas, difficult. My opinion: Head to the Nicoya Peninsula.

Tortuguero: This is the northern region of the Caribbean coast. It's wet, hot, and hard to get into. This means that unless you're willing to work hard and use local boats to get you around, you'll pay a lot for tours in this area. They may be worth it during peak turtle nesting seasons (see p. 330) or if you're into birding (400 species have been spotted in this region). Off this coast is some of the best snook and tarpon fishing in the world (see p. 280).

Wilson Botanical Gardens: Although this is quite a drive from San José, the gardens are worth a detour in the dry season from January to March. There are over 2,000 species of plants, including many orchids. There have been documented sightings of 220 species of birds, 80 mammals, 71 reptiles and amphibians, and 3,000 butterflies and moths. You can stay here, but make reservations in advance. If you come up from the coast to the gardens near San Vito, 4-wheel drive is essential. You'll climb incredibly steep and narrow paths. East of Golfito high in the mountains.

GUATEMALA

If it weren't for its political problems, this country would have a great deal more to offer. No one knows for sure how many people have been killed here in the last decades, but conservative estimates are well over 150,000. You get around the country safely by bus, minibus, plane, and taxi. Avoid any rural hikes. Avoid any political commentary or activity. Avoid taking photos of police or military. But, do see a limited part of the country. All of this can be done in 10 to 14 days. The chapter on Doing Things covers the following special activities: Archaeology, Festivals, Indian culture, Markets, Museums, Music, Photography, Shopping, and Study. The areas listed below are most visited and quite safe if you follow local advice at all times.

Antigua: Only about an hour southwest of Guatemala City by bus or cab is an old colonial city with cobblestoned streets. The city is surrounded by volcanoes, is relaxed and calm, and appeals to people interested in studying Spanish or spending months in Guatemala in a civilized place with good restaurants and decent accommodations at low prices. If you come here expecting to see an older city which matches the gems of Italy or Spain, you'll be sadly disappointed. But Antigua does attract fascinating people, lots of them—and, I believe that's its main appeal. Antigua boasts one of the finest festivals in Central America during Holy Week (*Semana Santa*). Reservations a year or more in advance are advised.

Biotopo del Quetzal: This preserve has been set up to protect the endangered Quetzal, but it is also a good area to see wild orchids (at their best in January and February). Since you're getting a little off the beaten path here, go with a tour. It's approximately 100 miles from Guatemala City.

Ceibal (El Ceibal): You have to be in really good shape and really into archaeology to visit this site. Part of your trip will include a 1-hour boat ride on the Rio de la Pasion from Sayaxche and then a 45-minute jungle hike. Getting there can be half the fun, right? Southwest of Flores in northern Guatemala.

Chichicastenango: This little, mountain town has the most famous market in Central America. The market is best on Thursday and Sunday. The market is held out in the open, but vendors are lined up in long rows in stalls covered by black plastic so you don't get this picture-perfect open market that you may have romanticized (I and everyone else I met had). I came here with an expert weaver who found little that couldn't be purchased in Panajachel at the same price. "Chichi" is famous for its December festival (make reservations months in advance). North of Lake Atitlán.

Flores: This lakeside town has a few hotels and restaurants. It's used as the access point to Tikal for people who fly into the local airport from Belize City or Guatemala City. Note that more people come here from Belize than from Guatemala. The town itself has a nice setting, but it's in no way spectacular. If you stay in Flores, you get up early in the morning while it's still dark to catch a minibus to Tikal (ask at your hotel about arrangements). The trip takes a little over an hour. Don't forget to bring local currency to pay for the entrance fee. Flores is in the north. Tikal is northeast of the town.

Guatemala City: You'll probably start your trip by arriving in Guatemala City. I haven't met a single person (including tour operators) who wouldn't agree that the city is noisy, polluted, and unpleasant. The residential area is the nicest. Many of the better hotels are located there for that reason. Most tourists go to the major museums (see p. 289) and the relief map, and then leave. In the southeastern part of the country.

Lake Atitlán: It's surprising how many times you read that this is the most beautiful lake in the world. Its water is clear, the volcanoes surrounding it stunning, and the setting magical. Many people visit a few of the Indian villages by boat from Panajachel. I suggest that a group of four people hire an individual boat with a guide and spend at least a full day seeing as many villages as possible. The cost is about double per person and worth every Quetzal. Each village is quite distinctive. You need a guide, because the Indians don't speak English or Spanish. If you're a photographer, come armed with plenty of 1-Quetzal notes since you'll be asked to pay for each photo. The trip will take you past multi-million dollar homes as well as into picturesque and authentic villages where many of the people continue to wear traditional clothing. The lake is northwest of Antigua.

Lake Izabal: The Rio Dulce leads you into El Golfete (a gulf with manatees) then to a lake noted for exclusive homes. Many people stop at the gulf and return to Livingston. Hire a boat locally or go with a tour. Note that fishing for snook off Livingston is good in September and October and virtually unknown. The area is rarely visited and included in a few adventure tours only. On the eastern side of the country just south of Belize.

Panajachel: This somewhat frenetic town is on Lake Atitlán, about an hour and a half by cab or minibus from Antigua. Bus service is also available, costs less, but requires more time (transfer). Panajachel is touristy and quite noisy. It's got a tremendous variety of shops selling fine fabrics and items made from handwoven wool and cotton. The collection of weaving here is extraordinary. There are many hotels and restaurants catering to tourists.

Quetzaltenango: Use this town as a base to visit surrounding Indian villages. Hire a guide, especially if you want to take photos. Don't miss **Zunil**. If you can time your visits to market days, so much the better. Note that Quetzaltenango is often called Xelha ("ahayla") by locals. Northwest of Lake Atitlán.

Quiriguá: If you're extremely interested in archaeology, this area (pronounced "kitty-gua") is famous for its carved stelae. The trip is included in some tours, but don't go out of your way to see it just for the sake of seeing it. Note, however, that the area is good for birding. Come with a skilled guide. It's in the eastern part of the country and most often visited from San Pedro Sula in Honduras.

Santa Catarina Palopó: This village is just a short bus or cab ride from Panajachel. I recommend staying in the Hotel Villa Santa Catarina as a way of escaping the tourist bustle.

Tikal: If you had only one archaeological site to see in all of Central America, this would be it. Words cannot do it justice. Climbing the ruins, up ladders and vines, almost into the sky for views of the surrounding jungle—this is what travel is all about. You'll practically be able to touch toucans and wild turkeys. The incredible, cat-like screeching sounds of the howler monkeys is unforgettable. This is a 5-star experience. Don't miss it. Note that you can stay in the park at lodges. No, they're not great, but they're okay. The advantage is that you can get up early to see birds before the crowds scare them away. If you're on a budget, commute from Flores as outlined earlier.

Uaxactún: Another spot for the ardent archaeologist. "Washucktung" is about an hour's drive from Tikal (15 miles to the North). Best to go with a guide.

Zunil: See Quetzaltenango.

HONDURAS

Honduras is not on most people's priority list because it offers very limited attractions. Most travel is by plane, although travel to the main archaeological site at Copan is generally by bus. On the Bay Islands you get around by boat, minibus, or taxi. You'll get much of what the country has to offer in a trip of 7 to 10 days. The chapter on Doing Things covers the following special activities for which the country is well-known: Archaeology, Birding, Diving, Shopping, and White Water Rafting.

Bay Islands: For many travelers the Bay Islands off the northern coast in the Caribbean represent the best that Honduras has to offer, namely excellent diving on a reef close to shore. This is a cluster of islands 35 to 70 miles off the coast. There are three main islands,

Guanaja, Roatan, and Utila. Morat, a fourth, is presently developing a large resort. The largest island is Roatan with varied accommodations and a few so-so beaches. The other islands offer mainly deluxe accommodations. Personally, I would only travel to these islands during the dry season from February to late August. Tip from a local: If you can afford it, stay on Guanaja and dive off Barbarat. See p. 306.

Copan: Most people who are extremely interested in archaeology make a trip to Copan, approximately 106 miles southwest of San Pedro Sula. The trip is best made during the dry season. In good weather conditions it takes less than 3 hours from San Pedro Sula. Impressions of the trip's value are not at all uniform, varying from "Don't bother!" to "It's pretty good. I liked it."

La Ceiba: You may end up going to La Ceiba whether you want to or not, especially if traveling in the rainy season. The reason? It's much easier to get to the Bay Islands from here than from San Pedro Sula. On the Caribbean coast northeast of San Pedro Sula.

Lake Yojoa (Lago de Yojoa): Very few tourists come here, but the lake does offer some bass fishing. Directly south of San Pedro Sula.

Pulhapanzak Falls: Depending upon who has done the measuring the falls drop 150 to 300 feet. The spelling also seems to vary by map or publication. Located just north of Lake Yojoa.

San Pedro Sula: A major industrial city in the northwest which serves as a hub for trips to the Bay Islands and Copan.

MEXICO

Mexico has extremely reliable winter sun. You can travel throughout the country by bus, car, plane, RV, taxi, and train. Because of the many charter flights arriving each week in major resort areas, Mexico continues to be an excellent choice for budget travelers. Yes, room prices have soared, but Mexico still offers good value for your travel dollar. Travel here requires flexibility. The country is known for its strikes, local uprisings, and travel curves. It's also known for health problems, although the government is working hard to cut down on the cases of malaria and has made considerable progress in combatting traveler's diarrhea. Theft continues to be rampant, as it is in most of Central America. Still, the country offers an incredible diversity of attractions, which explains why millions of travelers flock here each year. Mexico is an enormous country, one which would take years to explore in depth. You can get a nice break from the cold in a week, but to sample the country more fully takes at least three to four weeks. The chapter on Doing Things covers the following special interest activities: Archaeology, Art courses, Ballet, Beaches, Birding, Bullfights, Butterflies, Diving, Festivals, Fishing, Fossil hunting, Golfing, Hang gliding, Hiking, Horse racing, Hunting, Indian culture, Jai alai, Markets, Museums, Music, Night life, Nude bathing, Parasailing, Photography, Rodeo, Shelling, Shopping, Snorkeling, Spas, Spectacles, Study, Sun, Surfing, Tennis, Train ride (Copper Canyon), Turtle watching, Whale watching, White water rafting, Wildlife, Windsurfing, and Yachting.

Acapulco: Really a city curving around a broad bay with beautiful beach areas—noisy, crowded, and lively with prices for all pocket books. Known for its shopping and lively night life. Location and choice of hotel is crucial. Note that Acapulco is making a come-back, especially with Mexicans. On the Pacific coast south of Mexico City.

Archaeological Sites: A few are mentioned here because they are so outstanding. See p. 259 in the chapter on Doing Things.

Cabo San Lucas/San José De Cabo: Remote hideaways on the southern tip of the Baja. Geared to luxury travelers and jet setters seeking sun, fishing, and isolation in a desert-like setting. Easy access from California. One of the better government-sponsored touristic developments. Great beaches (some hidden), great weather, and sometimes great fishing.

Cancún: A bit like Miami Beach with a Mexican accent. Very commercial—lots of topflight, luxury hotels on a series of small, pure-white beaches. Appeals to couples or families looking for safety, sun, and varied activities. Lots of shops, restaurants, and aggressive types trying to sell just about everything. Nearly a million Americans come here each year. On the Gulf of Mexico in the Yucatán.

Chichén Itza: This is one of the most impressive archaeological sites in the country. It is accessible by a good road to the west of Cancún. Don't miss it.

Colonial Towns: A few of the most popular colonial towns are mentioned in this section, but there are actually 48. You could spend years traveling to and staying in these authentic places. They more accurately reflect a true picture of Mexico than the coastal resorts. Nearly half of them are accessible by train from Mexico City. So they are neither expensive, nor difficult to reach. With the exception of only a few they are relatively undiscovered. Contact the nearest Mexican Government Tourist Office for a detailed list of these towns and their attractions (see p. 26).

Cozumel: The place to go for diving and snorkeling—the preoccupation of most visitors, who demand little else. Remote and peaceful. Note that the most beautiful beaches are on the opposite side of the island than the town. Rent a motorbike to get to them. You won't regret it. Even if you've never snorkeled before, try it here (there's a park just outside town). Off the Yucatán coast south of Cancún.

Guadalajara: One of the favorite cities for retirement. It's quite large, but attractive. As an inland town, it has an excellent climate. Orozco's ceiling frescoes in the Hospicio Cabanas are famous. East of Puerto Vallarta in the central part of the country.

Huatulco: This is a planned development, similar to Cancún. There are a number of pristine bays which will have numerous tourist hotels and facilities built in the years to come. Development has already started with a Club Med in place. Much of the area is being protected to make this an especially attractive resort. Its location on the southern Pacific coast is ideal for winter sun.

Isla Mujeres: Laid-back, little island off Cancún. Appeals to backpackers and budget types content with sand, sun, seafood, and snorkeling. Frankly, it has lost much of its charm in recent years. The incessant noise of motorbikes is one of the main reasons.

Ixtapa: Luxury living in an enclave by the sea. Very fine commercial hotels with all the trimmings, including facilities for tennis and golf. A bit of a country-club atmosphere, cut off from the Mexico of Mexicans. Note that Club Med Ixtapa is ideal for families, especially those with babies or young children. On the Pacific coast southwest of Mexico City.

Loreto: Moderate resort geared mainly to avid fishermen and Californians seeking refuge from hectic Los Angeles. Nothing fancy. On the Sea of Cortez on the Baja peninsula.

Manzanillo: An "in" place with lots of charm. Geared to heavy spending and hard playing. Offers good sail fishing. Some of the finest accommodations in Mexico for someone willing to pay the price. South of Puerto Vallarta on the Pacific coast.

Mazatlán: Really a city/resort area. The best hotels and beaches stretch to the north. Varied restaurants, shopping, and night life. Passably good sail and marlin fishing (large fleet). Appeals to travelers on a moderate budget. Not far enough south on the Pacific for reliable winter sun. Not as hot and sticky as southern resorts in the summer.

Mérida: This would not top my list of travel destinations, but if you like vast, indoor markets, the one here is really interesting. In the Yucatán.

Mexico City: This is the largest city in the world and one well worth visiting. Some of the finest restaurants in the country are found here. Splurge. And, this is one of the few places in the country where dressing up is appreciated. Don't miss the Pyramids of Teotihuacán (30 miles north of the city), the Ballet Folklórico, a bullfight, and the National Museum of Anthropology (see p. 289). Ask for the location of murals by Jose Clemente Orozco and Diego Rivera (staircase in National Palace is one). In my opinion the Bazar Sábado (Saturday market) in San Angel is highly overrated. This city is at a high altitude, and daily naps are a good idea. Plus, in the winter months it can be quite cool (rarely cold). Located inland in the south central part of the country.

Oaxaca: A very popular Colonial city with an active market (best Saturday). The nearby ruins of Monte Albán and Mitla are worthwhile excursions. Don't miss the Sunday market in nearby Tlacolula. Well to the southeast of Mexico City.

Palenque: This is one of the finest, if remote, archaeological sites in the country. The buildings are in an open, slightly wooded area. The site is not nearly as impressive as Tikal in Guatemala, but it is very fine. Note that the nearby town is unpleasant. Northeast of San Cristóbal de las Casas.

Playa del Carmen: This is a sleepy little town across from Cozumel. It's really quite charming, but doesn't have the sex appeal of larger, more glitzy resorts. It makes a good base from which to explore the lower portion of the Yucatán.

Puerto Angel: What popular resorts were decades ago. Similar to Puerto Escondido in its attractions. Far south on the Pacific coast.

Puerto Escondido: Laid back, low key—for the budget and back-packing set. People who come here form a free-floating family, often staying for weeks or months. Good seafood at reasonable prices. Good, if highly unorganized, fishing. Surfing as well. Note that things are changing because the southern section of the Pacific coast is catching on rapidly. Note that it can be quite rainy here from May to September.

Puerto Vallarta: A mini-mining town with cobblestoned streets converted to a sophisticated and very popular resort. Best hotels are on the north and south of the city. Hotels in town are noisy and cheap. Broad beach, shopping, and frenetic night life. Fully discovered. Lively and fun. A great place to try parasailing. South of Mazatlán on the central Pacific coast.

San Blas: Lazy "jungle hideaway" with so-so to moderate hotels. Popular with explorer and hippie types willing to put up with nasty no-see-ums (bite like hell). The bugs have kept the area from developing despite its intrinsic beauty. North of Puerto Vallarta.

San Cristóbal de las Casas: The Indian market here was once one of the best in the country. Get up-to-date information before traveling here to see whether the market is again thriving and the area safe. When it was, it was worth a long detour. Note that photographers must be extremely discreet in this area. Indians are offended by it. Far to the south and quite close to Guatemala.

San Miguel de Allende: As an old, inland town with lots of charm and narrow streets atop a low hill, San Miguel has long been a favorite with foreigners. The pace here is relaxed and peaceful. The town is so well-known that there are excellent restaurants and hotels.

It's a good place to study Spanish and painting. Many people stay here for weeks, or even months. Northwest of Mexico City.

Sea of Cortez: That portion of the Pacific between the mainland and peninsula known as the Baja. This is one of the finest areas for birding, fishing, and observation of marine life in the region. Many tours operate in this area. See the appropriate sections under the chapter Doing Things.

Taxco: One of Mexico's most photogenic towns spills down a steep incline and is noted for its work in silver. Walking the streets here requires stamina. It's included on many tours and is easily accessible to the southwest of Mexico City. It is one of the older towns which has definitely been discovered.

Tulúm: A minor archaeological site with a spectacular seaside location. There's a good beach. Many people come here to snorkel. South of Playa del Carmen in the Yucatán.

Uxmal: This is a minor archaeological site in the Yucatán, but there's a Club Med here. Many people enjoy visiting the area. Southwest of Mérida.

Xcaret: Like a park set up for people who want to eat seafood and enjoy snorkeling in the Caribbean. South of Playa del Carmen to the south of Cancún. This entire coastline may be developed in coming years although there is a battle by conservationists to protect it.

Xelha: A national park and one of the most popular snorkeling areas in the country. It's easy to reach from Cancún.

Zihuatanejo: The Mexican counterpart to Ixtapa and only a short drive away to the south. Assorted beach and hillside hotels look onto charming bay filled with a handful of moored yachts. Small and manageable, but now well-known with constantly rising prices (no longer a bargain).

When to Go

You may not have much choice as to when you can travel. However, if you do, the following information will be extremely helpful. The seasons in Central America and Mexico are complex. Furthermore, if you're primarily interested in special interest travel, read the section on Doing Things (see pp. 258–338) before deciding when to travel. Timing can be critical for such activities as birding, fishing, flora, turtle watching, and so on. As an example, two famous movie actresses traveled to Playa Grande (Costa Rica) recently to see the leatherback turtles laying eggs only to find they were 3 months late. Timing is just as important in real life as in film.

When Should You Travel?

If you have a choice, match the time to your goals. It's pointless going to Central America to view off-the-beaten-path archaeological sites in the rainy season (you can't reach them) while this may be the best time to see the mass arrivals of turtles on certain beaches or to go white-water rafting. If you're primarily interested in sun and relaxation, then you'll want to go in the months which give you the best odds for this. Puerto Vallarta (Mexico) has practically no rain from November to May.

Charts on rainfall and temperature are available from the National Tourist Offices (see pp. 25–27). Charts are generally 10-year averages. Little information is given on humidity and wind. Both of these can be important to trip planning and enjoyment. I've included some tips regarding these often overlooked factors below. Using the following information in trip planning doesn't guaranty a great trip, but it will certainly help.

What's the Weather Like?

BELIZE
The weather in Belize is highly variable. The dry season is supposed to last from December to May. The most reliable months are mid-December to April, which explains why this is the peak season with all hotels packed. The hurricane season lasts from July through November. Typically the worst months for storms are mid-August to mid-September. Inland areas tend to be wetter than the coast, which is often quite windy even in the dry season. The rainfall charts frequently given for coastal Belize City are deceptive in that some inland areas experience up to 150 inches of rain a year.

Temperature fluctuates somewhat by month. It's very hot and humid during the summer inland, a little less so along the coast which is tempered by breezes. Some people find high humidity intolerable, others dislike wind almost as much. Few guides mention either.

COSTA RICA

In general, the dry season (summer or *verano*) lasts from December to April. The wet season (winter or *invierno*) runs from May to November. Note how the terms summer and winter can be confusing. The country is packed from mid-December to late March. This is the time most tourists travel to Costa Rica and for a couple of months Costa Rican schools are closed, which means the residents are traveling as well. November is a good risk, since there are few crowds and a good chance of sunny weather (mixed in with some poor days).

This general weather pattern has so many exceptions that you could write a small book on the micro-climates of this varied country. The so-called dry season doesn't really occur in the southernmost part of the Pacific coast (Golfito). The same can be said along much of the Caribbean, especially in Tortuguero (the northeast) where torrential rains occur year-round. On the Isla del Coco (Coco Island) it rains as much as 25 feet a year. However, about the only people who go there are divers, since it's 300 miles off the mainland.

In general, the northwestern part of the country is hot during the summer, warm during the winter (even a little cool at higher altitudes). The southernmost part of the Pacific coast stays hot all year as does the Caribbean coast. The mountainous inland section has an almost steady temperature (low to mid 70s) with the exception of the higher mountain areas, which get cool to cold depending upon elevation and time of year.

The northwestern part of the country can be extremely windy. On a mountain ride you may feel like you're in a wind tunnel. The Pacific Coast also gets quite breezy at times, even with a few storms occuring between May and October. Wind is difficult to predict. Along the Caribbean storms are most common from August to November. Since fishing is excellent in September and October, be cautious by staying close to shore.

GUATEMALA

The dry season (summer or *verano*) extends from late October to early May in the highland plateau (*alta*) where you'll find most of the touristic attractions. The rainy season (winter or *invierno*) from May to October is considerably wetter with rains lasting for a few hours at a time. Note that the terms summer and winter can be confusing. The highlands are also quite cool during the summer season, even occasionally cold as you get into higher elevations. It can also get quite windy at higher elevations. Tikal is in a low tropical area (*baja*). It's driest here from January to April, but come prepared for intermittent showers anytime. The region is warm to hot throughout the entire year and almost always sticky or humid. Avoid traveling to this area during the wet season (their winter, our summer).

HONDURAS

The Bay Islands, Copan, and the rivers used for kayaking and white water rafting are all in the same general zone around San Pedro Sula. The pattern is roughly this: January and February are frequently rainy. March has more rainy days than not, but the sun is beginning to return. April has more sun than rain, but there are still rainy days. From May to August it's hot and sunny with sporadic rains. From September to December it can rain two weeks straight, but weather patterns are totally unpredictable. August through November are months most prone to storms. Most divers come here in March. The best diving is actually in late spring and early summer. And, all of the above has so many exceptions that the Hondurans simply give up trying to predict weather.

MEXICO

Mexico is a huge country with weather patterns as intricate as those of Costa Rica. Still, there are a few generalizations which hold true most of the time for the mainland:
- The farther south you go, the hotter you get.
- The higher in altitude you go, the cooler you get.
- Winter (corresponding to ours) is dry, summer is wet.
- Storms are unpredictable along the Caribbean.
- The farther south you go, the more humid it gets.
- Many coastal areas are hot and sticky (even in winter which corresponds to our winter).
- Wind is usually pleasant relief in much of Mexico, but breezes bordering on gusts can become irritating.

The Baja: A peninsula extending south from California and cut off from the mainland by the Sea of Cortez. It has its own unique weather patterns.
- Much of northern Baja can be cool and frequently wet in winter (especially around Tijuana). Summers are hot to very hot, while deserts in the summer are torrid in the day and cool to cold at night. Visit Mountainous areas in spring and fall, since winters are very cold and summers are like a blast furnace.
- From La Paz south you'll find mild winters, although the best

weather is in spring and fall. Summers are very hot. It's cool in the desert areas at night, however. As in the north, the mountainous areas are cold in the winter and torrid in the summer. Unpredictable, violent storms (*chubascos*) are most common from July to October. Some resorts close down at this time. These storms do *not* come through every year, but are nasty.

INLAND TRIANGLE (GUADALAJARA, MEXICO CITY, AND OAXACA): In the inland area you'll find mild winter weather with occasional cool to cold spells at the higher altitudes including Mexico City. Summers tend to be hot and wet, with 2-hour showers in the afternoon. Weather from October to December is tops. January and February are cool but dry. It gets windy in February and March. By April it's getting hot with rains lasting through September. August is frequently the rainiest month despite what commonly published rainfall charts might indicate.

THE PACIFIC COAST: Much of the Pacific Coast tends to be windy in the winter with very mild temperatures and lots of sun. The most dependable winter sun can be found in the area from Puerto Vallarta south. Winter and early spring are the "in" seasons here. During fall and winter it's possible to have 5 or 6 months without rain, although there's usually a short (2-week) period in late December or early January when the weather is "iffy." Summers are hot to very hot, and you'll need a room with air-conditioning or with a hilltop location for breezes. From June 15 to October it can be sticky.

THE YUCATAN (SOUTHERN CARIBBEAN COAST): The Yucatán has two seasons—hot and hotter. The inland areas of the peninsula are usually 10 degrees (Fahrenheit) hotter than the coast. May is extremely hot. In the summer, the dry areas are torrid, the wetter areas steamy. The Gulf Coast is very unpredictable, and storms appear sporadically. Or, as the natives put it, hurricanes have no rudder. The *nortes* (north winds) sweep in from late fall to early winter, but from late winter to early spring the weather is ideal—the perfect time to visit the region.

Using Time Wisely

This section gives you a few tips on how to take advantage of whatever time is available for your trip.

How Long Can You Travel?

The length of your trip may be predetermined. However, extend your trip to the maximum length possible. Employers will often bend a little with enough advance notice. Minimum stays have already been suggested, but I'll repeat them. You need 7 to 10 days to sample Belize, 14 to 21 days to get a feel for Costa Rica (months to know it well), 10 to 14 days to see Guatemala, 7 to 10 days for Honduras, and a life time to get to know Mexico. However, for a relaxing seaside vacation in Mexico 7 days is fine. Following are some tips to keep in mind:

- Subtract two days of the overall trip as wasted—the first and the last.
- Use mileage charts and a map to plan your itinerary. Trace your route in red with a felt-tipped pen. Now add up the mileage.
- Divide the total mileage by the number of days you'll be in the region. (Don't count the first and the last).
- If you're traveling by bus, car, tour, or train, cover no more than 150 miles per day. You will sometimes wind up having traveled farther than the average distance. If you consistently cover more than 150 miles, your trip will be too time consuming, as well as too tiring.
- If you will be flying between two points, ignore the mileage between them—and simply write off one full day. Do this for each plane trip you'll be taking. Subtract these days from the total number of days you'll be in the region (minus the first and last days). This will give you a good idea of how many days you'll have left to enjoy your trip. You will simply not believe the delays and cancellations in regards to air travel.
- If you find that you'll be traveling too far in too short a period, admit it. Some options: Cut down on activities or sights, extend your trip, or plan a second trip for a later date.

Structuring Short Trips

The shorter the trip, the more organized it must be. Every phase of the trip should be planned to help you avoid waits (you'll still have some anyway). Have reservations for plane flights, hotels, and fancier restaurants made well in advance of arrival. If you plan to attend festivals, musical events, the ballet, or any popular tourist attractions which could be sold out—get reservations in advance if possible.

- Watch your schedule very carefully. Certain events take place on certain days (like the bullfights and *ballet folklórico*) in Mexico City, Mexico. Museums are often open at odd or restricted times like the Museo del Oro (Gold Museum) in San José, Costa Rica. Certain markets are open or best on certain days, like Chichicastenango, Guatemala. So if you're on a tight schedule, work out the smallest details in advance. The section on Doing Things (see pp. 258–338) will give you insight. Read it carefully, get as much information as possible, and plan accordingly.
- Limit yourself to one carryon bag. This will save you time.
- You pay more for a structured trip, but it's worth it.
- Consider taking a tour. These tend to be more expensive, but highly organized to take advantage of limited time.

Structuring Long Trips

A long trip in the peak season should be structured like a short trip, because hotels will be packed and planes booked solid. However, during the rest of the year a loosely-organized trip has lots of appeal.

- The big advantage of off-season travel is that you have a choice: You're never bound by a prearranged schedule, you can shift travel plans daily (and often do), you can move out of a hotel you don't like, you can seek out typical restaurants on your own—in short, you can do just about anything at whim.
- Loosely structured trips are less expensive.You'll discover how easy it is to cut costs if you think and act like the local residents and are willing to bend and bargain.

Who to Go With

Should you make a trip by yourself, with a friend or spouse, or with a group of people you like? Should you take the kids or a baby? The hints in this chapter should be helpful, not only in making your decision, but also in living with it.

Solo Travel

Advantages to traveling alone: You can do as you damn well please, when you damn well please, at your own pace, with or without someone else along, as you choose. You have total freedom.

On the other hand, you pay for such freedom. If you go on a tour, you may be socked with a single surcharge. If you're totally on your own, you will have no way of sharing expenses at mealtimes, in the hotel, and for personal transportation (mainly a car).

You may also be lonely—but loneliness can be converted into an advantage, as it will force you to get to know local residents and other travelers. You may also put yourself in danger, but much of this can be avoided by following basic safety guidelines (see p. 178).

Traveling Alone and Liking It
- As a loner, take short and inexpensive tours. You'll meet people and keep your costs down.
- Use public transportation. It's extremely inexpensive, and you'll meet many fascinating people.
- Share the cost of a room. A single only costs a dollar or two less than a double. If you're concerned about sharing a room with a stranger, put anything of value in the hotel safe.
- When eating alone, bring a newspaper, a book, or a journal. If you meet someone interesting, fine; if not, you'll catch up on your reading or note taking.
- Go a little before or after the peak dinner hours, to avoid running into poor treatment at the hands of waiters, as solo travelers sometimes do.

Women Traveling Alone
- Most women advise other women not to travel alone in Mexico. In Belize, Costa Rica, Guatemala, and Honduras there are fewer problems if you use common sense.
- Mexicans often hassle single women. Sometimes the hassling is

limited to hissing, whistling, and lewd comments. Occasionally, things get more serious.

- Women traveling alone are often considered sexually permissive, because they're breaking a social taboo. The older you get, the more this taboo breaks down.
- Read the section on personal safety (p. 278).

Single but Looking for Company

Singles who would rather not be alone can check into resorts and organizations catering to them. If this doesn't appeal to you, begin travel and hook up spontaneously with other singles. This is often quite easy to do in Central America and Mexico, because people feel safer traveling with another person and like to share costs.

- Cruises are a natural for someone looking for a travel partner, but ask many questions about the available cruises to match them to your personality and age (see p. 67).
- Probably better are the many resorts run by Club Med, oriented to couples and singles. These are world-famous and located in some of the most beautiful settings in Mexico.

Club Med (Head Office)
40 West 57th Street
New York, NY 10019
Tel: (800) 528-3100
    (212) 750-1670

- A number of companies set up tours for single people or put singles together through a networking system:

Gallivanting
515 East 79th Street,
    Suite 20F
New York, NY 10021
Tel: (800) 933-9699
    (212) 988-0617

Gramercy Singleworld
444 Madison Avenue
New York, NY 10022
Tel: (800) 223-6490
    (212) 758-2433

Mesa Travel Singles Registry
P.O. Box 2235

Costa Mesa, CA 92628
Tel: (714) 546-8181

Partners-in-Travel
11660 Chenault Street,
    Suite 119
Los Angeles, CA 90049
Tel: (310) 476-4869

Singleworld Cruises and Tours
P.O. Box 1999
401 Theodore Fremd Avenue
Rye, NY 10580
Tel: (800) 223-6490
    (914) 967-3334

Society of Single Travelers
3000 Ocean Park Boulevard,
   Suite 1004
Santa Monica, CA 90405
Tel: (213) 450-8510

Travel Mates International,
   Inc.
49 West 44th Street
New York, NY 10036
Tel: (212) 221-6565

Travel Companion Exchange
P.O. Box 833
Amityville, NY 11701
Tel: (516) 454-0880

Some agencies specialize in getting older, single people together:

Solo Flights
63 High Noon Road
Weston, CT 06883
Tel: (800) 266-1566
   (203) 226-9993

Suddenly Single Tours, Ltd.
161 Dreiser Loop
New York, NY 10475
Tel: (800) 859-8396
   (718) 379-8800

Saga Holidays
222 Berkeley Street
Boston, MA 02116
Tel: (800) 343-0273
   (617) 262-2262
Tries to match people up
on cruises or escorted tours
to avoid paying single supplements.

Twosome and Family Travel

The big advantage of staying together are shared company and shared costs. It costs far less for two people to travel together than to go independently. But savings mean nothing unless you're both doing what you really want to do and get along well.

Traveling as a Twosome
- If you and your partner cannot agree on the purpose of a trip, consider traveling independently.
- Meet again in places you'd both like to visit.
- Carry your own bags, unless you're willing to pay someone else to do it. It is unfair to ask a partner to carry your luggage.
- Share all responsibilities. Anyone who has to make all the decisions shoulders the burden for all mistakes.

- Iron out all money matters before you start. Good reckoning makes good friends.
- Each person of a married couple should have control of part of the money, including "mad money" for special occasions. Each person should be responsible for handling part of the payment for everyday expenses.

Family Travel

The more people involved in a trip, the more complex the planning is going to be. You can't expect to suit all tastes at all times.

- Talk about the purpose of the trip. Let each person contribute ideas. Is the trip for relaxation, stimulation, or some group activity (special interest)? Or will it combine these?
- Everyone should have some "mad" money. Teach kids about foreign currencies and let them deal with it on their own.
- Travel in non-peak periods. Yes, take your children out of school. Never let school interfere with your children's education.
- Dress casually. Everyone should wear comfortable shoes.
- Since each person will carry his own luggage, the size of the bag must match the size of the person.
- Travel light. Use backpacks.
- Pack several days ahead of time. Use a checklist. Let or help each child pack bags. Involve them in pre-trip shopping.
- Each person should have a map.
- Carry plenty of snacks. Lots of individually wrapped or packed items work best.
- If your kids like cameras, radios, or stereos, encourage them to bring one along. They can sell or trade them at the end of the trip.
- Bring a ball (for catch), books, cards, a frisbee, and toys. If a blanket or stuffed animal is permanently attached to one of your kids, bring it.
- Prepare for all minor medical emergencies with an appropriate kit containing items used regularly.
- Gear the pace of the trip to that of the youngest member of the group. Oftentimes less really is more.
- Book flights which include meals. Flights at normal mealtimes don't necessarily have meals. Ask.
- Select seats in advance. Choose a place best suited to your family's needs. If you can't choose a seat in advance, get to the airport early to get better seats.
- Travel non-stop whenever possible. At least, fly direct so that you don't have to change planes.
- If plane changes are required after a long flight, consider stop-

ping over for a day before continuing on. Make this stopover part of the fun of the overall trip. Plan something special.

- Agree that all responsibilities will be shared. If they're not, one person's always to blame—someone's got to be wrong, right? Actually, not, since travel often throws curves which no one has control over. But that doesn't stop people from getting angry.
- Children need numerous breaks: For a trip to the beach, a picnic, a pause for a cold drink. Slow down. Let go.
- Avoid constant long-distance travel by bus or car. It bores the hell out of kids. Marathon travel and families don't mix.
- Younger children appreciate markets, museums, and ruins—in small doses. Children are activity-oriented. They'd rather go swimming than to the ruins at Tulum—or would rather combine the two, preferably in a period of 20 minutes (here they can).
- Split up a party from time to time, so that those primarily interested in cultural attractions or shopping can have adequate time to enjoy them. Encourage separation at appropriate times so that each person feels in control and free.
- Central Americans and Mexicans like children. They absolutely adore babies.
- However, some hotels and resorts cater to adults.
- And, numerous restaurants catering to wealthy residents and foreigners detest the presence of small children. Eat outside or in places where noise and dropped food won't create hostility.
- When traveling as a group, always have a plan in case someone gets lost. Giving each child a "get unlost" card is an excellent idea. Explain to them exactly what to do.

Traveling with a Baby
- Stay in a place catering to families. For instance, the Club Med in Ixtapa has a program which allows parents free time by taking care of children off and on during the day.
- If driving, bring a safety seat. Car travel is tiring, but makes more sense than using local buses (see pp. 90–98, 194–205).
- When making plane reservations, schedule departure and arrival times not to coincide with the baby's feedings.
- Give the baby water (not milk) to drink during takeoff and landing: The sucking will help relieve pressure.
- Bring a towel to cover you during feeding and to place under the baby at changing time.
- Bring baby books, baby wipes, a small blanket, a cloth carrier, disposable diapers, life vest, plastic pail and shovel for beach, plastic bags for disposable diapers, small toys for the baby to play with, and a folding (umbrella) stroller.

- Disposable diapers are hard to find and expensive abroad.
- Baby food is often located in pharmacies (*farmacias*).

For Older People

The following organizations have information for older travelers. Elderhostel offers reasonably-priced courses worldwide for people over 60. Golden companions offers a networking system for people over 45. The term older may mean different things to different organizations, airlines, hotels, and so on. Many discounts begin at 50 (or younger).

American Association of
    Retired Persons
601 East Street NW
Washington, DC 20049
Tel: (202) 434-2277

Anderson Travel Tours
2707 North Loop West,
    Suite 390
Houston, TX 77008
Tel: (713) 864-2884
A tour wholesaler which caters
to older people. Sells tours to
Belize, Guatemala, and Mexico
(its main destination).

Canadian Association of
    Retired Persons
27 Queen Street East,
    Suite 1304
Toronto, ON M5C 2M6
Canada
Tel: (416) 363-8748

Elderhostel
75 Federal Street
Boston, MA 02110
Tel: (617) 426-7788
(Please do not call, write)

Golden Age Travellers
Pier 27
The Embarcadero
San Francisco, CA 94111
Tel: (800) 258-8880
    (415) 296-0151

Golden Companions
P.O. Box 754
Pullman, WA 99163
Tel: (208) 858-2183

Grand Circle Travel
347 Congress Street
Boston, MA 02210
Tel: (800) 248-3737
    (617) 350-7500

Interhostel
University of New Hampshire
6 Garrison Avenue
Durham, NH 03824
Tel: (800) 733-9753
    (603) 862-1147

Mature Outlook
6001 North Clark Street
Chicago, IL 60660
Tel: (800) 336-6330

Mayflower Tours
1225 Warren Avenue
Downers Grove, IL 60515
Tel: (800) 323-7604
    (708) 960-3430

National Council of Senior
    Citizens
1331 F Street NW
Washington, DC 20004
Tel: (202) 347-8800

Merry Widows Dance Tours
1515 North Westshore
    Boulevard
Tampa, FL 33607
Tel: (813) 289-5923

Saga Tours
222 Berkeley Street
Boston, MA 02116
Tel: (800) 343-0273
    (617) 262-2262

Younger Travelers

Generally, the young have more time, less money, and more energy
than other travelers.
- Pick up International Student ID or Youth Cards (see p. 4).
- Don't hitch—take inexpensive public transportation instead. It'll
  get you anywhere for next to nothing.
- Consider a pre-set time to call home each week, even if just for a
  few minutes (see p. 254).

For Women Only

Womantour organizes both group and individual tours for women alone.
Rainbow Adventures is aimed at adventure travel for women over 30.

Rainbow Adventures
1308 Sherman Avenue
Evanston, IL 60201
Tel: (708) 864-4570

Womantour
5314 North Figueroa Street
Los Angeles, CA 90042
Tel: (213) 255-1115

Traveling with Pets

You're allowed to take pets abroad, but why would you want to?
Mexicans thoroughly dislike pets. Very few hotels welcome them.

Tours and Cruises

Tours and cruises are extremely popular. Tours to Central America are especially good because they often include guides who know the region well and add a special dimension to travel there. Cruises are extremely relaxing ways to take a break, if just for a few days.

Tours

Tours can be the answers to travelers' prayers or forms of temporary damnation. Ask yourself, then, whether or not you are a good prospect for a tour. Loners should not take tours. Most people who are impatient standing in lines will not like tours. Impulsive, free-spirited people often regret traveling on tours. And, anyone on an extremely tight budget probably can't afford them.

On the other hand, people who dislike unplanned weekends, who are not very aggressive, who lead scheduled lives, and who don't speak Spanish find tours an excellent way to travel. For those in poor health, joining a tour may be more attractive than traveling alone. Furthermore, tours can take you safely into some areas where traveling alone might be ill-advised. In short, it's a question of personality. If you do decide to join a tour, its goals and yours should match.

Advantages of Tours
- Tours can save you money, lots of it in some cases. You're joining a group that buys everything as a block, which ensures substantial price reductions across the board.
- Tours can be prepaid, allowing you to know in advance how much the trip is going to cost.
- Tour packages, which cover all major expenses, allow you to pay in dollars. This avoids the currency exchange hassle.
- Tours are often tailored to individual needs or interest, from fishing to whale watching. These can be much better than anything you could arrange. Some of these tours are accompanied by highly-trained personnel, making something spectacular out of what could normally go unnoticed.
- Tours offer companionship and frequently humor for travelers prone to loneliness.
- Tours help less aggressive travelers to cope with the language barrier and avoid embarrassing situations.
- Tours get you into special hotels and restaurants in peak seasons. And get the most that place has to give.
- Tours save you time and energy by preventing potential hassles

and avoiding others. This can be a great advantage in Central America and Mexico, where things frequently go wrong. Note, however, that tours cannot necessarily control this either.

- Tours are excellent for people who are physically or mentally exhausted and don't want to be bothered with details. The resiliency required for independent travel is high.
- Tours are organized by experts who know the most interesting sights to see. Competent travel guides in each city help you understand its beauty, history, and tradition.
- Tours can take you to places which could be potentially dangerous on your own. Skilled guides, proficient in local customs and language, may help you get into an area and out safely, but still with full enjoyment of the area.

Disadvantages of Tours

- Tours herd people together. To find out how you react to this experience, go on a local tour in your home town. If it's enjoyable you may find a tour enjoyable as well. If it turns you off, then skip longer tours altogether.
- Tours can be hurried, impersonal, and flavorless affairs. Throughout the trip you are bound to follow a prearranged schedule, geared to a group and its needs. It takes the travail out of travel, but it also wrings the lust out of wanderlust.
- Most tour groups travel by bus. It's convenient and usually comfortable, but it can be equally boring and confining. And, it is not always as safe as operators may tell you.
- You pay for a tour sight unseen, which is something like marrying the same way. You don't know what you've got until it's in the boat. There's no real chance for a refund if things go awry.
- Tours are groups of people, people whom you may or may not like. Whatever your feelings, you're stuck.
- The words in tour brochures are just that—words. A "firstclass" hotel may end up being, well, second-rate, even in Saltillo.
- Most tour contracts squirm with loopholes and catches.
- If you don't like the hotels chosen for you or the restaurant's bland fare, your complaints may fall on deaf ears.
- In some cases, you can save money by planning an identical trip on your own. One veteran traveler calls this avoiding the "stupidity tax." This is true in many instances, but not all, especially on special interest tours.

Special Note on Special Interest Tours

A number of tours geared to special interests are covered in the chapter Doing Things (see pp. 258–338). They may be quite expensive for a number of reasons. The tours may require special knowledge, highly-trained guides, expensive equipment, pre-arranged permission from local governments, reservations made far in advance for unique jungle lodges, and so on. The value of these trips is often quite subtle. For example, you might be able to go for next-to-nothing to a good birding area and see next to nothing whereas with a competent guide who knows the area, the birds, and the right time to look for them, you might see as many as 200 to 300 species. So, if you were really into birding, the difference between total frustration and absolute exhilaration might be worth the extra money.

Tour Package Checklist

If you take the trouble to consult tour brochures or agents and find answers to the following questions, you will be in a much better position to judge the quality of any tour package you're considering.

- Is the tour operator a member of the National Tour Association, Inc. or United States Tour Operators' Association (see following)?
- How long has the tour operator been in business (the longer, the better)?
- Will the tour operator give a bank reference (good ones will do this as if by second nature).
- How much will the tour cost altogether?
- Will a service charge be added on? If so, how much will it be? Often you'll find that there is a service charge outlined in very fine print at the end of the brochure. Words like "extra," "optional," and "bonus" should also be red flags to you.
- What extra or supplemental charges will apply to you? What will optional packages cost you? How much is the deposit?
- What are the penalties for cancellation?
- Are substitutions allowed on the passenger list?
- Can the dates of the tour be changed arbitrarily?
- Can the schedule or itinerary be rearranged for any reason?
- Can the tour be canceled? How much notice must be given?
- Does the tour include transportation to and from the airport near your home? Most tours don't.
- Does the tour cost include the full price of airfare to and from Central America or Mexico? What are the dates and times of flights? Are the flights nonstop?
- Does the tour price cover all airport departure taxes?
- What kind of ground transportation is provided?
- Does it include all transfers from airports, bus, and train stations?

Does it include the cost of transportation to meals and night life?
- What kind of intercity transportation is provided: Bus, train, air?
- If it's a bus, is it air-conditioned, or "air-cooled" (a tour expression meaning windows can be opened)?
- What is the quality of the bus? Does it have a bathroom? If it does, it's probably a pretty decent bus.
- If it's a plane or a train, what class will you be in?
- How many nights' accommodation is included in the tour price? Are any nights left out?
- Is there a supplemental charge if you want a room to yourself?
- Which hotels will you be staying in? Get the names.
- Can other hotels be substituted arbitrarily? If so, get the names.
- What's included in the room? Bath or shower? Two beds?
- Where are the hotels located? Tell them to show you on a map.
- Are all tips and taxes included in the room price?
- Is there any charge whatsoever that's not included?
- Are all meals included in the price of the tour? Is any meal not included? If not, why not? Or if not, where not?
- Where will you be eating? In the hotel? In a restaurant? What restaurants?
- What's included with the meal? Is wine included? Is coffee included? Is dessert included? Is anything excluded?
- Do you have a choice from the menu at each meal? Can you make substitutions at no extra charge?
- Are all tips and service charges for meals included?
- Who pays the entrance fee to museums, galleries, and events?
- What is the pace of the tour? Does it leave you any free time?
- Does the tour spend enough time in each city or area to let you get anything out of the visit?
- Will the tour have an escort? Will the same escort be with the tour for the whole time? If so, that's an added value.
- Will the tour have travel guides for each city?
- Does the tour include insurance for accidents, health, baggage, etc.? If so, how much? Any deductible? Any exclusions?
- Who takes care of the baggage? Is there any extra cost? How many bags are *free*? Are all tips to porters included?

The Tour Payment Protection Plan

The American Society of Travel Agents (ASTA) offers a Tour Payment Protection Plan that is designed to protect people from agencies going out of business and leaving passengers stranded. The plan does protect you if the agency files for bankruptcy (many don't). The ringer is that if the agency doesn't, the plan is of little value. For information on present members contact:

ASTA
American Society of Travel Agents
1100 King Street
Alexandria, VA 22314
Tel: (703) 739-2782

Consumer Protection through NTA, Inc.

The National Tour Association, Inc., requires its members to meet certain requirements with the intention of protecting consumers against unscrupulous business practices and bankruptcy.

National Tour Association, Inc.
546 East Main Street
Lexington, KY 40596
Tel: (800) 682-8886
      (606) 253-1036

Consumer Protection through USTOA

The United States Tour Operators Association offers better consumer protection in that its members must post bond of $1 million dollars, which can be used in either insolvency or actual bankruptcy of a member company. For information write:

United States Tour Operators Association
211 East 51st Street, Suite 12B
New York, NY 10022
Tel: (212) 750-7371

Cruises

Going to Central America or Mexico by cruise ship is a romantic way to travel. Most lines sail out of Los Angeles, Miami, San Francisco, and Tampa. Common ports of call are Acapulco, Cabo San Lucas, Cozumel, Manzanillo, Mazatlán, Puerto Vallarta, and Zihuatanejo. And, of course, travel through the Panama Canal is a long-time favorite. Panama is not covered in this guide, but travel through the canal is usually quite safe.

Booking a Cabin

Travel agents specializing in cruises are your best resource. Booking a cruise is really booking a tour—the very heart of travel agency business. For information on agents specializing in cruises only, send a stamped, self addressed envelope to the National Association of Cruise Only Agencies, which represents approximately 700 agencies throughout the United States. Each of these must meet the associations standards (a form of protection for you). You may request information on agencies in any two states for free:

NACOA
3191 Coral Way, Suite 630
Miami, FL 33145
Tel: (305) 446-7732

The Cost
- The cost of a cruise varies dramatically by line, length of the cruise, and choice of cabin.
- If you're older, always ask about discounts. The age cut off may be lower than you think.
- If you want to travel alone (single cabin), the cost will be exorbitant (see below).
- The higher up you get, the higher the cost. Cabins on upper decks are quiet and offer the best views.
- Bigger rooms (or suites) cost more because space is precious. A bath instead of a shower adds to the cost for the same reason.
- Portholes, because they offer a view, add to the cost. This is an outside, versus an inside cabin.
- If money is a major consideration, ask whether there are any ways to reduce the cost, such as agreeing to standby status.
- Note that some cruises are fighting last-minute reductions by promising best rates to people who buy tickets first.

Extra Costs
- On some cruise ships tips are not included in the fare.
- Any land tours or excursions to the mainland cost extra on almost all cruise ships. These can be quite expensive, especially if they include a guide and transportation. However, if they are included in the overall price, that's added value.
- Wine, beer, cocktails—all cost extra. On some lines you'll get complimentary wine with a meal.

If Traveling Alone
- A number of cruises now offer a program which guarantees you'll get a roommate if you want to keep costs down.
- If they don't find a match, you'll be given a single room without supplemental charges.
- If a cruise does not offer such a program, ask whether it's possible to book a room without a supplement. If you book a room far in advance, some cruises will not charge the supplement. This

works best in non-peak periods. If you don't ask for this charge to be waived, it won't be—I can assure you.
- Some cruises even offer single rooms at no extra charge if they're having trouble filling the ship.

Length of the Cruise
- Most cruises last 1 or 2 weeks, providing adequate time for rest.
- A few cruises offer 3 and 4-day voyages (the first and last days are often write-offs).

Motion Sickness
Some people get sick at the sight of sea water (see p. 237).

Special Cruise Tips
- When booking a cruise, find out whether airfare is included to the port of embarkation. If it is, it may be a special fare and better than you can do on your own. However, comparison shop before signing the dotted line.
- Check on cruise prices by proposed sailing dates. Perhaps, by changing your travel plans slightly, you might cut costs.
- When comparing cruise lines and prices, ask how long the price is guaranteed. Some lines change fares on a moment's notice, others guaranty rates until a specific date. Ask about these dates. If you wait too long, you may have to pay extra.
- The lowest-priced cabins on most cruises go first.
- Some spur-of-the-moment clubs can get you the lowest rates possible if you're willing to take a cruise at the last minute.
- Since word about this has gotten out, ask whether room rates will be reduced to match any later reductions for other passengers. A few lines are now insisting that they will only give their lowest rates to people who book far in advance. Ask anyway and get it in writing.
- Get as much information on the ship as possible, including its age (has it been renovated?), its size, and its overall reputation for food and service. Smaller ships are rougher for those prone to motion sickness, but they are much more practical for shore excursions. Larger ships are much better for those interested in meeting people.
- Ask about the typical age and type of person attracted to a specific cruise. Some are geared to older people, others to a younger crowd. Some are sedate, others party-oriented.
- Many cruise lines have rooms for disabled people. This is one of the best options for someone who wants a glimpse of Central America or Mexico without the many hassles of land travel.

- Cruises are not geared to getting to know places. Central America or Mexico will be a backdrop, not the main performance.
- Cruises frequently offer shore excursions during mealtimes—very annoying, but a fact. Ask about the exact schedule when booking a cruise.
- Space is critical, so rooms on luxury liners are tight, and baths miniscule even for a midget.
- Bring a bottle of your favorite booze. Drinks may be overpriced, undersized, or watered-down.
- There are so many free snacks and edible extras on board that someone may whimsically remark that you board as a passenger, disembark as cargo.

Tipping on Board (see p. 170)

Flying to Central America and Mexico

Plane travel is the fastest and most convenient way to get to Central America and most points in Mexico. In some instances, it can even be the least expensive way.

Plane Travel

Plane travel is always the least tiring and time-consuming method of travel. Prices to Mexico are particularly reasonable since there are so many charters flying to its major destinations.

Saving Money by Comparison Shopping

Flying is often the only practical way to travel. Yet, on every flight, some passengers end up paying as much as 3 or 4 times what others pay. Smart travelers learn strategies to keep costs down.

- Call a local travel agent and ask what airlines fly to your destination. Ask the agent for the lowest possible fare to that city. This information is computerized.
- While the agent checks on prices, call different airlines. Use their 800 numbers to save money. Ask whether there are any unadvertised specials. Call the same number twice to get different airline agents. They will often work differently. One may offer you information that the other doesn't. This tip may seem absurd, but it isn't.
- Some foreign carriers to check into:
  Aero Mexico (Mexico—Tel: (800) 237-6639)
  Aviateca (Guatemala—Tel: (800) 327-9832)
  Lacsa (Costa Rica—Tel: (800) 225-2272
  Mexicana (Mexico—Tel: (800) 531-7921)
  Sahsa (Honduras—Tel: (800) 327-1225)
- Watch for introductory fares or special coupon offers. As airlines open up new routes, they offer incentives to new customers in the form of temporarily reduced rates. These tend to be heavily advertised in local newspapers—so stay alert to the possibility of coming up with a once-in-a-lifetime bargain.
- Once the travel agent has quoted you a price, ask whether there are any ways of reducing the price. Keep notes.
- If you live near Canada, consider flying out of that country. You may be able to take advantage of the weak Canadian dollar.

- Always ask about special passes. They may go under odd names like MayaPass or MexiPass or you name it. It is not unusual for these passes to go unmentioned unless you ask. They may give you numerous stopover privileges in more than one country at greatly reduced rates. Naming passes is a waste of time since they change constantly. Knowing that they often exist is the important tip.

Asking the Right Question
- Let the person know immediately that you're bargain-hunting by asking for the lowest fare from A to B.
- Ask if there are any incentive fares.
- Find out if there are reductions for midweek flights.
- Ask about reductions for night flights.
- After you've bought a ticket, continue to watch for better deals. If a bargain pops up, turn in your ticket and go with the better fare. In some cases, you'll save money even if you pay a cancellation fee.

Special Tour Rates on Scheduled Airlines
In most areas specialized tour companies buy blocks of seats on scheduled airlines. These seats are sold at rates far below those offered by the airline itself. This is most common with flights to Mexico, but as the market into Costa Rica expands, who knows?
- Know the companies in your area which specialize in low-cost airfare. They advertise heavily in Sunday papers.
- Call about any upcoming specials. You need an inside edge. Get to know an agent well enough so that he will go out of his way for you.
- These companies advertize on Sunday, but set their rates on Thursday. Call Thursday, since the lowest price seats are gone by Monday. *This is an extremely important tip.*

Comparison Shopping—Charters
Tour and charter companies rent planes for charters. In a few cases the company actually owns the planes and runs a sort of mini-airline. Presently, most charters fly to Mexico. Hopefully, as travel expands to Central America, you'll see charters to that region as well.
- Charters save you money, because seats are discounted as an incentive for quick sale.
- Charters often leave at weird times and rarely on time. But to save a buck, they make sense.
- Charter companies cannot cancel a flight within 10 days of the intended departure.

- There are stiff cancellation penalty clauses on most charter airlines. You can take out cancellation insurance (see p. 7).

Maverick Airlines

Small airlines come and go. Their offerings also come and go, but at the time of writing the following company was an example of a maverick airline offering good rates to Mexico. By the time you read this guide, it may have disappeared, been swallowed by another airline, or simply discontinued flights to Mexico. The tip is that maverick airlines exist, but are not highly publicized. Ask about these:

Morris Air
260 East Morris Avenue
Salt Lake City, UT 84115
Tel: (800) 466-7747
    (801) 466-7747

Comparison Shopping—Clearinghouses and Clubs

Clearinghouses and travel clubs offer reduced tickets. Basically, they pick up unbooked spaces on tours and flights.
- You pay a service fee to a clearinghouse or club.
- These clubs are geared to spur-of-the-moment travel. You may have only a few days to make up your mind.
- Once you pay your money, there's no time to cancel.
- Also, you have to get to the point of origin of the charter, cruise, or tour that's being offered.
- Many of these clubs have a "hot line." Make sure the club has a toll-free number for its clients.

Discount Travel International
114 Forrest Avenue
The Ives Building,
    Suite 203
Narberth, PA 19072
Tel: (215) 668-7184

Encore's Short Notice
4501 Forbes Boulevard
Lanham, MD 20706
Tel: (800) 638-0930
    (301) 459-8020

Hotline Travel
3001 East Pershing
    Boulevard
Cheyenne, WY 82001
Tel: (800) 543-0110

Last Minute Travel Club
1249 Boylston Street
Boston, MA 02215
Tel: (800) 527-8646
    (617) 267-9800

Moment's Notice
425 Madison Avenue
New York, NY 10017
Tel: (212) 486-0503

Spur of the Moment
  Tours & Cruises
411 North Harbor
  Boulevard, Suite 302
San Pedro, CA 90731
Tel: (800) 343-1991
     (310) 521-1070

Traveler's Advantage
3033 South Parker Road,
  Suite 900
Aurora, CO 80014
Tel: (800) 548-1116

Vacations to Go
1501 Augusta Drive,
  Suite 415
Houston, TX 77057
Tel: (800) 338-4962
     (713) 974-2121

Worldwide Discount Travel
  Club
1674 Meridian Avenue,
  Suite 206
Miami Beach, FL 33139
Tel: (305) 534-2082

Consolidators or Bucket Shops
- These companies or individuals sell tickets at wholesale prices. Look for them in travel sections of Sunday newspapers. Large cities, such as New York, often have the largest number of consolidators (bucket shops).
- Always pay for tickets with credit cards.

Consumer Wholesale Travel
34 West 33rd Street,
  Suite 1014
New York, NY 10001
Tel: (800) 223-6862
     (212) 695-8435

TFI Tours
34 West 32nd Street,
  12th Floor

New York, NY 10001
Tel: (800) 745-8000
     (212) 745-1140

Unitravel
1177 North Warson Road
St. Louis, MO 63132
Tel: (800) 325-2222
     (314) 569-0900

The following publication specializes in information on low-cost flights. Ninety percent of its information is on consolidators.

Jax Fax
397 Post Road
Darien, CT 06820
Tel: (203) 655-8746

Using Travel Agents

It costs no more to buy a ticket through a travel agent than to buy one directly from the airline. Unfortunately, though, many agents do not like working with discounted fares, because they make a commission on the total dollar value of tickets sold.

- Comparison shop with travel agents. Tell each you want to know the best deal to get you from A to B.
- A few agencies (not many) now guaranty that they will come up with the lowest possible rate or refund any overpayment.
- Sometimes a good agent will come up with a tour fare costing less than comparable airfare. This is hard to do.
- Agents who know how to wring low fares from the computer are invaluable. Reward them with all of your business.

Agencies Specializing in Cutting Airline Costs

The following are two travel agencies specializing in airfare cost reduction. Travel Avenue charges a set fee per person, so the more complicated your itinerary, the more valuable the service. However, it refunds from 5 to 23 percent of the fare as a way of covering this expense. It also searches for the lowest possible fares, including charters for your trip. Travel For Less specializes in keeping costs down for travelers who have to travel on a specific schedule but do not know how to jump through hoops to make substantial savings.

Travel Avenue
641 West Lake Street,
  Suite 201
Chicago, IL 60606
Tel: (800) 333-3335
    (312) 876-1116

Travel For Less
1301 47th Street
Brooklyn, NY 11219
Tel: (800) 223-6045

Student Discounts

All students and teachers should contact student agencies (see p. 4) for information on potential airline discounts.

Barter or Trade Exchanges

In most Sunday newspapers there is a section dealing with the sale of plane tickets. Many of these come from individuals with frequent flyer coupons. The legality is highly questionable, especially on international flights. Only buy a ticket if it can be issued in your name.

Free Travel Through Courier Services

Look for Air Courier Service in the Yellow Pages. These companies pay for all or part of your fare. Many books, magazines, and newsletters have named specific companies, only to have these inundated with inquiries. The companies then have no need for additional couriers. Major libraries have Yellow Page directories for most major cities. Librarians can help you get the addresses of courier companies. Write as many as you have the patience and stamina to try. Getting a job as a courier is not easy. Also check with major companies in your area to see whether they ever need courier services.

One company specializes in low-cost airfare from New York and Miami, which includes courier service, charter, and stand-by fares.

Discount Travel
  International (DTI)
169 West 81st Street
New York, NY 10024
Tel: (212) 362-3636

Discount Travel
  International (DTI)
801 Alton Road #1
Miami Beach, FL 33139
Tel: (305) 538-1616

Do not confuse this company with the discount travel club of the same name listed earlier.

Money-Saving Strategies

No matter how you decide to travel, you can usually save money by following certain strategies.

Buy Tickets in the United States
- Buy as many tickets as possible in the United States (or Canada). If you buy tickets abroad, you'll pay in foreign currency, often at a preset and unfavorable rate of exchange.
- Airlines cannot raise the price of a ticket once you've paid for it. However, simply making a reservation does not guaranty the price. Rules abroad may differ—ask.
- Hard to believe, but true: A round-trip ticket may be less than one-way fare. Always ask about this if you're traveling only in one direction.
- When getting an airline ticket price, ask if it includes all fees and taxes for international travel, including inspection fees and departure taxes on all legs of the flight.

Buying Tickets in Advance
Since only a certain number of seats are allotted for highly reduced fares, you can save hundreds of dollars by buying a ticket far in advance. In short, the early bird does get the worm. The exceptions to this have already been noted in the section on travel clubs and

clearinghouses (pp. 73–74), where the last in may get the best buy. Also, risk takers often steal tickets on charters by waiting until the last minute to buy a ticket in the off-season (see below).

Keeping Flexible About Travel Dates
- Be flexible to take advantage of lower rates. What if you have to leave on a Thursday instead of a Friday or return on a Monday instead of a Sunday? Isn't it worth $100?
- Ask about excursion rates, with minimum and maximum lengths of stay. By adding or subtracting a few days from your planned trip, you can save yourself a good deal of money.
- Ask about standby fares, good risks in the off season

Stopover or Extension Privileges
Frankly, this is rare in Central America and Mexico, but it never hurts to ask. If nothing else, by buying all your tickets to and within a country at once, you may reduce the overall price of travel.

Off-Season Travel
In Belize, Costa Rica, Guatemala, and Mexico the off-season runs from early April to early December. Most people travel to Honduras to dive. The peak season for diving is from mid-February to early September. This is essentially the reverse of the other countries.
- Check with the airline to see exactly when rates will drop for the off-season.
- Note the earlier tip regarding charters. Some of these fly in the off-season. If you're extremely flexible and patient, you can sometimes come up with a steal to a popular tourist destination by waiting to buy your ticket at the last minute.
- There are also discounts on what agents refer to as "shoulder seasons." Check with your agent or airline on exact cutoff dates for each type of fare. Shoulder season travel is great because airline rates are reasonable and rooms readily available.

Trouble-savers for Booking your Own Flight
- Call before 7 A.M. or after 7 P.M. to avoid a long wait.
- Be specific. Repeat the day and date several times to avoid mix-ups. Get the name of the person helping you.
- Early flights are less frequently delayed. The earliest flights rarely suffer the cumulative effects of earlier delays.
- Flights originating from your city are subject to fewer delays.
- Book nonstop or direct flights, wherever possible.
- Stay on the same airline to avoid long walks and check-in hassles at the connecting airport.

- There are exceptions to the above rule, especially in the United States. Smaller carriers don't carry the same clout as larger ones, so choosing a powerful airline puts the odds in your favor that you won't have a long walk from one gate to the next.
- Airline tickets can be purchased on credit. Compare these charges with rates available from your bank on a short-term loan to come up with the most favorable terms (lowest interest rate).

Special Meals

Scheduled airlines often offer special meals to passengers with specific dietary restrictions, either for cultural, health, or religious reasons. Specify your needs when making a reservation. Charters may or may not have special meals available. Either carry appropriate food and drink with you, or eat before or after your flight. Also, when you reconfirm your flight, specify once again that you have ordered a special meal.

Picking Up Tickets

- Pay for and pick up tickets in advance. It's a good feeling to have the tickets in your pocket, an assurance that now no one will be able to bungle your important reservation.
- If time allows, have your agent send tickets to you in the mail.
- When you get tickets, check the dates, flight times, and flight numbers for accuracy.
- Check to see whether all taxes and fees, including departure taxes have already been paid. If you're not sure, ask.
- Count the flight coupons to make sure there are enough to cover all legs of your flight. Usually, they're all there. However, coupons are missing on occasion. Without the coupon (slip of paper denoting a certain leg), you can't get a boarding pass.
- Photocopy the coupons twice. Leave one copy at home. Take one with you—just in case you lose your tickets.

Selecting a Seat

Find out about available aircraft and best seats at the time you pick up or pay for your ticket—don't wait until you're in the hurried atmosphere of the departure lounge. Ask to see a seating chart, choose where you'd like to be, and reserve a seat right away if you can. If you can't, mark down your preferred seats and several alternatives on your ticket folder so that you can ask for them when checking in. See p. 132 for tips on choosing seats.

Traveling by Private Plane

Once a private plane was the only practical way to see much of the Baja in Mexico. With the road heading from Tijuana to Cabo San Lucas much of what was once isolated has now opened up. Still, many areas and lovely hotels have runways geared to private planes.

Basic Tips from Frequent Flyers
- Pay someone to watch your plane.
- Much flying in Mexico is high-altitude flying—be wary.

Getting to Central America and Mexico by Land

Most tours into Mexico are by bus. Car and RV travel to and through Mexico is one of the best ways to get to know this vast country, but your trip will require time, energy, and patience. Although it's best to have 4-wheel drive in parts of the Baja, most of the country is accessible without it. New superhighways have been added, old roads improved, and the famous free road service "the Green Angels" continues to be one of the finest ideas ever conceived (see below). There are now 2,000 Pemex stations in 74 areas with unleaded gas.

Travel to Central America by land is certainly possible, but not recommended for anyone but the most adventuresome tourist with lots of time. You can get into Belize from Mexico, but to get to the other countries you must either travel through troubled areas or extremely rough terrain. If you are going to Central America by car, it should be 4-wheel drive.

Information

Before traveling to Mexico get full information on the document requirements and a good map. Free maps are available from the Mexican Government Tourist Office (see p. 26) and to members of auto clubs (see below).

Road Information for Mexico

The following office specializes in road travel. It offers free maps, a free "Directory of Road Services," a list of "Green Angels" numbers, and much more.

Mexican Government Tourist Office
2707 North Loop West, Suite 440
Houston, TX 77008
Tel: (713) 880-8772

Auto Clubs

Comparison shop when looking for an automobile club. Compare membership fees, emergency road services, emergency travel expenses, accidental death and dismemberment payoff amounts, arrest and bail bond, legal defense fees, and routing maps. Ask whether your club has any reciprocal agreements with auto clubs in Central America or Mexico. Find out too whether they'll take care of any paperwork necessary to get you into foreign countries.

American Automobile
  Association (AAA)
1000 AAA Drive
Heathrow, FL 32746
Tel: (800) 336-4357
Central America and Mexico.

Exxon Travel Club
P.O. Box 3633
Houston, TX 77253
Tel: (800) 833-9966
      (713) 680-5723
Mexico only.

Amoco Motor Club
P.O. Box 9046
Des Moines, IA 50368
Tel: (800) 334-3300
Mexico only.

Montgomery Ward Auto Club
200 North Martingale Road
Schaumburg, IL 60194
Tel: (800) 621-5151
      (800) 572-5577 (Illinois)
Mexico only.

Auto Club of Southern
  California
2601 South Figueroa Street
Los Angeles, CA 90007
Tel: (213) 741-3111
Mexico only. Handles a special
Baja California Guide and a
separate *Accommodation and
Camping Guide* for the Baja
(Mexico).

Shell Motorist Club
P.O. Box 60199
Chicago, IL 60660
Tel: (800) 621-8663
Mexico only.

United States Auto Club
  Motoring Division
P.O. Box 660460
Dallas, TX 75266
Tel: (800) 348-2761
Mexico only.

Chevron Travel Club
P.O. Box P
Concord, CA 94524
Tel: (800) 222-0585
Mexico only.

General Information on Car and RV Travel In Mexico

The Mexican Government Tourist Office, auto clubs, and insurance companies can all help you with the details on travel through Mexico, but it helps to know about a few things ahead of time, to prevent frustrating hassles which can easily be avoided.

The Best Cars to Take to Mexico
- Certain makes of cars are much easier to service and repair in Mexico: Chevrolet, Datsun, Dodge, Ford, Mercedes, Opel, Renault, and Volkswagen. VWs are the work horses of Mexico, and most mechanics know how to work on them.

Registering Your Car
- Register your car with U.S. Customs before crossing the border into Mexico. Don't lose the registration slip.

Auto Insurance
If you drive a car or RV into Mexico, you're going to need a separate insurance policy. Your U.S. or Canadian policy will not cover you there.
- Many companies offer coverage for car or RV travel in Mexico. The best known is Sanborn's. Compare prices and coverage offered by auto clubs and the following companies before making up your mind:

International Gateway
   Insurance Brokers
3450 Bonita Road, Suite 103
Chula Vista, CA 91910
Tel: (800) 423-2646
      (619) 422-3057

Lewis and Lewis
8929 Wilshire Boulevard,
   Suite 220
Beverly Hills, CA 90211
Tel: (800) 966-6830
      (213) 655-6830

MacAfee & Edwards Mexican
   Insurance Specialts
3435 Wilshire Boulevard,
   Suite 143
Los Angeles, CA 90010
Tel: (213) 388-9674

Mexico Services
12421 Venice Boulevard,
   Suite 2
P.O. Box 66278
Los Angeles, CA 90066
Tel: (310) 398-5797

Romero's Mexico Service
1600 West Coast Highway
Newport Beach, CA 92663
Tel: (800) 948-7477
      (714) 548-8931

Sanborn's
P.O. Box 1210
McAllen, TX 78503
Tel: (210) 686-0711
Also known for its "Travelog" with detailed information on trip routes.

Insurance Costs
Compare offerings from auto clubs, the insurance companies above, and the following travel clubs to come up with the most favorable coverage and rates:

CLUB MEX
3450 Bonita Road, Suite 101
Chula Vista, CA 91910
Tel: (619) 585-3033
Specializes in all aspects of
travel throughout Mexico.

Discover Baja Travel Club
3065 Clairemont Drive
San Diego, CA 92117
Tel: (800) 727-2252
     (619) 275-4225
Specializes in all aspects of
travel through the Baja.

Escapees
100 Rainbow Drive
Livingston, TX 77351
Tel: (409) 327-8873
Geared to RV travel.

The Good Sam Club
Customer Service
P.O. Box 500
Agoura, CA 91301
Tel: (800) 234-3450
     (805) 389-0300
Geared to RV travel.

Mexican Car Insurance
- All policies include a deductible for collision.
- U.S. and Canadian policies have comprehensive coverage, but Mexican policies do not. Glass breakage comes under collision, and a deductible applies.
- Mexican policies do not cover fines, bail bonds, and legal expenses. You have to take out a different policy for these.
- Partial theft and vandalism are not covered under Mexican insurance policies.

Trailer and Boats
- Insure a trailer or a boat.
- To insure a boat it has to be pulled on a trailer.
- Register your trailer and boat with U.S. Customs (see p. 130).

Legal Aid Insurance
If you're worried about fines, bail bond, or paying attorney's fees, you can take out legal aid insurance. This is not required in Mexico.

Temporary Importation Permits
If you drive a car into mainland Mexico (not the Baja), you are required to get a temporary importation permit for your car. The sole purpose of this permit is to make sure that you don't sell the car in Mexico. The car will have to leave with you.
- You are not required to have a permit for a car on the Baja, unless you intend to go by ferry to the mainland.
- Always get the permit as you cross the border into Mexico. This is true even if you enter Mexico on the Baja with the intention of taking the ferry to the mainland.

- The permit is combined in one document with your tourist card, which will be stamped *con automóvil.*
- You're allowed only one vehicle per person. If you're traveling by yourself, you cannot bring an extra moped or motorcycle or car towed behind an RV.
- Two people can bring in two vehicles, three people can bring in three, etc. Each one will be responsible for one vehicle. Each tourist card will be stamped appropriately.
- You have to be out of Mexico before your temporary importation permit expires. It can be extended with your tourist card to a maximum stay of 180 days.
- The period of validity of the tourist card and the importation permit should match since they're incorporated into one document. Some tourists have reported discrepancies.They had a tourist card valid for 90 days and a permit valid for fewer days. *Make sure that your tourist card and temporary importation permit are valid for the same number of days!*

What You Need to Get a Temporary Importation Permit

The border officials will give you a temporary importation permit if you have the following: A valid driver's license, valid license plates, a registration card, and proof of ownership.

- If the car is not yours, or has a lien on it, or is a company car, have a notarized affidavit authorizing its use from the owner or lien holder.
- If you cannot produce the letter, the car can be confiscated. This prevents stolen cars from coming into Mexico.

Who Can Drive the Car?

If you have the importation permit, you and your spouse can drive the car. If you're in the car, another person can take over the driving. But if someone else wants to drive the car while you're not in it, this must be indicated on the permit. Register this person at the nearest *Registro Federal de Vehículos.* If someone drives your car without being registered, the car can be confiscated!

Expensive Accessories

Expensive car accessories may be noted on tourist cards and must leave the country with you. If they don't (even if they're stolen), they'll be assumed to have been sold—you'll have to pay duty on them.

Large Trailer Permits

It is extremely difficult for vehicles with trailers to negotiate the narrow streets in Mexican towns.

- Any trailer more than 8-feet wide or more than 40-feet long requires a special permit to travel in Mexico. Contact the nearest Mexican Consulate for current regulations and fees (get the address from the nearest Mexican Tourist Office (see p. 26).

Citizen Band (CB) Permits
To use a CB in Mexico apply for a permit from the nearest Mexican Consulate.

Car and RV Preparation

Mexicans are excellent mechanics, but you could be stranded in a desolate area. Here are some basic tips:
- The tires on your car should be the best you can afford.
- You should carry a brand new spare. Check its pressure.
- Cactus spines can easily puncture radial tires. Consider putting inner tubes in *all* tires whether they're radials or not.
- Have the car serviced and checked completely. The cooling system and engine should be perfect. Hoses should be replaced if old. All fluids should be changed.
- Bring spare parts as outlined below.
- Install an accessible, in-line fuel filter and have someone show you how to replace it or clean it.
- Put a bug screen over the radiator and clean it off frequently.
- Take off all the lug nuts to make sure that you can get them off if you have a flat. Apply a little grease where necessary.
- Change the thermostat for the higher temperatures you'll encounter in Mexico.
- Reduce tire pressure for long hauls.
- If driving an RV, replace the spare battery with a new one. Clean out your water system and add chlorox to it. Then fill and drain it several times to get it completely clean. Apply a white reflective coating to the top of the RV to protect it from the sun. Consider buying a solar-cell battery recharger.

Special Note on Propane
Years ago the Mexican government made the sale of propane for vehicles illegal. Later it was illegal only within 75 miles of the U.S. border. Who knows what's going to happen in the future? So take the following precautions:
- Get your propane tank filled before entering Mexico.
- Have your fuel line adapted so that it can be attached to a portable propane tank. You can do this yourself or hire someone to do it for you. This way you'll never have to worry about the

propane problem (it has never been illegal for foreigners to buy propane in small, portable tanks).

Special Note on Dual Wheels
Dual wheels are great for everything but off-road travel. If you're going to the Baja or other areas with the intention of getting off the beaten path, get a vehicle without dual wheels. The reason? Ruts in the road have been carved out by cars and trucks without them.

Tools and Spare Parts for Safety
Mexico can antique a car overnight. Since spare parts and tools are extremely expensive in Mexico, consider taking them with you. Here's a checklist of suggested items for car and RV travelers.
- Expensive accessories, spare parts, and tools may be noted on your tourist card. If you sell or lose them, you'll pay a duty when leaving the country.
- Here's a checklist of documents and spare parts for avid motorists and RVers: Adaptor, air filter, air gauge, baling wire, battery cables, belts, bicycle, blocks (for tires or leveling), bolts and nuts, brake fluid, breaker points, bulbs, car permit, CB, CB permit, chains, chairs (folding), chamois cloth, condensers, distributor points, driver's license, duct tape, electric tape, extension cord, fan belts, fire extinguisher, fittings, flares, food, fuel filters, fuel pump, funnel, fuses, gaskets (for water hose), gasoline cans (preferably metal), generator brushes, grease (and grease gun), hammer (heavy rubber), hoses and radiator clamps, hose (water), hydraulic jacks, ice chest, ignition coil, inner tubes, jumper cables, keys (spares in hidden metal container), Liquid Wrench, lug wrench, motorbike, motor oil, paper products (towels), plastic bags, power steering fluid, radiator coolant, radiator sealant, reflectors, rotor (for RVs), shovel, siphon hose, spare tires on rims, spark plugs, tire inflator (aerosol), tire pump, tools, towels (old diapers), tow rope, trailer, trailer permit, triangle (reflective for breakdowns), tube repair kit, universal joints, valve cores, water can with sprinkler head, water cans (5-gallon), WD 40, whisk broom, window cleaner, and wooden blocks. Oh yes, a fly swatter.

Cutting Gas Costs in an RV
- Plan an exact route with mileage in mind.
- A tune-up may save 8 to 20 percent on fuel.
- Travel as light as you possibly can. Figure that you lose roughly 1 percent in gas mileage per 100 pounds of excess baggage.

- Buy radials for better mileage and safety.
- Don't fill your tank to the brim. Excess gas washes out and evaporates. It overflows on inclines. Tighten the gas cap.
- Buy locking gas caps.
- Check tires for proper pressure, avoid roof racks (they create drag), avoid peak traffic periods, travel early and late in the day (avoids air-conditioner use), and keep windows closed (prevents drag).

Car-Delivery Service

- You can get close to Mexico by offering your driving skill to a car-delivery service. These are often listed in Sunday papers.
- Most of these companies pay for gas only.
- Arizona, California, and Texas are common destinations, and the need for drivers is greatest in the fall and winter.
- Get your name listed with an agency. Be flexible in your travel plans to come up with a delivery assignment.

Tripshare

Although this may be obsolete by the time you read this guide, check into sharing a ride into Mexico. It's like a ride-board, so common in colleges. Never call Sanborn's to ask about this service. They have indicated that they will discontinue the service if people continue to call in. Write. Send in your name, address, telephone number, where and when you want to go to Mexico. All of this goes into a file sent out to prospective travelers.

Sanborn's
Department TS
P.O. Box 310
McAllen, TX 78501

Bus Travel to Mexico

A number of lines will get you to the border. Once there, you can either use bus or train to travel throughout Mexico, even going as far as Belize. Bus travel in Belize is inexpensive and extensive. From Belize you can get into Guatemala by bus, although I do not presently recommend this because of banditry on the route from Belize to Flores (the town from which you make excursions to Tikal).

Train Travel to Mexico

Because of time involved and relatively high cost, most people prefer to fly to Mexico or to save money on a bus. If you take a train, you'll have to get off at the border, no matter what time it is.

Hitchhiking

Hitchhiking has and always will be an option to get to Mexico. Once in Mexico, I do not advise it. However, tips are on p. 210.

Transportation in Central America and Mexico

This chapter covers all of the ways of getting around Central America and Mexico from biking and hitching to bus, car, plane, and train travel.

Plane Travel

Plane travel is the fastest and most convenient way to get to many cities and tourist sites in Central America and Mexico.

Advantages of Plane Travel
- Plane travel is much less tiring than car, bus, and train travel.
- It's the only way to get to some places, including remote ruins, jungle lodges, and fishing camps.
- You waste less time covering vast distances.

Disadvantages of Plane Travel
- Plane travel is more expensive than bus or train travel.
- Flights can and often are canceled on the flimsiest excuses.
- You've got to spend time and money on transfers from the airport into town. In some cases, this can be expensive.
- You can be locked in by bad weather. This is especially a problem getting to Roatan from San Pedro Sula in Honduras.
- You pass over, not through the countryside.

Reservations
Make reservations for flights in the United States whenever possible. If this can't be done, see pp. 188–190.

Bus Travel

Traveling by bus appeals to many people on a budget. In Mexico alone there are 700 bus lines going just about anywhere, which means most travelers will, at some time, end up on a bus. In Central America bus travel is extremely inexpensive and can get you to most destinations. Deciding whether or not bus travel makes sense for you means comparing the trade-offs.

The Advantages of Bus Travel

- You can get just about anywhere by bus, even to the most remote village or hamlet.
- Sometimes, bus travel is the *only* way to get to an area (unless you rent a car).
- Bus travel is incredibly cheap. It's truly a bargain in all countries, because the local residents rely on it so much.
- You meet fascinating people on buses, the kind of people who are veteran travelers, wily, and willing to put up with some discomfort to save a buck.
- Some people really like buses, no matter what the problems are. They can sleep and relax on them. If you're that kind of person, then buses leave you with lots of energy.

Disadvantages of Bus Travel

- Many bus stations are disaster zones with toilets so foul and waiting rooms so crowded you feel you're in a refugee camp.
- There are luxurious buses, but most first-class buses are second-rate. On many, people jam the aisles for standing room only. You barely have enough room to squirm in your seat.
- Buses do not stop frequently. Since many buses do not have bathrooms, this can be very uncomfortable.
- If you're finicky about sleep and rest, buses can be very tiring.
- The safety records of some bus companies are appalling.
- Buses do not follow exact schedules. Many stop to pick up passengers en route. If you're on a tight schedule, tough.
- Buses may arrive in towns at night. This can be difficult and potentially dangerous, especially so for women traveling alone (not advised).
- If you're allergic to smoke, if you can't stand stereos blasting for hours on end (noise is viewed as invigorating throughout the region), if quick fluctuations in temperature turn you off (it's often sweltering in some buses, nearly frigid in others), then buses are a turnoff.

Reservations

Rarely can you make bus reservations from the United States. Read the Inter-City Travel chapter (see pp. 190–194).

Car Travel

Car travel is for adventurous people who are willing to pay a price for freedom. Travel by car only in Belize, Costa Rica, and Mexico.

You can get to the main tourist sites in Guatemala easily by bus, minibus, taxi, and plane. I do not recommend travel by car into the rural areas of Guatemala, since these areas are not secure. Bus, minibus, plane, and taxi travel are all you'll need in Honduras.

Advantages of Car Travel

- Cars can get you just about anywhere. Occasionally, there are a few hidden corners accessible only by boat or plane, but you can reach most of the finest tourist sites by car.
- Cars get you to places much faster than buses. You're never tied to someone else's schedule. This gives you a great sense of freedom.
- You don't have to worry about reservations, tickets, and lines.
- You don't have to travel superlight unless you prefer to.
- You're free to change or rearrange schedules at whim.
- You don't have to put up with the poor conditions in train and bus stations.
- Avoid delayed or canceled planes, trains, and buses.
- You can stop whenever you like. Take a break for a picnic, stop for a pee, pause for a truly great photo—do whatever you like, when you like, pretty much as you damn well please.
- Most of all, you're part of the living jigsaw puzzle around you, which means you see and feel areas that many tourists miss.

Disadvantages of Car Travel

- Car travel is expensive. Rental rates are exorbitant.
- The cost becomes more manageable with more people.
- Car travel can be dangerous. Local drivers, especially bus drivers, are terrible. Costa Rica has the highest accident rate per driver in the world.
- In Belize, Costa Rica, and certain parts of Mexico (mainly parts of the Baja and rural areas) roads are incredibly bad (see p. 200). The term bad can mean dangerous.
- It takes time to travel to and through the region—lots of time. Distances can be overwhelming for anyone in a hurry.
- Car travel can be exhausting because of curving, dangerous, and poorly maintained roads. Your average speed may only be 10 to 15 miles per hour in some areas.
- Two or more people driving together can share the burden. But whether you're driving or not, you're still covering the same, long distances (or short distances which seem long).
- If your trip is oriented to major cities, you would save lots of time and trouble by taking a plane.

- Cars are a hassle in major cities where parking is expensive and sometimes difficult to find.
- Cars are constantly vandalized unless kept in guarded lots or garages.
- Car travel can insulate you from meeting local people, although in general the opposite is true.

Car Rental
Renting a car has the greatest appeal to travelers who really want to explore the hidden corners of a country. However, this mobility has a high price tag.

Travelers Who Need Rental Cars
- You need a rental car if you want to get off-the-beaten path to explore or to photograph unusual places and people.
- Anyone planning to visit many places in a short time without depending on public transportation needs a rental car.
- If driving is the way you *prefer* to travel, if it's emotionally satisfying, and if you exhilarate in the freedom it offers—then the high price doesn't seem too high to pay.

Travelers Who Don't Need Rental Cars
- Rental cars are almost useless in most resorts. All areas geared to heavy tourist traffic have public transportation that can get you just about anywhere for just about nothing.
- You can always supplement inexpensive public transportation with more expensive taxis—more expensive, yes, but still cheap compared to the high cost of car rental.
- You do not want a car in major cities. The hassles of weaving your way through rush-hour traffic or arguing over parking space is not worth it. You will not believe how inexpensive and good public transportation is in larger towns and cities.
- If you want to visit sights outside major towns, take advantage of local tours. Don't like tours? Then hire a cab at a set fare to take you there. You'll find that the cost is still less than car rental. And you've got a driver and guide to boot.
- The main point: If your travel is limited to one major city or resort with an excursion or two to certain sites, skip cars.

Who Can Rent a Car
- To rent a car in Central America or Mexico you need: Proof that you're not too young or too old (according to company rules), a valid driver's license, passport for identification, and a major credit card (or a large chunk of cash).

Reserving a Car in Advance

- Make reservations yourself or work through a travel agent. Use the toll-free (800) numbers in your telephone book if you prefer to use a well-known Canadian or U.S. company.
- During peak travel periods of Christmas, New Year's, Carnival, and Easter, reserve a car as far in advance as possible.
- Companies may give you a price break for a guaranteed reservation made far enough in advance. Note that there's a cancellation penalty for this special offer. Ask the company for full information on potential savings, restrictions, and penalties.
- When you make a car reservation, always get the name of the person you're talking to. Ask for a confirmation number so that you have proof that the reservation has been made.
- Have the exact address where you are to pick up the car. Ask for a map pinpointing this location.
- 4-wheel drive cars are at a premium during the peak season. Make reservations months in advance, especially for Costa Rica.

Car Rental Availability

- Major companies do not have cars available in every city and town of Central America and Mexico. However, smaller companies often fill the gap. If a travel agent tells you that cars are not available in town X, it isn't necessarily true.
- If you have trouble coming up with a car in a smaller town, go directly to the local tourist office and ask for rental information. You may be told about a car company you've never heard of.
- You can find out about all of these local companies by requesting a list from the National Tourist Offices (see pp. 25–27). Tell them to send you a complete list with addresses and local phone numbers in whatever town you intend to rent the car.

What Kind of Car Should You Rent

- Get by with the smallest car possible, especially if you'll be driving to isolated towns. Streets in villages can be narrow, torturous, and steep. Small cars can go almost anywhere. They guzzle less gas, are roomy enough if you're traveling light, can weasel into tiny parking spots, and cost less for ferries and toll roads.
- The most important point: Make sure that the car you rent is the newest one available, one with low mileage. If you're doing extensive driving, the condition and age of the car is crucial! Make this very clear when you're renting the car. Many vehicles are badly abused and will suffer a breakdown.
- I wish I could tell you that there would be some way to guaranty that you'll get what you ask for, but lying is so common in this

region that I can't. By working with major companies you may lower the odds of being lied to. I cannot tell you how many times I've been lied to by car rental companies in Central America and Mexico—it's a very sore area.

Stick Shifts
- If you don't know how to operate a stick shift, learn. Even if you reserve a car with an automatic shift, there is no guarantee that you'll get one. Furthermore, in an emergency you should be able to drive any car that's available. A competent driving instructor can teach you how to use a stick shift in 6 hours or less—from the basics to starting on a 45-degree incline.

Car Rental Costs
Car rental is much more expensive in Belize, Costa Rica, and Mexico than in the United States and Canada, so much more expensive that you may figure the price isn't worth it. The overall cost includes the basic charge, supplemental costs for air-conditioning or automatic transmission, insurance premiums, mileage charges, gas refill charge, and a tourist tax—more about each of these later.

Shopping Around for the Best Basic Rate
- In Belize you'll begin your trip from Belize City. The base rates vary by company. Comparison shop.
- In Costa Rica you'll probably start your trip in San José. Base rates vary here as well. However, only Tico and Elegante offer complete insurance coverage—at a higher base rate, of course. All other companies have deductibles.
- In Mexico car rental prices are government-controlled, so you'll find the base price is the same from all companies in the same city. All have deductibles.
- The secret: Prices vary by location. You might pay half as much for a car in Mexico City as you would in Acapulco. So you might start a trip from the Mexico City airport with no intention of visiting the city at all in order to save a few hundred dollars.

Things That Up the Basic Rate
- All car rental rates are related to the model and size of the car you rent. Rent the smallest car for your party. The many advantages of small cars have already been given.
- Most cars have stick shifts. You'll pay a surcharge if you want a car with automatic transmission. However, do not assume that you'll get an automatic car simply because you reserved one. It just doesn't work that way.

- During the sticky, summer heat of the Tropics you'll want air-conditioning—but it's an option for which you often pay a surcharge. During much of the year it's really not necessary. In some cases air is included in the base rate.
- Cars with 4-wheel drive are always more expensive and in great demand during peak seasons. Always rent these in the Baja (Mexico), Belize, and Costa Rica. I cannot emphasize this enough.

Avoiding the Mileage Charge

Many rental agreements add an additional charge for miles driven. The extra charge is actually per kilometer, roughly 6/10 of a mile. You can double the kilometer charge for a rough estimate of the per mile cost—and it's steep.

- If you rent a car for more than three days (in most areas), get a car at a set price without paying an additional charge for mileage. This is an *unlimited mileage agreement*.
- Some companies offer an unlimited mileage agreement when they are really not. For example, they offer a week's rental for a set price, but then you have to pay an additional charge after the first 1000 kilometers (or 600 miles). Avoid this trap by asking about any mileage restrictions. Most contracts are in Spanish, so write this on your contract: "Accepted on the understanding that this is an unlimited mileage agreement with no charge for kilometers driven."
- If you ask questions once in car rental agencies, you'll often be told later that you "misunderstood" because of the language barrier. The language barrier has a way of crumbling under a barrage of questions, all really the same question asked in a lot of different ways. Use the technique of *repeated* questions to get a straight answer. And make notes of your agreements directly on the contract as outlined above.

Insurance Premiums

- As in the United States and Canada, insurance charges jack up the total bill of a car considerably. Sometimes, insurance is included in the quoted rate. Ask to be sure.
- **Note**: Almost all car rental insurance has a deductible for which you're responsible. This applies to partial theft, glass breakage, and collision. So your insurance is really only partial insurance—a ripoff by anyone's standards.

Comparing Deductibles

- Deductibles vary greatly by companies. Find the company which offers not only the best base rate but also the lowest deductible.

For example, I compared the deductible of three major companies for Belize and Costa Rica. Belize varied from $450 to $1000, Costa Rica from $800 to $1500.

- In Costa Rica there are two companies (Elegante and Tico) offering full coverage (no deductible). Naturally, they cost more than their competitors. It is my understanding that these are sister companies somehow connected with the government. No other companies are allowed to offer full coverage (cozy arrangement). Check to see whether these companies still offer full coverage. If so, rent months in advance.

Covering Your Deductible

Whenever possible, cover your deductible with a credit card that offers primary coverage outside of the United States. Deductibles range from $450 to $1500 even if the base rate includes insurance for the rest.

- Call the 800 number of each of your credit card companies and ask whether they will cover the deductible on car rental in Central America and Mexico. Note that many operators say they do, when they really don't—read the following warnings.
- If renting in Belize or Costa Rica, ask your company whether it will cover 4-wheel drives. Most claim they do, but really don't once you read the fine print (see following).
- Ask the company whether there are any restrictions on this coverage, especially any clause which says you must drive on paved roads. This restriction essentially voids all coverage in Belize and Costa Rica where most driving is on dirt roads. Most contracts say that coverage is only on federally maintained roads, a euphemism for *paved* roads.
- Many credit card companies have chosen not to insure 4-wheel drive vehicles, because this is an expensive thing for them to do. Or, they insure 4-wheel drives *if* driven on paved roads, *if* never used off-road, and *if* the car is enclosed (not with open bed). This amounts to *no* insurance. So get a 4-wheel drive with the *lowest deductible* possible!
- Credit card coverage for car rental deductibles is primary outside of the United States, which means that the credit card company will have to pick up the whole tab for any damage to your vehicle. You can understand why these companies are so skittish about this coverage. In fact, as clearly pointed out above, many do *not* offer this coverage.

The Gas Refill Charge

- Rental cars are filled with varying amounts of gas depending upon the company you're dealing with.

- The amount of gas to the nearest quarter of a tank should be noted on your car rental agreement.
- You return the car with an equivalent amount of gas or pay a gas refill charge—always inflated (a worldwide practice).
- You pay a tax on the refill charge. So stop at a gas station before returning the car if you want to save money.

Drop-off Charges

- In most instances you cannot rent a car in one town and drop it off in another without paying a charge for this service. The charge is usually related to the distance between the two cities.
- Always ask about drop-off charges in advance and make sure to get the charge in *writing* before renting the car.

The IVA Tax

- On *all* of your rental car expenses you'll pay a government tax. Keep this in mind. Ask what the tax will be and whether it's included in the price being quoted. Get this in writing.

Car Rental Ripoffs

- Car rental companies, especially local ones, try to ripoff customers in a wide variety of ways. One is to have you sign an agreement stating how much the rental will be in dollars. You sign a credit card slip agreeing to pay X amount in dollars. However, when you return, they insist that the charge slip be converted to local currency—naturally at a horrendous rate of exchange.
- To avoid getting ripped off with this con pay them in dollars as originally agreed upon, using traveler's checks or hard currency. They have no defense against this, since your original agreement was for a dollar figure.
- You can flush out this con in advance by asking how much the rental would be in dollars or local currency. You can have them write down both figures. If the exchange rate is favorable, you can agree to pay the bill in the local currency. If it's not, pay with traveler's checks in dollars.
- Another con is to tell you that they cannot give you a copy of the charge slip until the car has been checked out. The car can be sitting right in front of them with absolutely no damage, but they can tell you it has to be inspected. Often, the clerks will lie about how long this inspection will take. They're hoping you'll leave the country. They then fill in any amount they choose, faking damage claims.
- Ask how quickly you'll be given back your credit card slip on returning the car. When told, ask them to write that on your rental

agreement. "The X car rental company agrees to inspect the car for damages and return the credit card slip within 2 hours of the car's return." If you don't have this in writing, you have nothing but anger propelling you to get your credit card slip back. This detestable practice is most common in Costa Rica. One company to avoid in this regard is Tricolor (Costa Rica).

- Another ripoff has already been implied. You may be given a car which is in such rough shape that mufflers are about to fall off, brakes about to fail, tires threadbare—you've got the idea. You're going to break down. The danger of using an older car is not worth it. Your life is too valuable. These cars are often pawned off on tourists during peak seasons.

- There is little certainty of avoiding this ripoff, again most common in Costa Rica where roads are really rough. In the peak season, use a major company based in the United States. The reason: When you bitch, the company may actually respond. If you're working with a local company, they'll just shrug you off. One company to avoid in this regard is Economy (Costa Rica). Naming this one company hardly helps, since others do it as well.

Train Travel

Train travel is only practical in Mexico. The famous rides in Central America are history. Skip trains there. Few people know very much about train travel in Mexico. Many Mexican Government Tourist Offices more or less discourage it. Travel agents in the United States and Canada ignore it because there are no commissions and no practical way of making reservations.

Advantages of Train Travel
- Trains are the cheapest way to travel in Mexico, less even than buses (as much as 50 percent less).
- Train travel is relatively safe and convenient, because it takes you from city center to city center with no transfers to pay and no weather delays (except in the high mountains).
- Train travel is far less tiring than car and bus travel.
- Trains are much less confining than buses.
- You can also go to the bathroom (rare on buses).
- You're allowed stopovers with many tickets.

Disadvantages of Train Travel
- Trains cannot get you everywhere in Mexico. You may have to rent a car, fly, or take a bus to get to remote areas.
- Many trains are quite old, jiggle badly, and make a racket.

- Some of the train stations in smaller towns are appalling—smelly, dirty, and even scary at night.
- For popular routes in the peak travel periods you may have to make reservations far in advance.
- Schedules change frequently and are hard to find out. You often have to go to the station to get accurate information.
- Trains are notoriously late. Trains make frequent stopovers in small places.
- Many trains have virtually no temperature control, meaning that in high mountains you freeze and in summer you swelter.
- Trains can be very crowded, but rarely like buses.

Information

If you plan to travel by train to or in Mexico, contact the following organization for information:

Mexico By Train
P.O. Box 2782
Laredo, TX 78044
Tel: (800) 321-1699
        (210) 725-3659

Boats

In a few areas places are accessible only by boat. Generally, you make arrangements locally for these short trips, which rarely last more than a few hours. Boats range from frail, tipsy dugouts to large ferries capable of loading numerous cars and semi trucks.

Reservations

You'll buy your tickets locally or bargain on boat transportation with the locals. If you're planning a trip out to a fishing lodge or to a dive site, see the appropriate sections in the chapter on Doing Things.

Motorcycling

Carrying a cycle or moped for excursions and off-road travel makes sense, but not as your only means of travel. You don't see very many bikes in Central America and Mexico for one simple reason—they get ripped off or vandalized in seconds. Stick to public transportation.

Biking

Biking is simply out of the question for the average traveler. Yes, adventurers have not only traveled through this region by bike, but written about it. If you have months or years to travel, then this is an option. Otherwise, write it off. See p. 264 for biking tours.

Hitchhiking

Hitchhiking is not recommended. Hitchhiking is quite common in rural areas of Costa Rica for short rides, but everywhere else it's a rarity. People are reluctant to pick up hitchhikers because of the strict drug laws making the driver responsible for anything in a hitchhiker's bags. Since public transportation is so cheap, why bother?

Where to Stay

You'll want to match the wide variety of accommodations to your budget and preferred style of travel.

Varieties of Lodgings

Following are some suggestions on the variety of places to stay in Central America and Mexico as well as some tips on making reservations before your trip. For more information on reservations and places to stay once abroad (see pp. 142–157).

Apartments. Contact the National Tourist Offices (pp. 25–27) for information on home or apartment rental. Note that the Tico Times (p. 31) has a section for people interested in renting homes or apartments in Costa Rica. Some helpful phrases: Furnished homes (*casas con muebles*) or private homes (*casas particulares*). The following organizations also have information on rental abroad:

At Home Abroad, Inc.
405 East 56th Street, Suite 6H
New York, NY 10022
Tel: (212) 421-9165
Mexico.

Creative Leisure
951 Transport Way
Petaluma, CA 94954
Tel: (800) 426-6367
Mexico.

Hideaways International
P.O. Box 4433
767 Islington Street
Portsmouth, NH 03802
Tel: (800) 843-4433
   (603) 430-4433
Belize, Costa Rica, Honduras
(the Bay Islands), Mexico.

Rent A Vacation Everywhere,
   Inc. (R.A.V.E.)
383 Park Avenue

Rochester, NY 14607
Tel: (716) 256-0760
Costa Rica, Mexico.

Vacation Exchange Club
P.O. Box 650
Key West, FL 33041
Tel: (800) 638-3841
Mexico.

Villa Leisure
P.O. Box 30188
Palm Beach, FL 33420
tel: (800) 526-4244
   (407) 624-9000
Mexico.

Villas International, Ltd.
605 Market Street, Suite 510
San Francisco, CA 94105
Tel: (800) 221-2260
   (415) 281-0910
Belize, Costa Rica, Guatemala,
Mexico.

Boardinghouses (*casas de huéspedes, hospedaje, pensión*): Boardinghouses or guesthouses go by a variety of names in Central America and Mexico. They vary from charming to dumpy. Some serve meals, others don't. Generally, they offer good value and are favorites of budget travelers. Ask about these locally. They're often overlooked in travel guides. Generally, they are small, often someone's home.

Bungalows (*cabañas*): Bungalows or cabins vary greatly by locale. Some are charming little huts in the mountains, others are more like motels by the sea. No definition really covers the category, except to say that they are usually geared to budget travelers. Some are truly dismal, others outstanding.

Camping: Camping is common throughout Mexico in organized campgrounds. It's also possible in some of the National Parks in Costa Rica. There are a few scattered camping areas in Belize, but not many. I would not suggest camping out in Guatemala or Honduras unless with an organized tour group. See p. 158.

Club Med: There are Club Meds in Mexico, but none in Central America. These vacation resorts combine elegance and casual living with good food and good times. Although they once appealed mainly to singles on the swing, many are now open to couples, and even to families as well. Costs tend to be on the high side, but are a good value. The Club Meds oriented to singles and couples are at Cancún, Huatalco, Playa Blanca, and Sonora Bay. The one in Ixtapa is aimed at families. There are also Club Meds at archaeological sites, including Chichén Itza (Yucatán), Choluca (Puebla), Coba (Yucatán), Posada San Francisco (Tlaxcala), Teotihuacán (México), and Uxmal (Yucatán). For information on all of these villages call the toll-free number and ask for the lovely, full-color magazine entitled "Club Med Vacations."

Club Med
40 West 57th Street
New York, NY 10019
Tel: (800) 258-2633
     (212) 977-2100

Fishing Hotels: There are certain people who go to Central America and Mexico to fish—and that's it. Fishing hotels are unique. They're friendly, club-like, and very original. In some hotels you won't find telephones and TVs, because no one wants them. Such hotels attract a special breed of traveler—sophisticated and fun. Many of these hotels can be reached by private plane or charter flights. See Fishing (pp. 273–282).

Home Exchange: If you'd prefer to exchange your home with a Mexican, contact:

> Vacation Exchange Club
> P.O. Box 650
> Key West, FL 33041
> Tel: (800) 638-3841
> Mexico.

Home Stays: If you would like to stay with a foreign family for a day or two, this can be arranged through:

> Home & Host International
> 2445 Park Avenue
> Minneapolis, MN 55404
> Tel: (612) 871-0596
> Costa Rica, Guatemala, and
>   Mexico.

> U.S. Servas
> 11 John Street, Suite 407
> New York, NY 10038
> Tel: (212) 267-0252
> Costa Rica, Guatemala,
>   Honduras, and Mexico.

Hotels: The variety in hotels is staggering. Some are truly first-class comparable to deluxe hotels anywhere. Others are small and unpretentious. Many are noisy. Price ranges from next-to-nothing to extremely expensive, just as it does in Canada and the United States. Travel agents and travel guides are having a hard time keeping up with new hotels in Central America and Mexico, especially in Costa Rica which is going through a tourist boom. Often, you'll find the best and newest hotels through word of mouth.

Huts: Small, thatched huts (*palapas*) are available for nothing or next to nothing in remote beach areas. These often are geared to people carrying their own hammocks. Most are right by the sea. Enclosed wooden huts on stilts are common in southern Belize. A few may have a sink with running water. These are slightly more expensive than open-air varieties. You go to the bathroom outdoors, either in an outhouse nearby or au natural.

Inns (*posadas*): These inns are similar to hotels, but usually consist of separate buildings spread out over a large area. Often, there are gardens or courtyards. Most serve meals, at least breakfast and dinner.

Jungle Lodges: Jungle lodges are as varied as their owners. Some are elegant, others extremely rustic. What most of them have in common is surrounding terrain which appeals to archaeologists, birders, hikers, and naturalists. Many of these are so famous that they are booked months and even years in advance, often by special-interest tour groups. Most jungle lodges are very expensive, even if rustic. Belize and Costa Rica have some of the finest. These are often quite difficult to get to by boat or plane, which adds to the overall expense.

Motels: For someone traveling by car in Costa Rica and Mexico these are convenient and often reasonably priced. However, the concept of motels is highly limited and not nearly as common as in Canada and the United States. In fact, there are relatively few. As with hotels, they vary in quality from abyssmal to utterly charming. Some motels serve as bordellos, and the word "motel" occasionally means just that—in case you can't figure out why someone is smiling when you ask for the nearest motel.

Mountain Inns (*albergues de montaña*): The only thing that these inns have in common is that they're located in mountains. Some are charming little homes, others like bungalows, still others more like hotels. Many offer meals. These are especially common in out-of-the-way areas of Costa Rica.

Restaurants: Travelers who really get off the beaten path may resort to staying in restaurants, especially in Mexico. Owners often ask for a token amount for overnight stays. This is safer than sleeping outside. Adventurer types get used to whatever's available. Don't shrug this possibility off.

Resorts: Travel agents are a good resource in helping you choose a resort and make reservations. Normally, there is no charge involved for reservations, but ask to be sure. However, since you'll probably be staying in a resort for a week or more, this is one time you should ask lots of questions. Below is a resort question checklist to help you get exactly what you want.

The resort hotel checklist is meant only to point out that glossy brochures are just that—paper with some words written on them. Photographers can do marvelous things with next to nothing. The questions you ask can help you get what you want.

Yet, you have to be realistic when traveling to Central America and Mexico, which means being willing to bend. Hot water, for example, comes and goes, even in deluxe hotels—you have to go with the flow. And that may mean taking baths or showers at odd times.

Requesting what you want is smart because it increases your odds of getting it. But don't count on it. Even such a basic thing as reservations can be bungled or disregarded.

Resort Checklist

- If you're using a travel agent, has he been to the hotel? Has he stayed there? How long ago?
- What is the overall area like?
- What does the resort specialize in? Some resorts are geared to golf, tennis, riding, while others offer pools with swim-up bars and flowers floating in pineapples filled with potent drinks.
- What is the price? Save the agent a lot of time by telling him your price range.
- What's the weather like? Is it humid? Is it windy?
- Where is the hotel in relation to the town? Is it a good location? Can you get a map showing the exact location of the hotel?
- Is there free transportation to and from the airport to the hotel? Is there a parking lot? Does the hotel have cars?
- Will the hotel provide free bikes to its guests (very nice touch)?
- What kind of people go to the hotel? Does it take tours? Is it family-oriented? Do many singles go there?
- Is it a large or small hotel? Would you call it intimate? Or is it a large, commercial complex?
- Is the hotel on or near the beach? Does the beach come right up to the hotel?
- What's the beach like? How wide is it? What's the sand like? Are there beach chairs?
- Is the water good for swimming? Is it clear enough for snorkeling? Can you swim in the area? Is there an undertow, rip tides, or any problem swimming in the area (very real concern)?
- Are there any rooms with access directly to the beach?
- What kind of rooms are available? Any special rooms? Any special suites? Any villas?
- Is there a road between the hotel and beach (very noisy and disagreeable)? How close are other hotels to this hotel? How far from a main road is the hotel?
- Does the hotel have a pool? If so, is it used or just a token pool?

Does it have water in it (no joke—some don't!). Is it kept up? Does it have a life guard (very few do)? Are there chaises lounges or hammocks for the guests? Is it in a good, open location or blocked off from the sun much of the day?

- Does the hotel have tennis courts? How many? Do you have to pay extra to use them? What surface do they have? Are they maintained? Is there a pro? What about equipment for sale? Are courts lit for night play? How far in advance do you have to make reservations? Do guests have priority?
- Is there a golf course? How far in advance do reservations have to be made? What are the greens fees? Are there carts and do they work? What's the best time of year to play? Is there a pro? Any equipment for rent or sale? What's the cost? Who has priority?
- Will your room face the ocean directly? Or will your room have an ocean view (a euphemism for seeing the water out of the corner of your eye while leaning over the balcony).
- Are hotel plans available showing where your room is located?
- The room has a balcony. Great! What size is it? Can it be used? Does it have a table and chairs? Can breakfast be served there? Is there any extra cost for such service?
- What's the food like? Do you have to eat in the resort (you don't want to be forced to)? What's included in the full-board price? What's not? Do you have a choice in what dishes you can order with full room and board?
- What size are the rooms? What kind of beds do they have? Is there a bath or a shower? Is there hot water (silly question—no one ever knows). Are beach towels provided?
- What kind of water sports are there? Are masks and fins available? What about boats? Windsurfing? Water skiing? Parasailing? Fishing? How much do they cost? Is the equipment in good shape?

Townhalls (*municipalidad*): You don't actually sleep in townhalls, but in Guatemala they are often a source of information for places to stay. Since I do not recommend off-the-beaten-path travel in this country at this time, you probably won't need to use this tip. Perhaps, things will calm down in the future. You ask for the mayor (*alcade*) when looking for help.

Villas (see *Apartments*)

Whorehouses: The word motel sometimes means whorehouse in Spanish, but not always. Bordellos are often hard to spot from tacky hotels. You'll rarely be turned away because you rent by the night rather than the hour. You may end up in one without realizing it—at least, at first. Just put in your earplugs.

YMCAs and YWCAs: There are a limited number of Y's, but if you're trying to keep your costs down, they are worth checking into. For complete information on these budget accommodations contact:

YMCA
101 North Wacker Drive
Chicago, IL 60606
Tel: (312) 977-0031
Belize, Costa Rica, Guatemala,
    Honduras, Mexico.

YWCA
726 Broadway
New York, NY 10003
Tel: (800) 992-2871
    (212) 614-2700
Belize, Mexico.

Youth Hostels (see p. 5)

Room Reservations

Reservations are not necessarily essential for enjoyable travel, but they certainly can help, especially for brief and highly organized trips. A poorly made reservation may be worse than none at all.

When Reserving a Room Makes Sense

- Have a reservation for the first night abroad. Since you'll be exhausted when you arrive, you don't want to look for a room.
- Make reservations if you want rooms of great charm or value, especially during the peak seasons.
- Always have room reservations in the period of Christmas (*Navidad*) to New Year's or at Easter time (*Semana Santa*).
- Local residents also jam hotels on three-day holiday weekends, particularly around major cities.
- During the summer, major tourist towns in mountain areas fill up on weekends, because they offer much cooler weather.
- If you're on a short trip with little time to waste, have reservations for every night.
- Resorts, fancy and famous hotels—these fill up months in advance during the peak seasons.
- Have room reservations for jungle lodges, often months or even years in advance for peak season travel.
- If you'll be going to a town during a festival, make reservations. You won't find a room in Mazatlán during Carnival, for example.

Disadvantages of Reservations
- You may have to pay a fee for room reservations and also foot the cost of faxes or telephone calls.
- You're usually renting sight unseen. Unless you have great confidence in your "source," you may end up disappointed.
- You'll pay the highest price a room will rent for. Reservations take away your bargaining power and make it very difficult for you to shift from one room to another.
- Reservations tie you down. On short trips, this makes no difference, but on trips three weeks or longer, a reservation schedule can begin to feel like an ill-fitting shoe on a 10-mile hike.
- Reservations are sometimes blatantly disregarded.
- If you cancel a reservation, you may not be able to get your deposit back. More about this later.

Avoiding Getting Bumped by Hotels
Many hotels routinely overbook by 10 to 15 percent. Even with written confirmations, you could be one of those bumped.
- Get your reservations confirmed in writing. Most hotels are now doing this by fax.
- If you know that you'll be arriving at a hotel after 6:00 P.M., make sure that the hotel knows this. And have this late arrival time noted on your room confirmation slip.
- Pay a substantial deposit on the room. With money in the bank, hotels are less likely to bump you. Deposits are common.
- If you get delayed unexpectedly (very common), notify the hotel. Few hotels will rent out a room if you have contacted them. Get the name of the person you talk to.

Canceling a Room
The refund policy varies with each hotel. In some instances, you may lose your entire deposit for canceling a room too late.
- Before making a reservation requiring a deposit, ask for a copy of the cancellation policy—preferably in writing.

Travel Agents' Reservations
- Most agents charge nothing at all for making room reservations, unless doing so involves a special service, such as faxing or telephoning (their commission is paid by the hotel).
- Ask the agent whether you'll be charged for faxes or telephone calls—or for anything else, for that matter.
- If the agent insists that there is no charge at all, ask whether a surcharge could be added to your hotel bill on the other end.
- If the agent says that no such commission need be paid, ask for a

letter typed on the agency stationery stating this in straightforward terms. If a hotel then tries to stick you with a surcharge, produce the letter and refuse to pay.

Making Your Own Reservations
- Larger hotel chains have toll-free (800) numbers listed in the phone book or available from information (call 1-800-555-1212). Dial the number and make a reservation. Repeat dates and ask them to send you some sort of confirmation in writing. Also ask for a reservation or confirmation number.
- Mailing for reservations is antiquated and unreliable. Hotels, even small ones, are moving towards the use of faxes. Use faxes to make reservations and request confirmation (keep it).
- Another method: Call the foreign hotel during local business hours (remember the time-zone difference). Ask for the front desk, where you'll probably find someone who can speak English. Talk very slowly and very clearly. Repeat the dates of your intended stay several times. Ask for a written confirmation. Get the name of the person with whom you're talking.
- Again, if you have a choice, use faxes rather than phones. Phone reservations are frequently bungled.

Credit Card Reservations
- Note that with some credit cards you can get a confirmed room reservation in major hotels. These guaranteed rooms have a penalty for cancellation. Call major credit card companies and hotel chains for current information on making these special reservations.
- Always get a confirmation number when making a reservation with a credit card. Produce this number as proof that the reservation was made if someone cannot seem to locate it.
- A confirmation number is nice, but a confirmation in writing is much better. Ask for one.

Discounts through Travel Clubs
A number of fee-based clubs offer both hotel and restaurant discounts for members. These offer cards or coupons to reduce hotel costs by as much as 50 percent. Most properties are in the expensive to very expensive category, so that savings can be substantial. Fees vary by club. If you want to stay in upper-bracket hotels, these cards make sense. Find out the number and location of hotels in making your choice of club or clubs. Once a member, make reservations as far in advance as possible. Note that in peak holiday periods these clubs may be of little value.

Entertainment Publications
P.O. Box 1016
Trumbull, CT 06611
Tel: (800) 285-5525
Mexico.

INFINET Travel Club
P.O. Box 1033
186 Alewife Brook Parkway
Cambridge, MA 02140
· Tel: (800) 966-2582

(617) 661-8900
Belize, Costa Rica, Guatemela,
Honduras, Mexico.

International Travel Card
6001 North Clark Street
Chicago, IL 60660
Tel: (800) 342-0558
   (312) 465-8891
Belize, Costa Rica, Guatemala,
Mexico

Hotel Representatives in the United States

The following companies handle hotels in Central America and Mexico. They have free brochures on numerous properties. You or your travel agent can make a reservation by dialing the toll-free (800) number of these hotel representatives.

Alexander Associates
(800) 221-6509, Mexico.
American International
(800) 223-5695, Mexico.
Belize Resorts (800) 333-3459
Belize, Honduras.
Best Western (800) 528-1234
Mexico.
Calinda Quality Inns
(800) 228-5151, Mexico.
Certified Vacations
(800) 233-7260, Mexico.
Camino Real (800) 722-6466
Mexico.
Club Med (800) 258-2633
Mexico.
Fiesta Americana
(800) 223-2332, Mexico.
Holiday Inn (800) 238-8000
Costa Rica, Mexico.
Howard Johnson (HoJo Inn)
(800) 634-3464, Mexico.
Hyatt International
(800) 228-9000, Mexico.
Krystal Hotels (800) 231-9860
Mexico.

Loews Representations
(800) 223-0888
Costa Rica, Mexico.
Magnum Americas
(800) 447-2931, Belize.
Omni (800) 843-6664, Mexico.
Pleasant Holidays
(800) 242-9244, Mexico.
Princess Hotels (800) 223-1818
Mexico.
Quality Inn (800) 228-5151
Costa Rica, Mexico.
Ramada Inns (800) 854-7854
Belize, Guatemala, Mexico.
Robert Warner (800) 888-1199
Mexico.
Runaway Tours, Inc.
(800) 622-0723, Mexico.
Sheraton (800) 325-3535
Mexico.
Utell International
(800) 448-8355, Belize, Costa
Rica, Guatemala, Honduras,
Mexico.
Westin Hotels (800) 228-3000
Guatemala, Mexico.

Packing

What to take, how to pack it—some of the most basic questions! Never forget to pack patience. You'll need it for border crossings; moved offices or incorrect addresses; non-existant signs; phone numbers that are not working, disconnected, or left unanswered; long lines to exchange money; and so on. Patience is the number one requirement for travel in Central America and Mexico.

Dress in Central America and Mexico

- Dress is extremely casual in most areas of Central America and Mexico. Rarely is a man expected to wear a coat and tie or comparable dress for women.
- Formal dress is only necessary for business meetings, in elegant restaurants , at a few major resorts, and at jai alai games.
- Get by with simple, casual clothes—nothing stylish at all. In fact, smart travelers keep a low profile.
- Casual clothing is fine. Dirty or patched clothing is offensive.

General Dressing Tips
- Read the section on when to travel so that you'll match your clothes to the prevailing weather.
- Remember that mountainous areas can be chilly to extremely cold. Even buses in tropical areas can be chilly at night or with the air-conditioning on in the day. Bring something warm even though 90 percent of the time you won't need it.
- Bring layers of clothes rather than bulky items. As the temperature drops, add layer upon layer.
- Most of your clothes should be cotton or cotton-blend. Cotton breathes in hot climates, which makes it the most comfortable.
- Wear light-colored clothes. Local residents wear a lot of white for obvious reasons. They reflect light.
- Keep your clothes loose. Tight-fitting clothing is uncomfortable in hot weather. On women it is sexually provocative and can cause serious problems (see p. 183).
- Have a hat. If you forget, buy one abroad. Caps, visors, tennis hats, sombreros—any of these are fine to protect you from the sun. You'll need it. Ideally, a hat will have a 4-inch brim to protect your nose and ears from serious burns.
- Keep shoes casual and comfortable. Forget style. Many young

and old travelers wear nothing but tennis shoes for the whole trip. No one cares in the least whether you're fashionable or not (except in discos and elegant restaurants). More expensive walking shoes are another good option with a spare pair of tennis shoes for getting into the water.

- If hiking, bring comfortable boots giving firm support but well broken in. They should tie tightly around your ankle.
- Coats, pants, shirts—all should have lots of pockets. Add pockets if necessary. Each pocket should close tightly with a button, velcro lining, or zipper. Use each of these pockets for a specific item or purpose. When traveling, you often get tired and disoriented. Always have specific places for specific items to avoid confusion.

Tips for Women

- Keep makeup extremely simple while traveling. Foreign women suggest no makeup at all, even though they wear it. You do not want to attract attention, you want to fade into the crowd to avoid robbery and sexual harrassment.
- Leave your valuable jewelry at home, including your engagement ring and wedding band. Don't even wear inexpensive silver and gold imitation jewelry. Robbers can't tell the difference between it and the real thing. Exception: If you're having trouble with male harrassment, wear a fake wedding band made from a cheap material. If it gets stolen, it won't matter. Wearing a band indicates that you're another man's "property." That comment may make your blood boil, but the band can cut down on unwanted attention.
- Remember that strong perfumes and cosmetics can make you sunsensitive. So can some antibiotics (see p. 241).
- Samples of beauty products are light, small, and easy to carry. Collect them for short trips. Get them free at department store.
- A loose skirt or a pair of cotton pants is more comfortable than jeans.
- Avoid any clothes which reveal your breasts. The bra-less look is not advised.
- Carry a flat, large purse for all your odds and ends—a folding umbrella, a camera (best kept out of sight), a snack—you name it. Keep your makeup in a makeup case (if you simply cannot do without it) and a little money in a wallet or change purse. These fit nicely into the larger purse.
- One of the most versatile items to pack is a *long*, cotton beach robe. Not only can it be used on the beach as a coverup or beach blanket, but it can pass as either casual or elegant dress. It's extremely easy to keep clean, weighs very little, and packs tight with little wrinkling.

Packing Light

- Do it like the pros—travel light. Get by with one piece of hand luggage. If you can't carry it on a plane, it's too large. If you can't carry it for a mile without setting it down, it's too heavy. There's a wonderful motto: "Take half as much clothing, twice as much money."
- It's natural for you to feel somewhat skeptical about traveling with only one piece of carryon luggage. If you choose your clothes wisely, you'll have no problem at all. The reaction to this style of travel is always the same: Are you ever smart! As long as you're clean and comfortably dressed, you'll exude an aura of contentment and confidence. Foreigners judge you by this attitude, not your clothes.

How to Pack Light

- Leave electrical items at home. They're heavy, bulky, and can be damaged by varying voltage.
- Pack only items you need to survive—the essentials. I met one person who considers a toothbrush the only essential item.
- Make each item serve as many purposes as possible. A bathing suit can pass as underwear. A one-piece woman's swimsuit converts into a dress by adding a wraparound skirt. Shampoo can wash not only hair but the body as well—think versatility.
- Go for comfort first, style last. But the two need not be mutually exclusive. As mentioned, style is less important than attitude.
- All clothes must be light, easy to wash, and quick-drying. Test them before you leave. Pick up heavier items for special needs (such as a *serape* for cool weather) abroad.
- Spray water repellant on any materials that are suited to such treatment. This will help keep them stain-free.
- Here's a typical wardrobe for a light-packing woman: Bathing suit (if appropriate—should be easy to dry); blouse (light and long-sleeved); coat (best if waterproof—GoreTex is great); dress (light, supple, easy to scrunch up material); handbag (as outlined above); pants (two—both cotton with lots of pockets); skirt (airy and light); shoes (comfortable, walking type—nothing fancy); socks; tennis shoes (for walking, beach, and getting into water); t-shirt or two (one thigh length); sweater (only if appropriate to weather); underwear (cotton panties and a couple of bras). Add or delete a few things as fits your personality, and you'll be carrying one small bag.
- A light packing man follows the same principles, replacing the dress with a sports coat and tie only if absolutely necessary.

Basics of Packing

Use the rolling technique to keep clothes wrinkle free and accessible in a small bag.

- Lay slacks or pants out on a flat surface (such as a bed) with the leg seams together. These will serve as a base.
- Fold such things as a sweater, t-shirt, or turtleneck in half lengthwise, with sleeves together. Lay these out evenly on both the top and bottom portion of the slacks.
- Roll the clothes into a loose ball, working from the pants legs up and hold them together with a large rubber band or slip the ball into a plastic bag—the latter is much easier.
- Clothes in a plastic bag slip in and out of luggage or a backpack very easily. The plastic also protects them from dust, dirt, and any liquids that might spill accidentally.
- You just unroll the ball to get to whatever item you need.

Packing Toiletries

- Put all liquids in plastic bottles. Place each bottle in a separate, locking plastic bag.
- To prevent leaking: Gently squeeze the bottle as you put the top on to create suction. Seal the top with tape for full protection (just for plane flights).
- As you use up your toothpaste and other creams in tubes, roll tubes up tightly so that they will take up less space. Carry two small tubes of such products instead of one large one, if you'll be traveling extensively.
- Keep all toiletries in one place, as in a makeup case, so that you can get to them easily at any time.

If You Can't Pack Light

If you've decided not to travel light, here are a few tips:

Use More Than One Bag

- Carrying two smaller bags is easier than carrying one larger one. They balance well in each hand.
- Pack each bag as if one of the bags may get lost. Split essential clothes and accessories. If you end up with only one bag, you'll make it.
- Carryon baggage should contain anything which if lost would ruin your trip. For example, if you were going fishing in Costa Rica, you would want your rods, reels, and lures in a carryon bag (see p. 274 on how this could actually be done).

Packing Larger Suitcases
- Plastic bags keep clothes from getting wrinkled. Slide each shirt, jacket, or skirt into a separate bag. The film of air between the plastic and clothes will keep them wrinkle free.
- Keep jackets and coats on hangers to whip out and hang in a closet. Cover each with plastic.
- Bags with rollers help you pull heavier bags over long distances. Sometimes, porters or carts just aren't available.

Packing Garment Bags
- Hang a number of clothes on no more than two hangers. If you use more, the bag becomes bulky and hard to handle.
- Light plastic hangers with rounded corners work best.
- You can stuff an incredible number of small items into the bottom of a garment bag. The temptation results in a heavy bag.

Protecting and Carrying Valuables

Protect and carry valuables such as a passport, plane tickets, traveler's checks, and money in a secret pocket (or pockets) which slides under your clothes. Attach it to your belt or hang it from your neck (see pp. 173–177).

Traveler's Checklist

A trip should start off relaxed, so pack well in advance of departure. This helps you remember things you've overlooked.

Use this checklist to help you pack. Take only those things essential to the enjoyment of a trip and matching your particular brand of travel. If traveling by car or RV, see the car travel section on p. 194.

Acetaminophen Replacement for aspirin, if you're sensitive to the latter (see Dengue Fever p. 226).

Address book Don't leave home without a small, light, thin address book to fill. Absolutely invaluable!

Adhesive tape A good item for backpackers and hikers.

Airline tickets Keep these in a safe place.

Alarm clock If you'll be traveling at off hours or are going to have important business meetings, take a tiny travel alarm. Many watches are now available with alarms.

Alcohol (*drinking*) Carry a flask of booze with you for flights or train trips. A bottle of imported wine makes a good gift.

Alcohol (*rubbing*) Backpackers and hikers might want to carry it.

Aloe vera gel This helps heal minor cuts and is good for sunburn.

Amoebecide You can buy similar products abroad, but it can't hurt packing this with other medications, especially for remote areas.

Ammonia solution See the medical section for possible uses.

Antacid Everyone should carry a few tablets. If you've got chronic problems, take all you could possibly need.

Antibiotic For bacterial infections causing traveler's diarrhea. Cipro is one of the best, but many others also work well.

Antibiotic ointment Bring a small tube.

Artificial tears Helpful for contact lens wearers.

Antihistamine Good for bee stings and insomnia. Benadryl is commonly recommended.

Antivenins (*scorpion and snake*) The average traveler will have no problem with snakes and scorpions, but if you'll be getting into remote areas, consider taking them. I'd prefer a good guide.

Art supplies Hard to find and expensive abroad.

Aspirin A must.

Backpack No matter what your age or style of travel, these can make sense. Get one of the smaller, canvas kinds with a pocket on top and two on the sides—comfortable and light.

Baking soda For campers and off-road travel.

Band-Aids Bring a few. Put them on blisters *immediately* to stop them from getting worse. The local versions of Band-Aids rarely stick.

Bandana Lightweight and very versatile. Used as a sweat band, table cloth, food wrap—you name it. See **Scarves**.

Bathing suit Bathing suits can double for underwear if they're easy to wash, quick-drying, light, and comfortable. Fifteen minutes is all it takes to dry out a suit in the sun after swimming or washing. Pick suits that don't bind or have tight elastic belts. Suits of different styles are best for those who want an even tan (dermatologists cringe at this advice).

Bathrobe Not essential and easily replaced by a beach robe.

Batteries Bring a few extra for portable radios and flashlights. If you forget, ask for *pilas*. Always test batteries before taking them with you (most hardware stores offer free testing).

Beach robe Essential. Make sure it's cotton and very long.

Beach towel Many hotels provide only the smallest and flimsiest towels for their guests. However, beach towels are hard to carry, heavy, and very bulky. Nice, but not geared to lightweight travel.

Belt Needed if you'll be carrying a secret money pouch.

Binoculars Useful for birding, whale-watching, bullfights, and ballet.

Birth control pills (*pastillas anticonceptivas*) Bring extra, just in case you stay longer than you expect.

Blanket Many times better and more versatile than a sleeping bag. Blankets (*cubiertas*) are easy to find abroad.

Blazer Fine if you'll be in formal situations, otherwise useless. Travel with one made of tightly woven material, dark-colored, and stain and wrinkle-resistant. Spray with water repellant.

Blouse Take two at most—one light-colored, one dark (or print). They should be light and easy to wash. Take only ones of cotton or silk. One should have long sleeves to protect you from sun.

Blue jeans No, not in the Tropics.

Boat A small, simple boat will help fishing immeasurably.

Boat permit You have to have one for Mexico (see p. 83).

Body lotion Good after bathing and suntanning.

Book Bring one book for interminable waits. If using a travel guide, rip out the sections you need to reduce weight.

Boots Bring a good pair if you'll be hiking or back-packing into remote areas. Old boots are best, but they should give plenty of support. Waterproof boots are essential for jungle travel. Get the kind which breathe easily to prevent fungal infections. Higher boots are best for areas with snakes.

Bottle Plastic bottles get warm quickly and take on the odor of whatever's been in them. Get light, durable ones with flip-up tops or screw-on lids.

Bottle opener One of the most useful and easy-to-forget items. Many Swiss Army knifes have openers on them, but you're not technically allowed to bring these knives onto planes in carryon luggage (although many people do).

Bottle stopper Many grocery stores have stoppers or plugs for glass bottles, if you prefer these to plastic ones.

Bra Bring no more than two. Substitute a bikini top if possible. In *resort* areas the bra is obsolete. Everywhere else—essential.

Bucket (*cubo*) Either bring or buy one abroad if camping.

Burner An absolute must for cooking. The alcohol burners abroad are really cheap as is alcohol (*alcohol*).

Burn ointment Essential.

Business cards Take a few.

Calculator Not a bad idea, if you take a slim, ultra-light kind.

Camera and film Great, but a hassle. Bring only if you're serious.

Camp cook set Keep it light and easy to use.

Camping gear See p. 159.

Can opener (*abrelatas*) Absolutely essential for camping.

Canteen For trekking, hiking, etc.

Cards (*playing*) Easy to forget, but wonderful.

Cassette tapes Nice to drown out noise on buses, trains, and planes. Relaxing at night.

Change purse You'll be carrying lots of change.

Chapstick Essential. Get the kind that contains sunscreen.

Chloroquine phosphate Usually sold as Aralen, an anti-malarial medication effective against bacteria carried by mosquitoes.

Clothesline A rubber braided one which stretches out is ideal.

Coats A medium-weight jacket is most versatile. Some of the newer kinds are light-weight, waterproof, and very warm. They're also very expensive, but worth it (GoreTex).

Comb Essential.

Compass A tiny pocket compass comes in handy. Some watches have removable compasses.

Contact lenses Take spares if necessary.

Contact lens solution Very hard to find.

Contraceptives Condoms made in the United States are the most reliable. If you're on the pill, bring all that you'll need.

Corn pads Hard to find when you need them.

Cosmetics Take as few as you can get by with.

Cotton swabs (see Q-tips).

Credit cards Very helpful, with many travel advantages.

Curling iron Can you get by without one?

Cup A metal, collapsible one is best.

Currency Bring as much U.S. currency as you can afford to lose. Bring *at least* fifty $1 bills for many smaller transactions.

Day pack Small day packs come in handy for a million uses. They should zip closed, be light, and scrunch up to almost nothing. One with an additional front pocket and shoulder straps is best.

Decongestant Prevents earache when landing in a plane.

Dental floss Cuts cheese and doubles for thread.

Deodorant If you're flying, don't take aerosol cans.

Desenex Bring one small tube if susceptible to athlete's foot or similar complaints. Stronger anti-fungals contain Nizoral, but require a doctor's prescription.

Detergent Fill a small plastic bag with some.

Diapers As if you could forget.

Diarrhea pills The best require a prescription.

Dictionary Get the little calculator-like kind. They're thin, light, and have a memory of more than 40,000 words. Get them at office supply stores. Just punch in either English or Spanish for quick translation. Much lighter and easier to use than a book.

Disinfectant Anything which will kill germs.

Diving gear Bring your own, especially your regulator (see p. 302).

Dixie cups Good item for short vacations.

Dress Take one which is easy to dress up or down.

Drugs Take as many prescription drugs as you'll need for the entire trip, plus enough for a week or two to spare.

Earplugs If you're sensitive to noise (and hotels can be unbelievably noisy), then these are a great item to bring along. Get the easy-to-mold kind, like *Flents*. The company also makes other protective devices, including eye masks. For a brochure contact:

Flents Products, Inc.
P.O. Box 2109
Norwalk, CT 06852
Tel: (203) 866-2581

Egg carton These are hard to find for campers.

Electric razor Small, light travel kits consisting of a compact safety razor and a few blades make more sense.

Emery boards Easy to forget.

Envelopes At least a few.

Eye drops Likewise.

Eyeglasses Bring a spare.

Eye masks Excellent for light sleepers. See **Ear Plugs**.

Extension cord Surprisingly useful.

Feminine hygiene products (see *Tampons*).

Film Bring lots. Take all film out of the cardboard boxes to show that they are not for resale.

Filters (*for lens*) Get a good Polaroid filter for each lens.

Fingernail clippers Very handy.

First-aid kit Gear it to your style of travel (see p. 20).

Fishing gear Bring your own. See p. 273.

Fishing license Get it before going to Mexico (see p. 273). For Central America, inquire at local tourist offices.

Fishnet shopping bag Essential. Light, compact, tough.

Flannel shirts Tough, easy to clean, versatile. Best for cooler areas (mountain hikes). Replace with similar style cotton shirts for warmer areas.

Flashlight Get a good pocket-size model. Essential for walking, groping, and seeing in dark places, including your hotel room. Also helpful in dark bus and train stations when the lights go out.

Flask The metal kind are best in warm areas. Wash flasks out frequently to avoid the growth of dangerous bacteria.

Fly swatter A must for the more casual, long-term traveler. More for spiders and mosquitoes than flies (unless you're camping out).

Food Have some at all times for inevitable delays and snafus.

Frisbee Fun and good for digging holes in sand.

Garbage bags The large, black plastic ones are thick and durable. Use these to protect the contents of packs in rainy areas.

Glasses One spare of both sunglasses and prescription glasses.

Gloves Golf gloves come in handy for skin diving.

Grill A small one for cooking out.

Guns Only with a permit.

Gun permit Hard to get and expensive. See p. 284.

Hairbrush Wonderful.

Hair conditioner Often hard to find.

Hair dryer Women for centuries got by without one. Can't you?

Hair spray Get by without it, if possible.

Halazone Or, similar tablets for water purification.

Hammock Pick one up abroad (preferably in Mexico) if you'd like to be a swinger (many hotels have hooks for hammocks in Mexico's Yucatán and in remote jungle areas of Central America).

Hankies Use disposable tissues instead. Buy as necessary.

Hat A hat with a 4-inch brim is the best. If it has a drawstring to pull it tight against your chin, all the better.

Hatchet A good tool for campers. A machete works just as well and can be bought in Central America or Mexico.

Heater (*immersible*) A clever gadget that heats up water quickly. Kills bacteria and giardia in impure water.

Helmets For motorcycling or biking.

Huaraches Sandals are a favorite in Mexico and quite cheap. Fine for beach areas, but useless for long walks.

Hydrogen peroxide Consider for your first-aid kit.

Immersible heater (see **Heater**)

Imodium A good medication for a bad case of diarrhea.

Insect repellent Get a liquid high in DEET.

International Student Identification Card See p. 4.

Iron Wrinkles are accepted everywhere.

Jacket Bring one.

Jeans Replace these with cotton pants.

Jewelry Leave it at home—just a come-on for crooks.

Juice squeezer Pick up an *exprimidera* abroad for camping.

Khakis Better than jeans.

Knapsack Accepted now almost everywhere.

Knife Technically, you can no longer carry knives, even small ones onto planes. A good knife is invaluable, however. And, many times security will let smaller Swiss knives pass. Note: Knives are allowed in checked baggage.

Laces Change laces before going abroad.

Lamp The light in many hotels is dim. Carrying a tiny lamp with a high-watt bulb isn't so dim-witted.

Laundry soap Get a few travel packets.

Laxative Just the opposite of what most travelers need, but a few people have problems with constipation.

Light bulb Pick up a *foco* of higher wattage to see in budget hotel rooms. A tiny little lamp is better.

Lighter Take one if needed.

Lip balm Bring something to protect and care for your lips. They'll dry out in the sun. Vaseline also works fine. See **Chapstick**.

Liquor If you absolutely insist on a specific brand of booze, bring in a bottle. Imported liquors are outrageously expensive.

Lomotil A strong diarrhea medication, but not recommended for ong-term use. Requires a doctor's prescription in the United States but is sold over the counter in Mexico for practically nothing.

Machete Buy abroad for camping. Be careful. Machetes are extremely sharp and cause many serious cuts.

Makeup pencil/sharpener No makeup (see pp. 183–185).

Malaria pills Take wherever recommended.

Maps Get ones which match your brand of travel. (see p. 33).

Matches Waterproof matches should be a part of every camper's gear. Place them in a waterproof container.

Mattress (*air*) Buy a good one. Bring a repair kit!

Medications Pack ones you use frequently.

Mesh bags Very light, compact, and useful.

Mirror One tiny pocket mirror is enough.

Moisturizer Your skin takes a beating in tropical sun.

Moleskin Dr. Scholl's adhesive felt—great for blisters.

Money belt or pouch Absolutely essential. Best to have several on different parts of your body. You can make your own or buy them. If you have trouble finding them, contact:

Austin House
P.O. Box 111
Station "B"
Buffalo, NY 14207
Tel: (800) 268-5157, or

Austin House
P.O. Box 1051
Oakvale, ON L6J 5E9
Canada
Tel: (800) 387-7101

Money tube The floating, waterproof type which you hang from your neck. Get it in any dive shop. For a better seal stretch electric tape around the grooves. The top will screw right over the tape. This is the best way to carry money at the beach because it goes with you into the water!

Mosquito netting (*pabellon*) Needed for camping out or sleeping in poorly screened hotels. If you have trouble finding netting, contact the following company (ask for a free catalog):

Travel Medicine, Inc.
351 Pleasant Street, Suite 312
Northampton, MA 01060
Tel: (800) 872-8633

Motion sickness remedies See p. 237.

Nail file Easily packed.

Nail polish and remover Can you get by without it?

Nasal spray Have trouble with your ears on flights? Use nasal spray before the plane makes its descent.

Needle and thread Bring one needle and a little thread (off the spool). Save travel packets given out in better hotels.

Nightgown Experienced travelers do without it.

Notebook Good place to write down names of hotels, restaurants, or contacts.

Nylons Not really necessary.

Overcoat The same.

Pajamas Ditto.

Panties Bring several pairs—all nylon for fast drying. Cotton only if you're prone to fungal or vaginal infections.

Pants Lightweight cotton pants are best. Two pairs at most, preferably with lots of pockets.

Paper A little pad is really useful.

Paper clips Bring a few.

Passport Not required in Mexico, but absolutely the safest and best form of identification. Required throughout Central America.

Passport photos Always bring 2 extra photos, just in case you lose your passport.

Pepto-Bismol Will prevent and cure mild diarrhea. Liquid is best, but bulky. Tablets are also available. Practical only for short trips.

Pen One of the most useful items abroad. Bring several.

Perfume Not recommended since it sets you up as a wealthy foreigner. It also attracts mosquitoes.

Permission for minor See p. 4.

Pillow Some veteran travelers carry a small, down pillow for rides in public transportation. These squeeze down to next to nothing.

Plastic bags These have dozens of uses. One of the best is to protect cameras from dust. Get the kind which lock tight.

Plastic plates Very useful, even if you don't plan to camp out.

Pocket (*secret*) See **Money pouch**.

Poncho Highly recommended in hot, humid areas where a raincoat won't breathe (see **Raincoat** for exception).

Prescription medications Bring extra just in case your trip is extended for unforeseen reasons.

Prescriptions Before filling out prescriptions for controlled substances, photocopy them. Carry a copy with you. If you lose the medication, you will have to see a doctor to get a refill abroad, but these photocopies prove that you're legally using the drug.

Purse Big and flat. One of the most useful items to have.

Q-tips Mainly for divers and snorkelers. Clean out your ears after each dive with cotton swabs dipped in rubbing alcohol or vinegar. Infections are common since water is often polluted (see p. 323).

Radio Tiny transistor and Walkman-type radios are prizes in Central America and Mexico.

Raincoat If you'll be traveling extensively in cooler areas, a lightweight one will do. GoreTex is best. If you plan travel in lowland areas which are hot and humid, forget the coat. A poncho which won't trap moisture is much preferred.

Rubbing alcohol (see Alcohol).

Safety pins Bring one or two. Use them to keep pockets closed to protect your wallet—a secret pocket works better.

Saltwater soap Pick this up abroad under the name *jabón de coco*. Great if you're camping out at the beach.

Sandals These are fine in beach areas and very cheap abroad.

Scarves Just like gold, because they're stylish, lightweight, compact, and versatile (they can be used as belts, skirts, and even shawls). Scarves replace jewelry, transforming one outfit into many.

Scissors Small travel scissors are useful, but not indispensable.

Shampoo Bring a small tube in toothpaste-style container. Doesn't leak easily and takes up less space. Tubes are getting hard to find.

Shaving cream Use soap instead.

Sheet Some campers prefer this to a sleeping bag in tropical areas. Good in cheap hotels and hostels. Excellent for picnics. Should be cotton, not polyester.

Shirt Match shirts to your style of travel. The best material is cotton. Shirts with lots of pockets are really useful.

Shoes Take one pair of your most comfortable shoes, preferably ones with soles that grip surfaces well. Don't bring shoes that need polishing. Many people get by with a pair of tennis shoes. If you have to dress up, buy a pair of shoes abroad.

Shorts Out of place except along the beach and in resorts. Many foreigners wear them in cities. This is considered offensive.

Skin cream For obvious applications.

Skirt Bring one that's easy to wash, lightweight, dark-colored to hide stains, and wrinkle-resistant.

Slacks (see Pants).

Sleeping bag Bring a thin, down bag that will scrunch down to nothing for high mountain or cool areas. Bring a synthetic one for hot, humid areas where bags could get wet.

Sleeping pills (see p. 234).

Sleeping sheet See p. 5 for youth hostel information.

Slip No more than one, if any at all.

Slippers Unnecessary. If you disagree, get the fabric kind that fold up into a tiny package. Or get slipper socks, the terry equivalent—found in most hospitals.

Snakebite kits Essential for anyone trekking into tropical forests on their own. Note, however, that different snakes require different antivenins. I'd go with an experienced guide.

Snorkeling gear Flippers are bulky so just bring a mask, unless your whole vacation centers around snorkeling. See p. 320.

Soap Even little dives provide soap for their customers, although it's often already opened and used. A few places don't have soap. Bring several bars, the tiny ones found in most motels.

Socks Two pairs—of synthetic material. Both wool and cotton are preferred for hiking and heavy use, but they're difficult to wash and take a long time to dry. To wash socks quickly: put them on your hands like surgeon's gloves and scrub them with a bar of soap.

Sports coat Rarely needed. A dark color is best.

Sports equipment All sports equipment is extremely expensive and sometimes impossible to find. There are no restrictions on equipment brought with you for personal use. A tip: Use gear once or twice to show that it's not for resale. Residents will love you if you'll give, trade, or sell them equipment at the end of your stay.

Spot remover If you travel with easy-to-wash clothes, you won't need this.

Suit Only necessary for business travelers.

Sunglasses Match the glasses to how they'll be used, but bring a pair. Mexicans, especially, love sunglasses and will trade the shirt off their back to get a good pair. If you're prone to eye irritation or skin cancer, get sunglasses which will afford 100 percent protection against ultraviolet rays. If fishing, get ones which are polarized.

Sun protective clothing (see p. 241)

Sunscreen The sun can cause a lot of damage in a very short time. Everyone should carry water-resistant sunscreen with at least an SPF (Sun Protection Factor) of 15 or higher. See p. 241.

Sweater Bring a sweatshirt instead.

Sweatshirt Much more versatile and comfortable than a sweater.

Swim suit Standard issue for parts of Central America and a must for Mexico (a country with 6,000 miles of coastline).

Swiss Army knife Technically not allowed in carryon luggage, but one of the most useful items imaginable. You'll probably get it through. A true Swiss Army knife has *stainless Rosrfrei* written on the large blade, *Officier Suisse* on the other.

Syringes Requires prescription and paperwork for customs. Available abroad. May require foreign doctor's authorization.

Tampons Quality and availability varies abroad. Bring some.

Tarp A must for campers only.

Tea bags Take up little space and weigh next to nothing.

Tennis shoes The kind you can slip on are best for beaches and walking in water (always wear them to prevent cuts or stings). Wear shoes on sand as well to prevent parasitic infections. If you're playing sports, more solid types are better.

Tent Campers only.

Thermometer Carry one without mercury (forbidden by airlines).

Tie Rarely required.

Toilet paper Tuck a small wad into your purse or wallet.

Toothbrush and paste Bring a small tube.

Tourist card (or similar entry document). Carry at all times.

Towel Very bulky and hard to carry. The best are the large, but thin beach towels which serve many purposes.

Towellettes These come in many forms.

Toys Small, light ones if traveling with children.

Tranquilizers Keep them in their original bottle.

Trash bags Can be used in countless ways.

Traveler's checks The only sane way to carry most of your money.

T-shirt You'll probably live in it. You can also sleep in it.

Turtlenecks Second-best to sweatshirts, but still good. Tend to be a little constraining and hot. Best for cooler areas.

Tweezers Ideal for splinters, cactus spines, and bushy brows. Not to be used on ticks (see p. 243) or to remove stingers from bees or wasps (see p. 223).

Umbrella Get the small travel kind that folds down to less than 14 inches. Umbrellas are also useful protecting you against sun.

Underwear Use the new, synthetic underwear; easy to wash and quick-drying. If prone to vaginal or fungal infections, wear cotton.

Velcro More durable than buttons.

Visas (see p. 3).

Vitamins Good idea for long-term travel.

Wash basin For campers.

Wash cloth Important to you? Bring one. They're rare abroad.

Watch Wear an inexpensive brand that can be replaced for a few dollars. If you need an expensive watch for a specific purpose, such as underwater diving, keep it packed away with your other valuables.

Water Always carry purified water. Get a pop-up, squirt top bottle at the grocery store. Refill it as necessary. The top pops up and snaps down. It won't leak. Only a few brands are sold this way. Bottles with screw-on lids are also good.

Water bottle Bring one as described under **Water**.

Water purification gear Water purification kits and water filter straws are available at quality camping or sporting goods stores. Filters should remove microscopic giardia from water (see p. 228). If you have trouble locating good ones locally, contact (ask for their free catalog):

Travel Medicine, Inc.
351 Pleasant Street, Suite 312
Northampton, MA 01060
Tel: (800) 872-8633

Wet Ones Another version of towellettes and just as good.

Whistle Basic survival gear for campers and off-road travelers.

Windbreaker Ideal for cool evenings and boat trips.

Woolite Bring a few travel packets. (see **Detergent**)

Youth Hostel card See p. 5•.

Zippers The zipper is the best and safest way to seal pockets.

Final Steps

Taking the few steps discussed below will ensure a smooth departure and will bring you peace of mind while traveling.

Plant Care While You're Gone

No one wants to spend weeks, months, or years growing beautiful house plants, only to return to a withered mass of brown mold or leafy splinters. To avoid these losses, use a plant-sitter, especially if you'll be gone 3 weeks or longer.

Using a Plant-Sitter
- Give the sitter a key and basic instructions on care.
- Put an identifying mark or a reminder note on each plant needing special care (misting, infrequent watering, etc.).

Doing Without a Plant-Sitter
If you'll be gone less than 3 weeks, get by without a plant-sitter.
- Remove all dead leaves, flowers, and buds.
- Place a plastic bag on the bottom of your tub and cover it with several layers of newspaper.
- Spray the paper with water until it's thoroughly moist.
- Cover the paper with another sheet of plastic.
- Soak plants thoroughly, and let drain completely before setting them on the plastic.
- Cover them with a clear plastic sheet and tape it in place. Poke some holes in it to let air circulate.
- Leave the bathroom shades up.
- If you have more or bigger plants than your tub holds, group them away from direct sunlight. Cover with plastic after a thorough soaking and draining. Poke holes in the plastic to ventilate plants.

Home Security

With more than 2 million burglaries a year in the United States, it's reasonable to be concerned about home security.

Home Security Checklist

- Prepay all utility bills in advance for extremely long trips.
- Cover or screen garage windows so that a potential burglar will not

know if your cars are gone. Bring tools inside from the garage.
- Set timers to turn your lights on and off at varying intervals.
- Put valuables and important documents in a safety deposit box.
- Never talk about upcoming trips with strangers.
- Get an engraving pen and ID number from the local police and mark your valuables. Use "Operation Identification" stickers.
- Lock basement windows and protect them with grilles.
- Lock all windows.
- Place removable drop bars on sliding glass doors.
- Never leave your spare keys in their "secret" hiding place.
- If you leave your car at an airport parking lot, don't leave a house key on your car key chain.
- Leave window shades and blinds in different positions, the way you would if you were at home.
- Stop mail and newspaper delivery a week before you leave. Pick up the mail directly at the post office for that short time.
- Ask a neighbor to pick up any letters, packages, or papers that may get through.
- Have a gardener continue to keep up your garden and lawn.
- Have snow plowed and shoveled if applicable in your area.
- Ask your neighbor to park in your driveway occasionally.
- Have a neighbor fill up a garbage can or two from time to time.
- Unplug your telephones or set the bells at their lowest ring so that any potential burglar will not hear the phone go unanswered from outside the house or apartment. If you have an answering machine, set it to answer after only one or two rings.
- If your trip has been announced in a local paper, hire a house-sitter. Burglars can read.
- Never leave notes outside the house.
- Steal valuable items from a potential thief by carting TVs, radios, stereos, guns, etc., to the house of a friend.
- Check that your insurance policy is paid and up-to-date.

The Last Few Days

Sensible handling of last-minute details can help avert problems.

Three Days Before Your Flight
- Reconfirm your flight reservation.
- Get the name of the person you are speaking to and note the day and time you call.
- This lowers the odds of your being bumped; but if you get bumped, you will have grounds for legal action.
- Reconfirm your order for a special meal if already requested.

The Day Before Your Flight
- Check to make sure no mail or papers are delivered.
- Take pets to the place where they'll be staying.
- Check through the things you'll be taking (see pp. 115–126).
- If you plan on checking baggage, place a label with your name and address on the inside of each bag. Make a list of what's in each bag. If a bag gets lost, you'll be able to identify its contents exactly. When the bag is opened after 3 days (airlines wait this long), you and it will be reunited quickly.

The Day of Your Flight
- Call to ask whether your flight will be leaving on time.
- To save money in cold weather turn down thermostats, close fireplace flues, and turn off the hot water heater. If you're gone for only a week, turn down the temperature on the hot water heater, but don't turn it off completely (it will cost more to reheat the water than you'll save).
- Water the plants for the last time as outlined earlier.
- Unplug appliances, hair dryers, irons, electric blankets, etc.
- Close the shut-off valves to all faucets and toilets. This stops them from accidentally running forever while you're gone.
- Go through all steps outlined in the Home Security Checklist.

Getting to the Airport
- Get to the airport at the time indicated on your ticket. Charters often request passengers to show up 2 hours ahead of time.
- Figure out how long it takes you to get to the airport. Then allow an extra 45 minutes for delays and traffic jams.
- Now add another hour if you intend to register items with customs (see p. 130).

At the Airport

All you want to do is get to the airport, get boarding passes (if this can't be done ahead of time), check your luggage (if you're not traveling light), walk through the security check, and board the plane with a minimum of delay and hassle. Today, that's asking quite a lot.

Parking
- At many international airports there are distant parking lots owned by the airport which cost less than those close in.
- Many private parking companies undercut the prices of the airport-owned lots. These have free shuttles.
- When parking in a private lot, ask how far it is from the airport and how often shuttles run (allow time for delays).

- Whenever you buy a ticket from an agency, ask whether they have coupons to reduce the price of parking at special lots. Many of them do, but tell you only when asked.

Checking Bags

Over a million bags are lost per year. Furthermore, theft from checked baggage is rampant both in the United States and abroad. However, you may need to check baggage.

- Check in with time to spare. Most luggage that's lost is checked in less than 30 minutes before flight time. Never use curbside baggage-check service if you're running late.
- Special tip: Con men are now posing as curbside baggage-check service people. Be careful if you use this service.
- Remove tags and stickers from past trips. They make handling difficult and may send bags in the wrong direction.
- At check-in, watch to make sure that each bag is tagged and placed on the conveyor belt. Never assume either.
- Keep your claim check in a safe place—or have it stapled to your ticket folder. You'll need to show it to claim your baggage.

Protecting Your Belongings

- Lock and strap every bag. Straps keep bags from popping open even under grueling conditions, and they discourage pilfering.
- Never pack cash, documents, fragile items, furs, jewelry, medicine—anything valuable or hard to replace—in your checked baggage. Carry these onto the plane.
- Never leave bags unattended for any reason. Ask someone to watch them or take them with you—even to the bathroom.
- Airport security is increasingly stringent. If you accidentally leave a bag unattended, it may be removed and immediately destroyed.

Registering Valuables

It's best to register valuable items before you get to the airport, but if you forget, do it there. Otherwise, when you come back to the United States or Canada, you may have to pay duty on items that you did not actually purchase abroad.

- You'll find registration booths in international airports as a part of the Customs Department.
- Occasionally, the booths are closed—inexcusable, but true. This is one reason why I recommend registration well before a trip.
- Fill out the form with pertinent information. You must have the items with you in order to register them. The slip is valid for all future trips, so don't throw it away.
- Never carry gifts to and from any foreign country for another per-

son. The unwary sometimes end up transporting narcotics in this way. If you are caught, then what?

Boarding a Plane

It all used to be so simple. All you had to do was tie a string on your finger and point yourself toward the plane. It's not quite so easy nowadays. To get on a plane, you need a ticket, a boarding pass, and in most cases a seat-selection card.

- If you don't have your ticket yet, you'll wait in a line.
- If you have to check baggage, you'll wait in a line.
- However, with a ticket in hand and bags either with you or checked, you can usually proceed straight to the boarding gate. If you arrive too late, you may lose your seat.

Security and Customs

To get to the gate, you'll have to pass through a security check. In a crowded airport, this can take 45 minutes or longer.

- If you're in danger of missing your plane, go to the front of the line and explain your problem to security.
- Under no circumstances should you make joking remarks about hijackings, bombs, or drugs.
- If you get hassled for carrying a Swiss Army knife, have them put it in a package to be given to a flight attendant on your flight. If they refuse this courtesy, have them put it in an envelope to be sent to your home. You'll have to pay the postage. Or, you can ask for it to be held in the security office until your return.
- If you're carrying film, remove it from the cardboard packages. Place the unwrapped containers in a plastic bag. Hand it to the inspector before going through the metal detector. You'll be told that this is unnecessary. Do it anyway (see p. 298).
- On some international flights, you'll pass through a customs inspection, which may add another 30 minutes delay. Start for the gate as soon as possible.

At the Boarding Area

- Unless you already have a seat assignment and boarding pass, you'll wait in line at the boarding area counter. You'll be given both at this time.
- Until you have a boarding pass in your hand, you essentially have nothing—except a contract that gives you specific legal rights. In short, you can still be bumped.
- When the plane is ready for boarding, the flight will be announced. If you don't board the plane when you're supposed to, your seat can be given to a standby.

- Occasionally, intercom systems do not work. Pay attention at the appropriate time to see whether boarding has started without any outward mention of the fact. Believe me, this happens!

Seat Assignments

Match the seat you select to your needs. Whenever possible, make seat selections as far in advance as possible. Ideally, select seats when you purchase your tickets. Unfortunately, this is not always allowed. You may have to do it at the airport on check-in.

- For leg room, ask for an aisle seat or for a seat behind a partition or bulkhead. The latter has lots of open space, but can be noisy if families are placed by you.
- For sleep, get a window seat.
- For quiet, avoid seats near toilets, the galley, or partitions.
- For travel with diarrhea, ask for a seat near the toilet.
- If you're traveling with children, ask for a bulkhead or partition seat unless you'd prefer one near a toilet.
- If you want to get off a plane quickly, ask which door will be used as an exit. Get a seat near that area. Note that the door used to get on a plane is not always the one used to get off.
- If prone to motion sickness, get seated over the wing.

Seating Strategies for Sleep

- If you are traveling with one other person, reserve the window and aisle seats in a three-seat section. Few people select middle seats unless a plane is fully booked. If no one shows up, one of you can find a single seat while the other person sleeps (simply pull up the arm rests and lie down).
- If you're traveling alone, be the last person to board. Look for a block of three unoccupied seats. If you board late enough, most flight attendants will allow you to sit anywhere.

Problems with Flights

This section gives you information about problems that you may run into when flying and strategies to help cope with them.

Lost Airline Tickets

- Whenever you buy an airline ticket, photocopy the flight coupons. Note the date and place of purchase as well as the method of payment. Carry this information separately from your ticket.
- If you lose a ticket or have one stolen, immediately go to or call the refund department of the airline from which you bought the ticket. You'll be asked to fill out a refund application.

- If you want to replace the ticket, you'll have to buy a new one. In most instances you must purchase the new ticket using the original form of payment. I suggest buying all tickets with a credit card. This way your account can be credited immediately for the lost or stolen ticket.
- If you paid with cash or by check, you will be reimbursed only after a 120-day waiting period. You may be given a card to send in for a refund after the waiting period is over.

Getting Bumped by Airlines

Your plane ticket is a legal contract with an airline. It guarantees your right to the flight, under specific conditions.

- An international ticket is valid only if you reconfirm your flight within 72 hours of departure. Get the agent's name when you reconfirm.
- You must arrive at the airport within the time limit specified on your ticket. If you do not reconfirm your flight or if you arrive late, the airline can sell your seat to another person (bump you from the flight)—legally! If you do reconfirm your flight and arrive on time, the airline cannot legally sell your seat. However, airlines do so—about 150,000 times a year.

Voluntary and Involuntary Bumping

Nowadays, airlines ask for volunteers to be bumped for a free round-trip ticket or a sum of money that varies with each airline and situation. If there are not enough volunteers, then some people will be bumped involuntarily. This could include you.

- If this happens to you, ask for a written statement outlining compensation for being denied boarding. Depending on the value of your ticket, you'll be paid a minimum to a maximum amount as denied boarding compensation (DBC). This money is yours for the inconvenience caused you by having been bumped.
- Note that DBC is only paid to passengers bumped from flights that actually take place (not canceled or delayed flights).
- If an airline cannot get you to your original destination within 2 hours of the scheduled arrival time for a domestic flight or within 4 hours for an international flight, the DBC must be doubled. The airline still must get you to your destination.
- Note that these regulations apply in the United States, but not necessarily abroad.

Taking it to Court

You are under no obligation to accept DBC, since you can take the matter to civil court. However, it's an unbelievable hassle.

- Don't accept DBC if you plan to take your case to court. Once

you accept compensation, you have no further legal redress.
- Have a case before you act. The airline does not have to pay DBC if the government takes over a plane (very rare), if a smaller plane is substituted for the original aircraft (occasionally happens), if you have not reconfirmed your flight, or if you check in later than the time specified on your ticket.

Flight Cancellation

If your flight is canceled, the airline should get you on the next available flight. It will do little good to complain about the cancellation.
- Note that each country has its own way of dealing with this situation. As long as you're being treated the same as other passengers, don't make a scene. You can certainly request free meals, a free room, etc., but the airlines decide.

Change of Fares

Once you have paid for and received a ticket, you cannot be charged more money to board a plane within the United States. However, in other countries you may have to pay whatever fare is applicable on that day.
- When buying a ticket, ask the airline about its policy in this regard. Remember that fares can change if you haven't already paid for the ticket. Reserving a ticket at a set price is no guarantee you'll get it at that price. You've got to pay for it!

Flight Delays

Flight delays have become quite common. Here are a few tips on avoiding and dealing with them when they do occur.
- Flights originating from your city are less likely to be delayed than flights coming from another city and continuing on.
- Flights beginning early in the day are less likely to be delayed. This rule has many exceptions in Central America and Mexico, but it is a good rule overall in the United States.
- When a flight is delayed after initial boarding has started, the airline is obligated to provide meals, lodging, transportation, and a free phone call to each passenger.
- If you have not started to board a plane and a delay is announced, you have no legal right to demand compensation of any kind. Nevertheless, many airlines will provide necessary amenities to stranded passengers.
- You will usually be given a voucher for a set-price meal and, in extreme cases, even a free hotel room.

- If the airline does not volunteer such things, don't hesitate to ask—and be polite, firm, and fair in your request.

Changing Travel Dates

Most discounted tickets require passengers to fly within specific time periods, with no changes allowed. If you try to make a change, the airline may ask you to pay full fare. Or, they may have a set amount added to the fare for each change. Always ask about this when buying a ticket. Fare increases are often not enforced for humanitarian reasons, such as death or severe illness of a close relative. Each airline makes its own decisions in this regard. All will require some sort of proof that your request is based on fact.

- Note that you can take out insurance to cover changes in travel plans caused by illness or death in the family (see p. 7). Because this insurance exists, a number of airlines are enforcing penalties on all ticket changes, no matter what the reason.

In-Flight Precautions

- Never leave money, valuable papers, or your passport unattended on a plane. Carry them on your person at all times—even when you go to the bathroom. This is doubly important if you are asked to get off a plane during a stopover.
- Get up and stretch regularly. This keeps your body relaxed and your blood circulating.
- The carbon dioxide build-up in planes is not good for your system. Use the overhead blowers to get fresh air.
- Drink lots of liquids. Dehydration is a problem at high altitudes. The more you drink, the better. Avoid alcohol which makes the problem worse. Fruit juices, soft drinks, and water are all recommended. Ask for the entire can when offered a drink.

Disinfecting Aircraft

Hopefully, by the time you read this guide the ineffective practice of disinfecting aircraft with a pyrethrin-like spray will have stopped.

- People allergic to ragweed can get sick from the spray.
- If spraying is announced, warn the flight attendant of your allergy. Ask for a wet cloth. Breath through this while the spraying takes place and for as long after as possible.

Special Safety Warning

The use of computers and electronic equipment on board planes may have resulted in crashes. Use them only as allowed or directed.

Clearing Customs

Here are a few of the main tips to keep in mind to avoid problems with officials when crossing borders.

Crossing Borders or Clearing Customs at Airports

Crossing the border can be a few minutes delay or a potential hassle. The same is true for clearing customs at an airport. Here are a few basics.

Basic Customs Vocabulary

age	*edad*	**make of car**	*marca*
baggage	*equipaje*	**marital status**	*estado civil*
birth certificate	*certificado de nacimiento*	**married**	*casado*
		minor	*menor de edad*
boat	*lancha*	**motorcycle**	*moto*
boat permit	*permiso de barca*	**number of doors**	*número de puertas*
border	*frontera*		
car owner	*propietario de automóvil*	**occupation**	*ocupación*
		outboard motor	*motor de fuera borda*
car permit	*permiso de automóvil*		
		passengers	*pasajeros*
chassis and motor number	*número de chasis y motor*	**passport**	*pasaporte*
		pets	*mascotas*
country	*país*	**profession**	*profesión*
customs	*aduana*	**rabies vaccination**	*vacunación de rabia*
cylinders	*cilindros*		
divorced	*divorciado*	**registration**	*registración*
driver's license	*licencia de manejar*	**single**	*soltero*
		state	*estado*
guns	*armas*	**suitcase**	*maleta*
gun permit	*cinegeticos*	**title (to property)**	*título (de propriedad)*
hunting license	*licencia de cazar*		
		tourist card	*tarjeta de turista*
immigration	*migración, inmigración*	**vaccination certificate**	*certificado de vacunación*
inspection	*revisión*	**visa**	*visado*
insurance	*seguros*	**widowed**	*viudo*
license plates	*placas*	**year of car**	*modelo*

Entry Cards

- Each country has its own formality in regards to entry. In Mexico you fill out a piece of paper, called a tourist card (*tarjeta de turista*). In other countries your passport might be stamped, or you might be given a paper to hang onto similar to the tourist card, or a slip of paper may be stapled right on your passport.
- Carry this or, preferably a photocopy, with you at all times.
- Don't write on or mutilate any document.

Immigration (*migración*)

- The immigration official will check the document you've been requested to fill out and match it to your passport.
- If you're a minor, you need a notarized letter signed by both parents allowing you to travel in Central America and Mexico.
- If traveling alone with a minor child, then you need a notarized letter from the other parent granting permission for such travel. You may not be allowed into a foreign country without this letter. My experience: They didn't even ask for it.
- Crossing borders by bus or car in Honduras can be frustrating. Honduran border guards are notoriously nasty.
- Special note: If your passport has been stamped in either El Salvador or Nicaragua, you may be denied entry into Honduras.

Customs (*aduana*)

- You must pass through a customs inspection which varies from a few quick questions to a thorough and meticulous search, which legally can include a body inspection.
- Most inspections are routine and very fast.
- If you come into Mexico by car or RV, you may be asked to pay a small gratuity (bribe) to pass through customs quickly.
- Your baggage will be sealed until you pass another inspection station farther inland. Don't tamper with the seals until you've been inspected the second time.

Tips on Going Through Customs

- Never volunteer information while going through customs.
- Impatience and anger are two things that irritate officials.
- If you don't think your profession will look respectable, change it. Become a secretary or a teacher for a day. It isn't what you are, but what they think you are that counts.
- Never tell an official that you're coming in on business or to study, unless you've got the appropriate visas. Just say you're a tourist—no one cares. However, if you're wearing a suit and carrying a briefcase, put something more casual on.

- Always be positive and respectful to officials. If you're negative or impatient, officials react badly.
- Customs officials can ask you to tell them the exact amount of money you're bringing into the country and in what form.
- They may require you to have a return or on-going ticket, if you arrive by plane. Legal, but rarely done.
- Say that your belongings are for personal use. Anything in its original package qualifies as a potential gift.
- Customs officials are suspicious of people carrying large amounts of tobacco and alcohol. Keep these to a minimum.
- Expensive items may be noted on your entry card. You must leave the country with them or pay a stiff fee.
- Certain items require special permits. Officials are very strict about guns, CBs, and movie cameras.
- If you have lots of film, get rid of the boxes to show the official that film is for personal use.
- A Swiss Army knife is useful. However, officials sometimes confiscate these, especially if they're new.
- If you're bringing an unusual item into the country, such as a typewriter, expensive tape recorder, special film equipment, tell the official that you're a professional. This word seems magical.
- Sexy magazines such as *Penthouse* will be confiscated and may result in a detailed search.
- Leave all prescription drugs in the original containers. They assume the pills are illegal otherwise.
- You can bring in almost anything for personal use, but if it hasn't already been used, watch out—it may get taxed.
- Don't carry fruits, vegetables, or plants across any border—they carry disease.

A Special Tip on Documents

- Keep your documents handy but in a safe place. Always keep them in the same spot. Having a special place for each item is one of the best ways to prevent its loss.

Hassles

Not everyone whizzes through immigration with a token wave of the hand. If you have little money, or, more importantly, look that way, you're in for a hassle. How you look affects how you're treated.

- These cause problems: long beards, long hair (the more unkempt, the worse), sloppy clothes, rings in your nose (women) or ears (men)—you've got it. Casual is fine, but be clean and conservative.

Where to Cross Borders into Mexico with Cars or RVs

Here are the points at which you've been able to cross the border at one time or another: Algodones, Brownsville/Matamoros, Eagle Pass/Piedras Negras, El Paso/Ciudad Juárez, Laredo/Nuevo Laredo, McAllen/Reynosa, Mexicali, Nogales, Tecate, and Tijuana.

- These border crossing points are sometimes open, sometimes closed depending upon political winds and whims.
- Border checkpoint hours change frequently. Any list would be out-of-date immediately. You'll have to call for information.
- Choose obscure checkpoints, to avoid long lines well-publicized during crackdowns and capers (like kidnappings).
- Don't cross at night. Border officials don't like to be bothered, and it's unsafe to drive at night in Mexico.
- Border officials can be tight on the importation of food. Any amount over the present allowed value can be confiscated.
- The number of vehicles may have to match the number of people in the car. For example, if you have a motorcycle or moped on the back of your RV or truck and you're traveling alone, you may not be allowed in. Try a gratuity.

Getting Into Town from the Airport

Getting from the airport into town is one area where many travelers get burned. Following are some helpful tips.

Ways of Getting into Town

There are several options on getting from the airport into town. Cost and convenience are usually the trade-offs.

Bus Travel From Airports

- Ask about local bus service at the information office. If it is closed, ask anyone who speaks English about departure times, cost, and location of the bus stop for the bus taking people into town. In some areas there is no bus service, and you have to take a taxi (more about that later). However, buses are always the least expensive way to get into a city's center. Buses are often slow, belch diesel, and can be packed. But, they are a real bargain. Also, check on how to get back to the airport using a bus, if you will be flying out at a later date.

Communal Cabs (*Colectivos*)

- More expensive than buses are communal cabs.
- In some airports, *colectivo* booths sell tickets at a set price related to distance .
- In areas without booths ask what a fair price is for cab fare at the tourist information booth. If that is closed, ask anyone who speaks English, preferably an airline attendant.
- Once you know the price, walk outside to the cab area and ask for a *colectivo.*
- Sometimes, you'll ask for a *colectivo* only to be put into a cab by yourself. Stop the driver at this point. Repeat the word *colectivo.* The driver may shrug his shoulders and say something like, "*No hay pasajeros.*" He's telling you that there are no other passengers. See next page.
- In a few areas (Cancún, for example) some of the so-called communal cabs are buses. Wait until the bus leaves and then ask for a communal cab. You'll pay the same fare, but get into town in half the time.

Where There are Only Taxis

- Some airports do not have buses or *colectivos* into town. In a few cities taxi prices are government regulated, but for the most part prices depend on your knowledge and bargaining skill.
- Ask a flight attendant or someone in the tourist office or information booth what a fair price is to where you're going before venturing outside. Otherwise, you won't know the going rate.
- A good strategy is to find other travelers heading in the same direction to get a group together to share costs. You're setting up your own "colectivo." This works more often than not.
- Never get into a cab without settling on the fare first. If there is a language barrier, have the driver write the fare down on a piece of paper. Don't be afraid to bargain. If possible, share a cab as outlined above.

From the Airport into Mexico City

Tips on getting into Mexico City from the airport follow and are arranged by mode of travel from least expensive to most expensive.

- If you have very little luggage, take the metro (least expensive) at the edge of the airport into the city. The metro from the air terminal subway station (*terminal aérea*) is a steal.
- There's a ticket booth in the airport for a SETTA bus which will take you to your hotel. There are different buses to different zones. The person in the booth will tell you which bus to take.
- SETTA taxis are more expensive than the bus. Go to the *boletos de taxi* booth. You pay according to distance traveled.
- More expensive than the SETTA taxis are licensed taxis. Negotiate your price. Do not take unlicensed taxis no matter what fare they offer. The crime rate at this airport is horrendous. Be wary.

Hotel Strategies

Getting the room you want with the amenities you want at the price you want—no mean trick. That's what this section's all about.

Basic Hotel Vocabulary

air-conditioned	*aire acondicionado*	**for...days**	*por ... días*
apartment house	*apartamentos*	**front**	*al frente*
back	*al fondo*	**furnished**	*amueblada*
baggage	*equipaje*	**garage**	*cochera, garage*
bar	*bar*	**good**	*bueno*
bath	*baño*	**hammock**	*hamaca*
with bath	*con baño*	**hangars**	*ganchos*
bathroom	*baño*	**hotel**	*hotel*
bed	*cama*	**house**	*casa*
double bed	*cama matrimonial*	**how much**	*cuánto*
extra bed	*cama extra*	**How much is...?**	*¿Cuánto cuesta...?*
twin beds	*camas gemelas*	**ice**	*hielo*
bedroom	*recámara*	**I like it**	*me gusta*
bellboy	*botones*	**I don't like it**	*no me gusta*
bill	*cuenta*	**inn**	*posada*
blanket	*cobija, cubierta, manta*	**key**	*llave*
boardinghouse	*pensión, casa de huéspedes, hospedaje*	**kitchen**	*cocina*
by the week	*por la semana*	**landlord, owner**	*dueño, dueña*
by the month	*por el més*	**maid**	*criada, camarera*
car	*coche*	**manager**	*gerente, dueño*
cheap	*económico, barato*	**matchbook**	*carterita*
cheaper	*más barato*	**May I see it?**	*¿Puedo verlo?*
child	*niño*	**minimum**	*mínimo*
clean	*limpio*	**motel**	*motel*
close (to)	*cerrar*	**name**	*nombre*
clothes	*ropa*	**last name**	*apellido, nombre de familia*
cot	*catre*	**nearby**	*cercano*
credit card	*tarjeta de crédito*	**night watchman**	*velador*
dining room	*comedor*	**noise**	*ruido*
electricity	*electricidad*	**no vacancy**	*completo*
elevator	*elevador*	**number**	*numero*
expensive	*caro*	**room number**	*numero de cuarto*
fan	*ventilador, abanico*	**office**	*oficina*
floor	*piso*	**open (to open)**	*abrir*
for rent	*se renta, se alquila*	**parking lot**	*estacionamento*
for sale	*se vende*	**pillow**	*almohada*

porter	*mozo de servicios*	sheet	*sabana*
quiet	*tranquilo*	shower	*regador, regadera, ducha*
refrigerator	*refrigerador*	soap	*jabón*
reservation	*reservación*	stairway	*escalera*
room	*cuarto, habitación*	stopped, plugged	*tapado, tapada*
single room	*cuarto sencillo*	stove	*estufa*
double room	*cuarto doble*	swimming pool	*alberca, piscina*
for two people	*para dos personas*	tax	*impuesto*
for three people	*para tres personas*	Are the taxes included?	*¿Están incluidos los impuestos?*
with bath	*con baño*	toilet	*baños, servicios, taza*
with meals	*con comidas*	toilet paper	*papel sanitario (higiénico)*
without meals	*sin comidas*	towel	*toalla*
safe (adjective)	*seguro*	view	*vista*
safe (for valuables)	*caja de seguridad*	water	*agua*
service	*servicio*	cold water	*agua fría*
Is the service charge included?	*¿Está incluido el servicio?*	hot water	*agua caliente*
		with	*con*
		without	*sin*

Getting into a Hotel with Reservations

Making a hotel reservation which will be honored is no mean trick in Central America and Mexico.

Getting Bumped With a Written Confirmation

With a reservation you've already decided where you're going to stay, but the hotel may have a different idea. You've been bumped.
- With written confirmation, insist upon a room.
- Patience often pays off. Park yourself in the lobby. Don't get angry. Assume they can handle the problem.
- If they can't find a room for you, ask them to get a room in a comparable hotel at a comparable price. Ask them to pay the cab fare to get you there.

Getting Bumped Without a Written Confirmation

Unless you have a written confirmation, you can expect no sympathy. That's why you get written confirmations.
- Again, don't get angry. Remain calm, patient, and friendly. Ask for help. People at the front desk admire courtesy and patience and will often help you out in this situation. You're thinking that it's all their fault. And they're just trying to get through the day.

They'll get to it, just don't expect it to be done immediately. Take out the paperback and start to read.

Finding A Room Without Advance Reservations

The big advantage of traveling without reservations is the overall freedom it gives you. Many people *prefer* to travel in this fashion. Another advantage is that you get to see the room (and the hotel) before you rent. That advantage pales in extremely crowded cities during the peak season, but the fact is that you often do better on your own than when others book rooms for you. It's quite easy and can save you a bundle if you know a few basic principles and techniques.

Tourist Offices
- If you come into a city during a peak travel period, during a holiday or fiesta, you may need help locating a room. Ask for the nearest tourist office (*turismo*).
- Most airports have tourist offices. In larger towns tourist offices are in city centers, usually around the main square.
- Tourist offices close at weird times and often take a break for a siesta (*descanso*). But they can help you locate a room where none are to be found. You may end up in a private home, but that in itself could be a great experience.

Local Travel Agencies
- Local agents often know of boardinghouses, homes, or small hotels looking for guests. You may pay a small fee for this service, but it can be worth it in the peak season.
- Travel agents are often your best resource for long-term stays. In Antiqua (Guatemala) the agents there can find you rooms in homes with meals at a fraction of the price of hotels.
- If you're on a budget, the key words are *bueno y económico*— good and cheap! There's only one way to come up with these places. Ask! Many remain totally undiscovered, even by companies producing budget guides.

The Grapevine
- Sometimes, simple is best. One of the simplest ways to find out about great little hotels is to ask people where they've been, where they've stayed, and whether they have any suggestions.
- Hotels are constantly opening up. Some are isolated and rela-

tively unknown. So just keep asking. The best hotels are often "gifts" from other travelers. In return, tell them about your finds.

- This informal grapevine is often more accurate and up-to-date than any travel guide. Travel in Central America and Mexico has a way of drawing people together. Sharing information helps the entire group overcome mutual problems.
- Once you find a hotel that matches your personality and budget, ask the hotel personnel to make recommendations in other cities. They often know spots that have never even been written about in the United States or Canada.
- Keep a log of all the places that offered good value and would interest others. It's easy to forget names, addresses, and telephone numbers. These can prove invaluable in the future.

Using a Travel Guide to Find Lodging
- Each travel guide is aimed at a specific market, usually according to budget. If you're on a tight budget, use a student or shoestring travel type guide. Not so tight? Try any of the more popular guides with varied listings.
- These guides are all out-of-date before they're printed. Many have given up listing prices—for good reason! But they all list a batch of hotels which fall into certain price categories.
- The tip: Go to *any* of these hotels which most accurately matches your idea of what you want. The hotel may or may not have a room available, but that really doesn't matter. What you need is help. And almost all hotels will suggest other hotels nearby, and many hotel owners will call those hotels for you.

Finding Hotels by Area
- If you're interested in a specific area of a town, if you want to be near or on the beach, if you want to be near the market or shopping, or whatever—check out the area.
- There are often a number of hotels around the main square (*parque central* in Central America or *zócalo* in Mexico).
- Hotels that fall into similar price categories often cluster together. If you're looking for budget hotels, you'll usually find a bunch of them in one location.
- The secret of this strategy is to be traveling light. Or, if you're with another person, have him watch over the bags while you go out in search of the "perfect hotel."

Staying Outside Major Cities
- Public transportation is cheap and good in Central America and Mexico. Sometimes, one of the best strategies for coming up with

a good, but reasonably-priced room is to stay on the outskirts of town or in a nearby town accessible by bus.

- Many of the inns in small towns around the capital of Costa Rica (San José) are much more attractive, quiet, and reasonably priced than hotels in town.
- If you're driving a car, get out of major cities into smaller ones with the idea of commuting by bus.

Calling Ahead for Reservations

- Major hotels will make reservations for you if you want to stay in another link of the chain.
- If you're in a budget hotel and know that you'll be arriving late at your next destination, consider having someone in the hotel phone ahead for a reservation. Their Spanish could be the key to getting you a room. You're out the cost of the call or calls, but you're assured of a place when you arrive.

Beating the "No Vacancy" Sign

It can be frustrating at times, this process of finding a room on your own. It's particularly frustrating when you find "No Vacancy" (*completo*) at every turn—a dirty word when you're looking for a room. When things look very bleak, try some of the following techniques.

- Find out when the check-out time is. Often people change their minds at the last minute and leave. Things are casual in this region, and in many places the staff really has no idea how many vacancies there will be—timing is key. So if someone tells you a place is booked solid, come back at check-out time.
- Many times you'll be told that there is no room simply because the clerk doesn't want to be bothered with the fuss of looking. Don't assume anything. Tell the clerk that you'll wait awhile to see whether anything opens up. Now he's got to look at you staring at him for the next half hour or so—this often produces a room. Obviously, this strategy works best later in the day.
- When you walk up to a clerk and the first thing you hear is, "How long do you intend to stay?" you've got to answer, "A week," or there may suddenly be no vacancies. Short stays cost hotels more in overhead. If the clerk tells you that they've only got a room for one night, take it. Once you're in a place, you're rarely booted out. And, if one night's enough, fine.
- The secret is patience, the aura of calm determination and tranquility. If there is absolutely no chance of your getting a room, they'll ask you to leave—often after making a call on your behalf to some other hotel.

Judging Hotels

- Never judge a hotel by its exterior or lobby. Some very bleak exteriors hide sumptuous interiors. And some charming lobbies with flower-filled gardens cannot make up for bug-infested and dirty rooms. Ask to see the room.
- Never judge a hotel by its official rating. A first-class hotel can have an empty swimming pool and surly staff while a budget inn with no stars may provide friendly service and rooms with fireplaces.

Checking Out a Room

- Make sure the room is clean. Don't worry about the glasses, half the time they haven't been washed.
- Does the room smell fresh? Well, does it smell okay?
- Are the faucets dripping? Is the toilet churning?
- Turn on the hot water to see if there is any.
- Check the bathroom. Are you willing to stand in the shower or bathe in the tub? Does it seem clean enough?
- Check the bedding. If it's cool, check for extra blankets.

Keeping Room Costs Down

Just as travelers pay different prices for plane tickets on identical flights, so do they pay different prices for identical rooms.

Bargaining on Room Rates

Although it may go against your grain, bargaining in various ways is acceptable. It's only effective with many open rooms, so it's more successful in the off-season.

- Ask whether there is an off-season discount if you're traveling in a non-peak period.
- Tell the clerk that the room is great, but that it's too expensive for you. Ask whether there are any other rooms available at a lower price. This will often bring the price down. Or, you'll be taken to a nearly identical room at a lower price.
- Tell the clerk that you like the room and will pay such and such an amount—a lower, but still fair, price.
- Very large hotels often offer payments to wholesalers (20 percent) and travel agents (10 percent). This gives you a hint on how to conduct a little negotiating in these places.

Room-Rate Discounts

- Rates shown in rooms are the maximum allowed by law. In the off-season there should be a discount.

- Always ask about discounts for prolonged stays (usually three days or longer).
- Ask if the hotel offers weekend discounts. This tactic works best in large cities.
- Some hotels will give discounts for people in different professions. Ask to see if such an opportunity exists.
- Occasionally, a hotel will offer a business discount if you make a reservation in your company's name.

Hotel Costs and Services

Check-in is the time to get everything straight on costs and services. Avoid any potential conflicts by asking questions right away.

- Ask to have the base price written down.
- In most hotels (but not all) you'll pay an IVA tax. Ask if any tax will be added to the base price.
- Occasionally, a hotel will tack on a service charge which ups the bill, usually by 10 percent. You'll want to know about this charge in advance. Again, ask.
- Note that single rooms are almost the same price as doubles, so you can't get much of a benefit by traveling alone.
- Ask if there are any additional charges for telephones and television.
- Air-conditioning may be expensive. If you're willing to settle for a ceiling fan, the cost drops dramatically.
- If you don't have a bath in your room, ask if there is an additional charge to take a bath. Find out if towels cost extra.

Room and Board

The term *American Plan* (full room and board) means that you're staying in a hotel and eating all three meals there. *Modified American Plan* (half room and board) indicates that you're skipping either lunch or dinner at the hotel. In most hotels it usually means lunch is left out. Hotels offer good rates for these plans.

- Some hotels will force you into an American Plan before they will rent you a room. In the peak season you may have to submit to this racket if you want to get into a particular hotel.
- Ideally, you want to choose to eat in any hotel. This gives you the option of eating out or deciding whether the hotel food warrants a full or half room and board plan.
- If you do stay on a room-and-board basis, find out if there is an extra charge for anything, such as wine, dessert, or coffee.
- Most hotels offering half or full room and board post specific meal times. If you miss the meal, you still pay for it.
- And most hotels offer a choice of two or more entrées with each meal, so that you have the feeling of some control.

Payment

- Fancy hotels will ask you to produce a major credit card at the time of check-in. They will imprint the information on a charge slip as collateral. When you check out, you can either fill in the total or pay in cash and have the credit card slip destroyed.
- Budget hotels will ask for a cash (*efectivo*) payment upfront for the first night's rental. Some places are very trusting and don't ask for any money until you leave.
- Avoid using a traveler's check to pay a hotel bill in most instances, because few hotels give a fair rate of exchange. Always carry local currency to pay your hotel bills. Or, ask what the bill would be in dollars. Paying in dollars is quite common.
- When you pay the bill, ask for a receipt (*recibo*). If you pay with a credit card, check the total before signing. Keep all receipts until the charges have come in. In many areas of Central America and Mexico surcharges are being added for the use of credit cards. Ask about this when checking in.

The Front Desk

- Always get the name of the person at the front desk. Use it. This is appreciated in Central America and Mexico (as it is everywhere). Surprisingly, few people make this effort. Those who do often end up with special favors and reduced rates.
- Always have room prices written down for you when checking in. This avoids any discussion of a language barrier at a later date. Consider paying for the first night to see whether the price being quoted is truly what you'll end up paying.
- Don't assume that your name is easy to spell or read. Write it down for the clerk.
- If you have valuables, ask about safe-deposit boxes. Normally, there is no charge for these. Better hotels have them, many budget hotels don't.
- If you don't have a map, ask for one at the front desk. They usually have tourist-oriented information.

Porters

- Porters expect a reasonable tip for carrying baggage, even if it's feather-light.
- If you're traveling light and don't want to pay for porters, be firm. Simply ask for the room key and the location of the room. Say you'll carry your own bags.

Idiosyncracies of Central American and Mexican Hotels

Half the pleasure of travel comes from discovering the difference between them and us. However, some differences come as a shock. Here are some bridges for cultural gaps in hotels.

Air-Conditioning
- Air conditioning can be a must during the hot, humid months of the rainy season. It may add a surcharge to your room.

Baggage Room (*garda equipaje*)
- If you're checking out before you have to leave a town, use the baggage room for storage. Your bags are secure there.
- Many hotels offer such a service free of charge.
- Always get a receipt for each bag stored this way.

Bathrooms and Showers
- In small hotels you'll find soap in the bathrooms, but it has usually been opened. If you're fussy, bring your own.
- Water barely escapes from the shower heads in some hotels. Enlarging the holes by force does wonders for the flow.
- Light a match in smelly toilets. The sulfur dissipates smells.
- If there are no plugs for the sink, just use a sock.
- Sometimes, a toilet won't flush. Lift off the back and see whether the tank is full. If not, fill it up with water from the faucet and flush—usually takes care of the problem, but not as well as a good plumber would.
- *Caballeros* is the sign on a men's bathroom, *damas* signals relief to ladies.

Bugs
- Insects are not only annoying, but carry diseases. If a place is obviously bug-ridden, consider another place to stay.
- You'll want to send bedbugs packing after your first experience with these invisible but voracious feeders. They leave little red spots that itch like crazy. Don't scratch them, they just get worse.
- Fleas are also a problem. As are spiders and mosquitoes. Shake out your shoes and clothing each morning.
- You can prevent most insect bites by wearing insect repellent.
- Whenever you see spiders, whack them with your shoe.

Concierge
- Luxury hotels have a concierge, a kind of jack-of-all-trades who

can arrange or get just about anything done. Use the concierge for any kind of unusual request and tip according to its difficulty. You will be amazed at what they can accomplish.

- If you're staying in a budget hotel without a concierge, go to a luxury hotel and ask for help. Always tip appropriately.

Curfew
- A few places close up early. When there's a strict curfew, someone will let you know. Get the key for the gate or front door. Don't forget to take it with you.

Electricity
- In some areas lights go off at the oddest times. In others electricity just stops being produced at certain times. If you see candles in your room, it's a good indication that this is a common problem. Get matches.
- Carry a pocket flashlight. It will help you get into the room when all lights go off outside, and it will help you from tripping over odds and ends on your way to the bathroom.
- Electric shocks are also common in older hotels or in ones using an electric apparatus above the shower to heat water. Never stand on a wet bathroom floor and plug in an electrical item or turn on a light.

Elevators
- The elevators in most hotels do not work like Swiss watches. The clunk when you push the call button means it's heard you. The whine means it's on its way. The second clunk means the maid has intercepted it on the third floor and will now head in the opposite direction.
- Once you've cornered the elevator, remember that PB (*piso baja* or *planta baja*) means main floor.

Fans (*ventilador*)
- Fans whine, moan, and make strange gyrating sounds.
- The switch on the wall controls their speed, usually a casual luffing to a kind of frenzy that seems to be pulling the fan off the ceiling as it jiggles and bumps in all directions.
- If you're tall, don't have a pillow fight or reach up to put on your sweatshirt. Many of the fans hover inches above your head.
- Fishing rods and spear guns will not stand up to the concerted attack of a ceiling fan—keep that in mind.

Fireplaces

- Fireplaces with a warm crackling glow and wonderful scent can be found in mountainous areas. Tip for extra wood—it's worth it.
- Starting fires is often difficult because of the shortage of paper. Candles are an excellent substitute and relatively inexpensive. Drip wax over the kindling and then lay the whole candle on top once it starts to burn. The fire often ignites at this point.
- Some fireplaces have extremely poor drafts. Smoke in your room ruins the romantic appeal. Unfortunately, it's often hard to test draft without starting a fire first.

Generators

- The only way to get electricity in some hotels is with a generator. These usually run for a set time each day and are noisy. They are most common in remote jungle lodges and fishing camps. If you are going to one of these, you might request being as far from the generator as possible if you're sensitive to noise.
- On a few islands power is provided by solar-charged batteries. In these areas you'll be asked to conserve power by using lights infrequently and flushing toilets only when absolutely necessary.

Glasses

- In better hotels you'll be given drinking glasses wrapped in plastic as proof that they've been sterilized. Unfortunately, this happens once—when you arrive. The glasses are then left in your room until you leave. The problem: The maids wash them out each day in tap water.
- In budget hotels there's far less pretense and protection—many of the glasses are filthy.
- Suggestion: Have a personal cup for traveling or carry some plastic cups which can be used and then tossed.

Guests

Hotels can be strict about inviting guests to your room.

- If you are expecting, or hope to find, a partner, pay for two from the start. It's rarely much more than the single price.
- It is *not* illegal for unmarried people to share a room, but in small inns it might be extremely indiscreet. Pretend to be "engaged."

Hammock Hooks

- Those strange claws on the walls of hotel rooms in the Yucatán are hammock hooks, perfectly suited to hanging hammocks so that they land squarely on a bed. Move the beds if you have to, and always ask for a discount if you're a swinger.

Lights

- To overcome the poor light in many smaller hotels carry a flashlight or a tiny portable lamp.
- If you want stronger light for reading lamps, pick up a high-watt bulb and carry it with you abroad.
- On some islands and in some remote areas generators go off at a specific hour. A flashlight is a necessity if you want to get around safely in your room.

Maids

- Unless you put small odds and ends in a drawer or in your luggage, they may disappear. They're usually not being stolen, but are being thrown away.
- However, maids sometimes accidentally misplace items in hidden corners. Their hope is that you won't notice them missing and will quietly leave without them.

Mattresses

- If you're the kind of person who doesn't have to jump to sink a basket, ask to see the bed in a room before renting it. You may have to settle for a double bed on which you can lie diagonally.
- You may run into a mattress which gives you a spinal tap for no extra charge. Just toss it on the floor and sleep there.
- If you want to slide two beds together to make one, place the box springs side by side, but always place the mattresses *across* them. If you don't, someone will disappear in the night.

Mosquitoes

- Mosquitoes hum and bum their way into rooms despite attempts at protection. They are annoying and carry malaria.
- If you're in a bug-infested area, invest in mosquito netting, insect repellant, and a long-sleeved shirt. If you're in a hammock, put a thin blanket down to protect your rump.
- Read the section on protecting yourself against mosquitoes (p. 236).

Noise

- Loud music, night-long fireworks displays, never-ending fiestas—these are a part of Latin culture. Loud talking at night and so on is not considered an invasion of your boundaries.
- If you're sensitive to noise, if you're a light sleeper, or if you prefer to listen to your own brand of music, bring earplugs.
- These countries are lands of constant crowing, mooing, mating of cats, grinding of gears, unloading of cement blocks—and a dozen

other noisy gerunds. You simply will not believe it!

- When checking out a hotel, pay attention to noise: Are you just above the lounge or disco? Are you right next to the reception area? Near the elevator or public toilet? Is your room overlooking the *zócalo* (main square), right on a busy highway, steps from the town's generator, or near the market?
- You never know how noisy a place is until night. Ask if noise is a problem. One of the prettiest places in Guatemala adjoins a disco which only begins blaring in late evening.
- Many Central Americans and Mexicans consider music as a part of a hotel's ambience. Either join the party, adapt to the cultural difference, or invest in earplugs.

Parking

- In major cities, hotels charge a steep fee for parking. There are exceptions, and you can save many dollars a day if the hotel offers free parking to its guests. Ask when reserving a room.
- Street parking is not advised, so no matter what the charge, it's worth getting your car into a guarded area or parking lot. Smaller hotels often have a courtyard where you can park overnight, and they rarely charge anything for this service.

Safety

- Women take note—there are pass keys, and some owners of hotels have been known to use them. Jam a chair under the door handle if you have any suspicion of this (or change hotels).
- Read the section on protecting your property and yourself (see pp. 183–185).

Servi-Bars

- The better hotels often have servi-bars in the room. You open these little boxes with your room or specially provided key. Inside, you'll find an assortment of drinks and snacks. You pay for these, often through the nose.

Sheets

- Budget hotels have fallen prey to the shrinking sheet epidemic which has swept across Mexico in waves leaving all sheets 6 inches too short for the bed—it is incurable.

Smells

- In some hotels you'll get nearly asphyxiated in the middle of the night if you're near the laundry room or if the wind shifts and the smell of diesel from the flues hits you with full force. This happens in even better hotels and suggests a quick look at the chimney line on the way to your room.

Telephone
- Most hotels charge a small fee per day for the use of a telephone or a small fee per local call.
- Most (but not all) hotels charge a surcharge for long-distance calls. You should ask ahead of time what the surcharge is.
- Hotels charge for collect calls as well. The charge can be higher if the collect call was not accepted. (see p. 254).

Television
- Quite a few hotels add a charge for television in the room. Some charge nothing at all, it's just built into the overall price of the room. You have to ask to avoid any surprises.
- In some of the most surprising places you'll find cable with dozens of channels, many of them in English.

Time
- Hotels work on the military system of time. Checkout at 13 hours equals checkout at 1 P.M. You'll see a placard in your room explaining the checkout policy. It will read: "*Su cuarto se vence a...*" ("Your room must be vacated by...")
- If you do not check out on time, the hotel can legally ask you to pay for another night's lodging.

Tipping (see p. 170)

Travel Agencies
- Moderate and upper bracket hotels often have travel agencies for city tours, excursions, and performances. Prices are inflated.

Views
- A good view can add considerable expense to a room. If one is important to you, make this clear upfront.
- Rooms higher up in the Tropics often get cooling breezes. The cross-ventilation serves as natural air conditioning.

Wakeup Calls
- If you use the front desk for wake-up services, wait until as late in the evening as possible to request the service. This way you have a good chance of talking to the person who will wake you up in the morning. Note that these are notoriously unreliable. Carry a light-weight alarm clock or a watch with an alarm.

Washing Clothes

- By hand-washing your clothes you'll save money and time (hotel laundries take forever).
- Roll clothes in a towel to collect excess moisture and speed up drying before you hang them up.
- Bring a braided rubber clothesline.
- Sinks in many hotels have no plugs. Wily travelers carry plugs or a small ball to fill up the hole. Frankly, a sock works just as well.
- Never hang your laundry out a window to dry in major cities. In budget hotels or resorts, you can lay out clothes on chairs or over the edge of the balcony to let them dry in the sun.
- In humid areas, the only way to get clothes dry is to get them into the sun or hanging in a strong breeze.
- If you have a car, lay out wet clothes on a towel in the back seat. As you drive around, they will often dry quickly.
- Don't lay wet clothes on stained wood surfaces, since they'll bleach the wood and end up stained themselves.
- When possible, separate the back portion of any wet clothing from the front. This speeds up the drying process.
- Use any kind of tape to pick up lint off clothes. Just wrap the tape lightly around your fingers and brush gently.
- Soak blood stains in *cold* water and scrub them vigorously.
- Sprinkle salt or soda on wine stains before washing.
- Note that some hotels have washing machines which guests can use for a set fee per load.
- If you don't want to wash your own clothes, save money over hotel laundry services by looking for a laundromat (*lavandería automática*). In some of these places you do everything yourself, in others you leave off your clothes. Laudromats are hard to find in many parts of Central American. A little less so in major cities of Mexico.

bag (plastic)	*bolsa*	**soap**	*jabón*
chlorine	*cloro*	**tokens**	*fichas*
dry	*secado*	**wash**	*lavado*

Water (for washing)

- Some hotels have minimal water pressure.
- In small hotels with a central water heating system you may be out of luck (and hot water). As a matter of fact, the same is often true in large, fancy hotels. You'll have to learn the best times for bathing if you're fussy about hot water.
- C (*caliente*) on a faucet means hot, which confuses many people from English-speaking countries. Cold in Spanish is *fría*.
- When taking a shower or bath, turn the hot water on first. Then

slowly turn on the cold. Cold water has priority over hot.
- In some hotels there are weird-looking gadgets as shower heads. These heat water as needed. Sometimes, they don't work. Never fiddle with these, since you can get a shock.

Water (for drinking)
- People who worry about water are not all wet. Skip tap water in hotels and don't brush your teeth with it.
- Some of the larger deluxe hotels claim to have pure tap water. They probably do. Some of the smaller hotels make the same claim. They probably don't. Be suspicious of tap water.
- In some hotels big jugs of purified water (*agua purificada*) are found in individual rooms or in the hallway. Just tip these to get water out, unless they have a little spigot at the base. Note: I'm convinced that in many cases this water has not been purified.
- Some hotels provide bottles of pure water by the sink. Or they have carafes filled with what they claim is pure water. Frankly, I'd be suspicious.
- Why not carry bottles of mineral water (*agua mineral*) with you? You can find them in some stores either in small or large bottles, with or without carbonation. Carbonated mineral water is the safest bet, since tap water could be placed in sealed bottles and sold as mineral water—it does happen.
- If you're suspicious about water, boil it for 30 minutes or longer. If you have an immersion heater and a small pot, this is easy to do. Again, I'd rather buy bottled water than go through this process which often precipitates a ghastly amount of sticky material in the pan.

Alternatives to Hotels

Not everyone can afford or even wants to stay in hotels. Following are some tips on alternatives.

Camping

Camping is geared to a loose, free-flowing style of travel that is not compatible with limited time. If you've got the time, however, you'll find that campgrounds are well organized in Mexico (rare in Central America), often offering facilities that include showers and stores. You'll find many of them in Mexico, even near major cities. Camping is also possible in parts of Costa Rica in some of the National Parks. Reservations in these are advised. Camping in Belize can be done on some of the cayes (islands) and in remote areas. Camping is possible at Tikal in Guatemala, but not recommended.

Official Warnings
- Never camp by yourself or in a small group in remote areas.
- Be wary about camping in beach areas, unless you're with a large group.
- In short, you're much better off in recognized campgrounds which offer protection in numbers.
- Note that many campers and even some writers of camping guides tell you that these warnings are not true. Yet, the police reports I've seen would indicate that they are.

Other Warnings—Not Quite So Official
- Listen to discreet warnings. Someone's trying to tell you that you're going to stumble into a marijuana or poppy patch.
- Shy away from borders, heavily patrolled and less than friendly places. If with a tour or local guide, these areas are safer.
- Never leave camping gear unattended unless in an organized and guarded campground. It will evaporate like water in the tropical sun. This is one of the main problems with freelance camping.

Solo Camping
- Officials say no one should camp out at anytime alone.
- Some ardent supporters of camping would say that the rule only applies to women. Nevertheless, everyone agrees that a woman camping alone is inviting serious trouble. Don't do it.

Camping-Gear Checklist

Here are a few items which you will find essential for camping.

Air mattress Get the best one available and bring a patching kit.

Alcohol burner This will be your stove. Alcohol is cheap in Mexico and easy to find. So are the burners. Kerosene lamps and stoves are more common in Central America. Propane is not.

Flashlight Absolutely essential. Bring a few extra batteries.

Grill This should be tiny, just large enough to cook something on. Carry it in a plastic or canvas bag.

Insect repellant Get a really strong one (no less than 35 percent DEET).

Knife Don't get anything too fancy or shiny. It will be confiscated by the police. A decent Swiss Army knife with a bottle opener is best.

Lantern Not essential, but really nice.

Matches One container of waterproof matches.

Mosquito netting The single most important item to carry.

Plastic containers Enough for a variety of solid and liquid foods.

Pots For cooking.

Sleeping bag Can be replaced with a blanket or hammock.

Tent Featherlight with excellent ventilation.

Toilet paper Needed everywhere.

Tools To match your brand of camping. Pick up a machete abroad.

Water containers Need a gallon of water per day per person.

Tips on Camping Equipment

- Know your gear. Nothing's worse than a so-called waterproof tent which leaks or a mosquito net that's worn through.
- Bring the minimum gear for your brand of camping.

The Value of a Good Hammock

One of the most enjoyable ways to cut costs and enjoy the warmer areas is to camp out with a hammock. Some hotels offer discounts to travelers who hook up their hammocks instead of using regular beds.

- Buy the S-shaped hooks made especially for hanging hammocks. They'll save you lots of time and are the easiest to use.
- Never hang your hammock so low that you'll scrape the ground. This will ruin the hammock quickly.
- Don't use the hammock as a place to sit or swing on. You should lie down in it, or you'll stretch the hammock in the wrong direction making it uncomfortable for sleeping.
- Mosquitoes are a problem in many areas where hammocks are

most enjoyable. Put a blanket down in the bottom of the hammock to protect your backside at night. Use mosquito netting over the hammock to protect you from night attacks. Spray everything with pyrethrin insecticide.
- Store your hammock in a bag or container to protect it from rodents or insects.

Where to Camp

You can camp out in many areas of **Belize**, particularly on some of the smaller cayes (keys) and on the beach at Placencia. Camping out in the jungle is also possible, but I'd do this with a guide or in a protected area. **Costa Ricans** camp out quite a bit, although there are few organized campgrounds. Camping is allowed in a number of National Parks, but reservations are often required. Camping out in remote areas should be done with a competent guide. Camping out in **Guatemala** makes little sense since accommodations are incredibly cheap in most areas. Furthermore, camping out is not always safe. The one exception is Tikal, a park with an area set up for camping. Camping out in **Honduras** makes no sense at all. There are dirtbag accommodations available on Roatan for a few bucks a night. Camping out in remote areas is simply not safe, unless you're with a tour or experienced local guide. You can camp almost anywhere in **Mexico** for free, since there are no laws prohibiting it. Note that beaches are public and cannot be privately owned (although access can be). Here are some free campsites:
- No-Cost Campsites: beaches (hassles with sand and salt mist), bridges (just off to the side), cemeteries (just outside), churchyards, dams (look for the sign indicating *presas*), gas stations (ask for permission), hot springs, microwave stations (look for *microondas* signs), national parks (some require reservations and a few charge), parking lots, plazas (only in the smallest villages), quarries, schoolyards, side roads, soccer fields, spas, thatched huts or *palapas* (in many areas these are abandoned and you can just fix them up for free), and town halls.
- Other popular places to camp may cost a token amount: campgrounds, cheap hotels (ones set up for hammocks), thatched huts or *palapas* (where they are tended), and trailer parks.

Where Not to Camp
- Certain campsites equal trouble: archaeological sites (officials discourage this), hills (noisy with lots of trucks), markets (busy at the break of dawn and full of thieves), riverbeds (flash floods), trails (dangerous), swimming holes (noisy with lots of kids), and windy areas (tough on you and tents).

Basic Camping Suggestions

- Always ask for permission to camp. It will rarely be denied. *"¿Por favor, podemos pasar la noche aquí?"*
- If you don't find anyone to ask, go ahead and camp. If someone shows up and asks you what you're doing, just say, *"Pasando la noche. Está bien?"*
- Leave the campsite spotless despite the incredible litter you'll see throughout the region.

Special Precautions

- Never camp or sleep under a coconut palm (*coco*). The coconuts drop with an alarming thud—one that can cause a great deal of damage to cars, tents, and unprotected heads.
- Don't eat any strange fruits. The manzanillo tree has both a poisonous sap and poisonous fruit.
- Always have a place that you can get to when the mosquitoes hit at night. In short, set up your tent well before evening.
- Read about scorpions on p. 239.
- If privacy is important to you, then have a place that you can block off as your own. Mexicans, especially, are fascinated with foreigners and will watch you for hours. Note that even in the most remote area you seem to run into people.
- **Repeat**. Never leave any camping gear unattended. It will simply disappear. This is one of the great disadvantages of camping in Central America and Mexico. Theft is commonplace. Furthermore, if you stow gear in a truck or car, thieves will smash in the windows to get to it.

Getting Your Body Clean

- One of the biggest problems is keeping clean.
- If you are by the sea, use coconut soap (*jabón de coco*) to wash with. This does the same thing as more expensive salt water soaps.
- Stop in at some of the RV and trailer parks and pay for a shower.
- In some areas, as on Islas Mujeres, you'll find showers in some of the beachside restaurants. If you watch closely, many beachside hotels also have a shower near their swimming pools.
- Cheap hotels offer yet another alternative to get clean. Some will allow you to pay for a bath only.
- Public baths (*baños públicos*) offer inexpensive showers (*regadores*).
- With over 10,000 hot springs in Mexico you may come up with an ideal bathing spot for free. Watch for quick changes in temperature! Don't bathe nude, even in remote areas.
- And you can bathe for free in any number of streams, rivers, and lakes. Note, however, that many of these can be polluted or con-

tain disease organisms. This is especially true in populated areas. Never, ever drink water from any outside source, no matter how cold and clean the water looks.

Tips on Bathing in Public
- Don't strip completely when bathing.
- Men and women should not bathe together, certainly not in public even if they are partially clad.
- The key word is discretion.

Getting Your Clothes Clean
- You may want to carry one set of clothes for special occasions and live in a second set.
- Clothes with holes, patches, and so on, are not regarded as "in." They are a sign of dire poverty.
- Many women will gladly wash your clothes for a token amount. Settle on a flat rate for the bundle and provide them with a bar of soap (*barra*) or with powdered soap (*jabón en polvo*).
- Be specific on when you want your clothes back—if you aren't, you may not see them for days.
- You'll find laundromats in Mexico, but they're rarely do-it-yourself operations. You'll pay a flat fee for a load. Finding laundomats in Central America is quite difficult (see p. 156 for laundromat vocabulary).

RV Living

RVs have become very popular with people traveling to Mexico, especially older people. There are now many trailer parks throughout the country. Much of the advice given in the camping section applies to RVers.

Tips Just for RVers
- You may no longer be able to buy propane for use in vehicles in Mexico. You can still buy the small containers, however. So fill up on propane before you come into Mexico, and convert your gas pipes to a hookup to portable tanks.
- RVs are big, and there are no shoulders on most Mexican roads. Never stop in the road, because you could cause a serious accident. RVs can make it through most towns and cities, but plan your route carefully and take the advice of others who have been there before.
- Trailer parks by the sea fill up fast. The sooner you can get to your appointed place in late fall or early winter, the better off

you'll be. If you can make reservations far in advance, do it.

- Some trailer parks double as bordellos, which are not illegal in Mexico. If you're traveling with a family, keep this in mind.
- An awning is invaluable in Mexico because of the bright sun. Have one installed if you haven't got one already.
- There are very few dump stations in Mexico, so don't spend a lot of time looking for them.
- In emergencies you can leave your RV in Mexico. Check locally for exact details if you have to leave the country without it.
- Mosquitos can get fierce in some areas. If your screens are old or filled with tiny holes, the bugs will get in. Replace them.
- Here's a club devoted solely to RVers and which has caravans to Mexico each year:

The Good Sam Club
International Headquarters
P.O. Box 500
Agoura, CA 91301
Tel: (800) 423-5061
       (800) 382-3455 (CA)

- Odds and ends that are easy to forget: a water hose with extra gaskets (these break with frequent use or get indented so that water leaks out), roof sealer (should be applied yearly), velcro (great for tying curtains back), paper towel rack (you'll be using a lot of paper products), fly swatter, small rugs, extension cord (plenty long), laundry bags (good for many uses), plastic garbage bags, soft soap, fire extinguisher, spare bulbs, nuts, screws, spare rotor, hydraulic lift (two of these are ideal for emergencies), and a superb tool kit.

Money Matters

Getting the most for your money is on every traveler's mind. Following are some straightforward tips.

Money Basics

Even if you've traveled a great deal, there are some oddities included in the following sections.

Cashing Traveler's Checks

Usually the easiest and sometimes the only place to cash a traveler's check is in a bank. Some banks refuse to cash certain brands of checks (mainly in Mexico), which means you have to find another bank or a money changer who is less suspicious. Fortunately, more and more hotels are now accepting traveler's checks. However, many of them offer a less favorable rate of exchange than a bank.

- Bring your passport to cash checks. You may have to write the number on each check. Do this ahead of time if you want to hurry up the process at the bank.
- Avoid getting your checks wet, because it is not easy getting mutilated or faded checks cashed. If no one will take your checks, rip them up and declare them lost.

Personal Checks

Leave your personal checks at home, unless you plan to pay for duty with them on your return home (see p. 345).

Credit Cards

These are as good as gold in much of the region. There is very little suspicion of credit cards.

- If you plan to be abroad for more than a month, send in a prepayment. If you send in enough money to cover your charges, you will not have to pay interest on the balance.
- Always find out if there is a way to call your credit card company toll-free from abroad before traveling. There often is.

Using Credit Cards to Get Cash

Many credit cards allow you to get cash in a pinch. The regulations and fees for such a service change frequently.

- If you think you'll be using this service, get a list of the places where it's available. Make sure that it's very specific.
- ATMs are available mainly in Mexico.

Protecting Credit Cards

Protect your cards like cash, and count them from time to time to make sure they're all there. Thieves are smart enough to steal just one, hoping that you won't notice.

Exchanging Currency
(*Cambio de Moneda*)

One of the realities of travel is the necessity of exchanging dollars into foreign currency.

Survival Vocabulary in the Bank

---

bank	*banco*	**exchange hours**	*horas de cambio*
bank draft	*cheque del banco*	**exchange (to)**	*cambiar*
bill (banknote)	*billete*	**local currency**	*moneda nacional*
cash (to pay *cash*)	*efectivo*	**money**	*dinero*
cash (to *cash*)	*cambiar*	**money changers**	*casas de cambio*
cashier	*caja*	**money order**	*giro*
change, exchange	*cambio*	**personal check**	*cheque personal*
check	*cheque*	**signature**	*firma*
coins	*monedas*	**teller's window**	*caja*
commission	*comisión*	**traveler's check**	*cheque de viajero*
credit card	*tarjeta de crédito*	**where's another bank**	"*¿Dónde*
dollar	*dólar*		*hay un otro banco?*"

Money Basics

- Here are the names of the respective currencies by country: Belize—Belizean dollar(s), Costa Rica—Colón(es), Guatemala-Quetzal(es), Honduras—Lempira(s), and Mexico—New peso(s).
- Both old and new pesos are still in circulation. Have someone explain the difference so that you don't get stuck with less than full value in any exchange. One new peso equals 1,000 old. Prices are often posted in both currencies, which can be confusing.
- You'll need a passport for each exchange. Many countries allow you to exchange as much money as you want into local currency, but have limitations on the amount of currency you can exchange back into dollars when leaving. So toward the end of your trip exchange only the amount you'll be using.

- Exchange rates fluctuate daily. "What is the exchange rate?" in Spanish is: "*¿Cuál es el cambio?*"
- Experienced traveler's study rates for several weeks before traveling to see whether the dollar is getting weaker or stronger in relation to a specific foreign currency. If the dollar is getting stronger, they exchange less money on arrival. If it's getting weaker, they exchange lots of money on arrival.
- Exchange money in major touristic areas. The more off-the-beaten-path you get, the lower the rate tends to be.
- No matter what the trend, always exchange the most money you can afford to lose. The reason is that you usually get a better rate of exchange for larger amounts of money.
- You almost always get a better rate of exchange for hard currency than traveler's checks.
- Never exchange currency in the United States or Canada. The exchange rates are absurdly low.
- In most European countries, you get a poor rate of exchange at international airports. My experience in Central America and Mexico was the opposite, especially in San José (Costa Rica) and Mexico City (Mexico).
- Generally, you get your best rate of exchange from a reputable bank. Rates of exchange do vary from one bank to the next. Knowing the rate of exchange is important, but you must also find out what kind of commission is charged. Before you exchange money, ask if there is a commission or service fee for the transaction—"*¿Cobran una comisión?*" ("Do you charge a commission?"). Commissions may vary according to the amount of money being exchanged. They may be a set amount or a set overall percentage of the amount exchanged. And, if you're exchanging traveler's checks, the commission may be per check. Ask. Without knowing how the bank charges a commission, you really don't know what the final exchange rate will be.
- In most instances you'll find the same rates at money changers (*casas de cambio*) as at reputable banks. Money changers are most common in Mexico. The big advantage: an instant transaction with none of the hassles of a bank. Always know the current rate of exchange before dealing with a money changer.
- You usually get a poor rate of exchange in hotels. Deluxe chains including Hilton and Sheraton have tried to reverse this in Mexico. Check them before going to a bank. But note that *most* hotels in Central America and Mexico consistently rip off their customers when it comes to currency exchange.
- The so-called black market usually matches or exceeds bank rates without all the hassles. And, sometimes it's the only way to get

local currency. For example, the first time I arrived in Honduras was at the San Pedro Sula airport on a Sunday. No exchange office was open. I had to exchange money outside on the street. Police were everywhere, but all the tourists were making black market exchanges at favorable rates.

- You'll find that money changers and savvy travelers carry little pocket calculators now. It's amusing to watch street transactions. Rates generally vary with the amount of money you're willing to exchange. The more money, the better the rate.
- If you can speak Spanish, you usually get a slightly higher rate. Remember that on the street there is no set rate. It's just like bargaining. Dollars are to locals what honey is to bees.
- Finally, note that it is often not necessary to exchange your currency at all. I have paid for a wide varied of accommodations, goods, and services with dollar bills throughout Central America and Mexico. In theory, you're not supposed to do this. In practice, money talks. Dollar bills talk very loud.

Tips on Money

- Study coins (*monedas*) for a few minutes until you're familiar with their odd shapes and sizes. Some of the smaller coins are worth much more than some of the larger ones—which is true of many coins in other countries.
- The bills or banknotes (*billetes*) come in a rainbow of colors to make them stand out from each other. Again, study the notes carefully. Note that with color photocopying possible forged notes occasionally are passed. But, this is less of a problem in Central America and Mexico than in other countries, especially Eastern Europe. Still, it's a good idea to see and feel notes of varying denominations right away.
- Never take marked, mutilated, or torn bills. These will be rejected over and over again when you go to use them. Let the bank or whoever's trying to pass them off on you have the headache. Hand them right back and demand good bills.
- Banks will try to stick you with as many large bank notes as possible. Large bank notes are fine if you're going directly from the bank to pay off a large bill, but they're next to useless in many shops, restaurants, and smaller hotels where change can be a major problem. Ask the bank to break down larger notes.
- Never carry coins across borders. Either use them up for a treat or newspaper or convert them to paper bills. Or, give small coins away to the poor children who hover around airports, hoping for just this sort of generosity.

Money Confusion in Mexico

- Mexico, Canada, and the United States share the $ sign for their national currencies. The $ sign in Mexico means pesos.
- Sometimes, an item for sale or an item on a menu will have M.N. (*moneda nacional*) written behind it. This means that the cost is in the national currency or pesos.
- If a store or restaurant wants to price an item in U.S. dollars, they'll do it by adding US CY (U.S. currency) or Dlls (dollars) after the price.

The Bad News About Banks

- What's the number one pet peeve of travelers to Central America and Mexico? Diarrhea—pretty good guess, but not quite right. Try banks. You'll only have to go to a bank once to know how agonizingly slow the process of currency exchange can be. Yes, there are a few exceptions, but not many. Lines can simply be amazing (I saw one in Guatemala that was two blocks long). And, the first line you stand in is often not the last.
- Bank tellers are often rude, insensitive, and incompetent. As bureaucrats, they often move at a slug's pace. They are almost always preoccupied with anything other than what they have to do. The endless stamping, the checking and rechecking, the okaying by a superior—it can be a traveler's nightmare.
- Particularly irritating in Mexico (less common in Central America) is how tellers allow "special customers" to butt into the line ahead of others who have been patiently waiting for an hour (or more) to get served.
- Banks can run out of local currency—no joke!
- Banks often refuse to exchange foreign currency after a specific hour, even though they are open. This is frustrating. So, before waiting in line, ask whether currency exchange is possible. Generally, local hotels know the ins and outs of local banks. They are not offended if you ask them about the system.
- In Mexico some banks won't cash traveler's checks. I never found this to be true in Central America, but it is certainly possible. However, in Central America some banks won't exchange cash— now figure that one out.
- Finally, banks are often closed. Perhaps, it's a holiday. Perhaps, it's time for lunch. Perhaps, it's a weekend.
- So if you can find a place to exchange currency at a fair rate of exchange outside of a bank, jump at the opportunity.

Taxes and Service Charges

Prices are often quoted without taxes or service charges added, especially in hotels and restaurants. Always ask what a price will be with taxes (*con impuestos*) and with service (*con servicio*). The Aggregate Value Tax (*Impuesto al Valor Agregado*—IVA) is the common name for the "tourist tax" and varies from country to country and from item to item. Some luxury goods have as much as a 20 percent tax.

- The only way you can avoid taxes is by eating in inexpensive restaurants and staying in inexpensive hotels and by shopping in the open market—these all cater to locals who don't have to pay the tax. In some instances, this doesn't work. They spot you as a tourist and add the legal tax anyway. The only place you'll never get taxed is in open markets, whether for food or goods.
- Since most tourists don't eat, stay, and shop exclusively in such places, they get socked with a tax that can really add up.
- This tax should never be confused with a service charge! You're still expected to leave a tip unless the service charge has already been added (see tipping below).

Tips (*propinas*)

Many locals depend almost entirely on tips for their living. Since wages are extremely low, tips take on an added importance:

- Tips tend to be much higher in major resorts and in major cities. Tip in these areas as at home.
- Tips can be much smaller in rural areas where any tip at all will be appreciated. Still, it is in these areas that need is greatest, and you might bear that in mind when tipping.
- Always carry lots of small change and small bills with you. These will be essential for tips.
- Although tour packages generally include all gratuities for services included in the tour contract, ask about the policy on tipping before signing a contract.

Tipping on Day Tours
Both the driver and tour guide will appreciate a tip for their services. A dollar a day is a fair tip, more if either person offered exceptional information or service. These tips are definitely optional.

Tipping in the Airport
Porters may tell you what their charge is for a bag. If they leave it up to you, tip less than in the United States, but don't underdo it.

Tipping on Cruises

- Some cruise ships include the tip in the price of the voyage. Ask.
- If tips are extra, tip the waiter and room steward appropriately.
- Give half the tip up front as an inducement for good service. Tell them you'll give an equal amount at the end of the trip if the service is good.
- Always tip the day before getting off the ship to make sure that the confusion of disembarkation doesn't make tipping impossible.
- Tip staff for any special services requested.

Tipping in Hotels

- Tip anyone carrying your bags the equivalent of the current price of a local beer for such a service.
- Chambermaids should be tipped for stays of longer than a few days—give at least $1 a day.
- If anyone in the hotel performs a special service for you, tip accordingly.
- In good hotels you should expect to tip the concierge for any unusual service, such as getting tickets to a sold-out performance or getting reservations at a restaurant which is nearly impossible to get into.

Tipping in Restaurants

- In most Central American restaurants both a tax and a service charge (tip) will automatically be added to your bill. If a service charge has been added, that's your tip.
- In Mexico, taxes are often added, but tips may or may not be. If there are two charges added to the base amount, both taxes and a tip have been added. If there is only one charge, ask what it is for. If it is for a tax, add a tip appropriate to the style of restaurant and quality of service. Confusing taxes and tips is quite common. Not leaving a tip causes a lot of resentment.
- Most guides tell you to tip 10 to 15 percent in all restaurants if a tip has not been added automatically to the bill. If you want to, fine. It will certainly be appreciated. However, this is not what the locals do. In a low-cost restaurant they tip just a little. If the bill runs over $5, they tip about 6 percent. If the bill tops $10, then they do tip 10 to 15 percent depending upon the service.
- Locals also tip less in small-town restaurants. In this way tips are related to the area. However, if you can afford to, tip 10 to 15 percent because these are exactly the areas where the residents are poorest and need money the most.

Tipping Taxi Drivers

- You are not expected to tip taxi drivers in most countries except Belize. However, a small tip is never inappropriate.
- However, if a driver provides any extra service (like carrying bags for you), then tip for that service.
- If you hire a taxi driver as a guide (often beats renting a car for a day), then a tip is appropriate.
- In some areas, it may take a taxi driver several hours to get you to an off-beat location. Even though you have established a firm price for this service, a tip is appropriate for such long-distance drives.

Miscellaneous Tipping

- Give tiny tips to kids who volunteer to watch your car if you have to leave it on the street. Yes, this is a tiny piece of extortion. Tell them you'll pay them on your return to the car. They'll often ask for half upfront. Refuse to pay it. Tell them they'll get their money when the job is done. Simply say *"Mas tarde"* which means "a little later."
- In Mexico give small tips to any gas station attendant who washes your windshield, checks your oil, or inflates your tires. Tips are not expected for such services in Belize or Costa Rica if you buy gas at the station.
- You should tip washroom attendants. Give them as little as you can get away with. Attendants are hardly common, but in a few fancy places they do exist.
- You should tip theater (and movie) ushers who guide you to your seat—again, a very small amount will do.

When Not to Tip

- Don't tip taxi drivers unless they perform some special service for you. The exception is Belize.
- Don't tip barbers and hairdressers.

Handling Beggars

Poverty is real throughout the region. Begging is most common in Mexico, but exists to a limited degree in all countries. There's very little any one person can do to alleviate the problem. So it becomes a matter of personal choice, who you give to and who you don't.

- Many travelers prefer to give food to beggars rather than money. Rarely will anyone turn you down. The hunger is real, not the scam that you'll find in other places.

Miscellaneous Money Tips

- Carry a change purse. It's helpful for tiny transactions. This way you don't have to take out your wallet. You can put in a few small bills as well. The less money you show, the better.
- If you're flying from a country, always save enough money for the departure tax. It is usually cheaper to pay this tax in local currency than in dollars.

Protecting Property

Suspicion and wariness require energy and are not very pleasant sensations, but they do prevent trouble, which can be even more unpleasant. Countries in this region are poor, and you'd have to be naive or careless not to take protective measures.

Protecting Your Belongings

Protecting your belongings requires a bit of preparation, lots of common sense, and enough street sense to stay out of trouble. Follow the strategies outlined below, and you'll cut the odds of losing things or being robbed to almost zero.

Basic Protection

- Mexicans have a saying about lovers kissing in public: "Don't count your money before the poor." This same saying can be taken literally as a warning to travelers. Never count or flash money in public. Local residents consider this cruel, stupid, and dangerous. You're asking for trouble if you do.
- Leave all expensive jewelry at home. Don't even wear imitation jewelry any longer. Thieves have a hard time telling it from the real thing. It's not worth getting hurt for an item worth pennies.
- Never wear an expensive watch. Get an extremely cheap one.
- Never carry all of your valuables in one place. Split up your documents and money. *This is basic street sense*, and absolutely essential in developing countries.
- Keep anything valuable out of sight. If you have to leave something valuable in a car (not a good idea), put it in the trunk. Stow your cameras in an inconspicuous bag.
- Never take public transportation, especially buses or trams, after exchanging a large amount of money. Get the money back to your hotel safe and take just what you need for the day.
- Just what you need for the day (or for the next few hours) is the key phrase.
- Dress casually.
- You cannot hide the fact that you are a foreigner. Just don't flaunt your wealth.
- Never, ever set your luggage down and leave it unattended, not even for a second.
- Carry a reduced photocopy of your passport with you abroad. Have it encased in plastic (*emplasticado*). This is done for all

sorts of documents in Central America and Mexico—right in the street, especially in San José, Costa Rica.

- Put your original passport in a safe and carry the little card with you for identification.

How to Carry Valuables When You Must—Pickpocket Proofing

There are times when everything you own is either on your body or in your bags. Violent crime is not common in Central America and Mexico, but ripoffs of bags and pickpocketing are (tens of thousands of cases are reported yearly). Here are some tips:

- A small, durable traveler's pouch which can be attached to a belt and worn under your pants or skirt is the *best* place to carry valuable documents and money. These can be improvised by anyone with a basic knowledge of sewing and should have a good zipper enclosure. Hidden pockets can also hang from your neck, be strapped to your leg, or placed anywhere else on the body. Having several pockets is a good idea. These hidden pockets are sold in catalogs and stores.
- Second best but good is the inside pocket of a coat or jacket, which has been modified with a zipper. You can alter these pockets so that they're twice as deep, and twice as hard to pick. The zipper is crucial. No zipper? Use a safety pin as a deterrent to nimble fingers.
- Never carry your wallet in a rear pocket! A pickpocket can rip it off in a second. A side pants pocket is only a little better. If that's all you've got, buy a nappy-surfaced wallet or put a rubber band around it—this can give pickpockets a fit.
- If you're carrying a purse, put it in front of you with your arms crossed over it. Your wallet should be at the bottom. If your purse is to your side or behind you, a thief will slash it open with a razor blade and be gone in seconds.
- Many travelers are now wearing fanny pouches for their valuables. They generally reverse them so that they are facing forward. Getting to passports and money is extremely easy with one of these pouches. So is stealing them. Despite their incredible popularity, avoid these at all costs. Your money and documents must be *under* your clothing.

Situations Pickpockets Like

- Pickpocketing is most common in crowded areas: markets, buses, the metro in Mexico City, and beaches.
- Pickpockets prey on careless, disoriented, and drunk tourists—in that order.

- Be wary of minor accidents: being bumped, having your foot stepped upon, being shoved.
- Avoid commotions of all kinds. Pickpockets love to create them. Move away from any commotion quickly.
- Pickpockets often pose as drunks. If someone wraps his arms around you, watch your wallet—he's probably feeling for it.
- Another trick is to push into you with a paper, as if the pickpocket were casually reading it in the street. If this happens, push the paper aside hard and move away quickly.
- Someone may point out that you have a stain on your clothes. React by getting away from that person immediately. If you want to worry about cleaning a stain, do it at the hotel.
- Don't get distracted by questions. Is that your money on the seat? Is that your purse over there? When a stranger starts asking you something, be wary.
- Watch out for the spilled money or contents of purse or bag game. When you see things spilling on the ground, don't reach over to help out. You're often being set up.
- If someone grabs at one part of your body or clothing, strike their hand away and move off quickly.
- Avoid any area where you can get trapped, as in an alley where there are no other people.
- If you're sure someone is trying to steal from you, shout *Ladron* (thief) and point at the person. If he's a thief, he'll immediately move off quickly, often at a gallop.

Protecting Valuables in a Hotel
- In some hotel rooms you'll find security boxes. Get a key and instructions on how to use these. Occasionally, there is a small fee, but it is usually reasonable. Often, there is no charge at all.
- Better hotels have safe deposit boxes (*cajas de seguridad*) at the front desk. Take advantage of them. There's usually no charge, unless you lose the key (very expensive).
- Some have larger safe deposit boxes. You put your valuables in an envelope, placed into the box until you ask for its return.
- When getting valuables out of a safe, be attentive. This is one time when thieves will try to distract you.
- If you're in a budget hotel, don't leave valuables unattended. Carry them into the shower or bathroom if you have to.

Protecting Valuables in Airports, Train, and Bus Stations
- If safety lockers (*gabinetes de seguridad*) are available, store excess baggage or valuables in them. These are relatively rare now, since terrorism has become a major concern. Most of them

have time limits, often with a maximum of one week.
- Never let anyone help you put your gear into one of these lockers. Keys are often switched in the process. If you don't understand how the lockers work, ask or watch someone else.
- If you're traveling at night, always carry a flashlight for blackouts in train and bus stations. This will be the only way to discourage thieves—one almost carted off my bags in this situation.
- Stick with your bags—assume that if they're left unattended for a second, they'll be ripped off. Chances are good that they will be.
- Travel light. That way you can carry your bags with you onto buses, planes, and taxis. The minute your bags are out of sight you have no way to keep track of them. On second-class buses you don't even get a receipt for your bags—good luck trying to prove they got ripped off, even if your Spanish is flawless.

Protecting Valuables in Cars
- Never leave anything valuable in a car. A good thief can get into a car or trunk in a few seconds.
- Always lock your car. If you don't, the tool set for changing tires will be gone when you get back.
- If in a major city, find a guarded parking lot where the attendant can see the car at all times. Put your gear in the trunk before going into the lot. However, it would be better if you would find a hotel first and leave your belongings there before parking.
- Before visiting popular tourist attractions in rural areas, find a hotel and leave your gear there first. Then go to the site. Thieves know exactly what areas tourists are interested in. For example, the inland Blue Hole in Belize is often visited by people traveling by car. Thieves routinely rip off all contents of cars at this spot. Yes, it may be a hassle finding a hotel first and possibly backtracking, but losing all of your baggage is even worse.
- If you travel to Mexico and on to Belize in your own car or RV, consider a built-in safe underneath the car. Many experienced travelers use this "hidden compartment" for valuables and documents—it's unlikely that someone will find it.
- Absolutely never leave your car out in a city street at night. It will be vandalized or stolen. In some areas, leaving cars on streets is illegal, anyway. Pay to have it put into a garage.

Protecting Valuables at the Beach
- Leave as much as you can at your hotel, preferably in a safe deposit box.
- Pin your money to a beach robe or piece of clothing which no

one would suspect as a hiding place. Leave nothing of great value in your purse or bag, which will be the first thing stolen.

Losing Things

It is very easy to lose things while traveling because you're constantly disoriented, frequently tired and fuzzy, and often moving at such a quick pace that it's hard to keep track of where you are or what you've got.

- Consider a special bag for things that are really important to you. Carry everything in that one bag (I'm not talking about money and valuables). You'll be less likely to forget the bag than an individual item.
- The quickest way to lose something is to set it down. You put a camera on the seat next to you and the next minute you're four blocks away and realize that the camera didn't come with you. What a sinking feeling and a mad dash to claim it.
- Try to establish a place for everything. This routine helps you know at all times where things are. This has a calming effect and really helps cut down on the loss of items through carelessness, fatigue, or simple oversight.

Personal Safety

Personal safety is a major travel concern in Central America and Mexico. Use common sense and do what the local residents do, to avoid problems. Fifty percent of life-threatening situations involve accidents, and 60 percent of these are road related.

What the Locals Advise

The local inhabitants follow certain precautions as if they were second nature. They've learned not to put themselves in situations that could turn nasty.

Up-To-Date Information on Personal Safety
- Updates regarding foreign travel are available from the U.S. Department of State. Write with specific questions to save on a long-distance call (the number below connects you with a recording).

  Bureau of Consular Affairs, Room 4811 NS
  U.S. Department of State
  Washington, DC 20520
  Tel: (202) 647-5225

- Updates are available in Canada from the Department of External Affairs in Ottawa at (613) 992-3705.

Tips on Registration
If you're planning on traveling extensively or if you plan to spend several months in one area, register with the nearest consulate.
- The consulates want to know where you are so that they can get messages or information to you in an emergency.
- Or, they may want to get information to your family in case you're hurt or possibly even killed.

Air Travel
- Ask locally about the safety records of regional airlines. Residents are quite aware of which ones have been losing planes.
- When traveling from one country to the next, ask about any stopovers. Avoid stops in either El Salvador or Nicaragua. Many agents won't tell you about these unless you ask.

Boating

- Locals often make a living by taking tourists out on boats. In a river this is not much of a problem. If you're going into the ocean, boats should have two motors, extra gas, and a good anchor.
- When boating in the Tropics, carry lots of food and water with you. Just in case the boat breaks down.
- If fishing in the Caribbean, watch the weather. The storms here are extremely violent.

Camping Out (see pages 158–162)

Driving

Driving can be quite dangerous. I have covered many more tips in the section on driving (see pp. 194–205). Following are critical safety tips.

- Don't drive at night. Not only could you have an accident, but you could expose yourself to the risk of robbery, rape, and murder.
- Know where not to drive. I do not suggest driving in Guatemala or Honduras. Guatemala is safe only in major tourist areas. Military death squads have killed over 150,000 people in recent decades, destroying no less than 400 villages. Guerrila activity is real. Use public transportation or taxis to get to major tourist destinations. Fly into Flores from Guatemala City (Guatemala) or Belize City (Belize) and take public transportation from there to visit Tikal. Do not take the bus from Belize to Flores. The route is commonly used by tours. It is notorious for theft at gunpoint. Tour operators will tell you it's completely safe. Most of the time it is. The exceptions are numerous enough to be taken seriously. Finally, if you want to visit Indian villages near Quetzaltenango, hire a guide.
- Certain routes in Mexico have been the source of more problems than others. Any person driving through the following areas should be especially cautious:

Highway 15 through Sinaloa.
Highway 2 in the Caborca area of Sonora.
Highway 15 from Nogales in Arizona to Mexico City.
Highway 40 from Durango to the Pacific Coast.
Highway 185 crossing the Isthmus of Tehunantepec.
Highway 57 between San Luis Potosí and Matehuala.
Highway off 185 from Palomares northwest to Tuxtepec
    in Oaxaca.

- Use 4-wheel drives in Belize and Costa Rica. Pay the extra money. It's worth every cent.
- Avoid off-road travel in arcas where marijuana or poppies are cultivated, especially in Nayarit, Sinoloa, and Sonora in Mexico. This includes some pretty large chunks of Mexico. Talk to consulates for advice. Avoid off-road travel in Guatemala and Honduras entirely.
- Don't sleep in your car by the side of the road at night, even if you're traveling in an RV. Find a campsite with other people or park in the lot of a gas station (*gasolinera*).

Drowning

- Many people drown in Central America and Mexico each year, most from carelessness. Ask whether an area is safe for swimming, particularly in Costa Rica and Mexico. Many of the most beautiful beaches have dangerous rip tides, even at waist level. Ask several people (not just one) about local conditions.
- A rip tide is a fast moving river of water within the ocean itself. It does not pull you down, but moves you along the shore very rapidly, then out to sea. Most people struggle against the water and drown from exhaustion. Rip tides may move out several hundred yards or more from shore but always go back in. Don't fight the water. Relax. Stay calm. Go with the flow. When you come back in toward shore with the tide, slowly swim across the current at a 45-degree angle. Eventually, you get to the edge of the current and can make your way into shore.
- If you get caught in a rip tide, throw your hand up into the air and yell a few times—possibly someone will see you're in trouble and come to your aid. Otherwise, relax and follow the preceding advice. It is difficult not to panic. If you can control yourself and stay calm, you will survive.
- If you see that someone is in trouble, get a surfboard, boat, or float and get to the person as quickly as possible. Ask the person whether they need help. Do not get close to them until they answer "yes." A drowning person is extremely dangerous until coherent. When they answer "yes," then help them.
- If a person is unconscious, act quickly. Begin artificial respiration from the moment you make contact, in the water. Get air into the person's lungs as *quickly* as possible.
- Note that 50 percent of people who drown have a high blood alcohol level. It's not just drinking and driving that don't mix.
- Special note: Never dive into water. Always slide in gently. It is often difficult to detect submerged structure.

Earthquakes (*tremblor*)

Earthquakes are common. In some years several hundred are detected, in other years very few. Here are tips just in case:
- Many larger buildings are constructed to sway (but not give way) during quakes. This motion is terrifying but normal.
- Get away from walls and windows, preferably under a table, desk, or bed.
- Standing in a doorway is a good option in smaller buildings or structures that may collapse.
- Never use elevators during a quake and avoid stairways as well. You're better off staying put in a room.
- If you're out on the street, go to the center of the road if possible—watch out for panicky drivers. The façades of buildings tend to crack and fall away, so keep clear of them.
- If you're driving, slowly come to a stop and simply sit the quake out in your car.
- Earthquakes are so quick and devastating that some of this advice may not be practical, but it's the best we've got to offer.

Fires (*fuego*)

Few travelers realize how common hotel fires are because most are contained and cause very little concern. However, in the event of a fire here are a few safety precautions that might save your life.
- Keep a flashlight and your room key next to you on the bed table. Or, keep them in the same place every night so you know exactly where they are in case of an emergency.
- Note all exits on your floor. Form an accurate picture of where they are in relation to your room. During a fire it may be impossible to see exits through the smoke. Count doors to the exit, to know where it is.
- Open these exit doors and check that the stairs leading down are clear. If doors are locked, find out why. Change rooms if the explanation seems fuzzy.
- Check on fire escapes from your room or from your floor.
- If a small fire starts in your room, put it out if you can. Smothering a fire works better than trying to douse it with water.
- If the fire's out of control, leave the room immediately. Close the door behind you to contain the fire and pull the fire alarm (if there is one). Rush to the front desk and report it *immediately*.
- If you see a fire start in another part of the building, pull the fire alarm (if there is one). Then immediately tell the front desk. Unfortunately, in many small hotels there are no phones. You may have to wake up guests to get them out.
- If you don't know where a fire is and are reacting to an alarm,

use the fire escape from your room or head immediately to a fire exit down the hall.

- If the door knob or door to your room feels hot, don't open it. The fire is too close and may sweep into your room as soon as the door opens.
- If the door is cool, head to the nearest fire exit.
- Always leave your room with your key in hand so that you can get back in if your escape is somehow blocked.
- If there's a lot of smoke, stay close to the floor. Cover your mouth and nose with a moist towel.
- In a fire *never use an elevator* as an escape route.
- If the stairwell going down is blocked by fire, go up to the roof. Many people are saved this way, and few people think of this alternative.
- If all fire exits are blocked completely, return to your room. Phone the fire department and the front desk so that they know you're in trouble (if you have a phone). Give them your room number. If you can't get through to the front desk, call the front desk of a hotel nearby.
- If you have a tub in your room, fill it with water. If you've only got a sink, fill that. Soak towels, sheets and even curtains in cold water. Stuff some of these into the openings around the door to keep smoke from coming in.
- Douse the door and surrounding area with as much water as you can. Soak the entire area thoroughly and as often as necessary.
- Try to cover vents (they can bring in smoke) if it's possible.
- If smoke filters into the room, stay low to the floor. Cover your face with a damp towel and breathe through it.
- If smoke becomes intolerable, open the outside window. The top of the window should be open twice as far as the bottom to draw the smoke from the top of the room.
- Never open a window if the air in your room is clear. You may inadvertently draw in smoke from the outside, and smoke is often more dangerous than fire.

Health Problems

Health is the number one problem with personal safety after accidents. Preventive measure are coverd in detail (see pp. 14–24) and other detailed advice is given in a second chapter (see pp. 219–244).

Hitchhiking

Don't hitchhike. You're too exposed if you do. Besides, people are afraid to pick up hitchhikers. And public transportation is so cheap that hitchhiking is unnecessary. Besides, if you do hitchhike, you're expected to pay a fare equivalent to that on a bus. The exception: in Costa Rica hitchhiking for short rides is commonplace in rural areas, especially in the mountains.

Military

- Never wear army or camouflage clothes. These clothes are often cheap and good for trekking, hiking, white water rafting, and other special interest activities, but not in this region. Avoid any association with the military.
- Never take photos of police or soldiers. Don't even think about it. Things can get really ugly if you do.
- Always stop at road checks or guard posts. If someone is carrying a weapon, stop. Usually, these are police or military checkpoints, common throughout Central America and Mexico. Occasionally, you may be stopped by guerrilas. This is very rare. If you don't stop, you may be shot.

Outdoor Activities

- If you engage in high-risk outdoor activities, be prepared for the worst. Plan a safety network in advance.
- If you're going with a tour specializing in outdoor activities, ask about their safety network. It must be specific.

Photography

- Never take photos of Indians without permission. Tourists have been stoned to death for doing this. Generally, when traveling into remote or rural Indian villages, go with a guide who speaks the local dialect. Many Indians do not speak Spanish.
- Taking photos of religious events or ceremonies is extremely touchy. Get permission first through your interpreter. You'll probably be turned down. Don't sneak a photo.

Politics

Stay out of local politics. Keep your mouth shut about your support for local resistance fighters, guerrilas, or left-wing (or right-wing) activists. Don't try to persuade anyone about anything. You could be killed for it. What you say can hurt you.

Rape

The basic rule for women is not to travel alone. Yes, many women do, especially in Costa Rica, but overall this is not a good idea. Single women are breaking a cultural taboo in many areas, and their behavior suggests sexual promiscuity. You're an easy catch (*conquista*).

This is true even on the beach. Following are tips from women who have traveled extensively in Central America and Mexico:

- Travel light. Remember that the weight of your luggage will affect both your attitude and your vulnerability.
- Get by with a single piece of luggage, one no larger than a car-ryon bag for a plane. This gives you freedom and mobility in every situation from public transportation to checking in at a hotel. Keep the bag with you at all times, even on buses.
- Two women traveling together are better off than a single woman, but be wary and avoid provocative situations.
- Whenever possible, travel with a group. If sightseeing, just blend in with a group if you think you might be hassled.
- Schedule most of your long-distance travel for the day. Try to avoid travel at night when you're more vulnerable.
- Women do not go out at night alone—with the exception of prostitutes and foreigners who don't know better. Find an escort for evening entertainment or go with a tour.
- Never tell a stranger your room number. Always meet strangers in the lobby at a pre-fixed time.
- Be unattractive! This is totally contrary to what most women have been taught. Watch your hair—cover it up, keep it in a tight bun. Skip makeup, any kind of nail polish, and no perfume.
- Don't carry or wear any jewelry. This includes even cheap imita-tion jewelry. Thieves can't tell the difference. Is it worth getting hurt over a piece of jewelry?
- Wear a wedding band (not real gold) even if you're not married. If you are, replace your real band with a fake one. Yes, you could get harmed for not giving it up if mugged.
- Watch your dress. Avoid tight-fitting clothes. Don't wear high heels. And don't expose much of your body, especially your breast and legs. Always wear a bra. If possible, wear a light, loose-fitting blouse or shirt which covers your arms completely. Wear cotton pants or a skirt that goes over your knees. Wear shorts only at the beach. Many women ignore this advice without serious consequences. However, their behavior is considered offensive by local residents.
- As silly as it sounds, wear glasses, even if you don't need them.
- Don't get into a cab by yourself and don't be the last person left off. You can almost always share a ride (see p. 140).
- Don't get into an elevator, alley, or any enclosed area with a man alone. Don't be anywhere alone with a stranger—period. And, that includes a beach or jungle path.
- In a hotel, have your key in your hand before reaching your room. You'll avoid fumbling through your purse this way.

- Almost all hotel rooms have bolt locks in addition to the regular lock. If the lock seems flimsy, jam a chair underneath the knob to make it difficult to open. Note that tiny, portable alarms can be attached to doors to go off with a forced entry.
- A proprietor may take advantage of a pass key to make a pass. Bear this in mind when bolting or blocking a door.
- Do not accept gifts from anyone, unless you want a sexual relationship. The meaning of the gift outweighs its value and may force you into a compromising position.
- Remember that many bars are off-limits to women. Your appearance in a cantina could set something off.
- Simply ignore hissing and staring in the street—don't respond to any comments. If someone starts to hassle you, turn and say, "*¡Deja me!*" which roughly means, "Leave me alone!"
- Whenever possible, don't say anything at all.
- Topless and nude bathing is absolutely taboo on most beaches. There are some exceptions. Follow the local lead. Never bathe topless or nude in an inland area.
- Find out where you're going before leaving a hotel. Have directions figured out so that you don't have to stop in the street.
- Walk confidently and rapidly. Look straight ahead. Don't look at men. Watch how the local women act and walk.
- Consider walking against the flow. This is a good way to see whether anyone is following you.
- Always carry the amount of money you'll need for the next few hours in small bills and change. You never want to ask someone to exchange large bills.
- In some areas police are not people you can rely on. They may be extremely aggressive with foreign women.
- If it's possible, always let someone know where you're going and when you intend to be back. This could be a friend or just someone at the front desk of a hotel.

Robberies
Most robberies do not involve personal injury. However, a few may. To avoid being hit or killed follow these tips (read pp. 173–177).
- Ask locally about dangerous areas. Stay out of ports, rowdy bars, and red light districts. These are particulary dangerous at night. Belize City in Belize; Puerto Limón, Puntarenas, and San José in Costa Rica; Guatemala City in Guatemala; and Mexico City in Mexico—all can be quite dangerous, some only in specific areas. I would avoid Belize City and Puerto Limón at any time.
- Finally, if you do get robbed, don't resist. Thieves are usually scared to death, they just want to get the money and run. Give it

to them. Say absolutely nothing. If you don't move, resist, or talk, your chance of bodily injury is minimal. Repeat—hand everything over without hesitation.

• Men should avoid all dealings with prostitutes, not only because of the threat of venereal disease including AIDS (SIDA), but also because robbery is so common, often with violence.

Terrorism

Dress casually. If you're on business, pack more formal attire. Avoid using fancy briefcases. Get to the departure area as soon as allowed in the airport. Talk softly. Read English papers only on planes or in your room. Avoid t-shirts with English sayings.

Trekking

• Dress appropriately. Carry food, water, and a good first-aid kit.
• In Guatemala tours take people on climbs up volcanoes. Bandit activity makes these climbs risky. Many people take these tours without problems. Others have been raped, robbed, and murdered. Do climbing in Costa Rica. There are many excellent areas which can be reached by horseback (see p. 302).
• Go into jungles only with professional guides, unless trails are clearly marked. Never go out at night. Insects, many carrying disease, bite furiously. Snakes come out at this time and are hard to see. And, in a few areas jaguars are a potential, if unlikely, threat.
• If you go out to take a sunset shot, bring a flashlight. Don't go too far from your base. Night falls like a rock in the Tropics. You can't see a thing.

Tropical Storms

There's an old saying that "tropical storms have no rudders." They are hard to predict. However, most storms occur in late summer through fall in the Caribbean. Whenever a storm approaches, get off the water or out of the area altogether for hurricanes.

Volcanic Eruptions

There are a number of active and semi-dormant volcanoes throughout the region. The active volcano near Fortuna in Costa Rica is a major tourist attraction. However, volcanoes can be extremely dangerous. Both lava and poisonous gases emitted from the cone kill people. Follow local recommendations to avoid danger. You'll be specifically told where not to go. People who ignore this advice put themselves and potential rescuers in great danger.

Walking at Night

Don't go out on beaches at night. This is a sad comment and *not* universally true, but in many areas beaches are no longer safe. Ask if you're in doubt. The exception: turtle watchers go out at night, normally accompanied by a local guide. In Costa Rica guides are required.

Travel Between Cities

How you decide to travel between major destinations will depend on how much time, money, and energy you have.

Plane Travel

Plane travel is the fastest and most convenient way to get to many areas in Central America and Mexico. People behind the desk at most airports (*aeropuertos*) speak excellent English in all countries.

Flying in Central America and Mexico
Much of the advice given on flying to Central America and Mexico (pp. 76–78) applies to flights within the region as well. But there are a few things to keep in mind that are quite different.

Domestic Airlines
- Each country has its own domestic carriers. These may offer international as well as domestic flights. In a few cases, there is one carrier for international, a separate for domestic.
- Prices on domestic airlines are often lower than on competing private lines. However, not all domestic airlines are reliable. Talking to locals is often the only way to know which airline is most reliable and safe.
- Since access to a number of areas is available primarily by air or by air only, you have no choice—you have to fly in.
- Whenever you purchase a ticket for a domestic flight, always ask whether all local and departure taxes (*Derecho de Uso de Aeropuerto*) are included. Have the agent show you where this is indicated on the ticket.
- Ask whether the price can be changed once you've paid for the ticket. Fares often go up at a moment's notice. You may be stuck with a surcharge if local law allows this.
- When you buy a full-fare ticket in the United States, you can make changes at no cost. Foreign countries have different regulations. When you buy a ticket, ask about charges for cancellations or changes in flights.
- The regulations in regards to no-shows are also quite different. For example, in Mexico you would pay 50 percent of the ticket cost for not showing up for your flight, no matter what the excuse. Ask about this when purchasing domestic tickets.
- In all instances, show up as early as possible to get your boarding pass and seating assignment. Getting bumped is routine abroad,

and there is no denied boarding compensation.

- Everything takes longer than expected in Central America and Mexico. Hurry up and wait and wait is the rule. Get used to it.
- Seat assignments are often disregarded. Don't bother to get in a huff. Anger is considered poor form. Worrying about seats is simply not considered worth the effort. So, if someone is sitting in your assigned seat, just find one which is open.
- Delayed flights are so common in Central America and Mexico that they are a nonoccurrence.
- In remote areas planes often show up late or not at all. In some of these rural airports there is no shelter from sun or rain. Bring an umbrella, a good book, snacks, and drinks.
- As mentioned earlier, flights are frequently cancelled because they are not full or full enough to make money. Getting angry and frustrated does nothing except get you angry and frustrated. You are not going to change the system.
- Write off every day of your trip that includes a plane flight. Getting to the airport, waiting for the plane to come or take off, the flight itself, the trip into town from the airport—these all burn up time. Accept the fact in advance.
- There is practically no compensation for lost luggage, which is a good reason to travel with carryon bags only.
- Getting reliable information over the phone is difficult. Work through a local travel agent or go directly to the airport.
- You will often be told by the airline, by travel agents, or by clerks at the airport that a plane is fully booked. Never assume that this is true. If you call an airline and are told a plane is fully booked, go to a local travel agent. Often, they'll get you right on the plane. If you go to a travel agent and are told a plane is full, leave and go to another agent. If told the same thing, then go to the airport. If you're told the same thing, ask to be put on the waiting list. The earlier you get to the airport, the better.
- Reverse the whole process if you arrive at an airport and are trying to make reservations there. If the clerk tells you the plane is full, then call the airline directly or work through a local travel agent. I cannot emphasize strongly enough that most planes listed as full really aren't. I have gotten on "full" planes over and over again using the above strategies.

Private Companies
- There are a number of small companies operating in Central America and Mexico. Most are charters to out-of-the-way ruins or fishing camps. A few have printed schedules, which they follow somewhat loosely.

- Flights offered by these companies tend to be more expensive than flights of a comparable distance offered by government-sponsored airlines. However, they are sometimes more reliable. You'll learn about this through word of mouth.

Private Airlines in Mexico

A few small airlines operate on a private basis in Mexico. One of these, Aero California, is presently expanding to include charter flights to the United States in some of the western states.

> Aero California
> P.O. Box 555
> La Paz, Baja California Sur
> Mexico 22109

Bus Travel

Bus travel can get you just about anywhere at a fraction of the price of plane travel. It is more expensive than train travel in Mexico, but still the major way for local people to get around in that country.

Helpful Phrases

arrivals	*llegadas*	How much is	*¿Cuánto cuesta un*
baggage (claim area)	*equipajes*	a ticket to...?	*boleto a...?*
bus	*autobús, camión*	I lost my	*Se me perdió*
bus with a toilet	*pullman*	baggage.	*me equipaje.*
bus station	*terminal, estación de*	intercity	*foraneo*
	autobúses	intercity bus	*camioneta*
bus stop	*parada*	Is it far (near)?	*¿Esta lejos (cerca)?*
city bus	*servicio urbano*	Is there space?	*¿Hay campo?*
deluxe	*super deluxe, de lujo*	I want to go to...	*Quiero ir a...*
departures	*salidas*	nonstop	*directo, sin escala*
destination	*destino*	north	*norte*
driver	*chofer*	passenger	*pasajero*
east	*este, oriente*	reservation	*reservación*
fare	*precio*	reserved seat	*asiento reservado*
card	*tarifa*	route	*ruta*
first class	*primera clase, deluxe*	seat	*asiento*
first-class bus	*pullman*	seated	*sentado*
gates	*llegadas*	second class	*segunda clase*
get in	*sube*	bus	*camioneta*
hour	*hora*	south	*sur*
How many hours	*¿Cuántas*	standing	*parado*
is it to...?	*horas a...?*	stop (bus stop)	*parada*

stop (stop the bus!)	*¡bajan!*	**west**	*oeste, poniente*
third class	*tercera clase*	**What is the**	*¿Cuál es el número*
ticket	*boleto, billete, ficha, ticket*	**number of**	*del autobús?*
ticket window	*caja, taquilla*	**the bus?**	
to	*a*	**What time does**	*¿A qué hora*
toilets	*sanitaríos*	**the bus leave?**	*sale el autobús?*
truck	*camión*	**Where does this**	*Dónde va este*
waiting room	*sala de espera*	**bus go?**	*¿autobús?*

Information on Bus Schedules

- Getting accurate information on bus routes and schedules is almost impossible. The only reliable way to do this is to go to the bus terminal or terminals (some cities have a number of them for different lines heading in different directions). Times change so frequently that no one can keep track of them. Since you buy tickets in person, this is the way to take care of the problem.
- During the peak seasons of Christmas, New Year's, Carnival, and Easter, buses can be packed. Buy your tickets in advance (if allowed). Buses are also packed on long weekends.
- Names are misleading. Nonstop (*directo*) often has a few stops. Drivers augment their income by picking up additional passengers en route.

Early Morning Departures

- Some buses leave very early in the morning. Make sure you can get out of the hotel at that time. Some have security gates or guards. These may be locked to prevent theft and more serious crimes. Always let the front desk know if you'll be leaving early.
- Pay for everything the night before.

Important Facts About Bus Tickets

- You cannot get bus tickets by phoning a bus terminal. You have to buy tickets in person.
- Tickets are rarely open-dated. If you miss the bus, you lose the money and have to buy another ticket.
- Tickets may be for specific seats. The number will be stamped somewhere on the ticket, often on the back.
- Reservations may be necessary, and sometimes can be made in advance.
- There are rarely stopover privileges with bus tickets.
- In most instances, there's no reduction for round-trip fares.
- You usually cannot refund or exchange tickets, but they're easy to sell to people waiting in line.

- Systems vary by country, so ask someone in a hotel to explain how each works. Often, clerks at stations speak no English.
- Never discard your ticket. Keep it until you leave the station at your final destination. Spot checks are common.

Getting Tickets for Inter-City Buses in Mexico City

- The inter-city bus situation is complex because there are many bus lines and a number of terminals. You can get to these terminals by using the subway (*metro*), but you have to know which terminal handles lines heading in the right direction.
- You can get this information from most hotels, the local tourist office, and a number of free publications.
- If you don't have the time or energy to pick up bus tickets in advance, you can pay an agency to do it for you for a fee. The following agency will buy tickets and deliver them to your hotel. The advantage of this agency is that it can compare fares and schedules to your advantage. Since each bus line has its own fare and varying routes, this can be quite difficult.

    Central de Autobuses
    SA de CV
    Plaza del Angel
    Calle Londres 161 Space 48
    Mexico City
    Tel: 533-2047/533-2097

Selecting a Seat

- Unless you speak Spanish, it's hard to select a specific seat. The basic vocabulary given earlier will help.
- Seats in the back near the bathroom can be smelly. However, many buses don't have bathrooms. In fact, few do.
- A window seat (*ventanilla*) or aisle seat (*pasillo*) are easy to specify according to your preference.
- On night rides get a seat on the right side (*derecha*) to avoid glare from oncoming cars and trucks.
- If you're prone to motion sickness, get a seat right behind the driver. Keep facing ahead.
- Always get on the bus as quickly as possible to get your seat, especially if there is open seating—first come, first served.

Bathrooms and Buses

- Not all buses have bathrooms. Even when they do, the bathroom can be hard to get to with people standing in the aisle or it can be so foul you wish you'd never reached it.

- Don't drink liquids before going on a long bus trip. Shy away from beer, coffee, colas, and tea.
- Go to the bathroom immediately before getting on the bus if you have a tendency toward a weak bladder.
- The bus will take a pee break every few hours, if you're lucky. Some travel all day without any break. Bus drivers and locals apparently have iron bladders.
- If you have a control problem, bring adult disposable diapers.
- Bring your own toilet paper. Buses with bathrooms may run out. And bathrooms at stopover points often have none.
- If you can't wait for a stop, ask the driver to pull over. Your pee will be in public. The most private spot is directly behind the bus. You'll probably return to a series of ribald comments and a little laughter—but you can handle that.
- If you have traveler's diarrhea, take lomotil or imodium well in advance or postpone your trip. Buses will stop for you in an emergency, but more than once is pushing it.

Temperature Control
- Some buses are air-conditioned. This can be a welcome treat in hot, sticky weather. If it gets too cool, you'll have to slip on a jacket. Always carry one with you.
- Some buses claim to be air-conditioned, but when you get on them, the air-conditioning turns out to be a series of open windows. This is often referred to in tour brochures as "air cooled."
- In the evening it can get cool in the Tropics. Another reason to carry a jacket. This is most often the case at higher altitudes, certainly rare along hot, humid coastlines.

Taking Care of Hunger Pains
- Never travel on a bus without a food pack filled to the brim with such things as fresh fruit, bread and crackers, some cheese, a chocolate bar, and something to drink.
- Many of the food stops are at restaurants that really can be quite scary from a sanitary point of view. If you have food with you, the greasy tacos won't tempt you for a second.
- Don't be self-conscious about eating in front of other travelers.

Stopovers
- Bus drivers stop every four or five hours to take a break on most (not all) routes. This gives passengers a chance to go to the bathroom or have a bite to eat.
- Occasionally, you wait around while the bus driver has his lunch. There may be a special place set aside just for drivers.

- Buses are usually locked during these breaks. You're allowed to stay on the bus, but if you get off, you have to wait until the driver opens the door to get back on.
- These breaks tend to be quite short, fifteen or twenty minutes. Don't let the bus take off without you. If the bus driver orders something to eat, you'll probably have a little longer break.
- If you're traveling with a group, have a contingency plan in case someone gets lost. If you notice that someone is missing on the bus, say, "¡Falta uno!"

Baggage on Bus Lines

- Traveling by bus with lots of baggage is a real hassle. Try to get by with one small bag that you can carry on the bus and stuff into an overhead rack or carry on your lap (if you have to). This way you can keep an eye on it at all times.
- If you've got a large bag or several smaller ones, you may have to put it in the luggage compartment where it can get lost or stolen. If you do put it in this compartment, watch it get loaded. You'll get a receipt for baggage in first class. But when you're traveling second class, no one bothers with such formalities.
- In some stations you'll find porters or free baggage carts (*carretillas*). Frankly, I'd never hand my baggage to anyone except the person loading it into the compartment on the side of the bus.
- Some stations have a baggage room (*guarda equipaje*) where you can leave your bags for little or no charge.
- If your bus is in an accident, baggage will often be held. That's right—held. This can tie you up for hours or days. If you're traveling with carryon bags, these bags will not be held.

Stopping Buses

- In remote areas there may or may not be bus stops. If there are, follow the locals to them.
- If you want to get on a bus, wave it down as it approaches. Often, buses will stop just about anywhere.

Car Travel

Whether you have your own car or intend to rent one, the following tips will be helpful.

Basic Car Vocabulary

air	*aire*	gas station	*gasolinera, bomba*
battery	*batería*	gas tank	*tanque de gasolina*
brakes	*frenos*	grease	*grasa*
car	*carro, coche*	headlights	*faros*
car hire	*alquiler de automóviles*	hood	*cofre*
change (to)	*cambiar*	horn	*claxon*
check (to)	*revisar, checar*	hose	*manguera*
clean (to)	*limpiar*	jack	*gato*
clutch	*cloch, embrague*	key	*llave*
drive (to)	*manejar*	leak (to)	*tirar*
exhaust pipe	*tubo de escape*	liter	*litro*
fan belt	*la banda del radiator*	map	*mapa de carretera*
filter	*filtro*	muffler	*mofle*
fix (to)	*arreglar, reparar*	noise	*ruido*
flat tire	*llanta ponchada*	mechanic	*taller mecánico*
	(desinflada)	oil	*aceite*
four-wheel drive	*doble tracción*	spare part	*refacción*
full	*lleno, full*	spark plug	*bujía*
funnel	*embudo*	spare tire	*llanta de repuesto*
gas	*gasolina*	tow truck	*remolque*
cap	*tapón*	transmission	*transmisión*
regular	*nova*	trunk	*cajuela*
unleaded	*sin plomo*	windshield	*parabrisas*
supreme unleaded	*extra*	wrench	*llave*

Car Rental

Although car travel is extremely expensive, it's often one of the best ways to see a country. Most of the people in car rental agencies speak good English. A few Spanish words are helpful: car hire (*alquiler de automóviles*) and highway map (*mapa de carretera*).

Crucial Questions

Before you leave the car rental office, have certain questions answered.

- What is the excess charge if the car is turned in later than expected? How much per hour? How much per day?
- If time and mileage come out to be less than the amount of your unlimited mileage agreement, will you be allowed to pay that smaller amount?
- Are all the necessary documents in the car? Get registration papers.
- Is there a map in the car?

- If the car breaks down, what should I do?
- Can we have two sets of keys? (This can really be a life-saver if you accidentally lock yourself out).

Special Mexico City Tip

Special stickers on your car indicate your right to travel in the city only on certain days. This is to cut down on pollution. Make sure you can return the car on the designated day of your sticker. Tourists face stiff fines for driving on the wrong day.

Get Directions Out of Town

Ask for directions to the road leading you to your first destination. This one step can save you an hour or more of frustration. Have the clerk show you the route on a map, if possible.

Checking Out the Car

- When you rent a car, pretend that you're actually buying it. The extra time you take will pay off.

Checklist

- Are there any dents or scratches on the car? If there are, have them *noted* on the rental agreement. That way you won't have to pay for them later. In some areas they note them on a separate sheet. Ask them to give you the sheet or a photocopy.
- Does the car have hub caps? Many don't because they get ripped off regularly. Have their absence noted.
- Check the antenna. Note if absent, bent, or broken.
- Check the spare tire. Make sure it's in good shape and fully inflated (a good reason to carry a tire gauge).
- Ask to see the jack. These are often stolen. In the Volkswagen they're located under the back seat—a good reason to leave your car locked at all times. Understand how the jack works. Have the attendant show you if you're not. Jacks for 4-wheel drives come in parts. Make sure that all parts are there. Have them show you how it works. Parts are often missing, which means you couldn't change the tire even if you wanted to and will pay for the missing part when you return the car.
- Try the horn, wipers, and lights. If two out of three work, you're ahead of the game. Don't settle for a car with any of these not working properly unless it's for a short, day trip.
- Many cars come with air conditioning. Check to see whether it works if you're driving during the torrid, summer season.
- Make sure all fluids are full.
- Stick a small coin into the treads of the tire to judge the depth of

the tread. Tires take tremendous abuse and should be in excellent shape before you start your trip.
- Check the emergency brake. Some simply don't work. You'll need these in mountainous or steep areas.
- Check all of the door locks. Make sure each one works properly. Roll all windows up and down.
- Check to make sure your key will open all doors and the trunk. Don't assume anything.

General Car Tips

Following are tips which apply to car travel in general.

Special Warning to Motorists in Mexico
You do not have to have a car permit to drive in the Baja. However, to go to the mainland you must get one. It's much easier and faster to get this permit when you cross into Mexico (see p. 83).

Gas
- The most common word for gas station is *gasolinera*. Sometimes, you'll hear *bomba*, especially in Costa Rica.
- In some areas gas is sold by the liter (a little more than a quart). So 40 liters is roughly 10 gallons.
- Since gas station hours and days of business are unpredictable, play it safe—top off whenever you have the chance!
- Gas stations run out of fuel—another reason to top off frequently.
- In off-the-beaten-path areas (mainly in Mexico) you may buy gas stored in drums. Filter this gas through a chamois cloth.
- Prices vary in Belize and Costa Rica, but are uniform in Mexico.
- The price of gas sold from drums is double that of gas sold in stations. Carry extra gas to avoid this ripoff.
- Have local currency with you to pay for all gas. Do not expect to pay for it with credit cards or traveler's checks. In some areas they will take hard currency (dollars), but don't count on it.
- Lead-free (*sin plomo*), is often hard to find (for those who travel into Mexico by car or truck). Some stations run out (more or less permanently) of unleaded gas. However, the situation is improving. Get information on the location of gas stations with lead-free gas before going abroad (see p. 90).
- Most rental cars do use regular gas—ask if you're not sure.
- Leaded regular (*con plomo*), is sometimes kiddingly called "*no va*" or "no go" in Spanish. You may want to mix higher (non-leaded) and lower (leaded) octane gases for extra power.
- Diesel is available and extremely inexpensive.

- In tropical areas water sometimes gets into the gas. Add cheap drinking alcohol (*alcohol*) as an additive to help burn it off.

Extra Tips on Gas Station Protocol

- Make sure the pump is set at zero before the attendant starts to fill your tank.
- Ask for a specific amount of gas in local currency rather than for a fill up. This way you'll avoid gas splashing over the car onto the pavement.
- Or ask for a specific number of liters (*litros*). If you don't, the attendant will try to squeeze every last colón, dollar, or peso out of you.
- If you ask an attendant to clean a windshield, check the oil, or inflate a tire, you're expected to tip for the service (in Mexico). Anytime you request a service make sure that it's actually done.
- Most drivers prefer to check the oil themselves. You may want to carry a few cans or plastic containers of oil with you.
- Carry small bills to pay for gas and any extra service. Attendants often claim not to have change for large bills.
- Always count your change. If it is incorrect, say, "*Me falto 30 pesos*" or whatever amount is missing.
- In remote areas, ask where the next gas can be found. "Where is the next gas station?" "*¿Dónde está la próxima gasolinera?*"
- Check to make sure the gas cap (*tapón*) is replaced with each fill. Occasionally, they are stolen.

Getting Better Mileage

- Keep tires inflated to the proper pressure. Carry a gauge.
- Drive slowly.
- If you have a truck with an open bed, put the tailgate down.
- If you're pulling a boat, keep it level with your car.
- Avoid all quick stops and starts.
- Accelerate rapidly but smoothly to your intended speed.

Directions

See the section on Communicating p. 252. Getting good directions is difficult unless you speak fluent Spanish. Often, you will be told the wrong directions anyway. Always confirm directions several times to avoid going in the wrong direction. The lack of good road signs is extremely frustrating at times. Just remember that you're never really lost, just temporarily disoriented and having a good time, right?

Theft From Cars

- Never leave gear in an unattended car. Thieves smash in windows, pull out everything, and are gone just like that. They know areas where tourists are most likely to stop.

- If you want to visit touristic areas where you have to leave your car unattended, find a hotel and leave all your gear there first. Then visit the area.

Driving in Central America and Mexico

Driving in developing countries is not at all like driving in the United States or Canada. This section explains the many major differences. However, using common sense, not drinking, wearing seat belts, and resting when tired are certainly stressed worldwide.

Speed Limits

- Maximum speed limits are posted in kilometers per hour (kph). Locals routinely ignore these. Being stopped for speeding is rare except in Costa Rica.
- To convert speed limits or mileage signs given in kilometers to miles, divide the figure by 10 and multiply by 6. For example: 80 kph ÷ 10 = 8; 8 × 6 = 48 mph.
- On superhighways slower traffic must stay to the right. If someone approaches you from behind, move over to make way. Often cars coming from the rear will blink their lights as a warning signal for you to move over. If you do not move over, you can cause a serious accident. Superhighways exist only in Mexico.

General Driving Conditions

- The only fast roads in the entire region are the scattered superhighways in Mexico. Other roads can be tied up with trucks (belching diesel smoke); broken-down, stopped, stalled, or stranded buses; and even herds of bleary-eyed cattle crossing the highway. Don't expect to drive quickly.
- Coastal and mountain roads must follow the natural contours of the hills, meaning hundreds of curves per mile. Passing is virtually impossible on many of these highways, although locals do it routinely—blind! You'll end up moving as slowly as the slowest link in the chain, which means at the tail end of a truck hauling a full load of timber up a mountainside.
- To avoid some of the traffic start trips early in the day, just after sunrise, if possible. End all trips early—definitely before dark.
- In the United States and Canada you may average 55 mph on many roads. In Central America and Mexico you might be lucky to average 15 to 30. Be realistic about driving times. Do not rely on charts given out by automobile clubs, the ones giving approximate driving times. They're just wishful thinking calculated by some bureaucrat with dust on his bifocals.

- City driving can be tough. The most intimidating place of all is Mexico City. Street names change without warning from one block to the next, the traffic circles (*glorietas*) swing you in all directions, and the traffic jams are appalling in rush hours. Come armed with a good map, lots of patience, and a sense of humor—they'll all be necessary to get you to your hotel. Once there, park the car and leave it parked until you move on!

Safety Hazards

- Driving at night is a nightmare. Don't do it! Animals are attracted to the warmth of the road and can total a car. Often vehicles break down and are impossible to see in the dark.
- Markings are extremely poor. You may suddenly find yourself driving across two lanes of traffic without even realizing what happened—don't assume anything.
- Be extremely wary at intersections. Buses think nothing of rolling through a stop sign at 80 mph. In short, don't trust signs.
- Desert areas are torrid. Avoid midday driving there.
- Always carry food and water. Each person should have one gallon of water per day of travel. In remote areas have a stockpile of food for two weeks. This is basic safety for off-road travel. But even in populated areas, carry something to drink and eat with you.
- The road surface varies from washboard to smooth tar. Shoulders do not exist. Rarely are there center stripes.
- Watch out for animals. They're often feeding by the side of the road. It is not unusual for a herd of goats or cattle to meander across a road. Burros and horses invariably find the grass greener on the edge of the pavement. Vultures light on carrion and can shatter a windshield in one quick beat of a wing. Sanborn's sums it up, "Burros don't wear taillights."
- Fog makes driving treacherous in high mountain areas. The Baja has fog in late spring and early summer along the coast.
- *Topes* or *tumulos*, speed bumps or "sleeping policemen", can wreak havoc on a car. These 3-inch high cement, asphalt, or steel bumps are not always marked, but you'll usually find them entering and leaving towns, even isolated ones with little traffic.
- Rocks, fallen or placed as markers on the road, can be hard to notice and especially hazardous. Rock slides (*derrumbres*) are very common after heavy rains in mountain areas.
- Watch for one-lane bridges (*puente angosto*) and one-lane sections of highway (*solo carril*). The driver who flashes his lights first has right of way—in theory. In fact, muscle and machismo determines all in these situations. Give way at all tight spots.

- *Vados*, dips in the road which act as creek beds, can be dangerous at high speeds. During the wet season the water sweeps
  across the pavement in these areas.
- Don't drive on sand, whether you're on the beach or out in the
  desert. You'll eventually get stuck. Who's going to get you out
  before the tide comes in?
- Always assume the worst. Assume that a bus is going to come
  sweeping around the next corner. It often will—in your lane.
- In Costa Rica there are many wooden bridges. Some of these
  have no railings. Some are so unstable that you have to go off the
  road, across the stream running under the bridge, and up the
  opposite bank. Iguanas sleeping on a bridge are a good sign that
  you may have to make a detour. Look for tracks off to the side
  indicating traffic doing just that.
- Driving can be tiring. If tired, choose a safe spot (a cafe or gas
  station) to pull over. Sleep for 20 minutes or so. Once refreshed,
  you'll have less chance of falling asleep at the wheel.

The Rainy Season
- If you're traveling in the rainy season (the summer months in
  most areas, the winter in the lowlands of Honduras), be
  extremely cautious of flash floods. Never ford low areas in the
  rain. Water can rise suddenly sweeping your car downstream.
- Watch downpours. These cause mud slides and washouts. Anyone who has traveled extensively realizes how serious these can
  be. In some areas entire concrete bridges collapse and are swept
  away like driftwood during a downpour.
- Have an escape route. If a bridge collapses, or a mountain slides
  over a road or gives way in a downpour, or if a river sweeps over
  the pavement—you can get stuck, literally for months, if there's
  no alternate route out!
- When in doubt, ask local bus drivers about road conditions. Bear
  in mind that only a catastrophe would seem significant to most of
  these men. Better ask in a hotel instead.

Hitchhikers
- Do not pick up hitchhikers. Your car can be confiscated if a
  hitchhiker is carrying drugs.
- Don't pick up people by a stranded car. This is a ploy for ripping
  off motorists. Let local residents stop.

Stopping on the Road
- Construction will often bring you to a halt. If a worker waves you
  back in Mexico, it may mean come ahead—something that can

confuse the average U.S. or Canadian driver.

- The lack of shoulders makes it difficult to turn around or stop for pit stops and picnics. Get well off the road if you do stop.
- Stopping for photos is dangerous because there's no way to get off the road. Be very careful in this situation.
- If you get sick or have to go the bathroom in the mountains, don't head into the brush on the edge of the hill. This brush is often just the top of tall trees. Each year people die in mountainous areas as they fall to their deaths in just this situation.

Parking in the Street

Parking is one of the more disagreeable aspects of traveling by car. And the rules of the game are a little different abroad.

- In most towns and cities you can park in the street during the day without any real problem. Lock the car.
- Just be sure that you're not parking in a no parking zone or in front of someone's driveway.
- In a few areas you'll find parking meters. Plug in the appropriate amount for the time you'll be parking.
- Never park near a market (*mercado*). Trucks will often double park in this area and lock you in for several hours or longer.
- In some areas kids or khaki-uniformed guards will watch over your car. Tip them a few pesos ahead of time to make sure your car doesn't have an "accident" while you're away. If you can speak a little Spanish, tell them you'll pay when you return.
- Occasionally, these guards will help you get into a tight parking place. Woodpecker tapping on the window means it's okay to back up, a loud rap means it's time to stop.
- In all cities park your car in a garage or attended parking lot at night. Many hotels offer garage parking to their guests, some hotels offer this at no charge. Consider this when choosing a hotel—it can save you many dollars a day.
- Cars left in the street at night tend to be vandalized even in smaller towns. If your hotel doesn't have a parking area, ask for a nearby garage. In some cities it's actually illegal to leave a car on the street overnight, so ask if you're planning to.
- Some garage attendants insist that you leave the keys with the car. In this situation you should never leave any luggage or valuables in the car.
- Mexican cops will remove the license plates of cars parked illegally. If this happens to you, hang around the car until the cop returns. You're in a fine (or bribe) situation.
- Some wily travelers put their license plate in the rear window or weld it to the car to avoid just such a situation.

Superhighways (*cuotas*)

- Most of the superhighways (*autopistas*) in Mexico are commonly referred to as toll roads (*cuotas*).
- If you're in a hurry, they may be worth the price. But secondary roads can get you to wherever you're going at no charge at all.
- Many travelers are avoiding toll roads altogether since prices for their use have risen dramatically in recent years.
- Tolls vary by the day you're traveling. Prices are highest on weekends and holidays.
- Tolls are related to the size of the vehicle. And you'll have to pay extra if you're pulling a trailer or hauling a boat. If you're driving an RV, you may be stunned by the fees.
- Always get information on toll roads before traveling. Outline alternative routes to avoid exorbitant costs.
- Note that Mexico is continually expanding the toll system. So make sure your information is current.
- Small tolls are requested or demanded along certain roads in Costa Rica. These are rarely very much, but it would be nice if the money would be used to improve the roads.

Road Signs

Road signs are relatively easy to understand. Travel clubs, automobile clubs, tourist offices, car rental agencies—all offer these charts free of charge.

Common Signs

aduana	*customs*	grava suelta	*loose gravel*
alto	*stop*	hombres trabajando	*men working*
atención	*caution*	maneja despacio	*drive slow*
aparcamiento	*parking lot*	—neblina	*—fog*
autopista	*superhighway*	no hay paso	*road closed*
bifurcación	*fork, junction*	obras	*road works*
camino en	*road repairs*	paso prohibido	*no entry*
reparación		pavimento	*paved road*
ceda el paso	*give right of way*	peatones	*pedestrians*
conserva su derecha	*keep right*	peligro	*danger*
cuidado	*caution*	playa	*beach*
curva peligrosa	*dangerous curve*	puente angosto	*narrow bridge*
despacio	*slow*	prohibido	*no passing*
desváción	*detour*	adelantamiento	
escuela	*school*	sentido único	*one way*
estacionamiento	*parking*	solo carril	*one-lane road*

Idiosyncrasies of Foreign Drivers

- Avoid contests and confrontations with drivers. You may find yourself in a macho confrontation. Tourists never win these.
- Railroads have stop signs. Mexicans never stop at these unless a train is coming. You shouldn't either, unless you want to be tail-ended by a Mexican who assumes you're smart enough to ignore the sign.
- Give priority to cars coming from the right. This is the easiest way to sort out traffic in any situation.
- No matter how fast you're going, someone will want to go faster, so look into your mirror before you start to pass.
- If you're following a truck, a left-turn signal means it's okay for you to pass, a right-turn signal means that there's a car coming, so don't pass. Or the signals mean the truck is turning left or right. No signal means you're on your own, the driver's asleep, or his signals are broken.
- If an oncoming car blinks lights at you, that means trouble ahead. Usually, uniformed trouble. If you're coming to a narrow bridge, it means, *Stop*, or I'll be the trouble ahead.
- **Belizean tip**: When you want to go left, the traffic from in front and behind both pose danger. If you have someone just behind you, pull over to the right. Let all cars pass, then make your left turn. Just putting on a left turn signal will not stop the car behind you from passing while you're making your turn.

Breakdowns

- Mexico has one of the finest emergency road services in the world. Green utility trucks, nicknamed *"Green Angels,"* cruise over 37,000 miles of highway twice each day from early morning to evening looking for stranded motorists on 230 designated routes. The Green Angels hotline in Mexico City is (905) 250-0123 or 250-0151. There is also a toll-free number with English-speaking operators: 91 800 90329. Use this number when in outlying areas.
- The Green Angels help get the car running again, providing service free of charge. You pay for parts, gas, and lubricants.
- In Mexico City you'll find *"Silver Angels"* offering comparable service. You can call them at 588-5100.
- When you have a breakdown, raise the hood of your car.
- If you don't want to wait for a Green Angel or if you're in an area where such a service is unlikely, ask a passing motorist to send help to you.
- Waving down a passing car is not always easy because of the suspicion of robbery and ripoffs. However, there is less suspicion of tourists.

- Under no circumstances should you leave a car unattended on the side of the road. Consider paying someone to watch the car if you want to find a mechanic.
- In Belize and Costa Rica no such service exists. Ask for help in Belize most people understand English. In Costa Rica ask for help (*ayuda*) and use sign language.

Repairs
- Local mechanics have learned how to repair just about anything with just about nothing.
- They'll often work on your car immediately realizing that you're a tourist in a tough situation.
- If you're traveling with adequate spare parts, this will often speed up the repair process. But how many of us do that?
- Mechanics will often improvise and use used parts to get your vehicle on the road again. If you insist on new parts, you may have to pay for these in advance. Ask for a receipt (*recibo*).
- Always get an estimate (*presupuesto*) in writing before allowing someone to work on your car.
- Stay with the car the whole time work is being done. You'll get the work done faster, the best mechanic in the shop will do it (often the owner), and you'll know what work has been done.
- Test drive the car. The person who repaired it will often come along. If you're not satisfied, let the mechanic know that something's still wrong. This process of repair is casual.
- If you're renting a car, call the main office before having repairs done. In some instances, they prefer to come and pick up the car rather than having it repaired. So, get an okay first.

Military Checkpoints
In Central America and Mexico you run into military checkpoints, set up to check on contraband, guns, and drugs. Or, in some cases to check papers and make sure that no one is coming in from troubled, neighboring countries. The soldiers are heavily armed.
- Soldiers wave most tourists through these checkpoints, although they'll check most buses very carefully.
- These checkpoints come up unexpectedly. You're required to stop. Sometimes, you'll have to wait in a long line of cars before you can continue on. This can get a little tiring if it's your third check in one day—just another of a dozen reasons why driving is much slower than you might expect.
- Never drive through one of these checkpoints without being waved through. You could get shot.

Train Travel

Few people know very much about train travel in Mexico. Many Mexican Government Tourist Offices more or less discourage it. Travel agents in the United States and Canada ignore it because there are no commissions and no practical way of making reservations. But vagabonds have already discovered that it's a cheap, reasonably comfortable, and a low-risk mode of transportation. In most other countries the train service is extremely limited and slowly dying out. For information on the famous Copper Canyon train ride in northern Mexico see p. 327.

Basic Vocabulary for the Train Station

arrival	*llegada*	railway	*ferrocarril, estación de trenes*
baggage	*equipaje*		
change here	*cambiar de tren*	second class	*segunda clase*
conductor	*revisor*	smoking car	*fumador*
connection	*correspondencia*	stop	*parada, apeadero*
departure	*salida*	ticket	*billete, boleto*
fare	*precio, importe*	ticket window	*taquilla de billetes*
first class	*primera clase*	timetable	*horario de trenes*
first class reserved	*primera especial*	train	*tren*
		train station	*estación ferrocarril*
no smoking	*no fumadores*	waiting room	*sala de espera*
pillow	*cojín*	What time is it?	*¿Que horas tiene?*
platform	*andén, parada*	Where is...?	*¿Donde está...?*

Information

If you plan to travel by train to or in Mexico, contact the following organization for information:

Mexico By Train
P.O. Box 2782
Laredo, TX 78044
Tel: (800) 321-1699
     (210) 725-3659

Buying Train Tickets

- Ask a Mexican to pronounce the name of your destination, so that the person in the ticket booth will understand you.
- Since popular trains may sell out, buy tickets far in advance.
- In some cases, you'll have to go to the train station and wait for

the ticket window to open. Tickets may only be sold an hour or so before the train actually arrives. You simply show up and hope there's space.
- Bring small bills to pay for tickets. You will not make a friend if you ask the ticket person to break a large bill.

What Tickets to Buy
- Don't skimp unless "local color" turns you on. Train tickets are so inexpensive that traveling in the best price category available is always advised.
- First class is not always the best class available. Ask for *primera especial*, which roughly translates to super first class. It is also called *primera numerada* and *turismo* on occasion.
- Baggage is watched over somewhat in the better classes. In second, or third, it's disregarded.
- Kids under five ride the rails for free, kids five to twelve pay half fare, and all the older kids pay full boat.
- If you get on without a ticket, you pay an extra 25 percent.

Provisions for Train Travel
- If you want to eat safely on many Mexican trains, bring your own food and drink. Bring a bottle of water, or a few cans of coke, or some juice per person.

In Train Stations
- Train schedules use the military (twenty-four hour) system of time; so that 12:00 means noon, and 24:00 means midnight. The system is designed to keep you from confusing 5:00 A.M. (5:00) with 5:00 P.M. (17:00).
- The bathrooms in many train stations are so foul that you'll prefer a hike into the woods. If you can stand the smell, be sure to bring toilet paper—there definitely won't be any.
- Some stations smell of urine, are covered with webs and strange hanging bugs, and can only be described as pits.
- Lights can and do go out at night in train stations. Always carry a flashlight with you and have it at hand!
- When the lights blink off, you can watch your bags by flicking on the beam. Keep your bags right by your side!
- Travel light. Traveling by train with lots of luggage can only be compared to frequent and unsuccessful attempts at suicide.

Getting on Trains
- Although trains make frequent stopovers, these can be brief. Don't dawdle! Get on the train and then find your seat.

Aboard Trains
- If you have an assigned seat, find and sit in it—unless it's already taken by someone with the same assigned seat. Be flexible, you'll probably find another available.
- Seats can swing around on many trains, but signs advise you not to do this. If you do, the conductor will undo it.

Sleeping on Trains
- Many trains have sleeping facilities for people willing to pay double or triple the cost of a first-class ticket. If you want to use this service, make a reservation when buying your ticket.
- The sleeper ticket is called a *primera dormitorio* and there is a surcharge according to how fancy your bedroom. You can sleep in a dormitory car (*dormitorios*) in either an upper (*cama alta*) or lower (*cama baja*) berth. The upper is cheaper.
- If you want your own room, ask for a *camarote* (private room), *camarote doble* (private room for two), *alcoba* (suite for two), *compartimiento* (suite for two), or *cabinette* (special suite for two). These are not available on many trains.

Getting off Trains
- Never get off a train until you've reached your final destination. You may be told that a train will be in a station for a specific time. Don't count on it. You never can be *sure* in Mexico.

Ferries

Useful Ferry Vocabulary

At what time?	*¿A qué hora?*	**next boat**	*la próxima lancha*
car ferries	*transbordadores de coches*	**passenger boat**	*lancha de pasajeros*
fare	*pasaje*	**pier**	*embarcadero*
ferry office	*oficina de transbordadores*	**toilet**	*baño*

General Tips on all Ferries
- Schedules change constantly, and there is no way for a guidebook to keep up with them.
- Local people are often as confused about ferry schedules as you are. Go to the ferry office to find out departure times and current costs.

- There is usually an inexpensive way to get to ferries, because locals use them regularly and don't have a lot of money to spare. If you want to cut costs, get to the ferry local-style.
- If you keep your luggage to a minimum, you can easily take advantage of public transportation to and from ferries.
- However, public transportation and ferry schedules do not always match, so that you may have a long wait.
- Bring food and water with you when taking any ferry, not only because you'll get hungry on board but because you may get hungry waiting.

Passenger and Car Ferries (*transbordadores de coches*)

BELIZE

Inquire locally about ferries to the main islands. Belize City is not safe. A number of ferries leave from here. Be wary. You can often find fishermen or local boats to get you just about anywhere along the coast. Often these boats aren't mentioned in travel guides.

COSTA RICA

The main ferries go from Puntarenas in the north to the Nicoya peninsula. One ferry carries passengers (to Paquera), the other cars (to Playa Naranjo). Farther north you can cross at Tempisque. This ferry carries both cars and passengers and leaves every hour or so. Use this ferry! There is also a ferry in the south from the port of Golfito to the Osa Peninsula (Puerto Jimenez). This may be your only way into that area during the rainy season. The road down the peninsula is often impassable during rainy periods. The road into Golfito is paved and good. There is also an intricate network of boats in the Tortuguero area of northeastern Costa Rica as well as many boats along the rivers. Fares are usually set for locals, negotiable for foreigners. Ask locally about fare prices. Motorboats are generally called either *lancha* or *panga*. In a few areas boats have no motors, and you're either paddled to your destination or drift down a river to your appointed rendezvous. It can be quite an experience.

MEXICO

The main ferries that concern travelers in Mexico are the ones connecting the Baja to the mainland and those heading to Isla Mujeres and Cozumel in the Yucatán. Reservations for car ferries can be very difficult to get in Mexico. Contact IMPA Mexican Information for help (see p. 27) for current information on ferries connecting the Baja with mainland Mexico.

Hitchhiking

Hitchhiking is not recommended. It is difficult to get a ride and potentially dangerous. Since public transportation is so cheap, why bother with hitchhiking? If you disregard this advice, here are a few tips.

Getting Rides

- Go to campgrounds and RV parks and ask whether anyone will soon be traveling in your direction. This is getting a ride without hitting the road.
- Wherever you see trucks, you may be able to pick up a ride (*un ride* or *aventon*). Women are not legally allowed on trucks, so bear this in mind if a driver wants to drop you and your lady off before a checkpoint or town.
- You may be able to pick up a ride at any Pemex station. Occasionally, it helps if you'll offer to pay for part of the gas.
- Carry all documents, money, and valuables on your person. Other important odds and ends should be in a little day bag which you take with you at all times—even to the bathroom.
- It's easiest getting rides in the early morning.
- Keep your gear light.
- Stay clean—this will help you get a ride, especially if you're asking tourists for help.
- Keep knives out of sight.
- Go through large towns using the public transportation system. It's incredibly cheap.

Motorcycling

Carrying a cycle or moped for excursions and off-road travel makes sense, but not as your only means of travel. You don't see very many bikes in Central America and Mexico and for good reason. Stick to public transportation.

Travel Within Cities

This chapter covers the basic information on getting around cities by walking or public transportation. By getting around the way the local residents do, you'll save a great deal of money.

Walking

Many times the simplest and fastest way to get around a small town or city is by walking combined with public transportation.

Some Walking Tips

- Wear extremely comfortable shoes, ones with good soles—the kind that grip surfaces and don't slide easily on wet pavement.
- Have a map with you. Have someone explain the way streets are laid out. Avenues (*avenidas*), neighborhoods (*barrios*), and streets (*calles*) may be laid out in what seems to be a strange pattern. Numbers may be confusing. The entire system may be completely different from what you're used to as in San José, Costa Rica. It only takes a few minutes to ask.
- Have someone pinpoint the exact location of the areas, museums, hotels, or whatever you want to visit.
- Make sure these are open before walking to them.
- In some instances building numbers are almost useless. As in Japan, it may be better to know where something is located in relation to a certain large building or well-known landmark.
- In some instances locations will be related to a landmark that is long gone. Get the location pinpointed on your map.
- Ask whether there are any areas where it's unsafe or unwise to walk. The locals will immediately tell you.
- Don't walk at night, unless you're told it's completely safe.
- Watch carefully for open holes in the street, large cracks, pipes sticking out, and so on.
- Never assume drivers will stop for signs or give you right of way. You may just be a nuisance. Your life is not highly valued.
- A few cities (not many) actually promote walking tours and give out maps for them. Ask about these.

All About Buses and Trams

Whenever possible, use buses or trams to keep costs down. Yes, they are crowded. They can be a little on the slow side, but they are incredibly inexpensive. They can also get you just about anywhere.

Bus Travel Within A City

Following are a few basic questions to get you off to the right start. Find someone who speaks English well either in the local tourist office or at the front desk of a hotel. If you're not staying at the hotel, tip accordingly to the amount of time and help given.

What is the best way to get from A to B?
What is the least expensive way?
Do you have a map of the area?
Where do you get tickets? How much are they?
How do I get on the bus, tram, or subway?
Should I know anything about street addresses?

Helpful Phrases for Bus Travel

bus	autobús, camión	south	sur
bus station	terminal, estación de autobuses	stop (bus stop)	parada
		stop (stop the bus!)	¡baja!
bus stop	parada	ticket	boleto, billete, ficha
departures	salidas	ticket window	caja, taquilla
destination	destino	to	a
driver	chofer	toilets	sanitaríos
east	este, oriente	waiting room	sala de espera
fare	precio	west	oeste, poniente
hour	hora	What is the number of the bus?	¿Cuál es el número del autobús?
How much is a ticket to...?	¿Cuánto cuesta un boleto a...?		
get in	sube	What time does the bus leave?	A qué hora sale ¿ el autobús?
north	norte	Where does this bus go?	¿Dónde va este autobús?
passenger	pasajero		
route	ruta		
seat	asiento		

- As you get on the bus, state your destination. The bus driver will say "sí" or "no."
- Have small change to pay for the fare.
- When you want to get off, shout "¡Baja!" ("Stop!") if you're stuck in the crowd. Don't be timid.

All About Taxis

Although you can use other forms of transportation for a fraction of the cost of taxis, the latter represent good value. Few taxis have seat belts, and in some areas meters do not exist.

Shared Cabs (*colectivos*) (see p. 140)

Jitney Cabs
Cabs which follow certain routes dropping off and taking on passengers as they go are common in Guatemala City (Guatemala) and Mexico City (Mexico). In Guatemala they're called *ruleteros* while in Mexico they're known locally as *peseros*. Ask about these since they are less expensive than regular cabs.

Regular Cabs (see p. 141)
- Before getting into a taxi, agree on the appropriate fare. Often by quoting the amount in hard currency (dollars), you'll get a better deal.
- You need to be able to say only two things: your destination and "*Cuánto cuesta?*" The latter means "How much does it cost?" If you can't understand each other, use pen and paper.
- In a few towns you run into a ripoff situation where all the drivers refuse to quote you a fair price. Keep trying different taxis until one caves in.
- Few taxis are metered. Some barely run. A few drivers may pull into a gas station and ask for money upfront. I kid you not.
- Payment should be exactly what you agreed upon. Most drivers do not try to cheat you once you've agreed upon a price, but a few will. Don't let the driver intimidate you into paying more—a good reason to get all prices in writing.
- If you alter your agreement by having the driver stop for an errand or shopping, by having him drive to a new or added location, or by making any change at all, then the driver has every right to charge you more than the negotiated price. So each time you ask for a change, discuss the *new* price.

Taxis with Meters (*taxímetro*)
- In most areas, taxis do not have meters (*marías*). In Mexico City most do, as well as an A on the license plate.
- If a taxi has a meter, it must be used to determine fares.
- Make sure that the meter has been turned back when you get into the cab. Just point to the flag and say *bandera* to let the cab driver know that it has to be turned back.

Other Tips on Taxis
- Only use official taxis in Mexico City. The odds of getting ripped off in unlicensed taxis are extremely high. Many of these unlicensed taxis seduce travelers with low prices and then really take them for a ride—watch it!

- Women traveling alone should always share a ride. Being alone in a taxi puts you into a vulnerable position.
- Taxis are not taking advantage of you in a few areas when they add a surcharge at night. Inquire locally about night fares.
- Be wary of asking a hotel to call you a cab, especially in a more expensive hotel. Many of these are served by special cabs—ones that offer extra comfort (or no extra comfort) at an extra price. Insist on getting an ordinary cab.
- Although some travel guides tell you not to use cab drivers as sources of hotel information, I've found drivers to be helpful. If you'll learn basic hotel vocabulary (p. 142), you can get the driver to take you to the kind of hotel that fits your style of travel and budget. Be explicit about what you want to pay.
- Some tours give vouchers for transportation from the airport to the hotel. Find out how to use the vouchers and whether you'll be reimbursed if they're not accepted.
- Taxis, including *colectivos*, can be very difficult to find in peak holiday periods including Christmas, New Year, and Easter.
- Taxis can be extremely difficult to get in rainy weather or late at night.

Local Tours

Besides getting you to some local sights for a reasonable price, consider the other advantages of local tours:

- Use them as an inexpensive way to get to another town without the fuss of public transportation.
- Tours offer a good way of meeting other people, who may be willing to join up with you as travel partners.
- City tours sometimes pass by the local airport. Take the tour at the appropriate time and ask to be left off near the airport. You get both the tour and ride to the airport for one price.

Public Transportation in Mexico City

Getting around Mexico City is an art, but one well worth learning. You can get everywhere in this huge town for very little.

About Addresses

- Mexico City is divided into 220 neighborhoods called *colonias*. In each of these areas you may have a street of the same name, a Calle Juarez, for example. It's important to know neighborhoods as well as individual addresses.
- The *same* street or avenue may have three or four different names. Get a cross street for each address.

- In some areas, building numbers don't run consecutively. Again, get a cross street for reference.

The Metro
The metro is the least expensive way to get around in Mexico City.

Basic Metro Vocabulary

---

andenes	*platforms*	**no pase**	*do not enter*
boleto	*ticket*	**salida**	*exit*
dirección	*direction*	**taquilla (caja)**	*ticket booth*
entrada	*entrance*	**viaje**	*trip*

- The subway (*metro*) is an incredible system now covering much of Mexico City. It is inexpensive, immaculate, quick, and safe—well-lit and heavily policed. An absolute gem.
- You pay for one ticket, no matter how far you travel and no matter how many transfers you have to make.
- Ticket offices in each station sell tickets at all hours.
- Pay for the tickets with small change—do not use large bills.
- Buy five (*cinco*) tickets at a time for a reduced price.
- You can get to most major tourist sights using the metro (occasionally combining it with other public transportation).
- Signs will lead you to the correct platform.
- Follow the flow in peak hours. Mexicans use any available space, not paying attention to right or left in aisles or stairs.
- Use escalators whenever you can. If you don't, you may get exhausted from the high altitude.
- Follow the Mexicans through the gates. Simply insert the ticket into the slot and give it a light push. The machine will suck it in, and you can then push through the turnstyle.
- The front cars usually have fewer people.
- When getting on the subway, don't be timid, shove and push the way the Mexicans do. The strange sound you hear signals closing doors—and they slam shut!
- Get away from the doors for more breathing room.
- But try to get close to the door as your final station approaches.
- Normally, you'll get out the right side of the car.
- In a few stations, you get out the left side. If you look at the route map in the subway car, you'll see these words in red under such stations: "*en estas estaciones la salida es a la izquierda*" ("in these stations the exit is to the left").

- If people are blocking your way, give a shove. Say, "*Con permiso,*" and the Mexicans will move for you.
- Rush hours are from 8 A.M. to 10 A.M. in the morning, and from 5 P.M. to 7 P.M. in the evening.
- If you're claustrophobic, avoid the rush hours.
- During the rush hour certain cars are reserved for women and children only.
- Crowds draw pickpockets, so you have to be wary.
- Technically, no backpacks or luggage is allowed in the metro. In reality, you can use the metro with a reasonable amount of luggage or a small backpack if you avoid the rush-hour traffic.
- To use the metro efficiently, get a color-coded subway map which outlines all routes and stops.
- The map is available from information booths in the subway stations. Look for a booth labeled with a black "i" in a yellow circle. These booths are sometimes closed on weekends.
- The map is also available in some hotels, in free tourist publications, and from tourist information offices.
- Find out what metro stop is nearest your destination. You can get close to most hotels; the bus terminals, train station, and airport; to many of the finest and favorite tourist sights; and to most of the major shopping districts and department stores.
- In some cases, you'll have to combine the metro with bus, tram, pesero, or taxi rides, to get to where you're going.
- Each line has its own color. The direction the subway is going is usually the last station on the line. In some cases, it's the second-to-the-last station, which can be confusing the first time you use the system, because both stations may be used to designate one line. Example: Line 1 may be called *Observatoria* (end of the line) or *Tacubaya* (station next to the end). It's the same line heading in the same direction.
- To get to your destination you'll often have to make a connection from one line to another. Connections are made through gates marked *correspondencia.* Some of these involve quite long walks, so take a route with the fewest connections, even if it seems longer on the map!
- Maps are posted in every car. Each station has its own symbol for quick reference and for those who can't read.
- By having your route planned from the start, you'll make fewer mistakes.
- Coming out of the subway to the street is often where you get disoriented. A small compass can help you a great deal (even though it sounds funny) and so can a good street map.

Jitney Cabs (*peseros*)

- Jitney cabs, cars, or combis, are *colectivos* which zip along desig-nated routes with up to eleven passengers or more.
- These are lime green or white with green stripes.
- Wave them down to get in. If they're full, they won't stop. Some drivers hold their hands up to indicate open space.
- Some jitneys have automatic doors, and the driver will give you a dirty look if you try to shut them. Others don't and the driver will give you a dirty look if you don't try to shut them.
- Know how to pronounce correctly the name of your destination. If the driver gives you a quizzical look, you flunked, go back to school. If the driver shakes his head or wags his finger, get in a different jitney (he may indicate which one), and if the driver nods and waves you in, you're heading home.
- The amount you pay is related to the distance you go. Pay when you get off. State the place where you got on so that the driver knows how much to charge.

Regular Taxi

- The regular taxi is more expensive than the metro, buses, and jit-ney cabs, but fares are still quite reasonable.
- In Mexico City the fares on the meter do not represent pesos but a number which corresponds to a fare quoted on a price sched-ule (*lista*). The meter ticks for distance and time.
- You have every right to ask to see the fare schedule to make sure that the quoted fare really does match the number of units regis-tered on the meter.
- If you have any problem with a cab, write down the cab number and license plate. Have someone who speaks Spanish convey the complaint to the following number (588-6526). Lost items? Call 571-3600, ext. 14 or 15.

Sitio Taxi

- Cab stands are listed in the yellow pages under *Sitio*.
- They always charge more than regular cabs, even if they're hailed in the street. *Sitio* is written on the sides of these.
- You can call them to your hotel, but you'll pay for the service.
- Always establish a price immediately for any trip. You may end up relying on regular taxis after a bad experience with a *sitio*.

Turismo Taxi

- Turismo cabs sit outside hotels like salmon-colored, sleeping sharks.

- The drivers usually stand next to the revolving door with a solicitous grin and a constant "*taxi, señor*" on their lips.
- The meters in these cabs are usually covered with a black hood. Don't let the wake be yours! These cabs charge exorbitant rates. Skip them and hail a regular cab in the street.

Getting from Mexico City to the Airport

- If you have little or no baggage, backtrack to the airport using the metro. Go to the *terminal aérea* metro stop, not the *aeropuerto* stop (the latter doesn't get you all the way to the terminal).
- If you prefer to take a cab, ask your hotel to get a *colectivo* for you. Make sure you get the price clearly understood from the hotel employee. When the cab arrives, verify the price.
- These *colectivo* cabs don't always show up as scheduled. You may end up hailing a regular cab in the street.

Staying Healthy Once Abroad

This chapter covers the basics on health care abroad plus detailed information on how to prevent or cure common health problems once in Central America or Mexico.

Basic Health Vocabulary

chest pain	*dolor de pecho*	**I am sick.**	*Estoy enfermo.*
dentist	*dentista*	**I need a doctor.**	*Necessito un*
doctor	*doctor*		*doctor.*
fever	*fieble*	**pain**	*dolor*
headache	*dolor de cabeza*	**pharmacy**	*farmacia*
hospital	*hospital*		

Health Care Abroad

Hospitals generally can't provide quality care. Local blood supplies are definitely not safe. However, doctors abroad often recognize common health problems and tropical diseases quickly because they have seen so many cases. Health care costs, including the price of drugs, is usually reasonable.

Hospitals

Hospitals in major cities are generally more reliable than those in rural areas. If possible, get to one of these. When in doubt, call the nearest embassy for information on where they send their staff in emergencies. In most instances, you're better off returning home for health care if blood transfusions or serious operations are involved— even to the point of being airlifted out (see p. 24). The opposite may be true for tropical diseases.

Symptoms to Watch Out For

Go to a doctor during or after a trip if you have any of the following symptoms: bites which turn color or won't heal, chills, coughing (chronic), diarrhea that lasts over a week or is recurring, diarrhea with blood or mucus, excessive gas, fatigue, fever, headaches, itching, pain, rash, sweats, vomiting, welts or spots on your skin, or undue weight loss. Important tip: Tropical diseases may take weeks, months, and even years to appear. Keep a record of all countries you visit in case symptoms occur at a later date. Again, see a doctor specializing in tropical medicine.

- If you need a doctor for a minor illness, you can trust someone in your hotel to come up with a name.
- If you feel that language will be a barrier and you're in a larger city, call the U.S. or Canadian consulate and ask for the name of an English-speaking doctor.
- If you belong to one of the organizations mentioned earlier (p. 23), use one of their doctors if available.
- Most doctors will come to your hotel if you request or need it.
- Doctors charge relatively low fees. So do most laboratories.
- Don't hesitate to call your home-town tropical disease specialist or travel clinic if you're concerned about the diagnosis or proposed treatment. The long-distance charge is worth your peace of mind, and a second opinion can't hurt.
- Always get the diagnosis and treatment plan in writing.
- Get a written receipt for all charges so that you can be reimbursed by your insurance company when you get home.

Pharmacies (*farmacias*)

Foreign pharmacies carry a wide assortment of drugs. Many of these require prescriptions. A number of drugs are available in Central America and Mexico over-the-counter which would normally require a prescription at home. A few newer medications may not be available, but effective alternatives usually are. If you buy a controlled substance abroad, always get a doctor's prescription if you intend to bring it back into Canada or the United States. Some controlled substances are sold over-the-counter. Almost all drugs are sold at a fraction of the cost you pay at home.

- The maximum legal price is listed on containers.
- When filling a prescription (*receta*), make sure that you get the drug prescribed.
- Pharmacists give shots in some countries. If you need an antibiotic, you can get it here, but buy a new syringe (one sealed in paper).
- Late-night pharmacies are listed in the yellow pages of the phone book as *farmacias—servicio de 24 horas, farmacias de turno, farmacia de la guardia*, or *farmacia de la vigilancia*.
- A number of drugs sold abroad are considered dangerous by the FDA. One of the most common is entero-vioform for traveler's diarrhea. This can cause blindness.

Toilets (*servicios sanitariós* or *baños*)

- Toilets in restaurants or hotels of rural or remote areas are often extremely dirty. Toilet paper is frequently absent.
- Carry your own toilet paper.
- If you take toilet paper from a hotel, just take a little. Paper is expensive, and hotels are angry about its theft.
- Note that lighting a match often reduces the foul odor in toilets.
- Where toilet paper does exist, there is often a basket to the side of the toilet where you are supposed to put used paper.
- Some travelers prefer to go to the bathroom outdoors in remote areas.
- In major cities go to finer hotels and ask for the toilet. Or, go to a better restaurant.
- Many toilets are communal. *Caballeros* means men, *damas* or *señoras* means women.

Alcohol

Alcohol interferes with many medications. Alcohol does not kill germs. It is also a problem at higher altitudes where its effect is much greater than at lower ones. It increases fatigue on plane trips. View it as a drug, often one which is contraindicated.

General Health Problems

Certain health problems crop up frequently abroad.

AIDS

AIDS (SIDA in Spanish) is a serious problem in developing countries.
- To be totally safe, refrain from sex altogether.
- If sexually active, practice safe sex using latex condoms purchased in the United States.
- Avoid needles. If this is not possible, buy wrapped needles at a pharmacy for vaccinations or transfusions.
- Local blood supplies in Central America and Mexico are not safe. In a life-threatening situation, you'll just have to take the gamble.
- If a transfusion is needed and if you have time, get air lifted to Canada or the United States.
- Never have acupuncture.
- Have dental work done before going abroad.
- Tattooing is absolutely out of the question.
- So is allowing a barber to shave you with a blade.

Altitude Sickness

In Mexico City and other cities in higher altitudes you may experience loss of appetite, nausea, mental confusion, fatigue, and shortness of breath—that's altitude sickness.

- The simple solution is to go to a place at a lower altitude.
- Diamox, a medication, can prevent most symptoms if taken a day or two before arrival.
- Slow down. Your body needs time to adjust.
- Drink lots of liquid to counteract dehydration, which causes severe headaches.
- Eat less at noon, and mostly carbohydrates.
- Sleep more. Nap after a tiring trip.
- If climbing volcanoes or mountains, ascend slowly. Rest for one day after each ascent of 1,000 feet.

Amoebic Dysentery

This is caused by tiny living organismas called amoebas (*amibas*). One of the most dangerous is *Entamoeba histolytica*. Symptoms are severe diarrhea containing blood and mucus. Follow the standard tips given under the diarrhea section. There are a number of drugs which will kill amoeba. There is another form of dysentery with symptoms of high fever, headache, vomiting, and stomach pains. Since all forms of dysentery are serious, get to a doctor immediately.

Ants

Ants, especially the variety *Paraponera clavata*, are nothing to play around with. Their sting can last for days. These ants make lots of noise and emit a foul odor warning you to keep away. Some people are highly allergic to ant bites. In such a case get that person to a doctor immediately.

Anxiety

Some travelers feel out of their element abroad and experience anxiety or stress.

- Plan ahead. Avoid any tight scheduling.
- Slow down the pace, don't feel compulsive about tours and sightseeing, get plenty of rest, and eat well.
- Natural tranquilizers are beer, the fruit *zapote*, and herbal teas.
- Exercise relieves stress. It's hard to be uptight after two hours of snorkeling in the Caribbean or walking in a rain forest.
- Practice deep breathing (see **Headaches**).

Bed Bugs

In developing countries bed bugs are found in cheaper hotels. They do carry disease.

- Wear insect repellant at night.
- If you can stand the smell and aren't allergic to it, use a spray to kill insects.
- No spray? Keep a light on. Bed bugs don't like to come out into light. Wear a mask to shut out light.

Bee Stings

Any person who has ever had an allergic reaction to a bee sting, should carry along antihistamines or an appropriate kit such as EpiPen (requires a doctor's prescription). Get someone to a doctor if they show signs of severe swelling, difficulty breathing, or a rash. Approximately one in twenty people is allergic, about one in a hundred will die from bee stings. For immediate relief from stings use ammonia and an ice pack. If a stinger is in the skin, do not pull it out with a tweezers. Gently scrape it out with the side of a knife blade to avoid squeezing poison still in the stinger into the skin. Killer bees have made their way into Central America and are extremely dangerous in that many bees can sting you at one time. When running from bees, run in zigzag patterns. Note too that an allergic reaction can show up in a person who has never had one before.

Bleeding

If you're bleeding internally, get to a doctor *immediately*. Apply pressure to any external bleeding until it stops—it can take time.

Blisters

Nothing can ruin sightseeing or hiking faster than a blister.

- Wear comfortable walking shoes or boots.
- The minute you feel a blister forming—stop! Cover the tender spot with a Band-Aid or some Mole skin.
- Clean blisters with soap and sterile water. Apply alcohol. Cover with a Band-Aid.

Broken Bones

A rough surf can do a lot of damage in seconds. Never get in front of a boat coming into a beach. Be careful climbing.

- Don't try to set a broken bone. Immobilize the area as best you can. Get the person to a doctor.
- Anyone involved in potentially dangerous outdoor situations should have first-aid training. Go with competent guides with professional, medical training. Ask about their qualifications in advance.

Burns
Someone in a group of campers always manages to get a burn.
- Clean the area with soap and sterile water.
- If ice is available, apply it to the burn.
- Rub vitamin E oil or cream on the burn.
- Cover it with a sterile bandage.
- Drink lots of liquids.
- If you have severe burns, get to a doctor immediately.

Cactus Spines
Watch where you sit and don't walk around in bare feet.
- If you have a tweezer, you may be able to remove some cactus spines. Don't count on it.
- A better method is to cover the area with melted wax (try not to burn yourself doing this). Let the wax harden and then pull it off—the spines will come with it.

Chagas' Disease
High fever is the most common symptom of this desease. Others include convulsions, swollen lymph nodes, stiff neck, and vomiting. A bite which swells, turns color, and gets hard is another warning sign. Note, however, that the disease may not have any symptoms at all. The disease is caused by vampire-like biting insects called assassin or kissing bugs (*vinchugas*), which infect the blood with a parasitic protozoa (*Trypanosoma cruzi*). Bugs carrying this disease are most commonly found in dilapidated buildings, mud dwellings, thatched huts, and palm fronds. Protect yourself with netting and use insect repellants. Don't delay getting medical help since the disease is most easily cured in its early stages.

Cholera
Cholera is always a potential problem because of poor sanitary conditions.
- Never eat raw shellfish or raw fish anywhere—never. This includes *ceviche* (raw seafood bits soaked in lime).
- Follow tips on preventing diarrhea (p. 226).

Ciguatera (fish poisoning)
Fish poisoning is caused by a toxin (*ciguatoxin*) in reef plankton and results in a tingling in the mouth, nausea, and diarrhea. It can also cause persistant neurological problems. Fish to avoid are barracuda (usually ones over 2 feet), jacks, moray eels, parrot fish, and snappers. In Central America and Mexico barracuda are routinely sold and eaten. The problem is sporadic, but it does exist and is worth noting.

Coconuts

Watch for coconut bombs! Don't walk, stand, camp, or park your car under coconut palm trees. This is not a joke.

Colds

Popular cold remedies include honey and lime juice, hot tea with lemon, warm salt water, garlic, chicken soup, and large doses of Vitamin C. All work as well as common cold medications.

Constipation

Studies indicate that constipation is a problem with as many as 50 percent of travelers. Women suffer from it more often than men.

- If you're prone to constipation, bring medication with you.
- Drinking lots of mineral water is highly recommended. The more water you drink, the less likely you'll get constipated.
- Don't delay going to the bathroom. While traveling this is sometimes hard to do. Go as soon as possible.
- Eat regularly. Carry snacks if necessary.
- Eat foods containing lots of fiber. Beans, fruits, nuts, and vegetables all contain lots of fiber and are readily available.
- Walk frequently. Of course, ask whether an area is safe or not before venturing out.
- Locals insist that drinking coconut milk or eating fresh coconut acts as a natural laxative.

Coral

Keep your hands off all coral—for two reasons. Some coral is highly toxic, and every time you touch coral you kill it.

- If you do get stung accidentally, clean the area with warm salt water and apply cortisone cream.

Cramps—Muscle and Menstrual

- Strenuous activity can easily bring on muscle cramps. Take high concentrations of Vitamin E. The older you are, the more effective this is.
- Drinking quinine (tonic water) may be helpful.
- Once you have cramps, the best solution is usually a steaming hot bath. Let muscles rest to work out the lactic acid.
- To cut down cramps associated with menstruation reduce your salt intake for one week before your period. Carry medication for this problem. If you forget, take an aspirin-free pain reliever.

Cuts (see Bleeding and Wounds)

Wear sandals or old tennis shoes to avoid cuts and abrasions—even on beaches or in the water. If using a machete or filet knife, be extremely careful.

Dehydration (see Cholera and Diarrhea)

In tropical climates you lose water quickly. The signs of dehydration are not sweating when you should, infrequent urination, a dry tongue, or extremely dark (deep yellow) urine. Dehydration is a common side effect of diarrhea. Dehydration is dangerous for everyone, but especially so with young children. Drink lots of fluids regularly (every 5 minutes), even if you aren't thirsty. Add salt to all fluids. Drink so much fluid that you have to urinate. Keep drinking until your urine is pale. No matter where you are, carry water or soft drinks with you as a safety precaution against dehydration.

Dengue Fever

Dengue fever is a flu-like illness causing high fever and aches in your joints. The virus is carried by a mosquito which normally comes out at dawn and dusk. Prevent the disease by avoiding mosquito bites. If you do get dengue fever, drink lots of liquids, take acetaminophen (not aspirin), and rest. Important: A few people develop hemorrhagic dengue about one year after having dengue fever. Signs of this disease are high fever, rapid pulse, measle-like spots, and vomiting blood. Go immediately to a doctor specializing in tropical medicine, since this can be fatal if not treated immediately.

Diarrhea (see Dehydration)

Diarrhea is not a disease, but a symptom of an underlying problem. In most instances, a bacterial infection. In some cases overeating, too much drinking, stress, dietary changes, loss of sleep, or fatigue may be the cause. Occasionally, viral infections occur. Diarrhea is sometimes a side effect of chloroquine phosphate, an anti-malarial medication. It can also indicate a much more serious underlying illness if it persists for a long period of time.

How To Prevent Diarrhea—The Standard Advice

- Take Pepto-Bismol (bismuth subsalicylate) for short trips.
- About 15 percent of currency carries germs. Wash your hands frequently. And, dry them with clean paper.
- Avoid raw or undercooked fish.
- Avoid *all raw shellfish*, *ceviche* (raw seafood salad in lime), and cold fish.
- The advice regarding raw fish and shellfish is especially important for anyone suffering from diabetes, gastrointestinal problems, immune disorders, and any liver disease.

- Never eat raw or undercooked meat. Ask for your meat well-done to kill bacteria and parasitic worms.
- Avoid food sold from street stands.
- Avoid cold foods that were once hot—leftovers, snacks, anything. In effect, eat cold foods cold, hot foods hot.
- Be suspicious of mayonnaise and egg-based custards unless they're refrigerated (they rarely are).
- Avoid sauces and condiments left out on the table.
- Many foods are very spicy, and these can cause diarrhea.
- Drink only purified or bottled water (*agua mineral*)—preferably carbonated (*agua mineral con gaz* or *soda*). Or, buy a soft drink—they're sold just about everywhere at low prices. Use a straw (*pajilla*) since bottles are frequently wet or dirty.
- Never drink water from lakes or streams, even if the water is extremely cold.
- Tap water may or may not be safe.
- Ice is often fine in better resorts. If you don't want ice, ask for drinks *sin hielo*.
- Coffee often causes diarrhea. Switch to tea.
- Alcohol lowers your resistance to infection. It actually promotes the growth of harmful bacteria. Furthermore, it interferes with the effectiveness of many medications.
- Avoid all milk or milk products unless they've been pasteurized. Yogurt is usually safe and may actually help prevent diarrhea. It can kill E-coli bacteria, one source of traveler's diarrhea.
- Don't eat food cooked or served in pottery unless you're certain it's lead-free. Watch out especially for pottery glazed green.
- *Carry food and water with you wherever you go.* This way when you're thirsty or hungry, you won't be forced to eat or drink whatever's handy at the time. Best snacks are those which are wrapped, like packets of peanuts, granola bars, raisins, candies, dried fruit, chocolate bars, and so on.
- Sewage runs directly into the sea in some resort areas. This is a problem rarely pointed out by hotels. In fact, many go to great lengths to avoid discussing it.
- After a storm stay out of the water until it is completely clear. You can be sure the water contains high degrees of *E-coli.*
- Pools can be a source of infection if improperly chlorinated. If you can't smell chlorine, stay out of pools.
- Purify all fresh vegetables and fruits by soaking them in appropriate solutions (information follows). The fact that you can peel them (the usual advice) is totally meaningless. You can contaminate what you eat in the peeling process.

My reaction to the standard advice

- The advice is excellent, because it's basically true. However, no matter how many precautions you take, you can still get sick.
- It only takes one fly on one piece of food to undo all the precautions that you've so religiously taken not to get sick.
- Some bugs causing diarrhea are airborne. You can't do a thing about these.
- Warnings to eat in upscale restaurants or hotels doesn't solve the problem. It simply weighs the scales in your favor. You can get just as sick in these as from fly-covered food handed to you from a street vendor.
- Finally, while most doctors tell you not to premedicate for a trip abroad, many of them ignore their own advice. If you're traveling for only one week, I'd consider taking a broad-spectrum antibiotic as a preventative despite advice against it. Yes, it does kill helpful bacteria in your system and will not prevent all forms of diarrhea, but it does prevent many. And, that's why doctors who recommend one thing for their patients, do another for themselves.
- You're either going to get sick or you're not. Follow common sense, yes; hope mostly that God is looking over your shoulder.

Purifying Water, Fruits, and Vegetables

- Water purification straws are now available. Read labels carefully and use them only for the amount of water indicated.
- Some people carry water purification systems. Purifiers are made by First Need, Katadyn, and PUR. Some of these claim to have filtration systems so refined that they can filter out even the smallest microorganisms. Note that these kits are somewhat bulky and have been known to get clogged. They will not necessarily destroy all viruses.
- The safest way to purify water is to boil it for 30 minutes at sea level, for 45 minutes at higher altitudes. Boiling water kills giardia. Chemical purification does not. Note that some filtering systems may. Read the package carefully. Boiling does not get rid of any chemical pollution.
- Water purification tablets (*pastillas para purificar agua*) will kill most bacteria if left to soak for 30 minutes. They're very expensive, and it takes many of them to purify each quart of water. Use them only in emergencies. Some types break down in time or in high heat. Read labels carefully.
- Liquid bleach (*blanqueador*) will kill most bacteria. If it's a 1 percent solution, add ten drops to each quart of water. If it's a 4 to 6

percent solution, add two to four drops per quart. Let the chlorine do its work for thirty minutes. If water is especially cloudy or dirty, you may want to add a little more. Iodine (*yodo*) can be substituted for bleach in this process. Add 5 to 10 drops of a 2 percent solution of Iodine per quart of water and let stand for three hours. Use the smaller amount for clear water, the larger for cloudy. Too much iodine is not good for you, but you need enough to kill whatever bacteria are present. Note that these methods do not kill giardia.

- To kill bacteria on fruits and vegetables, soak them in the above-mentioned chlorine or iodine solutions for 30 minutes.

How To Treat Diarrhea

- If diarrhea is accompanied by high fever, chills, severe dehydration, blood or mucus in the stool, then see a doctor immediately. If you can't get to a doctor quickly, take antibiotics. Get to a doctor as soon as you can.
- Note that many antibiotics can make you sun sensitive or sun reactive (you get a rash). Ask about this ahead of time.
- If you have none of the above symptoms but have to travel immediately (as on a bus without a toilet), take something like Imodium (preferred) or Lomotil.
- As soon as you can, stop taking these. Never take them for more than 3 days.
- Pepto-Bismol is milder and good for minor infections. This medication frequently causes stools to be black. In some people, it causes ringing ears (*tinnitus*). Stop using the medication in this case. Aspirin does the same thing for a few people.
- If diarrhea keeps coming back, go to a local doctor. If you know ahead of time that getting to a doctor will be difficult, carry something like Cipro with you. This is one of the newer and more effective antibiotics. Unfortunately, it's very expensive. The price is worth it when you're isolated and on a long trip. However, other antibiotics are available and quite effective if the cost seems unreasonable. Note that Cipro cannot be taken with antacids.
- The main danger of diarrhea is dehydration. So here's a diarrhea potion: In one glass put 8 ounces of fruit juice, 1/2 teaspoon of sugar (or honey), and a pinch of salt. Fill another glass with 8 ounces of purified or carbonated water and 1/4 teaspoon of baking soda. Alternate swallows from each glass until both glasses are empty.
- Or pour salt and soda into a bottle of coke and drink that.
- Also highly recommended is chicken broth with lots of salt.

- *Warning*: Diarrhea can make anti-malaria drugs, oral contraceptives, and some cardiovascular medications less effective. Use a physical contraceptive if you've got diarrhea.

Diptheria (see Tetanus)

Dogs

Dogs are lovable, but they cause health problems.
- All dog bites should be taken extremely seriously. You may have to get rabies shots.
- Never pat dogs. Their fur often contains cysts for parasitic worms. These get on your hands and begin to burrow into your skin. So keep your kids away from dogs.
- Wear tennis shoes or sandals on all beaches because dog feces also contain cysts for parasitic worms.

Ear Problems

- If your ears begin to hurt during the landing of a plane, yawn.
- You can also pop your ears by holding your nose and blowing gently. This is what scuba divers do to equalize pressure.
- If you'll be flying and have a stuffy head, use a decongestant before landing.
- Babies should be given a bottle to suck on during a landing. The bottle should contain water, not milk.
- If you can't get water out after a swim, have someone pour warm (not hot) water into the ear. Let it sit there for a minute and then roll over.
- Bug in your ear? Use a flashlight to draw it out.

Exhaustion

Travel may catch you off balance. Exhaustion can lead to more serious health problems. Listen to your body, which speaks in sign language. It will always tell you what pace to keep.
- If you're traveling with people who want to move at a faster pace, split up and plan to meet them at a later date.
- If you're caught on a whirlwind tour, skip part of it. Don't worry about missing something you've paid for—a trip is for fun.
- Match your style of travel to your energy level. If you don't feel well, pamper yourself with a nicer hotel or more comfortable transportation. Consider making your trip short but sweet.

Eye (contacts)

- Bring spare contacts with you. Bring comfort drops, daily cleaner, disinfecting solution, saline solution, weekly cleaner, and wetting-

soaking solutions if needed for your type of lenses.
- Remove contacts on all flights. Humidity is extremely low.
- Alcohol and antihistamines can also cause problems.
- Always plug a sink if you remove lenses there.
- Use only pure water to clean lenses.
- Always clean lenses after swimming.

Eye (Something in it)
Nothing is more frustrating than getting something in your eye and being unable to get it out. Here's the secret:
- Pull your upper eyelid out and down as far as you can. Let go. The irritant will often come off on the first try.
- If that doesn't work, have someone else look for the spot. Have them touch it gently with the end of a tissue. The grit will usually adhere to the tissue and be out of your eye in an instant.

Eyestrain
- If you wear contacts, remove them while flying. Cabin air is extremely dry, and irritation results if contacts are kept in.
- Bright sun can also cause eyestrain. Prevent the problem with a quality pair of sunglasses.

Fever
For mild fever take aspirin, drink lots of liquids, and keep cool. A high fever signals a trip to the doctor.

Fish Poisoning (see Ciguatera)

Fleas
Fleas carry disease. Use insect repellant. Avoid "fleabag" hotels.

Food Poisoning
Headache, nausea, vomiting, and diarrhea (often all at once)—these are the signs of food poisoning, which can only be described as the next worst thing to death. Occasionally, you'll also experience either chills or fever as well. On rare occasions blood poisoning occurs.
- Prevent food poisoning by following the advice given in the section on diarrhea.
- If you have the above symptoms, see a doctor at once. Some food poisoning can be fatal. Food poisoning normally lasts 3 days.
- Anyone with diabetes, gastrointestinal problems, immune disorders, or liver disease is at especially high risk.

Frogs

Native people use the toxins produced by tropical frogs to tip their arrows with poisons. Many of the most colorful types are the most dangerous. Do not touch frogs or other amphibians in tropical areas.

Fungal infections

Some people are especially prone to fungal infections. Many of them are related to an immune system somewhat out of whack. Even if you're healthy, you can still have trouble. Your fingers, toes, and crotch area are especially prone to minor infections in warm, hot areas. Wear loose-fitting clothing (preferably cotton), change it frequently, and dry off whenever you can. Carry a strong anti-fungal cream (such as Nizoral or Spectazole) and apply it at the first sign of trouble. Yeast infections of the mouth and vagina are most often caused by *Candida albicans*. Everyone has this in their system, but it sometimes flares up as pitted, white sores in the back of the mouth or the common vaginal yeast infection. For oral problems liquid Nystatin is extremely effective. If you're prone to vaginal yeast infections, carry something with you, especially if you'll be traveling for longer periods of time. A number of over-the-counter products are quite effective. For serious, long-term fungal infections the newest recommended drug is Itraconazole (Sporanox). It is reported to have fewer side effects than Ketoconazole (Nizoral). Both of these are taken as pills. These medications require close monitoring by a specialist (blood samples will be taken regularly).

- Stay out of pools which don't smell of chlorine.
- If whirlpools are not crystal clear, don't go in them.
- Stay out of the ocean after heavy rains.
- Clean out your ears with rubbing alcohol after swimming.
- Wash off after swimming with soap and hot water.
- If you notice any skin infections, apply creams immediately.

Giardia

Giardia, a tiny little organism, is spreading and causing problems in water worldwide, especially in cold-water lakes and streams. Boiling water for at least 30 minutes (more at higher elevations) kills it dead. Some of the new water filters claim to be so fine that giardia cannot pass through them. I'd be wary. Diarrhea which comes and goes every few weeks and pain are two common symptoms of giardiasis (infection by these microscopic organisms). The most commonly prescribed drug is Metronidazol (Flagyl), a synthetic anti-protozoal and bacteria medication. Treatment with more than one medication may be necessary since giardia are good at hiding in the intestinal tract, reproducing into small colonies, and causing trouble after you think the problem has been eliminated. Whenever you have diarrhea for more than a week or recurring bouts, you should definitely see a doctor. Don't drink any alcohol.

Hangovers
Prevent some of the effect of a hangover by drinking lots of water during a night of hard drinking. This helps prevent dehydration. Note that clear beverages (such as Vodka) generally cause fewer hangovers than colored ones (the latter contain flavorings which cause headaches). Before going to bed drink lots of fluid with two aspirins. Mexicans say that dog tea (*té de perro*) diminishes the effects of a hangover. A little tea of the dog that bit you. Tonic water, which contains quinine, may also be helpful. Lots of fruit juice and carbohydrates including bread reduce hangovers. Finally, capsaicin, the chemical which gives chili peppers their fire, is believed to help relieve hangovers. Note that the effect of alcohol is much more noticeable at high elevations, including plane flights or stays in places like Mexico City.

Headaches
- If prone to frequent headaches, bring medication.
- Relax muscles as frequently as possible. Stretch regularly if confined. Walk around on flights.
- Practice deep breathing. This is one of the basic principles of relaxation and yoga. Lie down on a bed and breathe in deeply. If you're breathing properly, your stomach will rise, your chest will barely move. Many people do not know how to breathe properly. In fact, they've been taught to hold their gut in—just the opposite of what you should be doing.
- If you get a headache, place ice immediately on your forehead and back of neck.

Heartburn
Carry some antacid with you—heartburn is inevitable. Experts say not to eat too fast, not to eat too much, to avoid spicy foods, to loosen your belt, to avoid big late-night meals—how many of those experts have traveled in this region?

Heat Prostration/Sunstroke
Tropical sun can cause a lot of damage, especially between 11:00 A.M. to 2:00 P.M. If you're going to be out in the sun for long periods of time, never underestimate its effect.
- Wear light-colored, lightweight, and loose clothing.
- Never travel without a wide-brimmed hat.
- Drink lots of fluids. Carry drinks with you.

- Put more salt on your foods than you normally would.
- Avoid strenuous activities in the middle of the day. Do these in early morning or late evening when it cools off.
- If you get too hot, get out of the sun.
- Lie down and rest.
- Anyone who gets flushed, hot and dry skin, and runs a rapid pulse should get to a doctor immediately. If ice is available, get into an ice bath. Sunstroke can be fatal.

Hepatitis (see p. 15)

Get vaccinated. Eat in clean places. Drink pure water. Kiss and have sex only with a partner you trust. Avoid bad blood or dirty needles.

Hypothermia

Campers and hikers should be wary of this condition. It gets very cold in the higher mountain regions. It even snows there. However, it doesn't have to be freezing outside to get hypothermia. Danger signals: uncontrollable shivering, difficulty talking, confusion, puffy face, or unconsciousness. *This person needs help.*

- Prevent hypothermia by staying dry.
- Keep your head, neck, and hands covered to prevent heat loss.
- Wet clothes lose 90 percent of their insulating value and drain heat from the body 240 times faster than dry clothes. If you get wet, find shelter and change into dry clothes immediately.
- If a person has hypothermia, act quickly. Strip and put him into a dry sleeping bag, preferably with another person. Don't rub his skin. Just keep him warm and dry. Make him rest.
- Give him something warm to drink. Feed him high-energy foods. Never use alcohol which leads to heat loss.

Infections

All infections should be taken seriously, even if they seem minor.

- Clean them frequently, preferably with alcohol and treat them with an antibiotic ointment.

Insomnia

- Exercise, lots of liquids, and a good diet high in protein will help you avoid insomnia.
- Drink a little beer to take advantage of its lupulin (a product of hops). Eat a light snack with milk. It contains both L-tryptophan and calcium—both cause drowsiness.
- Take a warm bath just before going to bed.
- Carry earplugs.
- Keep the room dark.

- Follow a routine which triggers sleep. For many people this is reading a book or magazine or listening to a soothing tape.
- Certain things cause insomnia: heavy drinking, late meals (the norm in Mexico); spicy foods (also very common); chocolate and colas, which contain caffeine; and afternoon naps.
- Sleep-inducing drugs work, but they are not advised
- Antihistamines, such as Benadryl, are often good substitutes for sleeping pills. They cause drowsiness but have few side effects.

Jellyfish

If you find yourself surrounded by jellyfish, dive down and try to swim under them. If you're already in the tentacles, dive down to get out of them. Leave jellyfish stranded on shore alone. They may still be able to sting you.

- Here are a few things that might take away the sting: ammonia (mild), antihistamine cream, Benadryl (*jarabe*), cortisone cream, meat tenderizer, Windex, papaya juice, rubbing alcohol, vinegar, or warm salt water. A Belizean fisherman told me that urine (as awful as it sounds) is the most effective and immediately available cure.
- If you're trying to help someone else, wear gloves. Rub the area off with salt water and sand. Never use fresh water.
- If a person faints or can't breath after a jellyfish sting, get him to a doctor immediately.

Jet Lag

Since the time differences are minimal from most U.S. and Canadian cities to Central America and Mexico, jet lag tends to be a minor problem. It's much more serious when crossing many time zones. However, flying can be quite tiring.
- Sleep well before a flight (pack well ahead of time).
- Eat on a regular schedule. Carry snacks if necessary.
- Fly during the day if possible.
- Fly in the non-smoking section and use ventilation provided from above. The carbon dioxide build-up in planes is becoming more of a problem each year as airlines try to save money by using outside ventilation less.
- Drink lots of liquids, but nothing containing alcohol. Cabins are very dry and dehydration results.
- Get up and walk around. Do minor exercises such as tapping your toes or squeezing your hands together.
- At the hotel, take a hot shower. This gets moisture into your lungs and nose. It also relieves tension in your muscles.
- Take a long walk about 3 hours before going to sleep.

Lead poisoning

Mexican ceramics are notorious for containing extraordinarily high amounts of lead. The brilliantly colored and decorated ceramics are stunning art pieces, but should not be used for eating. For more information get the pamphlet "What You Should Know About Lead in China Dishes" from the following organization:

The Environmental Defense Fund
257 Park Avenue South
New York, NY 10010

Malaria (see Mosquitoes)

Prevent malaria by taking Chloroquine phosphate and protecting yourself properly from mosquito bites.

Meningitis

This bacterial disease is normally spread through saliva. Symptoms are convulsions, fever, headache, purplish skin spots, stiff neck, and vomiting. It can be fatal if not treated promptly. Fortunately, a doctor can prescribe antibiotics to cure it. It is rare in Central America and Mexico.

Mosquitoes (see Dengue Fever and Malaria)

Central America and Mexico are prime breeding grounds for some of the world's most prolific and potentially dangerous mosquitoes. Surveys indicate that 40 percent of people traveling to the Tropics do not protect themselves against mosquito bites.

- Stay in a protected area, especially from dusk to dawn when the breed of mosquitoes carrying malaria comes out. Early morning and early evening are prime times to be bitten by the type of mosquito (*Aedes aegypti*) carrying dengue fever.
- Keep windows closed if screens are absent or have holes.
- Consider a covering even while indoors. Contact:

Inside Tent
Long Road Travel Supplies
P.O. Box 638
Alameda, CA 94601
Tel: (800) 359-6040
    (415) 865-3066.

- Wear loose-fitting clothes. Cover as much skin as possible.
- Avoid scents of any kind.
- If sleeping in a hammock, lay a blanket down on the hammock. Cover the hammock with a mosquito net.
- Use an insect repellant with a high degree of DEET (diethylolu-amide, N.N. diethylmethyl benzamide, or N.N. diethylmetatolu-

amide) in it. The higher the better (no less than 35 percent). Note
that 100 percent DEET may now be illegal, but it is highly effective if placed on clothing. It will not damage natural fibers, but
may make holes in synthetic materials. Concentrations of DEET
above 10 percent should never be used on children, who may
suffer skin irritation to serious seizures from its use. Mild, slow-
release formulas are okay.

- On hot days reapply insect repellant frequently as it runs off from
  perspiration. On rainy days do the same. Reapply after swimming
  for the same reason.
- Always carry mosquito netting (*pabellon*) for camping or staying
  in smaller hotels without good screens on the windows. *It's
  absolutely essential in some areas.* If you buy it before going
  abroad, get netting treated with permanone.
- Carry a pyrethrum (pyrethrin) insect spray. Use it in smaller
  hotels or in tents unless you're allergic to it (anyone allergic to
  ragweed should be careful with this spray). Apply it to bedding
  (sleeping bags) as well.
- If a mosquito lands on your skin, kill it by brushing it off your
  skin with a sweeping motion.
- A strong breeze will often keep mosquitoes away. If you're
  camped in a low area, consider moving up into the wind or
  closer to the sea shore.

Motion Sickness

You're either susceptible to this, or you're not. Common symptoms
are nausea, dizziness, and vomiting. To prevent this illness take a
medication. Follow directions exactly, since many have to be taken
well before travel to be effective.

- Drugs may have side effects, and some of them must be prescribed by a doctor.
- If you forget to get pills in the United States, ask for *pastillas para
  mareo* at a pharmacy (*farmacia*) abroad.

If you forget or can't take motion sickness pills

- On a **boat**: On a cruise stay on deck in the fresh air in the middle
  of the ship. Lie down. Try to sleep if possible. Eat frequent, light
  snacks. Avoid alcohol. On smaller boats lie down as far away
  from the motor as possible. The noise and diesel smell from
  motors makes many people sick. Ask people not to smoke
  around you. If not able to lie down, never stare at waves or moving objects. Look out above the horizon.
- On a **bus**: Try to sit right behind the driver. Look straight ahead,
  not off to the side. Open a window slightly for fresh air. Do not

read maps or books. Eat light snacks. Try to go to sleep.

- In a **car**: Ask to drive. Drivers rarely get motion sickness. If you're not able to drive, ask to ride in the front seat. Look straight ahead at the road. Avoid reading or looking at maps. If the driver needs help, ask him to pull over so that you can look at the map while the car is still. Open your window to get lots of fresh air. Ask people not to smoke. If your seat reclines, push it back as far as possible. Close your eyes. Go to sleep.
- On a **plane**: Ask to be in the non-smoking section. Ask for a seat over the wings (if in non-smoking section). Turn the knob for ventilation on to get as much oxygen as possible. Eat frequent, light snacks. Avoid alcohol. Lie down if possible, lie far back if not. Try to sleep. Do not read. Do not watch movies.

Pain
Since pain is only a symptom of a medical problem, see a doctor.

Parasites (see Dogs and Giardia)

Poisoning
Avoid eating any plants, leaves, or fruit in tropical areas unless you're sure of what it is. Manzanillo trees are common in the Tropics. The fruit is poisonous and even the leaves cause a poison ivy-like rash. Ask locals to point out dangerous plants. If traveling with children, induce vomiting if they eat an unknown leaf or fruit. Get them to a doctor immediately (bring a sample of what they've eaten—use a handkerchief or cloth to pick it up).

Polio (see p. 17)

Rabies
If you're traveling with small children, tell them not to play with stray animals. Anyone exploring caves should consider rabies shots as prevention. Anyone bitten by any animal while traveling abroad should see a doctor immediately.

Sandflies
These miniscule insects attack tourists in many beach areas, mainly at dawn and dusk. In some areas they are so bad that they discourage tourism altogether. Caye Caulker (in Belize), the Bay Islands (Honduras), and San Blas on the Pacific Coast of Mexico—all are examples of areas infested with no-see-ums (*purrujas*) and sandflies (*jejenes*). They most commonly bite your legs. Insect repellant works. Wading in the water also stops immediate attacks. Sandflies carry dis-

eases. If a bite gets larger than a dime, begins to ulcerate or turn a strange color, see a doctor specializing in tropical medicine. You may have Leishmaniasis (*Papalomoyo*). This disease normally takes several weeks to develop, and, in some cases, longer. The earlier it's treated, the better.

Scorpions

In Mexico scorpions kill 10 times more people than snakes. They are very common, especially in the states of Colima, Durango, Jalisco, Michoacán, and Nayarit. They are generally more painful than deadly. Stings also may cause you to sweat, vomit, or have severe diarrhea.

- Scorpions come out mainly at night. Wear shoes and carry a flashlight.
- Scorpions hide in things. Shake everything out before going to bed and in the morning.
- If you get stung, lie down and relax. The calmer you are, the less severe the reaction, usually no worse than a bee sting.
- If you have an antihistamine, take it.
- Antiscorpion serum is sold in pharmacies as *Antialacran*. But you must be tested to see whether you're allergic to it. If you are, you'll immediately be given adrenalin. It is said that more people die from the serum each year than from scorpion stings.
- If ice is handy, put it on the sting.
- Drink anything loaded with vitamin C, such as lime juice.
- Don't take opiates or morphine derivatives, which means *no codeine, Darvon, Demorol, or paregoric.*
- Don't eat or drink dairy products, don't smoke, and don't drink alcohol.

Sea Urchin Spines

If you step on a sea urchin or get pushed into one by a wave, you will get pricked by one of the sharp spines which may lodge in your skin.

- Use a tweezers or needle to get it out. Make the wound bleed slightly.
- Squeeze lime juice or cortisone cream on the wound.

Shock

Any serious accident or injury can cause a person to go into shock. Common symptoms include pale and clammy skin, rapid pulse, a general feeling of dizziness or weakness, intense thirst, and shallow breathing. If a person is walking around, get him to lie down on his back with his feet raised. Loosen any tight-fitting clothing and cover the person with a blanket or coat if available. Do not give him anything to drink! If a person needs CPR, administer it immediately. Do not move the person at all. Have someone call for an ambulance right away.

Snakes

Snakes are most prevalent at night, although you occasionally see one during the day. If you intend to hike in tropical forests, go with a knowledgeable guide. Rattlesnakes are common in desert areas of Mexico. All snake bites are very serious. If you are bitten, kill the snake. Do this only if you're sure you won't get bitten twice (note that a severed head can bite people). If you are by yourself, walk slowly to the nearest place for help. Bring the snake with you. If you are with a group or with a very strong person, get carried out. The less movement, the better.

- If you see a snake, stop. Snakes attack movement.
- If a snake is far away, move away quickly.
- Prevent bites by wearing boots and using thick gloves if you'll be picking up things while camping or climbing.
- Watch where you put your hands, especially when climbing. Snakes often strike your hand if you put it too close to them.
- If sleeping outside, get off the ground.
- Never swim in areas surrounded by mangroves.
- You'll find some coral snakes (*Micrurus rotanus*) in Central America and Mexico. They have extremely small mouths and rarely bite people. There is no cure for a coral snakebite.
- There is also no cure for the brilliant green death snake (*Muerte verde*).
- Antivenins are often available at resorts or research stations where tourists trek through marked trails. If you get bitten, kill the snake so that the proper antivenin can be used. Naturally, anyone killing a snake should not risk getting bitten.
- Do not drink any alcohol after being bitten.
- If you do serious desert or tropical rain forest trekking on your own, learn to identify poisonous snakes and carry proper antivenin kits with you. The most common snakes are bushmaster (*Lachesis muta*), coral snakes (*Micrurus rotanus*), and fer-de-lances (*Barba amarilla* in Spanish and *Bothrops atrox* in Latin).
- If you have to travel through jungle at night, use a powerful flashlight. Night travel is dangerous. Night in a jungle equates to total blackness. You can't see at all.

Spiders

The bird, black widow (*Lactrodectus mactans*), and brown recluse (*Loxosceles reclusa*) spiders cause the most trouble. The average tourist rarely sees them. There are other poisonous spiders as well throughout the region. If you get bitten by any spider and have any of the following symptoms, apply ice to the bite and see a doctor immediately: severe pain, stomach cramps, difficulty breathing or speaking, sweats or chills, nausea, and vomiting. Tarantulas (*Latrodectus tredecemgattarus*) are also common. They are ugly (to some) and frightening (to many), but generally harmless.

- Kill any spiders you see by whacking them with your shoe.
- Close all windows at night.
- When you get up, shake your clothes. Turn your shoes upside down and tap them several times against something hard.

Stingrays (*rayas*)
Stingrays like to rest in the sand along the shoreline. When in the sea, shuffle your feet instead of taking big steps.

Stress (see Anxiety)

Sunburn
With cases of skin cancer increasing each year (there are now hundreds of thousands reported) doctors insist that *no* sun bathing is best. As you approach the Equator the power of the sun increases by as much as 25 percent. The same is true at high altitudes. Damage to the skin is cumulative. Unfortunately, if you're older, most of the damage has already been done. Locals often refer to tourists as *backra*, local trees with stringy bark. Our backs often end up looking like that tree.

Preventing Sunburn

- Buy protective clothing which blocks out both types of ultraviolet light. Most clothing offers minimal protection, especially when wet. Anyone with skin cancer should follow this advice, even though protective clothing is expensive.
- The following companies specialize in gear for sun protection. Frogskin creates products for kids. Solar Protective Factory specializes in hats and umbrellas. Sun Precautions offers a wide selection of products. Write or call for catalogs:

Frogskin
10105 East Via Linda,
  Suite 103-256
Scottsdale, AZ 85258
Tel: (800) 328-4440
  (602) 968-1992

Solar Protective Factory
564 La Sierra Drive, Suite 18
Sacramento, CA 95864
Tel: (800) 786-2562

Sun Precautions, Inc.
105 Second Avenue North
Seattle WA 98109
Tel: (800) 882-7860
     (206) 441-6688

- Protect your nose and ears with a hat with a 4-inch brim.
- Wear sunglasses guaranteed to block out ultraviolet rays to protect your eyes and eyelids.
- Cover your arms and legs with loose-fitting blouses or shirts and pants, preferably ones with sun blocking ability.
- Wear shoes or boots to cover the top of your feet.
- Use a sunscreen with an SPF (sun protection factor) of 25. Reapply as necessary if washed off by perspiration, rain showers, or swimming. Creams guaranteed not to wash off in water are highly recommended, but reapply anyway.
- Use sunscreens which protect against both UVB and UVA rays.
- Use sunscreen before traveling to check on allergic reactions. When in doubt, see a dermatologist.
- Apply sunscreen 45 minutes before going into the sun.
- Gradually increase sun exposure over a period of days, especially if you haven't been in the sun recently or are fair-skinned.
- The sun is extremely intense midday when locals eat lunch or take a nap. Follow their lead.
- Don't fall asleep in the sun.
- Wear a wet suit or sun protective t-shirt when snorkeling since the sun's rays penetrate water.
- Drink lots of water when you're out in the sun.
- Certain drugs make you sun-sensitive including diabetic medications, sulfa drugs, tetracyclene, and tranquilizers.

Dealing With Sunburn

- Use water-based moisturizer on your skin to help it heal.
- These things may help: aloe vera, lime juice, Neosporin, papaya (make a paste of the pulp), Solarcaine, or vinegar. Rub these gently on the skin.
- Also, if you get burned, drink lots of liquids with a good dose of salt. Lots of fresh lime juice should be added to the drinks. But do not drink alcohol. Aspirin is also recommended.
- For serious burns see a doctor immediately.

Tarantulas (see Spiders)

Tetanus/Diphtheria
Prevent these diseases by being vaccinated. If you get a puncture wound, clean it out well. See a doctor if it gets red.

Ticks
Smother ticks with vasoline. Oil, kerosene, or fingernail polish also work in a pinch. Wash the area well and apply an antibiotic ointment or clean with antiseptic.

Tuberculosis
The chances of an older traveler getting TB are relatively remote. Vaccinations are certainly recommended, especially for children under 12.

Typhoid
Get typhoid shots. Read the section on Diarrhea (pp. 226–230).

Typhus (see Ticks)
This serious disease with symptoms of high fever, severe headache, delirium, and a red rash is caused by being bitten by lice or ticks, which carry tiny micoorganisms (*Rickettsia*). Get to a doctor immediately. Avoid sleeping in "fleabag" hotel. Use insect repellant to keep lice and ticks off your body.

Vomiting
The danger of vomiting is dehydration. Drink liquids if possible. Since it is a sign of a more serious illness, see a doctor.

Worms
Sterilize all fruits and vegetables, avoid all rare or undercooked meat (or fish), avoid petting animals, avoid swimming in fresh water areas, and wear sandals or shoes at all times. Stool tests, and sometimes biopsies, are necessary to detect worms. If not destroyed, worms can cause serious health problems.

Wounds (see Bleeding)
Any cut or wound in the Tropics is very serious. Wash out with purified water and a disinfectant. Apply a sterile bandage. See a doctor if the wound gets hot, particularly painful, red, or throbs.

Yellow Fever

Yellow fever shots are not required for travel to countries covered by this book with the exception of Honduras, which requires inoculations for journalists (don't tell officials). If you intend to travel into Panama or into South America, get yellow fever shots.

Eating and Drinking

The food in this region can be excellent ranging from *cabrito* (goat) cooked on a spit in Monterrey, Mexico, to *camarónes* (shrimp) drenched in garlic butter in Costa Rica. Most of the time it is average, and occasionally it drops to bad.

Meal Times

- Breakfast (*desayuno*) time is elastic, stretching from early morning to noon. Some hotels and boardinghouses have strict schedules for breakfast, usually 7:30 to 9:30 A.M.
- Locals like to eat lunch (*almuerzo* or *comida*) at about the same time we do. In Mexico lunches are a bit later.
- Dinner (*cena*) times vary considerably. In fashionable restaurants you might not begin to eat until 9 P.M. In average restaurants dinner begins a couple of hours earlier. Many places catering to both tourists and locals have an early and a late sitting. Dinner time is later in big cities and some resort areas. Dinner is served at its latest in Mexico.

All Inclusive Resorts

- A number of resorts include meals in their overall price. With the exception of Club Med avoid being forced into eating at a hotel.
- In some isolated areas, especially on islands, you're stuck. Sometimes, the food's great, sometimes marginal.
- In jungle lodges and fishing camps, the same is true. You might be served gourmet cuisine or basic survival food. Ask about this when making reservations if the quality of food is really as important as seeing a jabiru or catching a 25-pound snook.
- If the food is not meeting your expectations, talk to the manager directly and discreetly. This may work miracles.
- Breakfasts vary from continental to copious. Good breakfasts include a wide variety of choices
- You might think that food quality will be directly related to the price you're paying. It's the place, not the price that counts.
- So if you're planning on staying somewhere for a week, get the name of someone who has already stayed there. If food is important to you, ask what they served and how good it was.

Moderate to Expensive Hotels

- Some hotels include meals in their overall room price. Avoid all-inclusive agreements. If you find that your hotel serves great food, great. If not, move on, sometimes to a tiny, informal hut next door which serves fantastic food at a fraction of the price.
- Still, in more isolated areas and on a number of islands, the better hotels are often the best choices for good food.
- Whenever checking out a hotel, always ask about breakfasts. Don't simply ask whether breakfast is included in the room price, ask what breakfasts are.
- Many hotels offer non-residents access to their dining rooms. If you're staying in an inexpensive hotel with poor food, check with better hotels about eating there.
- Throughout Central America and Mexico hotel food is often better than local restaurant food. There are exceptions, but this rule is a good one, especially in rural areas.

Fashionable Restaurants

Fashionable restaurants are found in the major cities, in world-class resorts, and occasionally, but rarely, in remote areas. Mexico City is especially noteworthy in this regard. San José isn't bad (eat at the National Theater for lunch).

If you really want to know about superb restaurants, go to a luxury hotel and ask the concierge. If a restaurant is difficult to get into, tip the concierge and ask him to make reservations. Eat at the same time that locals would for best service and food. Dress appropriately.

Reservations

Better restaurants usually require reservations, especially in Mexico City and major resorts like Acapulco.

- Call immediately on arrival to get into a restaurant with a fine reputation, especially during peak seasons.
- Reservations are most difficult in the evening, so if you're willing to eat at noon, you'll have a better chance of getting in.
- If you're dining alone (restaurants dislike this), reserve early for lunch and early for dinner. You'll have better and friendlier service.
- It's more enjoyable to go to a fine restaurant with another person, because the livelier atmosphere at the peak dining time is part of the fun. If you're a single woman, avoid hassles by finding a dinner partner for the evening (see p. 349).

- If you have difficulty making a reservations and absolutely must eat in a certain place, ask your concierge or one in a luxury hotel to make reservations for you. Tip appropriately.

Dress Requirements
When making a reservation at a fine restaurant, ask about dress requirements. Very few places have stringent dress codes—mainly in Mexico City.

Drinking with Meals
Fashionable restaurants charge fashionable prices for drinks. If you order any imported liquor or wine, you're going to be stunned by the bill. A bottle of imported wine could double your entire bill.
- Start off with a purely local drink made from local liquor. Or order beer with your meal. Local beer is excellent.
- If you want to sample some local wines (*vinos del país*), ask your waiter or wine steward for advice.
- If you're in doubt about wines, try a glass first. A few terms: *blanco* (white), *tinto* (red), *rosado* (rosé), *champaña* (champagne), *dulce* (sweet), and *seco* (dry).
- Wines imported from Chile are reasonably good and more reasonably priced than other imported wines.
- Know the price of any bottled wine that you order.
- Finally, wines may not be stored properly despite the restaurant or resort's best efforts. You may order a "good" wine only to find that it has deteriorated because of poor handling.

Service
Slow service is not considered bad service. Fine restaurants allow you to enjoy a meal at a leisurely pace.

Seafood Restaurants

Locals love seafood and are willing to splurge for it, especially when they're on vacation with their families.

Getting the Most and Best from Seafood Restaurants
- The best seafood restaurants are right on the sea, often right on a beach. They don't have to be fancy to be good.
- Ask to see whatever you intend to order. Make sure that what you're ordering is fresh.
- Smaller lobster are more tender than larger ones, larger shrimp are nicer and more expensive than smaller ones, large fish tend to be more expensive than small fish.

- Eat fish, shrimp, and spiny lobster only. Avoid clams, mussels, oysters, and scallops. The latter are rare anyway.
- Never eat *ceviche*, small chunks of fresh fish marinated in lime juice—can cause food poisoning and cholera.
- Avoid barracuda. The fish can cause an illness called ciguatera. Larger barracuda are worse than smaller ones.
- Go to seafood restaurants at noon. Keeping seafood cool and fresh until evening is a problem.
- Seafood must be fresh to be good. If it smells strong or tastes like iodine, don't eat it.
- Cold beer goes extremely well with fresh seafood.

Good but Cheap Restaurants

In most Central American countries, it's easy to find good (*bueno*), but cheap (*barato*) restaurants. In Mexico it's getting harder all the time, although it's still possible.

Finding Budget Restaurants
- If you're staying in a budget hotel, ask someone where a good, but cheap restaurant is located.
- Define the amount of money you're willing to spend to avoid a wild-goose chase.
- Your idea of good is very subjective. Be more specific. Who has the best chicken in town? Where can I get *fresh* fish? Who makes the best guacamole? Which place has the best local food? Which offers the most food for the best price?
- You may discover that you're thinking in terms of cheap, but good dishes, rather than cheap, but good restaurants.
- Ask other travelers about their finds. This is one of the simplest and most effective ways to come up with current information.

Regional Specialties

Each country has specialties particular to that country alone, but many dishes are common throughout the region. Unusual regional dishes (*comida típica*) rarely found or eaten on special occasions are fun to try, although few travelers are going to eat mosquito eggs, once the caviar of Mayan Indians. However, the ordinary tourist will rarely find certain items on the menu, even though they are mentioned in numerous travel guides. Things like armadillo, iguana ("bamboo or jungle chicken"), rabbit stew (*mole de conejo*), wild turkey stew (*chunco*), and so on. However, the following dishes and drinks are commonly available:

Popular Dishes and Drinks

Café: Coffee is as popular in the mid-afternoon with a sweet roll or pastry as it is in the morning. Locals do not drink coffee with lunch or dinner. They wait until the end of the meal to have it. Helpful words: black (*negro*); milk (*leche*); cream (*crema*); and sugar (*azúgar*). In some areas cream is not available and will simply be replaced by milk. *Camarónes*: If you like shrimp, you'll find some of the biggest and best in this region. *Casado*: Very popular in budget restaurants throughout Costa Rica is a dish of rice and beans supplemented with fried bananas, cole slaw or salad, and usually a piece of chicken. Rice and beans eaten in the morning are known as *gallo pinto*. *Cerveza*: Beer is the most popular regional drink. Helpful words: light (*clara*), dark (*oscura*), semi-dark (*semioscura*), and draft (*cruda* or *de barril*). Mexicans often sprinkle salt and lime on the lid of a beer can before drinking. *Chiles rellenos*: A stuffed pepper cooked in egg batter and smothered in sauce. *Coco*: Coconut milk known as coconut water (*agua de coco*), is safe and refreshing to drink. Stands offer green coconuts (*pipas*) from which you drink the milk with a straw. Mature coconuts are brown. The white flesh is known as *carne*. Both the flesh and milk can cause diarrhea. *Elote*: Boiled or broiled corn-on-the-cob is sold on most street corners by sad-eyed little old ladies who would be delighted if you gave it a try. Often served with lime juice and chili powder. *Flan*: This custard dessert, often called crème caramel, is a favorite throughout the entire region. *Frutas*: There are so many tropical fruits that this is heaven for anyone who likes them. *Langosta:* Spiny lobster is delicious throughout the region. Buy it only in season. *Licuados:* These are blended drinks of fresh juice, water (or ice), and milk (sometimes). Fresh juices (*jugos*) are equally good and a little safer. *Pescado:* Fresh fish is delicious and reasonably priced.

Saving Money

- Miscellaneous charges in restaurants include the cover charge (*cubierto*), service charge (*servicio*), and taxes (*impuesto*). Always ask whether these have been included in the bill before adding a tip (*propina*). The service charge is a tip.
- Eat regional food (*comida típica*) and drinks as outlined above. Good buys are set-price meals (*almuerzo ejectivo, comida corrida* or *corriente*) and daily specials (*menú* or *plato del día*).
- Try picnics. Buy food in open markets (mercados or tianguis), little stores (*tiendas* or *pulperías*), or supermarkets (*supermercados*). Some shops specialize in one item: baked goods (*panadería*), pastries (*pastelaría*), tortillas (*tortillería*), and so on.

Communicating

Don't let the language barrier discourage you from getting what you want out of a trip. You can have a good time with very little knowledge of the language. The Spanish spoken in Central America and Mexico has a different pronunciation and variations in words than that spoken in Spain.

Speaking

When you get off the beaten path, you'll run into a language barrier. You'll get by combining a few key words with sign language.

The Fundamentals

Take the time to learn a few basic expressions and how to count. No book can show you how to pronounce foreign words correctly. Have a native speaker pronounce them for you (don't be afraid to ask).

Basic Expressions

These are the everyday basic expressions that you should know. People will really appreciate it if you use them.

Do you have	*¿Tiene usted?*	**Is (are) there. . . ?**	*¿Hay. . . ?*
Do you speak English?	*¿Habla usted inglés?*	**I want**	*quiero*
		Miss	*Señorita*
Excuse me	*permiso, disculpeme*	**Mr.**	*Señor*
good-bye	*hasta luego, adiós*	**Mrs.**	*Señora*
good night	*buenas noches*	**My name is. . .**	*Me llamo. . .*
hello	*buenos días (in the morning)*	**no**	*no*
hello	*buenas tardes (in the afternoon and evening)*	**please**	*por favor*
		slowly	*despacio*
How are you?	*¿Cómo está usted?*	**sorry**	*perdón*
How do you say. . . in Spanish?	*¿Cómo se dice . . . en español?*	**thank you**	*gracias*
How much is it?	*¿Cuánto cuesta?*	**thank you very much**	*muchas gracias*
How much time?	*¿Cuánto tiempo?*	**very well**	*muy bien*
I am from Canada (the United States).	*Soy de Canada (de los Estados Unidos).*	**what**	*qué*
		What does. . . mean?	*¿Qué significa. . . ?*
I don't understand	*No entiendo; no comprendo*	**when**	*cuándo*
		where	*dónde*

Where are you from?	¿De dónde es usted?	yes	sí
who	quién	you're welcome	de nada, con mucho gusto
why	por qué		

Numbers

Knowing numbers is essential for anyone interested in keeping costs down and knowing what's going on around them.

0	cero	11	once	40	cuarenta
1	uno	12	doce	50	cincuenta
2	dos	13	trece	60	sesenta
3	tres	14	catorce	70	setenta
4	cuatro	15	quince	80	ochenta
5	cinco	16	diez y seis	90	noventa
6	seis	17	diez y siete	100	cien (ciento)
7	siete	18	diez y ocho	200	doscientos
8	ocho	19	diez y nueve	500	quinientos
9	nueve	20	veinte	1000	mil
10	diez	30	treinta		

Days of the Week

Monday	lunes	Saturday	sábado
Tuesday	martes	Sunday	domingo
Wednesday	miércoles		
Thursday	jueves		
Friday	viernes		

Helpful Adjectives

bad	malo	dirty	sucio	happy	contento
beautiful	hermoso	drinkable	potable	heavy	pesado
broken	roto, quebrado	early	temprano	high	alto
cheap	barato	easy	fácil	hot	caliente
clean	limpio	expensive	caro	ill	enfermo
closed	cerrado	fair	justo	large	grande
cold	frío	far	lejos	late	tarde
comfortable	cómodo	fast	rápido	long	largo
dangerous	peligroso	friendly	amable	low	bajo
difficult	difícil	good	bueno	old	viejo

open	*abierto*	**short**	*corto*	**small**	*pequeño*
pretty	*bonito*	**slow**	*lento*	**ugly**	*feo*

Tricks for Communicating

- Don't be complicated. Say "Menu, please", not "I would like a menu, please."
- Repeat statements or questions only once—slowly and without raising your voice. No go? Smile and say, "*Gracias.*"
- If your comprehension is limited, communicate in writing. Carry paper and pen, and get prices written for you.
- Say something, even if in English. Silence is considered rude.

Some Confusing Words

- A library is called a *biblioteca*, while a bookstore is a *librería*.
- The Gulf of California is the Sea of Cortez (*Mar de Cortez*).
- Mexicans refer to the Rio Grande as the *Río Bravo*.
- *Monte* doesn't mean mountain, but jungle, forest, or brush.
- *Señorita* (Miss), applies to all women unless you know they're married. If they are, say *señora*.
- México can mean Mexico (the country), Mexico (the State), or Mexico City.

Asking Directions

Asking directions is a real art and varies with each country. You don't have to speak fluent Spanish to travel widely, but it helps to know a few words relating to directions:

Useful Vocabulary

---

far	*lejos*	on the corner	*en la esquina*
here	*aquí*	**straight ahead**	*(sempre) derecho*
How far is. . . ?	*¿A qué distancia está. . . ?*	**there**	*allí*
in front	*en frente*	**to the left**	*a la izquierda*
near	*cerca*	**to the right**	*a la derecha*
one block	*una cuadra* or *cien metros* (in Costa Rica)	**Where is. . . ?**	*¿Dónde está. . . ?*

Tricks to Asking Directions

- Ask directions from men, especially in rural areas where women will often avoid contact with foreigners.

- Always greet someone before any questions. This is considered basic good manners. *"Buenos días, señor,"* is all it takes.
- Keep your question ultra-simple. Don't get fancy.
- The simplest way is to use the word *a* in Spanish. This means *to* and is pronounced "ah" as if you're showing your tonsils to a doctor. Follow *a* by the place you want to get to. For example, "ah" San Miguel de Allende? Now say this as a question, and you've found the simplest way to ask a direction.
- If you're not going in the right direction, the person will shake his finger and point you in another direction. If you're going in the right direction, he'll just nod and say, *"sí."*

Sense the Nature of the Response
- It is considered more polite to give a wrong answer than none at all.
- Some people may be confused by your accent or your looks.
- If you don't trust an answer, ask again—but this time ask someone else. If you get a different answer, ask yet another person.

Things Not To Do
- Don't take out a fancy, multicolored map and ask a peasant to show you the right direction to San Miguel de Allende. The odds are he's never seen a map before, and you'll spend the next twenty minutes showing it to him.
- Don't get angry if someone doesn't understand you. It's not their fault that you're lost. In fact, never think of yourself as being lost. You're just experiencing a part of the country you've never seen before.

Other Tips on Directions
- A small compass can be very useful. If you're traveling in remote areas, this gets you headed in the general direction.
- Some areas may have more than one name. This can be very confusing and is usually only a problem in off-road travel.

Faxes

In many areas of Central America and Mexico faxes are now the best way to communicate. Some hotels have no phones. Faxes are sent to a central location, then delivered by the mailman to the appropriate address. If you know where you'll be going, try to get fax numbers. Faxes are much more reliable than mail service.

Telephoning

Telephone systems have improved greatly in Central America and Mexico. This is an easy way for people to keep in touch.

Basic Telephone Vocabulary

busy	*ocupado*	**(international)**	*(internacional)*
call	*llamada*	**person (calling)**	*de parte de*
call (to)	*llamar*	**person to person**	*persona*
code (city or area)	*clave*		*a persona*
coin-operated	*teléfono*	**station to station**	*a quien contesta*
telephone	*monedero*	**telephone**	*teléfono*
collect	*a cobrar*	**telephone office**	*oficina de*
cost	*costo*		*teléfonos*
Hello	*Hola, Bueno*	**time and charges**	*tiempo y costo*
long distance	*larga distancia*	**token**	*ficha de teléfono*
number	*número*	**United States**	*los Estados Unidos*
operator	*operador*		

Where to Make Long-Distance Calls
- You can make long-distance calls in most hotels, in the telephone offices of many towns and cities, at the airport, and at many booths displaying the sign *servicio de larga distancia.*

Ways to Make Calls
- You can dial directly to Canada or the United States following directions provided with whatever calling card you have.
- You can easily call collect or with a telephone calling card by dialing these AT&T numbers: Belize (555), Costa Rica (114), Guatemala (190), Honduras (123), Mexico (95 800 462 4240). Operators understand both English and Spanish. Calls go through almost immediately. Collect has a higher surcharge, but the minute rate is the same.
- If you have another long-distance carrier, simply ask whether access codes exist before traveling abroad.

Messages
Check with your local company about how to use "voice mailbox" and message services. Each has its own method. This allows you to communicate "indirectly" with someone.

Miscellaneous Charges and Rip-offs

- The *hotel surcharge* is probably the single biggest rip-off in travel today. The hotel jacks up your phone bill by whatever amount it can get away with, calling it a service charge. Ask what this charge will be *before* making a long distance call. Note that you pay this charge even on a collect call.
- Another interesting charge: You may pay a fee if no one answers. You may pay a larger fee if someone refuses to accept your collect call. Try to work out an *exact* time to contact someone if you plan to call long distance. But make sure that the other party knows that it may take several hours for you to reach him. For example, tell the person that you'll call Sunday evening between 9 P.M. and midnight.
- Finally, you pay a steep IVA (Value Added Tax) on calls.
- Hotels often lie about surcharges. I'd make all calls from a pay phone or post office if possible.

Keeping the Costs Down

- Each company has varying times when rates are lowest. There is no uniformity among companies. Ask your company what the best times are to call if you want to save money.
- Finally, if you'll be on the line for a long time, have the other party call you back station to station.

Local Calls

- Never make local calls using your telephone card from the U.S. or you will be stunned by the charges.
- The simplest place to make a local call is from your hotel.
- If you have a phone in your room, you may be charged a small daily fee for its use. Or you may be charged on a per call basis. Or, nothing at all. Ask about the cost.
- If there's no phone in your room, make local calls at the front desk.
- You can also use public pay phones, as in the United States and Canada. These phones are for local calls only. Calls can be incredibly inexpensive. Coins needed may be of such little value that they're actually hard to find.
- Many pay phones are broken.
- Ask locally how to make calls. The system varies by country.

Mail

Mail to and from Central America and Mexico is notoriously unreliable. Use faxes or phones.

Telegraphing

Telegraphing only makes sense if you're having trouble getting through by telephone, since the cost of a telegraph often matches that of a telephone call.

Basic Telegraph Vocabulary

---

address	*dirección*	**telegram**	*telegrama*
night letter	*carta nocturna,*	**telegraph office**	*officina de*
	carta de noche		*telégrafos*
regular	*ordinario*	**urgent**	*urgente*

- You have to pay for telegrams. They cannot be sent collect.
- An urgent telegram will be sent immediately, a regular telegram will be sent on the day it's paid for, and a night letter goes out the next day at the latest.
- Night letters sometimes get through as fast as regular ones, but you can never be sure.
- The price you pay is related to the speed at which you want the telegram to get through.

Nonverbal Communication

People pick up on a lot more than you say. You don't even have to open your mouth, and they begin to have a reaction to you.

A Relaxed Attitude
- If you smile and seem relaxed, people let their guard down. Anyone can pick up on your tension and fears.
- If you're impatient at a front desk or waiting in line, residents tend to react negatively to you and make you wait a little longer. Patience is seen as a virtue, and the more your manner mirrors this quality, the better you'll be treated.

Simple Gestures Denoting Respect
- A simple nod or bow goes over well as an acknowledgement.
- Shaking hands when meeting and leaving people means a lot.

Things That Say Sex
- What says sex to one person may seem innocuous to another. In this region the following things say sex: bare skin, especially breasts (says sex in a lot of places); tight-fitting clothes (look at

how local women dress); long, free-flowing hair (especially blond); lipstick, fingernail polish, and lots of makeup; and any overt flirting or drinking in public.
- Finally, a woman traveling alone says sex—no matter how unfair that may seem to you.

Poor Communication—Causing Trouble

Occasionally, what you say or do can cause some embarrassing moments. Here's what to watch out for.

What Not to do
- It is polite to admire things in the United States and Canada. In Mexico if you admire something that belongs to someone else, they may give it to you. Imagine how guilty you'd feel if it were something personal or valuable?
- Machismo is an obsession with one's manliness. Many men fall into this Latin mode. So lay off the horn, don't get into drinking bouts, refuse any gifts graciously, and let lies lay—you can't win in a confrontation with a macho (see p. 349).
- Women should never respond to any comments in the street. Even negative responses are seen as an open invitation to more harassment. Pretend the hissing, whistling, and open sexual invitations don't exist. You're above it all—the only attitude to have.
- Don't sit back and take abuse. Get in there and push the way the locals do—they'll admire you for it.

Doing Things

This section is devoted to special-interest activities. Each appeals to different people in different ways and can make any trip to Central America or Mexico especially memorable.

Special Tips on Special Interest Activities

- In most categories you'll find several companies specializing in that activity. There are tens of thousands of agencies, so these represent only a sampling of those available. If you find a terrific company to add, just send the name in.
- The advantages of working with specialists are numerous. Trips are meticulously scouted and prearranged. Sometimes, the only way to get the very best is to go through these companies. For example, certain isolated lodges may be prebooked years in advance at the prime time for the special interest activity.
- The cost of trips arranged through these companies are often quite high. If you have lots of time and energy, you could make arrangements at lesser cost in a number of instances. However, you would have to find local guides to match the ones offered by the tour companies to get the most from your trip.
- In short, if a company offers a great trip, expect to pay for it, just as you would expect to pay for a vintage wine.
- Read the section on Tours (pp. 63–70) carefully, since you want to match your interest to the tour you choose.
- Many of these companies offer trips which would go into other special interest categories as well, particularly into "soft" and "hard" adventure. The terms are travel jargon for relatively easy exploration to roughing it in the jungle.
- Take tours which match your physical ability. Some trips are extremely strenuous. Even trips called "soft" adventure may require stamina in certain segments. Don't get in over your head.
- Some of these companies work together. Some work with foreign travel companies, others arrange everything on their own. Ask how the tour is being arranged.
- Many foreign companies arrange travel similar to that of companies listed below. If you want a list of these, ask the appropriate tourist office. Dealing with foreign travel agents from a distance is not always easy. But, you certainly have that option. If you have lots of time, you may want to make arrangements with local companies on arrival. However, if time is limited, don't even think about this, especially in the peak season.

Adventure Travel

Practically all of the companies listed in this chapter have some form of adventure-travel orientation. Here are some which offer a wide range of activities from "soft" to "hard" adventure (again, don't count out other companies listed below as alternatives):

Adventure Center
1311 63rd Street, Suite 200
Emeryville, CA 94608
Tel: (800) 227-8747
    (510) 654-1879
Belize, Costa Rica, Guatemala,
Honduras, Mexico.

Mountain Travel
6420 Fairmount Avenue
El Cerrito, CA 94530
Tel: (800) 227-2384
    (510) 527-8100
Costa Rica, Guatemala,
Mexico.

Explorers
499 Ernston Road
Parlin, NJ 08859
Tel: (800) 631-5650
    (201) 721-2929
Belize, Costa Rica, Guatemala,
Honduras, Mexico.

Tropical Travel
5 Grogans Park, Suite 102
The Woodlands, TX 77380
Tel: (800) 451-8017
    (713) 367-3386
Belize, Costa Rica, Guatemala,
Honduras, Mexico.

Archaeology

Throughout Central America and Mexico there are thousands of archaeological sites, many of them not even explored. Never remove anything from any of these sites, not even a little piece of stone. Leave all sites as you found them. Follow local regulations in regards to climbing, photography, and touching inscriptions to the letter.

Clark Tours
9 Boston Street, Suite 9
Lynn, MA 01904
Tel: (800) 223-6764
    (617) 581-0844
Guatemala, Honduras.

Far Horizons
P.O. Box 91900
Albuquerque, NM 87199
Tel: (800) 552-4575
    (505) 822-9100
Belize, Guatemala, Honduras,
Mexico. One of the best for
people interested in Mayan
archaeology and culture.

CVI Group (Vagabond Tours)
P.O. Box 2664
Evergreen, CO 80439
Tel: (800) 538-6802
    (303) 674-9615
Belize.

Mayan Adventures, Inc.
P.O. Box 15204
Seattle, WA 98115
Tel: (206) 523-5309
Belize, Guatemala, Honduras,
Mexico—does educationally oriented tours in archaeology only.

Mundo Maya Travel
P.O. Box 31000-193
Phoenix, AZ 85046
Tel: (800) 362-2875
    (602) 971-0031
Belize, Costa Rica, Guatemala,
Honduras, Mexico.

Mountain Travel
6420 Fairmount Avenue
El Cerrito, CA 94530
Tel: (800) 227-2384
    (510) 527-8100
Guatemala, Honduras.

BELIZE

There are dozens of archaeological sites in Belize. Only a few have been excavated. Many have been vandalized or are being vandalized, and funds don't exist to protect them. The most visited sites are Altun Ha, Caracol (noted for its sky palace—Canaa), Lamanai, and Xunantunich ("shoo-nahn-too-kneetch"). The latter has a lovely location overlooking a river. The experience of getting to the sites is often the most memorable part of the trip. Caracol is only accessible during the dry season from January to May, although recent reports indicate that the road is being upgraded.

GUATEMALA

Tikal is the finest archaeological site covered in this guide. The area is large. Only some of the buildings have been cleared and restored, but they are incredibly impressive. They are located in a jungle, filled with howler monkeys and exotic birds.

- More people get to Tikal from Belize than from Guatemala City. There is a bus to Flores. This has been robbed frequently by armed bandits. The road is sometimes impassable because of mud. Tourists coming from different directions wade through the mud and transfer to buses on the other side. Many local tour operators travel in this way, insisting that the danger is minimal.
- The other option is to fly into Flores. Stay overnight there and pick up a minibus early the next morning to take you to Tikal, approximately an hour away.
- The hotels at Tikal are much more expensive than those in Flores, but more convenient. The advantage of staying at Tikal is that you can get up early to see more birds and wildlife.

- The other sites in Guatemala are relatively obscure and for the ardent archaeologist. They include Piedras Negras (see Usamacinta under White Water rafting in Mexico), Quiriguá ("kitty-gua"— famed for Mayan stelae), and Uaxactún ("washocktune"—15 miles north of Tikal).

HONDURAS

Copan (3 hours from San Pedro Sula in dry weather) is this country's most popular site. Reconstruction has been haphazard. The stone carvings are intricate. If you ask people whether a trip to Copan is worth it, you'll get divided opinions. If you decide to visit Copan, arrange to go to Quiriguá across the border in Guatemala. Expect nothing but hassles at the border. It's all part of travel here.

MEXICO

It is estimated that there are 11,000 archaeological sites in Mexico, many still unexplored and undiscovered.

- The major sites are Chichén Itza (Mérida), Monte Albán (Oaxaca), Palenque (Villahermosa), and Uxmal (Mérida). The towns closest to these are in parentheses.
- The most impressive is Palenque. But it's isolated. Chichén Itza is only a few hours from Cancún. Down the coast from Cancún is Tulúm, a minor site with a spectacular seaside location. It has a fine little beach and good snorkeling.
- Monte Albán on the outskirts of Oaxaca has been closed occasionally by strikes. Always ask in advance if the site is open before making a special trip to see Oaxaca.
- On the outskirts of Mexico City you'll find the Pirámides de Teotihuacán. These pyramids are very impressive and worth seeing. You can get to them by car (via tollway), tour, or public transportation. (Take the subway to the Indios Verdes metro stop. From there go to the Zona Arqueologico by bus.)
- Special note: In Gainesville, Florida, you'll find the best reproductions of the art of Bonampak, a site which has been left to deteriorate over the years.
- All sites charge a small fee for parking (tip the attendant) and for entry. Fees drop on Sundays.
- Always get information locally on hours and days of closing. Try to arrive as early as possible to avoid the crowds.
- If you're into photos, don't look too professional. You can't *legally* use tripods, flash, or movie cameras in archaeological zones without special permits. So, be discreet.
- Sound and light shows are given in English at many ruins from October to May. Inquire about exact hours. Bring warm clothes during the winter—it can get quite chilly!

Ballet

MEXICO

The Ballet Folklórico de México is a *must* for all tourists.

- The ballet is usually performed in the Palace of Fine Arts (*Palacio de las Bellas Artes*) in Mexico City.
- It is sometimes in the National Auditorium in Chapultepec Park or at the Museo de la Ciudad near the zócalo in Mexico City.
- Similar performances take place in Acapulco and Cancún.
- There are three performances a week in Mexico City. Usually, these are on Wednesdays at 9:00 P.M., and on Sundays at 9:30 A.M. and 9:00 P.M.
- Many agencies sell tickets at inflated prices.
- You can get your own at the box office at the Palace of Fine Arts (Bellas Artes metro station).
- The office is open 10:30 A.M. to 1:00 P.M., and 4:00 P.M. to 7:00 P.M. Note the break for a siesta.
- It is easiest to get tickets for the Sunday morning performance (leaves you time for the Sunday afternoon bullfight).
- The price is very reasonable and varies by section. Pay extra to be on the main floor, close up.
- If you want to save money, settle for the highest seats in the house (bring binoculars). Skip these seats if you're prone to vertigo.

Beachcombing

MEXICO

Some of the best beachcombing beaches are the ones isolated on the Baja facing the Pacific.

Basic Beach and Beachcombing Vocabulary

beach	*playa*	sand	*arena*
coconut	*coco*	shell	*concha*
coconut palm	*palmera*	sun	*sol*
current	*corriente*	tide (high) (low)	*marea (alta)*
it's cloudy	*está nublado*		*(baja)*
it's (very) hot	*hace (mucho) calor*	undertow	*resaca*
it's raining	*está lloviendo*	water	*agua*
it's windy	*hace viento*	wind	*viento*

Beaches

BELIZE

Don't go to Belize because of beaches. Most are mediocre compared to those in Costa Rica and Mexico. Placencia is touted as the country's best and longest beach, but overrated. The isolated beaches around some of the off-shore islands and atolls are far lovelier.

COSTA RICA

The beaches at Manuel Antonio south of Quepos are lovely. The area was damaged badly by a storm in 1993, but is still a good spot for sunbathing and swimming. The most stunning beaches are on the Nicoya peninsula in the northwestern part of the country. Getting to these is a battle because the roads are so bad. As these improve, tourism in the area will flourish. The best way to see many of the beaches is by 4-wheel drive. Planes do fly into isolated spots with pickups by nearby hotels. Always ask locals whether a beach is safe before swimming. Many have extremely dangerous riptides.

HONDURAS

There are a few mediocre beaches on Roatan. The best beaches are on the northern coast of the mainland and rarely visited.

MEXICO

With 6,000 miles of coastline Mexico offers just about any kind of beach for any kind of personality.

- The water in the Pacific is not as clear or turquoise-colored as the water in the Gulf of Mexico or Caribbean.
- The water is poor around Tampico and Veracruz.
- The water is calm in the Gulf of Mexico and in the Sea of Cortez.
- The Pacific beaches have dark, hot sand—wear sandals. (Remember Dudley Moore in the movie *10*).
- The white sands of the Caribbean stay cool—fantastic.
- There's tar on some of the beaches, a good reason to wear sandals. You can get it off with kerosene.
- Before you get into the water, ask the locals if it's safe!
- Some of the finest beaches are Bahía Concepción near Loreto and isolated beaches at Cabo San Lucas on the Baja Peninsula; Chacahua Beach on the Manialtepec lagoon near Puerto Escondido (reached by boat or *panga*); the many beaches south of Puerto Escondido to Bahías de Huatulco; the lovely beach at Tulúm on the Caribbean south of Cancún; and on and on.
- Blight has killed many palms. The sand remains pure, the water clear.

Biking

While I don't recommend biking as a way of getting around Central America and Mexico, specialized trips are fun.

Backroads
1516 Fifth Street
Berkeley, CA 94710
Tel: (800) 462-2848
    (510) 527-1555
Costa Rica, Mexico (both the Baja and Yucatán).

Remarkable Journeys
P.O. Box 31855
5231 Arboles
Houston, TX 77231
Tel: (800) 856-1993
    (713) 721-2517
Costa Rica.

Nantahala Outdoor Center
13077 Highway 19 West
Bryson City, NC 28713
Tel: (704) 488-2175
Costa Rica.

Birding

Following are some tips which apply to birding throughout the region.
- Birding requires patience and stamina. Getting to good areas by boat or foot is often difficult. Some areas are remote. It might take a week or more to spot a specific bird, if at all.
- Getting to prime birding areas can be extremely expensive.
- Your odds of seeing birds increase dramatically with a good guide, whether local or a part of your tour.
- Birding is similar to hunting. The fewer people, the better.
- The time of day can be critical. Many birds are spotted early or late in the day.
- If you want to see a specific bird, timing is critical. Find out ahead of time exactly what months are best for spotting that bird. Find out exactly where recent sightings have taken place.
- Books are helpful for identification, but few people are really able to use them properly. Guides say that only the most expert birders can make accurate identification from books.
- When birding, move extremely slowly and stop frequently.
- Birds are often difficult to see. You may hear them at the tops of trees, but never get a glimpse of them. A good guide knows the calls and can help you spot them. He may also be able to call birds in. Look closely and carefully wherever you hear even the

smallest sound. Birds are often sitting right in front of you with-out you're knowing it (until you become more expert).
- Watch for tiny flickers of movement.
- Binoculars are a must.
- Birds are spooky. Don't talk. Walk quietly.
- Never point at birds. Simply nod your head in the direction of the bird if you want to indicate its position to a friend.
- Birds see colors easily. Wear subdued colors (light green).
- The best strategy may be to locate a bird's food source or nesting site. Let it come to you as you patiently sit nearby.
- Never disturb birds during courting or nesting by getting too close, no matter how badly you want that photo.

Academic Travel Abroad
3210 Grace Street Northwest
Washington, DC 20007
Tel: (800) 556-7896
Costa Rica, Mexico.

Betchart Expeditions
17050 Montebello Road
Cupertino, CA 95041
Tel: (800) 252-4910
      (408) 252-1444
Well-run wildlife tours to the Sea of Cortez in Mexico and diverse areas of Central America. Birding with experts is included.

Biological Journeys
1696 Ocean Drive
McKinleyville, CA 95521
Tel: (800) 548-7555
      (707) 839-0178
Mexico's Baja peninsula and off-shore islands in the Sea of Cortez.

Borderland Productions
2550 West Calle Padilla
Tucson, AZ 85745
Tel: (800) 525-7753
      (602) 882-7650

Owned by one of the finest birders in the country. Superb birding trips to the Copper Canyon (see Trains below) in Mexico. Also, excellent trips to Belize, Costa Rica and Guatemala.

Clark Tours
9 Boston Street, Suite 9
Lynn, MA 01904
Tel: (800) 223-6764
      (617) 581-0844
Guatemala.

Field Guides
P.O. Box 167023
Austin, TX 78716
Tel: (512) 327-4953
Belize, Costa Rica, Guatemala, Mexico.

Holbrook Travel
3540 Northwest 13th Street
Gainesville, FL 32609
Tel: (800) 451-7111
      (904) 3777-7111
Belize, Costa Rica (owns Selva Verde—great birding area), Guatemala, Honduras.

National Audubon Society
700 Broadway
New York, New York 10003
Tel: (800) 765-1228
     (212) 979-3066
Belize, Costa Rica, Mexico
(see Whale Watching).

Victor Emanuel Nature Tours
P.O. Box 33008
Austin, TX 78764
Tel: (800) 328-8368
     (512) 328-5221
Belize, Costa Rica, Guatemala,
Honduras, Mexico.

Osprey Tours
P.O. Box 832
West Tisbury, MA 02575
Tel: (800) 645-3244
     (508) 645-9049
Focuses on birding in Costa
Rica and Honduras, but does
travel to Belize and Guatemala.

Wings
P.O. Box 31930
Tucson, AZ 85751
Tel: (602) 749-1967
Birding is this company's only
business. It runs tours into
Central America (Honduras
excepted) and Mexico.

BELIZE

Birding is excellent here. Throughout the year you can spot approximately 500 species of birds, some of them quite rare.

* You have the best chance to spot the Jabiru Stork at the Crooked
  Tree Wildlife Sanctuary. This enormous bird with a wingspan of
  up to 12 feet is frequently spotted by chance in varied areas
  throughout the year, although your best chance is in the sanctuary in March.

COSTA RICA

This is one of the best birding countries in the world. You would
have to spend months here to see all of the different varieties (848
species have already been spotted). Popular birding areas are Barra
del Colorado (traveling by boat), Braulio Carrillo National Park
(Quetzales are often spotted near the Barba entrance in season),
Carara Biological Reserve (Scarlet macaws), Corcovado National Park,
La Selva, and Monteverde—with many other areas to go. Visiting
National Parks sounds easier than it is. Expect to spend five to seven
days in more remote parks to get full value out of it. Special lodges
are geared to birders. The Organization of Tropical Studies (*Organi-
zación Para Estudios Tropicales*) at La Selva Biological Station has
marked trails for birders. The daily fee is quite steep, but birding is
good. Selva Verde, a lodge close by, is a nice place to stay. Note that
the area is extremely hot and humid. Rara Avis is difficult to get into,
but one of the prime birding lodges in the country.

- One of the goals of many birders is to see the Quetzal, ironically the national bird of Guatemala. When you come to Costa Rica affects your chances of seeing the bird, as it does other species. For example, if you came in July with a good guide, you might see a dozen or more Quetzales. If you came in November, you'd be lucky to see one or two (with expert help).

GUATEMALA
If it weren't for political unrest, this would be highly recommended for birding. In fact, your chance to see the rare Quetzal (the national bird) is greater here than in Costa Rica. However, the prime sites are located in remote areas—not recommended at this time. Trips to the Biotopo de Quetzal are fine with a tour. Your best chance to see a Quetzal is at dawn or dusk. They court from February to March, nest in April and May. Local guides know where they feed. Do not disturb nesting sites. Best time to see them is April to June. The superb archaeological site of Tikal offers birders a sanctuary for over 220 species. Best to come here in the dry season from January to April.

HONDURAS
Birding is just catching on in Honduras. Go with professionals into areas rarely visited by tourists. The Quetzal is commonly spotted in Consuco National Park from late March to early June.

MEXICO
Some of the best birding spots are Coba in the Yucatán (200 species a year pass through), Isla Contoy off Isla Mujeres, Isla Raza in the Bahía de los Angeles in the Baja, Rancho Liebre Barranca north of Mazatlán, and Río Lagartos (flamingo sanctuary in the Yucatán). The areas around Colima, Oaxaca, and Palenque are also recommended.

Boat trips

For basic boat trips in Belize and Costa Rica work with local agencies or guides. For trips along the Rio Dulce to Lake Izabal in Guatemala (may see manatees in El Golfete en route) you might want to contact:

Best of Belize
31 F Commercial Boulevard
Novato, CA 94949
Tel: (800) 735-9520
    (414) 884-2325.

Ocean Connection
211 East Parkwood, Suite 108
Friendswood, TX 77546
Tel: (713) 996-7800
Same as above.

BELIZE

Just getting around Belize often requires you to get on small boats. Some of the ruins are most easily accessible in this fashion. Naturally, there is quite a bit of boat traffic to smaller islands. All of these trips are fun.

- Highly recommended is a canoe trip down the Macal River.

COSTA RICA

Access to many areas in Costa Rica is by boat only, especially in the Tortuguero area in the northeast. Here you'll see lots of birds and wildlife (the area is extremely hot, humid, and wet).

- A trip on the Sarapiquí can be viewed either as a mild white water trip or a wilderness, jungle adventure depending on where you start.
- The latter begins in Puerto Viejo de Sarapiquí (don't confuse this with Puerto Viejo on the Caribbean coast).
- The best time of year to come is before the peak season. November and early December are highly recommended.
- If you come in the peak season (December to March), the increased boat traffic often scares away birds and wildlife.
- Plan on renting a boat for an all-day trip. The reason is that birds tend to come out early and late, while wildlife varies depending upon the animal. To see the most of each you must travel slowly and quietly for an entire day.
- The person running the boat will act as a guide, pointing out animals and birds which you might not even see.
- Trips can be arranged into Nicaragua with stays in tents or huts there. Locals insist that there is no problem. Be wary. However, the advantage is that you'll see many more birds and wildlife if you stay overnight in the jungle. Note: If you're passport is stamped in Nicaragua, you may not be allowed into Honduras. Carry a spare piece of paper, have them stamp that, and keep it with your passport.
- The cost of any trip will depend on your bargaining skill. If you deal directly with boat owners and can speak a little Spanish, you will not have to pay as much for the trip as one arranged through a local hotel or lodge.
- However, if a hotel or lodge can set you up with an English-speaking guide, the extra money may be worth it.
- Some of the local hotels and lodges run abbreviated trips along the river which give you a feel of what a longer trip would be like. These tend to be overpriced, but fun.

GUATEMALA

Some more adventurous types will want to travel from Livingston up the Rio Dulce to the area called the gulf (El Golfete). This is a manatee reserve. Tour operators have been mentioned earlier.

MEXICO

The Usamacinta trip is an archaeological, nature-lover kind of boat ride (see White Water Rafting below).

Bullfight (*corrida de toros*)

Let's skip the cruelty debate and get right to the point—Mexicans love bullfights and so do a lot of tourists.

- The best bullfights take place in Mexico City. The stadium holds 50,000 avid fans and attracts the top matadors.
- The best matadors perform from December to March. Apprentices (*novilladas*) take over in the off-season—these fights are not recommended (poor bulls, poorer fights).
- Fights start at exactly 4:00 P.M. on Sunday—the one thing in Mexico that's always on time.
- The best tickets are called *barrera*, the second-best *primer tendido*. You won't get these unless you have an "in" or a dynamite concierge (tip well).
- All travel books tell you to get tickets in the shade (*sombre*) and to avoid the sun (*sol*). Since Mexico City floats under a sea of smog, most of the time this advice is irrelevant.
- You can buy tickets at a steep price from tour operators and travel agencies. The extra money is probably worth it since tickets can be hard to come by, and the tour does provide transportation to the ring.
- However, you can get tickets at the ring from scalpers. And, if you're daring and willing to wait, you'll pick them up for face value just as the fight starts.
- Bring binoculars. These will add immeasurably to the spectacle.
- Wear a hat, and if it's sunny (it can happen), bring sunglasses for the *sol* section.
- Bring a newspaper or rent a cushion for fanny fatigue.
- Bring small bills and coins to pay for snacks and drinks.
- Don't bring valuables with you—this is a favored area for pickpockets.
- If you don't like a fight, leave. Showing disgust or getting upset is offensive to Mexicans who view bullfights as an art.
- Finally, most bullfights fall far short of art. If you see a great one, you'll know it.

Butterflies (*mariposas*)

There are an estimated 90,000 varieties of butterflies in the world. Butterflies come out in the day, close their wings, have slender bodies, and dots on the end of their antennae. Moths come out at night, rest with wings open, have thick bodies, and fuzzy or hairy antennae which end in a sharp point. When an irridescent Blue Morpho flits past, it's a thrilling moment.

COSTA RICA

Costa Rica boasts 10 percent of the world's butterflies and more than in all of Africa. Exhibits are found in La Garita (Zoo Ave) and La Guacima (The Butterfly Farm). In San José visit the Museum of Entomology (Museo de Entomologia) at the University's Faculdad de Agronomia. It's free, but open only for a few hours each week. Ask the local tourist office about current times.

MEXICO

Two hours from Toluca in the town of Donato Guerrero you'll find the winter resting area for millions of monarch butterflies. They arrive in October and leave in March. There's a butterfly reserve close to the town of Angangueo, at its peak from January to March. Photography at this time is sensational. Butterfly viewing is weather dependent.

Betchart Expeditions
17050 Montebello Road
Cupertino, CA 95014
Tel: (800) 252-4910
    (408) 252-4910
This is the company that originated tours to this area. These upscale tours accompanied by expert guides are geared to people *serious* about entomology and photography of the monarchs.

Joseph Van Os Photo Safaris
P.O. Box 655
Vashon Island, WA 98070
Tel: (206) 463-5383
Normally takes photo trips to two areas, Herrada (near Valle de Bravo) and Rosario in mid-February.

Wildland Adventures
3516 Northeast 155th Street
Seattle, WA 98155
Tel: (800) 345-4453
    (206) 365-0686

Caves (*cuevas*)

Some people really enjoy cave exploration. This can be extremely dangerous. Be vaccinated against rabies. Many areas are filled with sinkholes. Some of the underground caves have rivers running through them. Good shoes, water and food, proper lighting equipment, ropes, and an experienced guide are absolutely critical.

BELIZE
The Rio Frio caves in the Pine Ridge Mountain area are open.

COSTA RICA (see National Parks)
Costa Rica has a number of caves. The best are in the northwest and on the Nicoya Peninsula. Ask the tourist office in San José for more detailed information.

MEXICO
The fresh-water springs (*cenotes*) near Akumal can be explored by divers, who should be certified for this kind of activity. You crawl down a hole with a rope and then begin the dive. If you would like to do this with a group, contact:

Caradonna Caribbean Tours
P.O. Box 3299
Longwood, FL 32779
Tel: (800) 328-2288
    (407) 774-9000

Climbing (*alpinismo*)

There are many volcanoes throughout Central America and Mexico. Mountains are popular for hikers and mountain climbers in season. Note that volcano climbing is still not recommended in Guatemala. Following are companies which specialize in this activity:

Above The Clouds Trekking
P.O. Box 398
Two Tory Fort Lane
Worcester, MA 01602
Tel: (800) 233-4499
    (508) 799-4499
Costa Rica (including a climb to Chirripo at the highest point in the country—requires lots of energy and advance planning).

Great Adventure Travel Company
645 North Michigan Avenue, Suite 800
Chicago, Illinois 60611

Tel: (800) 874-2826
    (312) 880-5764
Belize, Costa Rica, Guatemala, Honduras, Mexico. A "soft" adventure company which emphasizes trekking.

Mountain Travel
6420 Fairmount Avenue
El Cerrito, CA 94530
Tel: (800) 227-2384
    (510) 527-8100
Specializes in arduous climbs in Mexico, including popular volcanoes.

MEXICO
- You're on your own if you get in trouble. Bear this in mind on all climbs. Have or ask about a safety network.
- Some of the rock is extremely weathered and potentially dangerous, and much of the terrain is covered with dense jungle.
- The three most popular volcanoes are Ixtaccihuatl (17,400'), Orizaba (18,800'), and Popocatepetl (17,700').
- Breathing is difficult on ascents. Spend no less than 2 days in Mexico City and one at the base of each mountain.
- Climbing is best from November to early December. It's okay in January and February.
- Start ascents very early, about 2 to 3 A.M.
- You should be accompanied by an experienced climber or guide who knows glaciers and crevasses.
- You should carry appropriate gear, including ice anchors, axe, crampons, rope, warm weather clothes, and so on.
- You'll need food and water.
- Take these climbs seriously. They are not for amateurs.

Cruises

Most of the companies offering whale watching trips also are nature-oriented with truly fascinating tours. See Whale Watching below.

Clipper Cruise Line
7711 Bonhomme Avenue
St. Louis, MO 63105
Tel: (800) 325-0010
       (314) 727-2929
Specializes in nature-oriented trips to see bird and sea life in Costa Rica and Mexico.

Tauck Tours, Inc.
11 Wilton Road
Westport, CT 06880
Tel: (203) 226-6911
Combines land and sea travel along Costa Rica and then on through the Panama Canal.

Diving (See Scuba Diving)

Exploration (see Adventure and Jungle Trekking)

Festivals (*fiestas*)

Mountain Travel
6420 Fairmount Avenue
El Cerrito, CA 94530
Tel: (800) 227-2384
     (510) 527-8100
Guatemala.

Remarkable Journeys
P.O. Box 31855
5231 Arboles
Houston, TX 77231
Tel: (800) 856-1993
     (713) 721-2517
Mexico.

GUATEMALA

Festivals with lots of fireworks are an everyday occurrence. One festival stands out—Holy Week (*Semana Santa*) in Antigua. If you plan to come here at this time, make reservations at least a year or more in advance. It is one of the great celebrations in Central America. The local residents cover entire streets with colored sawdust laid out in intricate patterns and build immense floats with full-size, carved wooden figures. The celebration "Fiesta de Santo Tomas" takes place in December in Chichicastenango and is second to the festival in Antiqua in color and importance. In smaller towns the fiestas can get quite raucous. Drunkenness can become a problem.

MEXICO

There are so many festivals in Mexico that a list fills a 200-page book *Fiestas in Mexico*. Every day there's a major festival somewhere.

• Reservations are hard to make in towns with major festivals, such as during Carnival in Mazatlán. So plan ahead.

• Some hotels offer perfect views of festivals, and if you can make reservations in these, you have a ringside seat. For instance, the rooms at the Hotel Majestic or Gran Hotel overlooking the zócalo in Mexico City are in demand on the night of September 15.

• Certain towns are known for being the "best" in certain festivals. Holy Week in Taxco draws thousands of spectators. So if festivals are a major interest, study the options ahead of time and make reservations accordingly.

• Tourist offices (see pp. 25–27) have lots of *free* information on festivals and a calendar of major events. Get these in advance.

Fishing

Listed below are popular game fish. Spanish names change by region and can cause confusion, but the following list will help you.

Basic Fishing Terms

albacore	*albacore*
amberjack	*pez fuerte*
ballyhoo, balao	*escribano*
barracuda	*barracuda, picuda*
bass (black)	*lobina*
bass (black sea)	*cabrilla*
black marlin	*marlín negro*
blue marlin	*marlin azul*
bobo	inland fish in Costa Rica
bonefish	*macabí*
bonita	*bonito*
catfish	*bagre*
corbina	*curbina*
dolphin, dorado	*dorado, dolphin, mahi mahi*
grouper	*cherna, mero, garropa*
guapote	Inland fish found in Lake Arenal (best fished in May)
jack (crevalle)	*jurel (toro)*
jewfish	*mero*
lady fish	*pez dama*
mackerel (Spanish)	*sierra*
marlin	*marlín*
mojarra	*mojarra* (like a bluegill)
mullet	*lisa*
needlefish	*picuda, aguja*
parrotfish	*perico, pez loro*
pompano	*palometa, pampano*
porgy	*mojarra*
rainbow trout	*trucho arco iris*
red snapper	*huachinango, pargo rojo*
roosterfish	*pez gallo*
sailfish	*pez vela*
sardine	*sardina*
seabass	*mero, corvina*
shark	*tiburón*
snapper	*pargo*
snook	*robálo*
striped marlin	*marlín rayado*
swordfish	*pez espada*
tarpon	*sábalo*
triggerfish	*pez puerco, bota*
trout (rainbow)	*trucha (arco iris)*
tuna (yellowfin)	*atún (cola amarilla)*
wahoo	*sierra golfina, peto*
white marlin	*marlín blanco*
yellowtail	*jurel*

Companies Specializing in Fishing

Following are companies specializing in fishing in Central America and Mexico. Here are a few tips about these companies:

- These companies know differences beween lodges. They know how to match you to your destination.
- Contact them for their brochures and current offerings to compare accommodations, fishing, and prices.
- If you're after a specific type of fish, companies know exactly where and when to go after it. So be specific in what you want.
- Companies often reserve space in peak fishing periods. You may need their help to get into a lodge at a specific time.
- Some companies get reduced airfare. Compare what they offer to what you can arrange on your own.
- Confirmations from some lodges can be time-consuming and difficult. By working through the listed companies, there is less chance that your reservation will be bungled or difficult to make.

- Companies insist that you pay no more working through them than you would if you contacted the lodge directly.
- These companies will tell you exactly what you need to bring for the type of fishing you'll be doing. Their checklists are detailed and come from years of experience.
- Some of the companies even have catalogs with suggested equipment and prices.

Angler Adventure
P.O. Box 872
Old Lyme, CT 06371
Tel: (800) 628-1447
   (203) 434-9624
Belize, Costa Rica (both coasts),
Mexico (Baja and Yucatán).

Anglers Travel Connection
1280 Terminal Way, Suite 30
Reno, Nevada 89434
Tel: (800) 624-8429
   (702) 324-0580
Belize, Costa Rica (east and west coasts), Honduras, Mexico (Baja, Yucatán, and inland bass fishing).

Chapman's Executive Resorts, Inc.
P.O. Box 12163
El Paso, TX 79912
Tel: (915) 581-3580
A good contact for bass fishermen, who would like to take a tour to Mexico.

Fisherman's Landing
2838 Garrison Street
San Diego, CA 92106
Tel: (619) 221-8500/222-0391
Short and long fishing trips to the Baja (Mexico).

Fishing International
4775 Sonoma Highway
Santa Rosa, CA 95409

Tel: (800) 950-4242
   (707) 539-3366
Belize, Costa Rica, Guatemala, Honduras, Mexico.

Frontiers International Travel
(Fish and Game Frontiers, Inc.)
P.O. Box 959
100 Logan Road
Wexford, PA 15090
Tel: (800) 245-1950
   (412) 935-1577
Specializes in light-tackle fishing in Belize, Costa Rica, Mexico. Works with 4 lodges in Belize. Has been in business for more than 25 years.

Golfito Sailfish Rancho
International Reservations
   Center, Inc.
P.O. Box 290190
San Antonio, TX 78280
Tel: (800) 531-7232
   (512) 377-0451
One of the best-known fishing resorts on the southern Pacific Coast of Costa Rica. Marlin, roosterfish, and sailfish. Accessible only by boat. Guarantees you'll catch a sailfish or you get a return trip free. Sailfishing best January to May.

CLUB MEX
3450 Bonita Road, Suite 101
Chula Vista, CA 91910
Tel: (619) 585-3033
A club with lots of information
on fishing in Mexico.

Outdoor Adventures
P.O. Box 608
McAllen, TX 78505
Tel: (800) 375-4868
    (210) 618-1168
Costa Rica (both coasts), Mex-
ico (large-mouth bass fishing
on inland lakes).

PanAngling Travel
180 North Michigan Avenue,
  Suite 303
Chicago, IL 60601
Tel: (800) 533-4353
Belize, Costa Rica (both coasts),
Guatemala (west coast), Mexico
(Baja and Yucatán).

Parismina Tarpon Rancho
International Reservations
  Center
P.O. Box 290190
San Antonio, TX 78280
Tel: (800) 531-7232
    (512) 377-0451
This is one of Costa Rica's best
lodges for snook and tarpon.

Sunbelt Hunting and Travel, Inc.
P.O. Box 3009
Brownsville, TX 78520
Tel: (210) 546-9101

This is another good source for
information on bass fishing in
Mexico.

Tamarindo Sportfishing
Apartado 188
Santa Cruz, Guanacaste
Costa Rica
Central America
Tel: 011 (506) 67 40 90
Costa Rica. Specializes in
advanced catch and release
techniques of large fish.

Tropical Travel
5 Grogans Park, Suite 102
The Woodlands, TX 77380
Tel: (800) 451-8017
    (713) 367-3386
Belize, Costa Rica, Honduras,
Mexico (Cancún and Cozumel).

United Sportfishing, Inc.
2803 Emerson Street
San Diego, CA 92106
Tel: (619) 222-1144
Mexico.

World Wide Sportsman, Inc.
P. O. Drawer 787
Islamorada, FL 33036
Tel: (800) 327-2880
    (305) 664-4615
    (305) 238-9252 (Miami)
Specialists in bonefish, snook,
and tarpon in Mexico. Can set
up billfishing in Costa Rica as
well.

Special Tips on Fishing at Lodges

- Some lodges are geared just to fishing. Others are suited to both fishing and relaxation (for the non-fishing partner).
- If the quality of rooms, food, and extra amenities is important because you're traveling with someone who really cares little

about fishing, ask about these. Make it clear that you need all of the above to be satisfied (or, at least, your companion does).

- Some lodges are really close to the action, others farther away. Ask how long the run is to the fishing grounds.
- In some lodges you can fish from sunrise to sunset, really fishing your heart out. In others, the fishing day is much shorter. If you want to fish long hours, ask about this ahead of time.
- Always bring packaged snacks with you. You may be given a good breakfast, but when you're out fishing, you may want more than the guides bring with them to eat or drink.
- Protect yourself from the elements. Bring two sets of raingear. One often gets ripped. It should be the best you can afford. It can get extremely hot and humid in some areas. Get fully waterproof clothing which breathes (GoreTex).
- Protect yourself from the sun with a wide-brimmed hat, sunglasses (bring an extra pair), sunscreen, long-sleeved shirt, long pants, and so on. When you get close to the Tropics, the sun can be extremely dangerous. Besides, it reflects off water.
- Buy rods which break down. These traveling rods are popular because you can carry them onto the plane. Have spare rods and reels. Never put these into checked baggage.
- Check all your equipment out carefully. Make sure it works well. Buy new line. Carry extra line.
- Mark your dufflebag or backpack with permanent marker. This way your bag won't be confused with someone else's. People often have similar bags, and the confusion is annoying.
- Place clothing into plastic bags before putting them into your backpack or duffle. Mark each piece with a permanent marker (as if going to camp). Spray your duffle or backpack with water repellant. When it rains, it really rains—torrents.
- Whether you're fishing with guides or independently, sharpen your hooks. Carry a file with you and sharpen tips constantly.
- Never stay out in a storm. Don't let guides take you into rough seas with inappropriate boats. Some are very macho.

When Not Fishing at a Lodge
- Many guides who work at lodges also free-lance on off days. If you just want to fish for a day, ask about these locally—not easily done in the most remote areas.
- If you want to go deep-sea fishing on charter boats during peak seasons, you must reserve a boat far in advance.
- Most charters offer one-half or full-day fishing at set rates.
- Although rates tend to be similar, they're rarely identical. In non-peak seasons get special, reduced rates for fishing trips. Bargain.

- When striking a bargain with a captain or charter company, get the price in writing.
- Prices for full-day charters usually include a lunch, but rarely include drinks, license, or any extras.
- Prices for half-day and full-day charters usually include the boat, equipment, and bait. You should ask about the policy on lost or broken rods, reels, and lures.
- Don't assume that boats will have all necessary equipment. Some have just about everything. Others very little.
- Look at the boat carefully. If an outboard, make sure it has two motors if you'll be out in the open sea.
- Ask to see the fishing rods, reels, and line.
- Bring steel leaders, if appropriate for the kind of fishing you'll be doing. Many local guides have heavy line, but no steel.
- For isolated areas where you know there are few boats or guides bring all of your own equipment.
- Fishing is expensive. By asking around, you can almost always find someone else to share costs.
- Ask the guides what kind of bait they'll be using. Having enough live bait may be the difference between great and lousy fishing. It is extremely frustrating to pay a lot of money, get to an area, and run out of bait.
- Each guide may vary in what is meant by a half or full day of fishing. Ask to be sure.
- Be very specific about the kind of fish you're after. Ask how far the run is to good fishing. If the run's too far, you might be smart to fish from a different location.

If Fishing is All Important

- In general, fish follow certain patterns each year. People have come up with fishing calendars to give a rough idea of what fish are in season when. Try to match your trip with the best time for catching the kind of fish you're after.
- Year in and year out certain boats have the most "luck." Getting this information is difficult unless you're able to ask questions in person. Talk to other fishermen in the area for their advice on boats and captains. A good question: Who's the most sought-after captain for fishing tournaments?
- Some areas claim to have lots of good "big-game" fishing. When you check into the hotel, check the bulletin boards for pictures of fish caught that year. If they're not the kind of "big-game" fish you're after, consider moving on.

If You Have Your Own Boat (see p. 83)

- Boats give you lots of freedom, but watch tides and winds. Inquire locally about potential danger.
- Keep your boat and equipment as simple as possible.
- In some areas, good fishing can be found right off the shore. For boaters these areas are the safest and simplest to fish.
- You may have to get a launch permit before you can put your boat in the water. Inquire locally about regulations.

Surf Fishing

- Bring all the fishing equipment you'll need. It's extremely expensive and very difficult to find.
- Bring all the hooks, line, and lures you'll need as well. One of the best and most versatile lures is the Rapala in a variety of sizes. Most effective colors are white, white and blue, and white and red.
- Good live bait: chitons, clams, conch (endangered), fish, limpets, mussels, oysters, and worms.
- Shore or surf fishing can be fabulous, but be sensitive. For example, shore fishing on Cozumel has been described as the equivalent of hunting in a zoo.
- When surf fishing, keep moving along the shoreline until you get action. Don't leave bait in one place for more than five minutes. No strike? Move another 50 yards down the shore and try again. Keep doing this until you find the fish.

About Tarpon

Your local guide will give lots of advice on catching tarpon and will know tricks for that area. One special tip from an expert:

- Most fish you hook by pulling up sharply. For tarpon, pull sharply toward your stomach.

BELIZE

Belize offers a wide variety of fishing on all types of tackle. The Belize River Lodge is on the mainland and in a region where it rains frequently. It has easy access to the airport. It offers bonefish (year-round), snook, and tarpon (late spring through summer). El Pescador on Ambergris offers bone and tarpon fishing. However, there are a number of small boats for charter in town if you would like to fish for black grouper or wahoo. Black grouper congregate off the northern part of the island in January. Bring steel leaders, since locals don't have them. Make sure the guide has plenty of bonefish for bait. Fishing around Turneffe is also excellent for bonefish and tarpon, but especially for bonefish. You can walk the flats to spot large fish in large schools (mostly bonefish). Blue Marlin Lodge on Southwater Caye has some of the best permit fishing in the world. Many other areas are represented by the tour operators listed earlier.

COSTA RICA

Costa Rica is a mecca for fishing. Just over 100 people caught and released 1691 sailfish and marlin in a 4-day period in May of 1991.

- Billfishing is best on the Pacific. The billfish move along the shoreline so that areas vary in quality by the time of year, but there are always some billfish somewhere along the coast at any time of year. In general, the southern part of the coast is best from November to April, the northern best April to December. However, each specific resort is best for a specific fish at a certain time of year. Knowing this is critical information.
- Snook and tarpon fishing is best off the mouth of the Colorado River in the northeastern part of the country (Tortuguero). There are numerous fishing camps in this isolated area (new ones are opening up). Most are accessible by boat and plane only and are quite expensive. Snook fishing is possible from January to May. You can catch lots of small fish in January. Camps vary in recommendations for large snook, but most agree that the September to mid-October period is great. A few claim that May can be sensational for large fish. Tarpon are caught from January to mid-May, but they peak in March. A few are caught off the river mouth in September and October. Note that netting of fish (mainly snook) has been taking place on this coast and hurting the fishing in recent years. Ask about this in advance. It can reduce fishing to almost zero. The netting is illegal, but the government has a hard time stopping it.
- Lake Arenal, close to the Arenal Volcano, has a season for rainbow bass (*guapote*). You fish for these just as you would for largemouth bass. The rainbows can get up to 12 pounds. Ask in advance about the season.

GUATEMALA

For the truly adventurous fishing can be quite an experience near Livingston. Tarpon run in the Rio Dulce from March to June. There are also snook in Lake Izabal and off Livingston, the best month is October. Snook are also said to be in Lake Petexbatun in the Peten in July and August. Bring all of your own equipment and hire a boat with a guide locally. Note that the Golden Sail Lodge has recently opened on the West Coast and offers billfishing. Note that very few people go to Guatemala to fish.

HONDURAS

This country is just beginning to attract tourists. Snook and tarpon fishing along the coast are just beginning to be offered. Use one of the companies listed above.

MEXICO

One of the primary attractions of Mexico for many tourists is its fabulous deep-sea, surf, and specialized fishing. It offers some of the finest fishing in the world.

- Some of the better fishing hotels in southern Baja include Cabo Baja, Cabo San Lucas, Finisterra, Hacienda, Los Barriles, Mar de Cortez, Palmas de Cortez, Palmilla, Punta Colorada (fabulous roosterfish fishing), Punta Pescadero, Rancho Buena Vista (World Festival of Fishing), and the Twin Dolphin.
- Reservations should be made as far in advance as possible in these hotels during the peak seasons.
- One of the finest billfish areas is the stretch of water off the Baja south of La Paz to Cabo San Lucas. Special fishing camps have been attracting sportsmen to this area for years.
- On the mainland both Manzanillo and Mazatlán claim to be the "sailfish capital of the world." Neither are.
- If you have your own boat, some of the finest fishing areas are the ones none of the sports fishing fleets even service. The area off the west coast to the south of Puerto Vallarta is superb.
- Zihuatenejo also offers fabulous billfishing at the right time.
- In the Yucatán, excellent fishing resorts are Ascension Bay Bonefish Club, Boca Paila, and Pez Maya on Ascension Bay. Farther south is Casa Blanca. Here you'll fish for bonefish, permit, snook, and tarpon on light tackle. Tarpon are also found inland in the Paradise Lake chain. Note that there are other camps in the area as well. I've just mentioned the best-known.
- On Cozumel off the Yucatán there's bonefishing in the "Monte Cristo" and "Rio de la Plata" lagoons.
- Near Cancún you can find excellent bone fishing. Ask locally about guides specializing in day fishing.
- If you're into largemouth bass fishing, El Salto 100 miles north of Mazatlán has trophy bass (in the 7 to 12-pound range). Smaller, but plentiful, bass are in Comedoro. But, there are a number of other lakes as well. Fishing is usually poor during the summer as water is drained off for irrigation purposes.
- For up-to-date information on fishing regulations and licenses, contact the following organization or work through one of the companies listed earlier:

Mexican Department of Fisheries (Oficina Recaudadora de Pesca)
2550 Fifth Avenue, Suite 101
San Diego, CA 92103
Tel: (619) 233-6956

Flora

Central America and Mexico have an enormous diversity of plant life.
Frangipani (*plumeria*), ginger, hibiscus, poinciana (*flamboyana*), and
hundreds of other plants will be of interest to the botanist, nature
lover, or serious photographer. The Central American countries are
notable for bromeliads and thousands of varieties of orchids.

- Many people are tempted to bring exotic plants, especially
  orchids, back to Canada or the United States.
- This is illegal without the proper paperwork. You must have permission from foreign governments to remove any plants. This
  regulation is strictly enforced.
- For information on importation of plants get in touch with the
  local branch of the Customs Department. Importing plants must
  be done within extremely tight controls for numerous reasons—
  primarily to protect our own plants from disease and endangered
  plants from extinction.

BELIZE

Much of the country is covered in jungle. Experts on orchids are
Godoy & Sons in Orange Walk. They export them.

COSTA RICA

The diversity of plants in Costa Rica is a natural marvel. This is a
botanist's heaven. Very popular are the Lankester Gardens (4 miles
east of Cartago with 800 varieties of orchids in bloom in March and
April) and the Wilson Botanical Gardens near San Vito (a long drive
from the Capital into a mountainous area in the South). The latter is
part of the Organization of Tropical Studies and is best visited from
February through April.

- For information on orchid shows (usually held in March and September) contact the National Tourist Office or the following;

Orchid Association of Costa Rica
Apartado 6351
1000 San José
Costa Rica
Central America

Golf

Costa Rica has several 9-hole golf courses and one 18-hole course at Cariari Country Club. Few people come to Central America for golf. On the other hand, Mexico has dozens of courses, many of which are superb. Golf is an aristocratic sport in Mexico with prices to match. Many courses are open to the public, but others are difficult to get into. Note that many resorts have their own courses. Travel agents are familiar with these. For a list of courses contact the Mexican Government Tourist Office nearest you (see p. 26).

- On weekdays some private clubs will let nonmembers play.
- If you have a letter of introduction from your club and if it is associated with the U.S. Golf Association, you can sometimes get into a private club.
- You can get into a private club if a member vouches for you.
- If you're staying in a fine hotel, the concierge can sometimes arrange for an entry to a private club.
- Do not try to get into a private club on weekends, since restrictions at this time are tight.
- Bring your own equipment and lots of spare balls. All sporting goods are ultraexpensive in Mexico.
- Golf carts are often scarce or "in the shop" being repaired. If you have to have a cart, check on availability far in advance.
- If golfing is really your bag, you may want to contact the following company:

Best Golf
332 Forest Avenue, Suite 27
Laguna Beach, CA 926651
Tel: (800) 227-0212
      (714) 752-8881
Mexico.

Green Wave

Look for the green wave (*ola verde*) off the Manzanillo to Jiquilpan Highway at Cuyutlan in April and May. This giant wave breaks on the shore and shimmers green from the phosphorescent creatures in its curl. Note too that on occasion you may walk along a Costa Rican beach and see glowing footsteps. I've been told that these are particles of jellyfish, one of the turtle's favorite foods.

Hang Gliding (*papalotes a las delta*)

Not a big sport in Mexico, but growing. You have to bring all of your own equipment into the country, because none is available for rent locally (hang gliders don't rent out their gear). Note that there are some excellent hang gliding areas in Guatemala, but this is still not recommended until the political situation is more stable.

- You should have credentials from a free flight club in the United States and Canada.
- The south winds from December to April are the best.
- Some good spots (states in parenthesis): Acapulco (Guerrero)— The broadcast tower, Cantamar (Baja), Chapa de Mota (México— Best June to September), Cumbres de Acutzingo (Puebla), Guadalajara (Jalisco—Tequila Hill), Iguala (Guerrero—The micro-wave (*microonda*) tower), Jocotitlan (México), Tapalpa (Jalisco), Tulancingo (Hidalgo—best June to September), and Valle de Bravo (México).

Hiking

Costa Rica and Mexico are sensational areas for hiking or trekking. Belize also has some excellent hiking areas, but fewer. The following travel organizations specialize in hiking:

Backroads
1516 Fifth Street
Berkeley, CA 94710
Tel: (800) 462-2848
    (510) 527-1555
Specializes in long hikes in Costa Rica, but also offers trip to Baja California (Mexico).

Wilderness Travel
801 Allston Way
Berkeley, CA 94710
Tel: (800) 368-2794
    (510) 548-0420
Guatemala.

Hunting

Bird shooting is excellent in Mexico. Hunting for whitewing dove is one of the most popular sports because the birds are abundant. Hunting is best from August through October. Duck, geese, and quail are normally hunted from November through January.

Game Birds

duck	*pato*	**quail**	*codorniz*
goose	*ganso*	**white wing dove**	*paloma de ala*
morning dove	*paloma huilota*		*blanca*
pheasant	*gallo de montés,*		
	faisán de collar		

Mexhunt Bookings
3302 Josie Avenue
Long Beach, CA 90808
Tel: (310) 421-6215

Mexico Services
12421 Venice Blvd., Ste. 2
P.O. Box 66278
Los Angeles, CA 90066
Tel: (310) 398-5797

Outdoor Adventures
P.O. Box 608
McAllen, TX 78505
Tel: (800) 375-4868

(210) 618-1168

Sunbelt Hunting and Travel,
   Inc.
P.O. Box 3009
Brownsville, TX 78502
Tel: (210) 546-9101

Wildlife Advisory Services
P.O. Box 76132
Los Angeles, CA 90076
Tel: (213) 385-9311

Basic Tips

- You bring your own guns into Mexico if possible. Although you can rent them in some camps, gun repair is difficult in Mexico and many rental guns are in poor condition.
- Prepare for a hunting trip far in advance since regulations on the importation of guns are strict.
- If you intend to bring game back to your area, check with customs on current regulations.
- Bring as much ammunition into Mexico as possible.
- Note that if you travel by plane, you will have to have the gun put in a case. Get the kind which will protect it even when checked—some airlines provide these cases at a reasonable price to customers (especially airlines flying to Canada).
- Ask if it's possible for the gun to be carried on by a flight attendant to limit the risk of damage or theft. Some airlines will do this, others won't.
- Have your gun insured for full *replacement* value.

Gun Permits

You are not allowed to take a gun into Mexico without a special permit. Bringing a gun across the border without a permit is a serious offense. If you're caught, you'll be put in prison.

- Getting a gun permit involves high cost and lots of red tape. Contact the nearest Mexican Consulate for current regulations and fees. Do this as far in advance as possible—getting a permit can take a long time!

Indian Culture

GUATEMALA

The Indians, who prefer to be called *naturales* or *indígenas*, are struggling to survive in Guatemala. Many continue to speak any of 95 different dialects based on two underlying languages. Many Indians continue to live as they have for centuries, following ancient traditions, and wearing traditional costumes. It is best to take a guide to any of the more remote villages. Photography is accepted in some areas, not in others. Be extremely sensitive. Your guide will help you in this regard. In the more heavily visited villages people will allow photographs to be taken if they are paid. In general, Indians turn away from anyone trying to get a photo unless payment has been agreed to or permission granted in advance.

MEXICO

- Your first stop should be the Archaeological Museum in Mexico City. The displays on the second floor will amaze you.
- Indian cultures thrived in Mexico and achieved greatness hundreds of years before the Europeans arrived on the scene. Many of these cultures are still alive. If you're willing to get off the beaten path, you'll find them for yourself.

Jai Alai (*Frontón*)

The best jai alai is in Tijuana. But you can also see it in Mexico City.

Jungle Exploration

Many companies can get you into the National Parks of Costa Rica. The following is one of the few which deals with travel into the remote areas of Belize and Honduras:

Get Lost Adventures
1171 East Putnam Avenue
Riverside, CT 06878
Tel: (800) 955-5635
     (203) 637-4920

- **Warning:** Much of Central America and Mexico remains to be explored. This is a highly specialized activity, and most experienced explorers recommend a guide, especially for remote, jungle areas. I would avoid any exploration in Guatemala. Certain areas of Mexico turn hot from time to time, so keep your ear to the ground, and your nose into the wind.

Kayaking—Inland (see White Water Rafting)

Kayaking—Sea

Sea kayaking is gaining in popularity because it takes you into areas barely touched by other tourists. Outfits will tell you exactly what to bring, but at the very least you'll need a bathing suit, extra clothing in a waterproof bag, food, helmet, kayak, life jacket, paddles, tennis shoes, and lots of water. The following companies are geared to this aspect of adventure travel:

Baja Expeditions, Inc.
2625 Garnet Avenue
San Diego, CA 92109
Tel: (800) 843-6967
     (619) 581-3311
Trips to Costa Rica and the
Sea of Cortez (Mexico).

Mountain Travel
6420 Fairmount Avenue
El Cerrito, CA 94530
Tel: (800) 227-2384
     (510) 527-8100
Trips in the Baja area of Mexico.

Eco-Summer Expeditions
1516 Duranleau Street
Vancouver, BC V6H 3S4
Tel: (800) 688-8605 (US)
     (800) 465-8884 (Canada)
     (604) 669-7741
Belize, Mexico (Baja).

Nantahala Outdoor Center
13077 Highway 19 West
Bryson City, NC 28713
Tel: (704) 488-2175
Trips in the Baja area of Mexico.

Remarkable Journeys
P.O. Box 31855
5231 Arboles
Houston, TX 77231
Tel: (800) 856-1993
    (713) 721-2517
Honduras.

Safari Centre International
3201 North Sepulveda Boulevard
Manhattan Beach, CA 90266
Tel: (800) 223-6046
    (310) 546-4411
Belize, Costa Rica.

Rothschild Travel
900 West End Avenue,
    Suite 1B
New York, NY 10025
Tel: (800) 359-0747
    (212) 662-4858
Trips from Placencia in southern Belize.

Slickrock Adventures, Inc.
P.O. Box 1400
76 South Main Street No. 1
Moab, Utah 84532
Tel: (801) 259-6996
Runs sea kayaking out of Glover's Reef (a lovely atoll) in Belize.

BELIZE

Sea kayaking is popular out of Placencia in southern Belize. Trips take you out to isolated cayes, including Laughing Bird.

COSTA RICA

Although this sport is relatively new here, the Pacific coastline is 750 miles long and magnificent.

MEXICO

The Sea of Cortez is one of the most beautiful areas to explore by water. Kayaking here is an adventure.

Manatees

Your best chance of spotting these endangered animals is in Guatemala. You head up the Rio Dulce from Livingston to El Golfete. Only a few tours or tourists go into that area, although quite a few Guatemalans have fancy homes around a lake farther inland. A safer place to spot manatees is in the Crystal River Sanctuary in Florida (but then this isn't a guide on Florida).

Markets (*mercados*)

GUATEMALA

The markets in Guatemala are among the best in the world. The most famous is the market at Chichicastenango on Thursday and Sunday. Here you'll find almost any kind of weaving available from the surrounding Indian villages. Although the market is outdoors, it's really like a series of pathways with countless stalls covered in black plastic. It's fascinating but not what many travelers picture in their minds. Every Indian village has its market day. Particularly popular are the markets in villages surrounding Quetzaltenango, including Almolonga, San Francisco El Alto, Totonicapan, and Zunil. The latter is noted for its colorful costumes. Markets in the villages around Lake Atitlán are also fun. A number of Indians continue to wear native dress there as well. If traveling to more remote villages, go with a guide who speaks the Indian languages. This is not only for safety but for added enjoyment.

MEXICO
The best market in Mexico is the one you're closest to. They're all interesting, some are unbelievable in color and action.
* Here are favorites: Guadalajara's *San Juan de Díos*, Mexico City: *La Merced*; Oaxaca: *Juárez*; Puebla: *Tepeaca*; and the markets at San Cristóbal de las Casas and at Toluca (on Friday). The large indoor market in Mérida is colorful and interesting.

Museums

COSTA RICA
The two most popular museums in San José are the Gold Museum (Museo de Oro) and the Jade Museum (Museo de Jade). The Gold Museum is only open Friday to Sunday at limited times—a problem for many travelers. The Insect Museum (Museo de Entomologia) is popular with butterfly collectors. It too is only open at limited times.

GUATEMALA
In Guatemala City visit the Museo Ixchel de Traja Indigena (5,000 pieces of Indian costumes), Museo de Arqueologia y Etnologia (Mayan Carvings), and Museo Popol Vuh (Mayan Art). The relief map showing a topographic rendering of the country is popular with some.

MEXICO
The Anthropology Museum in Mexico City is one of the best in the world. It is closed on Mondays, so plan your trip accordingly. It can easily be reached by subway or bus—just ask. Many visitors prefer starting on the second floor of this museum.

Music

GUATEMALA

You're most likely to hear music on religious holidays and during festivals. Most fascinating are the *chirimia* (flute), drums, and *marimba* (xylophone-like instruments in varying sizes with a haunting sound similar to the African *limba*). Festivals are extremely common in Indian villages. Ask locally about them.

MEXICO

Guadalajara and Mexico City offer the most to music-lovers on a formal basis.

- *Mariachis*: These late-night entertainers are everywhere in Mexico, but one of the most famous areas is Garibaldi Plaza in Mexico City. Note that this area can get wild.
- You're expected to tip mariachis if they perform at your table anywhere in Mexico.
- *Happy hour*: This U.S. import is becoming very popular in Mexico in areas frequented by tourists. Normal happy hours are 4:00 P.M. to 8:00 P.M. The tradition is getting strong in the better hotels of Acapulco and Mexico City. What makes these happy hours stand out is the wide range of music.

National Parks

Each country has protected zones, either in the form of reserves or national parks. Some of these are easily accessible, others really are geared to adventure travel.

BELIZE

The most popular restricted areas are the Baboon Sanctuary, Jaguar Preserve, and Pine Ridge area on the mainland. Off-shore several atolls and marine parks are superb for diving, fishing, and snorkeling.

COSTA RICA

This country has an extensive park and reserve system. Because information on these is getting more difficult to get, here's an outline:

- Barra del Colorado is an extremely wet area (240 inches a year) accessible only by boat. It's noted for birding, fishing, and wildlife. It's driest from February to April. Note that the area is being destroyed rapidly by illegal logging.
- Barra Honda is noted primarily for its caverns. You have a good chance to spot a coati here. There are hiking trails and campsites. It's driest from January through March.
- Bolanos Island (*Isla Bolanos*) is noted as a fine birding location.

You reach it only by boat. Shelling is said to be good on the eastern end. The area is often windy. It's driest from January through March.

- Braulio Carrillo is an extremely large, popular park noted for birding (333 species have been seen here). It's easily accessible from San José and does have trails. A lovely park with primary rain forest and lots of waterfalls. Considered a must by many. Camping allowed.
- Cabo Blanco lies on the southeast tip of the lovely Nicoya Peninsula. Noted primarily for its cliffs and marine birds. Trails wind through the reserve. Driest from November through April.
- Cahuita is on the Caribbean coast. It's noted for acres of coral. These have been damaged by earthquakes but are still quite lovely when the water is clear (hard to predict). Call ahead to check on weather conditions.
- Cano Island, accessible only by boat, offers trails through an evergreen forest. This is a good place to snorkel. Camping is permitted with prior permission. Driest from January through March.
- Cano Negro is a popular birding area. Most birding is done in a dugout. It's driest from January through March. When the water recedes, it's sometimes possible to spot animals in the southeastern corner of the lake.
- Carara is another area close to San José and famed for its birding and beauty. Best to go with a guide. Camping is permitted with advance permission. Driest from November through April.
- Chirripo is known for its fantastic hike up to the highest point in the country. On a clear day you can see both coasts. The hike is tough and must be prearranged. Camping permitted with prior permission. The area is noted for its fantastic birding (more than 400 species) and diverse flora. Driest January through March. Note: Much of this area is unexplored. Go with a competent guide. Allow plenty of time.
- Corcovado is one of the country's great parks. The birding is terrific (367 species), but the park is difficult to get to in the wet season. You may choose to stay in one of the lodges here, but there are simpler accommodations through local guides and hotels. Camping is permitted with permission. This jewel is being damaged by illegal mining. If you intend to come here, give yourself plenty of time and lots of advance preparation.
- Curu is a private refuge. Get permission to enter. It's near Paquera on the Nicoya Peninsula. You have a good chance to see white-faced Capuchin monkeys here. The beaches are good for swimming. Driest from January through March.
- Dr. R.L. Rodriguez refuge is noted for its waterfowl and wildlife.

Camping is allowed with prior permission. The best time to visit
is January through March.

- Gandoca-Manzanillo refuge is located on the Caribbean coast
close to Panama. It's noted for birding and a rocky shoreline. The
snorkeling is excellent. If you have a boat, you may see manatees
here. Best visited in February and March.
- Golfito refuge appeals to people interested in birding and local
flora. Hiking is allowed, but no real trails exist. Camping is permitted with permission. Best to go with a local guide from January through March. It is extremely wet here the rest of the year.
- Guayabo National Monument is one of the country's few archao-
logical sites. Camping is permitted.
- Guayabo, Negritos, and Pajaros Island reserves must be reached
by boat and offer great birding. Best visited January through
March, although rainfall is limited at any time of year.
- Hitoy-Cerere reserve is for the ardent adventurer willing to put up
with extremely wet conditions. You must be in superb physical
condition to explore this area, noted for its verdant flora and
lovely orchids. Go with a guide.
- Irazú is a popular volcano. You are allowed to walk the rim. It
can be quite cool and windy at 11,260 feet. Best visited from late
December to early April—fewer clouds.
- Isla del Coco (Coco Island) is 332 miles off the coast. Getting to it
is extremely expensive. Its main attraction is to divers. Driest
from January through March. Note that more than 500 expeditions have been made to this area in search of lost treasures.
- La Amistad (see Chirripo).
- Las Baulas is just north of Tamarindo and includes Playa Grande
where huge leatherback turtles arrive from early to late fall. You
must go out with a guide to view them.
- Lomas Barbudal appeals to birders (130 species) and entomolo-
gists (more than 250 species of bees alone). You'll probably see
monkeys here. Camping is allowed. Driest from January through
March.
- Manuel Antonio is one of the most famous parks. Just a few miles
south of Quepos with good beaches. Unfortunately, the area was
recently damaged by a bad storm. You'll still see birds (184
species) and monkeys. Swimming is good. Lovely at any time of
year.
- Monteverde is a private cloud forest famed for its birds. Nearly
30,000 people come here each year. There are many places to
stay. Special tip: Some of the more expensive lodges have their
own private birding areas.
- Ostional Refuge near Nosara is famed for its mass arrivals of tur-

tles in early to mid fall. Contact a hotel in this area for current information on regulation regarding turtle watching. Things are getting tighter. Come prepared with good rain gear.

- Palo Verde is famed for its waterfowl. Driest January through March.
- Penas Blancas has 70 species of birds and wildlife, including monkeys. Trails hug the river. Driest January through March.
- Poás Volcano is easily accessible and one of the most visited parks in the country. Views into the crater are excellent. Driest from December to April.
- Rincón de la Vieja consists of 9 volcanic cones. There are many hot springs and boiling mud pots in the region. Consider going to the Rancho Buena Vista and making a spectacular horse ride into the mountains near this park.
- Santa Rosa is a popular area for camping. Nearly 100,000 turtles come to Nancite beach in late summer and early fall. It can be very wet at this time. Driest from January through March.
- Tamarindo is famed for its turtle watching. Inquire locally about guides. Turtles usually seen in mid to late fall. Come prepared for wet weather.
- Tapanti is a cloud forest (mainly evergreens) with many species of birds. The Quetzal has been spotted here in late spring. Hiking trails are limited. Camping is permitted with permission. Driest from January through March.
- Tortuguero on the northeastern coast is one of the wettest areas in the country. The area is explored by boat. This is a naturalist's heaven with varied fauna and flora. It's especially noted for mass arrivals of turtles in summer to early fall. Go with a guide. Come prepared for torrential rains.

GUATEMALA

Although it has more parks than mentioned here, the two areas most visited are Tikal (a 5-star attraction) and the Biotopo del Quetzal (noted as much for orchids as birding). Both have been mentioned in the section on Where to Go (see pp. 42–44).

HONDURAS

The park system is in its infancy. Adventurers are just beginning to explore many of the areas. Go with a tour or competent local guide.

MEXICO

Mexico, like Costa Rica, has an extensive national park system. Information is more readily available. Contact the closest tourist office for specific details (see p. 26).

Natural History

Specifics on birding, butterflies, manatees, turtle watching, whale watching, and so on, have been mentioned in other sections of this chapter. However, natural history is such a broad subject and one so important to the region that I'm including a partial list of companies you might want to contact for information on tours to Central America and Mexico. Note that many of the companies mentioned in other categories spill over into this one.

Betchart Expeditions
17050 Montebello Road
Cupertino, CA 95014
Tel: (800) 252-4910
    (408) 252-4910
Belize, Costa Rica, Guatemala, Mexico.

Biological Journeys
1696 Ocean Drive
McKinleyville, CA 95521
Tel: (800) 548-7555
    (707) 839-0178
Mexico (many trips to the Baja and Sea of Cortez).

Extraordinary Expeditions
P.O. Box 1739
Hailey, ID 83333
Tel: (800) 234-1569
    (208) 788-2012
Costa Rica, Honduras.

Geo Expeditions
P.O. Box 3656
Sonora, CA 95370
Tel: (800) 351-5041
    (209) 532-0152
Belize, Costa Rica.

Geostar Travel
1240 Century Court
Santa Rosa, CA 95403
Tel: (800) 624-6633
    (707) 579-2420
Specializes in Costa Rica.

Holbrook Travel
3540 Northwest 13th Street
Gainesville, FL 32609
Tel: (800) 451-7111
    (904) 377-7111
Belize, Costa Rica (owns Selva Verde—superb birding area), Guatemala, Honduras.

International Expeditions, Inc.
1 Environs Park
Helena, AL 35080
Tel: (800) 633-4734
Belize, Costa Rica.

Mountain Travel
6420 Fairmount Avenue
El Cerrito, CA 94530
Tel: (800) 227-2384
    (510) 527-8100

Nature Encounters, Ltd.
3855 Lankershim Boulevard
North Hollywood, CA 91604
Tel: (818) 752-7363
Belize, Costa Rica, Guatemala.

Oceanic Society Expeditions
Fort Mason Center, Building E
San Francisco, CA 94123
Tel: (800) 326-7491
    (415) 441-1106
Mexico (mainly the Baja and Sea of Cortez). Note that programs for researchers are available in many countries.

Osprey Tours
P.O. Box 832
West Tisbury, MA 02575
Tel: (800) 645-3244
    (508) 645-9049
Belize, Costa Rica, Guatemala,
Honduras.

Overseas Adventure Travel
349 Broadway
Cambridge, MA 02139
Tel: (800) 221-0814
    (617) 876-0533
Costa Rica.

Pacific Sea Fari Tours
2803 Emerson Street
San Diego, CA 92106
Tel: (619) 226-8224
Mexico (mainly the Baja and
Sea of Cortez).

Preferred Adventures
1 West Water Street, Suite 300
St. Paul, MN 55101
Tel: (612) 222-8131
Belize, Costa Rica, Honduras
(limited).

Special Interest Tours & Travel
10220 North 27th Street
Phoenix, AZ 85028

Tel: (800) 525-6772
    (602) 493-3665
Costa Rica.

Temptress Cruises
1600 Northwest LeJeune Road,
    Suite 301
Miami, FL 33126
Tel: (800) 336-8423
    (305) 871-2663
Costa Rica.

Voyagers, Intl.
706 Cayuga Heights Road
Ithaca, NY 14850
Tel: (800) 633-0299
    (607) 257-3091
Costa Rica.

Wilderness Travel
801 Allston Way
Berkeley, CA 94710
Tel: (800) 368-2794
    (510) 548-0420
Costa Rica.

Wildland Adventures
3516 Northeast 155th Street
Seattle, WA 98155
Tel: (800) 345-4453
    (206) 365-0686
Belize, Costa Rica, Mexico.

Tips on Protecting Nature
- Travel in small groups without making a lot of noise.
- No radios.
- Stay on all marked trails.
- Don't hassle animals by getting too close to them, especially during reproductive cycles.
- Don't remove any vegetation or collect wild plants without permission from local authorities.
- Never feed wild animals. This means not dropping food on the trail as well as directly feeding birds or monkeys.

- Never smoke.
- Taking photos is fine, but never with a flash—never.
- All garbage should be picked up, especially plastic.
- Never buy any products from endangered species, especially feathers, skins, or turtle shells.
- Don't disturb any research project by moving stakes or any other obvious object related to study.
- Never enter protected areas with a 4-wheel drive. Always ask about this ahead of time. You could face huge fines, but, more importantly, do incalculable damage to the area.

Night Life

Mexico comes alive at night when the temperatures drop and expectations rise.

Discos

- Most discos are closed on Sundays.
- The action starts very late in the average disco and runs into the early morning hours. If you arrive before 10:30 P.M., you'll just watch the help clean the floors.
- Discos often have a high cover charge and steep prices for drinks. Very few people "disco hop."
- Often, there's a minimum consumption to boost sales.
- Drinks made from Mexican liquor will be 20 to 50 percent less than those made from imported booze.
- In some areas, reservations are necessary on popular nights.

Nude Bathing

- Nude bathing is tolerated in part of the Yucatán, especially along the coast to the south of Tulúm. But remember that it is illegal in Mexico and highly offensive to many Mexicans.
- On beaches frequented primarily by foreigners, the sight of bare breasts is commonplace and doesn't seem to be ruffling official feathers as it did in the past. However, these safe havens are *limited* to resort areas.

Painting

Of course, it's possible to draw and paint anywhere. However, art schools are quite popular with foreigners.
- Check with the nearest Mexican Government Tourist Office about

the courses offered in San Miguel de Allende—many famous writers and artists have taught there.

- Bring as many of your own supplies into the country as possible. They may be impossible to get once you arrive or extremely expensive when available.

Parasailing

It's a thrill, dangling several hundred feet above the water and being buffeted by the wind like a kite. Give it a try (mainly in Mexico).

- Prices are negotiable. Bargain.

Photography

Central America and Mexico offer a visual feast for photographers. I'm assuming that you have a 35-millimeter camera. If you have some other type, some of these tips won't apply to your outfit. Joseph Van Os Photo Safaris (listed under Butterflies) and Nature Encounters, Ltd. (listed under Natural History) offer trips geared to serious photographers.

Cameras and Lenses

- If serious, bring a 50-millimeter lens, a wide-angle, and a telephoto lens—but don't go overboard, keep it as light and compact as possible. If you specialize in extreme close-ups of insects and flowers, bring an appropriate lens.
- A light-weight tripod can be invaluable.
- A broad camera strap makes taking pictures easier and carrying cameras more comfortable.
- Be familiar with your equipment. Run a few rolls through the camera to make sure that things are working properly. Camera repair abroad is difficult.
- Change all batteries and carry a spare for each body.
- Equip each lens with a Polaroid filter. Leave the filter on at all times (not only to improve photos but to protect the lens).
- Bring photographic lens tissue or liquid lens cleaner to clean lenses.
- Don't forget your instruction book if you're not completely familiar with your camera or haven't used it recently.

Register Your Equipment

- Don't forget to register equipment with customs (see p. 130).

Film

- Bring more than the "legal" amount of film. Simply take the film out of the cardboard containers.
- Put the film in a plastic bag, which you hand to an inspector at security checks at airports. Although the inspectors will tell you that the x-rays do no harm, don't take any chances.
- Figure one 36-exposure roll for each day of shooting.
- Avoid "professional" film which requires refrigeration.
- Heat hurts all film, so keep it as cool as possible—often quite difficult in hot areas. Never put film in glove compartments.
- Slide film allows you to view every photo before deciding which ones you want made into prints—a real savings.
- Get films with different ASAs (ISOs in some areas). ASA, referred to as speed, is a measurement of light sensitivity. Lower speed films (most commonly ASA 100) are excellent for outdoor use. Much higher speed films are necessary for indoor shots.

Security Inspections

- Don't have film in cameras when you go through security inspections at the airport. They may be opened. If you forget or can't help having film in the camera, ask the inspector not to open the back. Just run it through the machine.
- The X-ray machines do damage to film, particularly if over 400 ASA. Moreover, the effect is cumulative.
- Ask the inspector politely for a visual inspection. If you carry film in a separate plastic bag, this takes only seconds.
- Don't put film in checked luggage, which can be subjected to high-level radiation. Even lead pouches are no guarantee that the film will not be harmed. Carry all film on board with you.
- Note that the affect of x-rays on film is highly controversial. Personally, I believe those who say it can do damage.

Protecting Camera Gear

- Dust, sand, and salt are problems—bring a locking plastic bag for each lens and camera, even if they're already enclosed in a leather carrying case.
- Humidity is also a problem. So in highly humid areas get cameras out of plastic bags as soon as possible. The same applies to rain. Protect cameras from downpours, but get them out of bags once indoors.
- If you carry cameras in plain bags, potential thieves will be less likely to know what you've got—namely, something they want.
- Always zip up the bag, even if you're nearby. Leave nothing exposed to chance and sticky fingers.

- Hand carry all camera equipment onto a plane or bus. This way you won't lose it if you're luggage is lost or crushed.
- Wear a camera around your shoulder rather than around your neck. A thief snatching at your camera can easily hurt your neck in his eagerness. Yes, it is easier to steal this way.
- Do not leave cameras in car trunks or glove compartments. Not only are they vulnerable to theft, but the heat of the closed compartment can damage the camera.
- Have a fully waterproof camera for all water-related sports and underwater photography. Try it out before you leave. There are disposable cameras of this kind for limited photos.

Photography Etiquette

- In some areas, you must be sensitive about taking photos. Indians especially resent photos.
- In some remote villages photography is associated with witchcraft, something taken very seriously by many people in these areas. Photographers have been stoned to death in such areas.
- Never take pictures of police or soldiers.
- Certain restrictions apply for photography in archaeological zones (no tripods, no flash, and no movie cameras).
- You can often get good shots of people with a telephoto lens, and this can be done inconspicuously.
- However, if you're close to a person, don't sneak photos. If you want to take someone's picture, be forthright and friendly—it often works. "Can I take your photo?" "*¿Puedo sacar una foto?*"
- Just lift the camera slowly, nod your head, and smile. If the person turns away or tosses his hand at you, don't take the photo. Or just say "please" as you lift the camera, to get a reaction.
- In the marketplace, an orange or tomato splatting against the side of your head or ricocheting off your shoulder is a good indication that photos are not tolerated.
- If you really want to get pictures in an area where this is tough to do, consider hiring a guide or an interpreter who can ask for photos as you go along. You may be asked for a small payment for some of the photos, which seems reasonable enough.
- Some professionals look for a good background and then just let people walk into the frame while they sit at a table or pretend to be doing something else.
- In touristic areas, especially in Guatemala, you're expected to pay a small amount for taking photos. Ask what the going rate is. The people here often make more money from photos than from their daily work.

- Don't dawdle once you've taken a picture. Smile, shake hands, offer a gift—then go about your business.
- Unless your camera is always at hand, you're going to miss some of the best, spontaneous shots. Have your camera handy.

Developing Film
- Do it at home. It's the safest place to develop film which represents special memories or a lot of effort.

Tips on Taking Good Photos
Following are tips from professional photographers. These generalizations are not iron-clad rules, but often result in great shots.
- Focus carefully so that the subject is clear, not at all fuzzy. If you cannot hold the camera steady, use any handy object to help you keep the camera still. If you have a tripod, use it.
- The key ingredient in good photography is light. In most instances, you want light shining on your subject. This means the sun should be behind you. Sometimes, light may be shining through your subject, such as a flower, to intensify the colors.
- Light just after sunrise and before sunset is extremely rich.
- Look carefully at your subject. Cameras are objective. Whatever appears in the viewfinder will show up on film. Check all edges of the photo to make sure that nothing unwanted is left out.
- Keep photos simple. What do you want the photo to say?
- Keep photos simple by having a clear-cut background; and, by getting close to the object you're photographing, whether it's a person, flower, insect, butterfly, or fabric. Fill the entire frame with your subject.
- Vary angles of your shots. Shooting down on a market can lead to an excellent shot. Shooting up at people can be dramatic.
- Move your camera from vertical to horizontal when trying to decide what kind of shot to take. You develop an instinct over time as to which position is really working.
- When you know that you have a really interesting subject, take many photos from different angles and at different speeds.
- Composition requires a good eye and an ability to create interest. Avoid placing subjects directly in the middle of the frame. Horizons across the center of a photo are deadly. Look for powerful diagonal lines; rhythmic curves (especially sensual S-curves along rivers or shorelines); unusual patterns in shapes, texture, and color.
- Use the appropriate film for the situation. A low speed film is excellent for outdoor shots, but worthless in low-light conditions or for photographing things in rapid movement. For this reason,

consider carrying two camera bodies—one loaded with low speed film, the other with high speed.

- Shoot lots of film—quickest way to learn what works, what doesn't. Again, the camera is objective. It feels nothing. It simply records. It takes lots of shooting to see how what is subjectively so beautiful in person can be so objectively dull on film.

Retirement

Tips On Retiring Abroad

AIM
Apartado 31-70
45050 Guadalajara
Jalisco, Mexico

Newsletter for people interested in retiring in Mexico.

Costa Rican Residents' Association (*Asociación de Pensionados y Rentistas de Costa Rica*)
Apartado 700-1011 y Griega
Calle 5, Avenida 4
San José, Costa Rica
Tel: 33 80 68 or 33 10 17
Strictly aimed at people who want to retire in Costa Rica.

- Find out if there is a local branch of the American Chamber of Commerce. Get tips from them.
- Books on retirement are available in foreign stores.
- Remain in an area for a full year to decide whether you like it.
- Never buy property without talking to people who have already done the same thing. They know many of the ins and outs.
- Land sales are a scam artist's heaven. Don't make any quick moves. Land which cannot legally be sold often is. Be wary.
- Never convert all your money into local currency. Keep as much in Canada or the United States as possible.
- Always consider the possibility that you could lose everything if laws change. You may not be able to sell your property and take money out of the country legally.
- Weigh renting against owning.

Riding (*equitación*)

Equitour
P.O. Box 807
Dubois, WY 82513
Tel: (800) 545-0019

(307) 455-3363
Rides take you past some of Belize's remote Mayan ruins.

FITS Equestrian
685 Lateen Road
Solvang, CA 93463
Tel: (800) 666-3487
   (805) 688-9494
Belize (Pine Ridge Mountain area), Mexico (Etzatland, 2 hours northwest of Guadalajara).

Mountain Travel
6420 Fairmount Avenue
El Cerrito, CA 94530

Tel: (800) 227-2384
   (510) 527-8100
Costa Rica (riding part of overall trip to volcanoes and rivers).

Rothschild Travel
900 West End Avenue,
  Suite 1B
New York, NY 10025
Tel: (800) 359-0747
   (212) 662-4858
Belize, Honduras (near Copan).

Tips on Riding

- When going into remote areas, particularly mountainous ones, wear clothing which will protect your legs and fanny.
- Wear appropriate shoes. Boots are best.
- Let horses rest when exhausted. Some climbs are unbelievable.
- Let the horses drink whenever they need to. If crossing a mountain stream, encourage them to stop by letting the reins go loose. They'll often stand in the middle of the water and drink for several minutes.

COSTA RICA

The most fascinating rides are into the mountainous areas around volcanoes. Highly recommended: the Rancho Buena Vista north of Liberia and trips up to the Turrialba Volcano from the Guayabo Lodge.

MEXICO

A few recommended spots: The Meling Ranch in Ensenada, the Hacienda San Miguel Regla in Pachuca, Parras de la Fuente in Rincón del Monterro, Hotel Jurica in Querétaro, Rancho El Morillo in Saltillo, and Rancho El Atascadero in San Miguel de Allende. The latter is the best known and offers a riding school.

Sailing (see Yachting)

Scuba Diving (*buceo*)

- Get certified in the United States, no matter what anyone tells you about foreign certification. Your instructor should be sanctioned by PADI (Professional Association of Diving Instructors).

- Take all your own gear except for tanks (airlines go nuts when they see these) and weights (bulky and heavy). This means bringing your own regulator, mask, fins, and wet suit.
- The water ranges from 75 to 80 degrees Fahrenheit and reaches up to 250-foot visibility under ideal conditions.
- Evaluate the conditions for each dive. They should be equal to or better than your training. Always be willing to say "no."
- Consider each dive as if it's being made only by you, but follow the buddy system as you've been taught.
- If you haven't been diving recently, take a refresher course.
- Local "dive masters" are often just guides.
- When choosing a resort, read dive magazines. Only the best resorts can afford to advertize in these. Magazines include "Scuba Times", "Skin Diver", and "Sport Diver".
- Consider making travel arrangements through an agency specializing in dive travel (check your yellow pages).
- Travel at the right time of year to avoid rough, windy, or dirty water. Best dive times are generally in an area's dry season.
- Protect coral: Don't touch it, don't spearfish, never hand feed fish, don't drag anchors over it, don't leave any debris in the water, and keep your hands out of openings (eels).
- Basically, don't touch anything. As one Belizean put it, "If you get stung by a scorpion fish, it hurts so bad you'll see your grandmother naked."
- After any decompression dive, do not fly for 24 hours. After any dive, do not fly for 12 hours.
- When checking live-aboards, ask about boat size, number and power of engines, number of compressors, type of electronic and communication gear.
- Diving is one of the main reasons people go to Central America and Mexico. Here's an extensive list of companies specializing in this activity:

Adventure Scuba
330 Jewel Street, Suite D
New Orleans, LA 70124
Tel: (504) 282-6047
Belize, Costa Rica, Honduras,
Mexico (Cozumel).

Aggressor Fleet
P.O. Drawer K
7810 Highway 90 East
Morgan City, LA 70381
Tel: (800) 348-2628

(504) 385-2628
Belize, Costa Rica (Coco Island), Honduras (Bay Islands).

Baja Expeditions, Inc.
2625 Garnet Avenue
San Diego, CA 92109
Tel: (800) 843-6967
Specializes in diving in the Sea of Cortez (Mexico) either from hotels or live-aboards.

Boulder Scuba Tours
1737 15th Street
Boulder, CO 80302
Tel: (800) 826-9834
      (303) 449-8617
Belize, Costa Rica (Pacific
Coast), Honduras (Bay Islands),
Mexico (Cozumel area and the
Baja).

Caradonna Caribbean Tours
P.O. Box 3299
Longwood, FL 32779
Tel: (800) 328-2288
      (407) 774-9000
Belize, Costa Rica (Bat and
Coco Islands), Honduras, and
Mexico (Baja and Yucatán).
Much diving off liveaboards.

CVI Group (Vagabond Tours)
P.O. Box 2664
Evergreen, CO 80439
Tel: (800) 538-6802
      (303) 674-9615
Offers dives in Belize.

Ocean Connection
211 East Parkwood, Suite 108
Friendswood, TX 77546
Tel: (713) 996-7800
Belize and Cozumel (Mexico).

Oceans of Living
2015 Ogden Avenue
Lisle, IL 60532
Tel: (800) 466-1400
      (708) 769-4900
Belize, Costa Rica (Coco Island
and Pacific Resorts), Honduras
(Bay Islands), Mexico (the Baja
and Cozumel). Offers land and
liveaboard dives.

Poseidon Venture Tours
359 San Miguel Drive
Newport Beach, CA 92660
Tel: (800) 854-9334
      (714) 644-5344
Belize, Costa Rica (Coco
Island), Honduras, Mexico (the
Baja and Cozumel). Many live-
aboard opportunities.

Rothschild Travel
900 West End Avenue, Suite 1B
New York, NY 10025
Tel: (800) 359-0747
      (212) 662-4858
Belize, Costa Rica (El Ocotal),
Honduras, Mexico (the Baja
and Cozumel).

Safari Centre International
3201 North Sepulveda Boule-
vard
Manhattan Beach, CA 90266
Tel: (800) 223-6046
      (800) 233-5046 (Canada)
      (310) 546-4411
Belize, Costa Rica, Honduras.

Scuba Tours
P.O. Box 366
5 Paterson Avenue
Little Falls, NJ 07424
Tel: (800) 526-1394
      (201) 256-9115
Belize, Honduras.

Sea and Explore
1809 Carol Sue Avenue, Suite E
Gretna, LA 70056
Tel: (800) 345-9786
      (504) 366-9985
Belize, Honduras.

Sea Safaris
3770 Highland Avenue,
    Suite 102
Manhattan Beach, CA 90266
Tel: (800) 821-6670
      (310) 546-2464
Belize, Costa Rica, Honduras,
Mexico (Cabo area).

See and Sea Travel Service
50 San Francisco, Suite 205
San Francisco, CA 94133
Tel: (800) 348-9778
      (415) 434-3400
Belize, Costa Rica, Honduras,
Mexico (the Baja). Liveaboard
opportunities.

Temptress Cruises
1600 Northwest LeJeune Road,
    Suite 301
Miami, FL 33126
Tel: (800) 336-8423
      (305) 871-2663
Costa Rica (south Pacific coast
and Coco Island).

Terra Firma Adventures
10097 Cleary Boulevard,
    Suite 287
Plantation, FL 33324
Tel: (800) 524-1823
      (305) 370-2120
Belize, Costa Rica, Honduras.

Tropical Adventures
111 Second Avenue North
Seattle, WA 98109
Tel: (800) 247-3483
      (206) 441-3483
Belize, Costa Rica, Honduras,
Mexico (the Baja and
Cozumel). Liveaboard opportu-
nities.

Tropical Travel
5 Grogan's Park, Suite 102
The Woodlands, TX 77380
Tel: (800) 451-8017
      (713) 298-2238
Belize, Costa Rica (El Ocotal),
Honduras (Bay Islands), Mex-
ico (Cozumel).

Diving Emergencies
Although the need for airlifts and decompression is rare, it's helpful to know the location of the nearest chambers (assuming they're working). See p. 24 for other air evacuation companies:

DAN (Divers Alert Network)
P.O. Box 3823
Duke University Medical Center
Durham, NC 27710
Tel: (800) 446-2671
      (919) 684-2948
Offers accident insurance plus emergency evacuation services.

BELIZE
There are a number of fine dive sites. The reef itself extends for approximately 175 miles, making it the second longest in the world.

Not often mentioned is the other 180 miles of reef around the atolls (Glover's Reef, Lighthouse Reef, and Turneffe).

- Diving and snorkeling off Ambergris Caye (island) is popular. Get on a liveaboard for more far-ranging dives. Many of the cayes are lesser-known, but spectacular dive sites.
- Not to be missed is the Blue Hole on Lighthouse Reef, roughly 40 miles by sea from Belize City. Stay on the reef or get there on a live-aboard. This is a great, if expensive, experience. It is a wall dive. The hole is over 400 feet deep and pictured on many brochures promoting the country.
- All of the atolls offer excellent diving. Many consider lesser-known dives to be far more interesting than the famous Blue Hole. Highly recommended are Turneffe ("The Elbow" with numerous fish is a great dive), Glover's Reef, and Caye Bokal.

COSTA RICA
Costa Rica, often overlooked, offers some fine dives.

- Isla del Coco offers excellent pinnacle and wall dives as well as a good chance to see hammerhead sharks. Since the island is far off the mainland, much of your trip is spent getting to and from the dive site. As you would guess, it's an expensive trip.
- There are also excellent dive sites along the northern portion of the Pacific Coast. El Ocotal is well-known for its diving. If the water is clear, this can be a great dive.

HONDURAS
Honduras is famous for its diving. Come at the right time of year, or you'll be sadly disappointed. Go only in the dry season. The best months for diving are April, May, and June.

- Here you'll find very good reef and wall dives. All of the islands have good dive sites. The best sites are said to be off Barbarat. Resorts specializing in diving are very expensive.
- If your funds are limited, stay on Roatan in an inexpensive place. Pay to go out with a guide. Trips are expensive, but less than staying in a resort.
- You may also strike a better deal in the off-season, but the waters are often disturbed or cloudy.

MEXICO
Mexico offers superb diving, but has a reputation for erratic and unethical operations. Go with a reputable outfit.

- Scuba diving is excellent in the Sea of Cortez and off certain areas of the Baja. Trips here usually combine diving with birding and observation of sea life, including whales.
- Scuba diving is most popular off Cozumel. Half the people who come here are interested in exploring the area's famous reefs.

The most famous are the Columbia, Palancar Maracaibo, Punta Sur, San Francisco, and Santa Rosa reefs. However, there are many more (40 sites in all).

- Boats often take divers and snorkelers from here to Tulúm, with an archaeological site and beach right by the water.

Shopping

Useful Vocabulary

another color	en otro color	old	viejo, vieja
bargain (to)	regatear	palm	palma
bark drawings	amatl	pink	rosa
black	negro	purple	morado
blanket	poncho	red	rojo
wool	chamarras	reed mat	petate
blouse (traditional)	huipile	religious paintings on tin	retablos
blue (dark)	azul (obscuro)	sandals	caites, huaraches
brown	café	sash (waist)	faja
carpet	alfombre	shawl	perraje, rebozos
cheap	barato	shirt (embroidered)	guayabera
cotton	algodón	shop	tienda
costume (native dress)	traje	shoulder bag	bolsa, morral
expensive	caro	silver charms	milagres
gray	gris	skirt	refajo
green (light)	verde (claro)	wraparound	enredo
grindstone (for corn)	metate	small	pequeño
handcrafts	artesianias	supermarket	supermercado
How much?	¿Cuánto cúesta?	white	blanco
large	grande	wool	lana
market	mercado	yellow	amarillo
new	nuevo, nueva		

Where To Shop

You may be one of those people who enjoys shopping, who loves every minute spent in fashionable stores, street markets, and typical boutiques. If so, you will find Guatemala and Mexico a delight. Belize, Costa Rica, and Honduras offer little in comparison.

Comparison Shop in the United States and Canada

- Since many articles are imported, study prices before going abroad. Unless you do this, you will not know if you're really getting a bargain or a unique item.

- Unless an item is much lower in price or of much higher quality than you can get at home, don't buy it. You'll lose on the currency exchange, you'll have to lug it home, and you may even have to pay duty on it if you exceed your personal exemption. If you can't make a 40 to 50 percent saving, skip it. In many instances a savings of 80 percent is common.

Comparison Shop Once Abroad

Once you arrive, get to one of the state-managed stores or better boutiques, selling authentic local goods. There are two good reasons: the products are thoroughly genuine, and they are chosen because of their high quality. Furthermore, the prices are high, so that if you know the price in one of these stores, you know the very *most* you should pay for anything from embroidered dresses and blouses to fascinating ceramics and candle holders. In Mexico some of the state-managed stores are known under the title FONART (*Tiendas Artesanales del Fomento Nacional de Artesanias*). Others are found in regional folk art museums (*Museos de Arte Popular*), civic centers, and art galleries. Ask locally for their location.

Department Stores in Mexico City

Check out the Galería in the Zona Rosa, Liverpool, Palacio de Hierro, Paris Londres, and the huge complex Perisur at the end of Insurgentes Sur (don't miss this one).

Specialty Shops

Once you've visited a FONART and some of the department stores, you'll enjoy comparison shopping in the many specialty shops and boutiques, especially in the Zona Rosa of Mexico City.

Artesans (*artesanos*)

If you've got the interest and time, you may want to locate the artesans who make goods sold in specialty shops. This can take a lot of legwork and patience, but many people enjoy the search.

- When you go to the artesan's home, studio, or shop, consider taking someone who speaks Spanish (if you don't).
- You may be able to buy a truly unique piece from an artesan directly, the kind of piece that won't show up in shops or markets.
- All of this takes time, lots of it.

Duty-free Shops (*tienda libre de impuestos*)

You'll find so-called duty-free shops in airports. Prices are often higher in these shops than in many comparable specialty shops. The term duty-free is just hype.

Markets (*mercados*) (see p. 288)

Factory Outlets
Many tours and tour guides lead people to factory outlets, usually just retail shops offering the tour guides a kickback. Be wary.

Street Vendors
You can't walk anywhere without being hustled. It's just part of the culture. Hustling is most common in Guatemala and Mexico, because these countries have the most to offer.
- If you're not interested, just say no. A polite way of turning vendors off is to say that something is very nice, but that you don't want it. *Muy bonito, mas no lo quiero.*
- Some vendors offer some pretty good deals on some fairly decent items, but many offer junk at not-so-good prices.

Timing in Shopping
- Some vendors are superstitious about the first sale. You often get the best price of the day if you're the first customer! This is particularly true in Mexico.
- One of the most pleasant times to shop is in the late evening— lots of action, nice temperature, and an easy-going pace. Just as street vendors start to pack up is a good time to get a bargain.
- Hours of shops vary greatly, but tend to be from late morning to late evening with a break for a siesta (*descanso*) or lunch.
- Shopping in certain towns is best at certain times of year. For instance, the pre-Christmas period is very good in Oaxaca because the peasants bring in handmade goods at this time.

Bargaining (*regatear*)
It's actually improper for you to pay the asking price for goods when you shop at open markets, small owner-operated shops, antique shops, art galleries, and flea markets. Bargaining is inappropriate only in state-managed and department stores. Bargaining is not only accepted in most settings, it is also expected. If you're not used to bargaining, here's a chance for you to become an expert.

Basic Bargaining
Bargaining is an attitude, a position, a style. The attitude is wariness; the position is: "I won't buy unless it's a fair price." The style is tough but breezy, with a good sense of humor.
- The basic rule of bargaining: He who cares least wins.
- Take your time and comparison shop. When you've decided on

what you want, begin the bargaining game. Frivolous bargaining is unfair and a waste of the merchant's time.

- Ask for the price. Undercut the stated price by whatever you think you can get away with. Start with a fraction of what's asked (Mexicans sometimes ask ten times the real value, Guatemalans often two to three, although there is no set rule).
- Tell the vendor that you'll have to shop around because you want to come up with the best price and are willing to spend the time to do it. Prices will often slide down on the spot.
- Let a missing person play the bad guy. "Oh, it's beautiful, but my husband (wife) would be very upset if I spent that much."
- Be complimentary but shrewd, saying, "It's one of the finest pieces I've seen, but I really think it's overpriced."
- Evoke the expert. "I've got someone who really knows about these things. I'd better ask his advice before I spend all that much." As a matter of fact, get some helpful advice.
- Use tour guides for information about what is authentic, but be wary because many of them get kickbacks from certain stores.
- Find a flaw. Almost everything has one, especially high-quality, handmade articles. I don't like this, but it does work.

Advanced Bargaining
- Play the add-on game. "I'll pay your price if you'll throw this extra item in." That so-called extra item may be exactly what you were after in the first place! This lets the vendor save face.
- Play the lump-sum game. "I'll pay you this much for this, that, and that." You play the lump-sum game after finding out the prices for the individual items. Naturally, you shave off a fair percentage for buying them as a group. This is another face-saving device (very important in Latin cultures).
- Take out the money and put it in front of the vendor. Tell him that this is your last offer. If he shakes his head, put the money back into your wallet and leave. Often, this will bring on a sale.
- Note that advanced bargaining is more difficult in areas where foreigners have been paying inflated prices for local goods. But don't believe it if someone tells you that you can't bargain in such and such a place. Everything is negotiable.
- An important note: If you're bargaining in local markets or with street vendors, you're often negotiating a price with people who work extremely hard and are quite poor. So what if you pay a few dollars more than someone else for an item that took from three weeks to three months to make by hand?

Luxury-shop Bargaining

- Some shops have a *precios fijos* (fixed prices) sign in the window. In short, you're expected to pay the full price. Nonsense! Try some polite bargaining anyway.
- Will the item soon be on sale?
- Is there a discount for paying cash?
- Will you give me a favorable rate of exchange for dollars? Some shops build in a discount by giving you more foreign currency per dollar than a bank.
- Or, bargain anyway. Everything is negotiable.

Bargaining Etiquette

- Treat the people with a "hello" and "good-bye." This is minimum manners in a region where courtesy counts.
- If a vendor agrees to your price, it's considered poor form for you to walk away. A deal's a deal.
- Displays of anger, disgust, or annoyance are inappropriate. No one is forcing you to buy anything. Locals expect bargaining to be polite, quiet, and respectful. If you're not satisfied with the price, simply say "Gracias," and walk away.
- If the bargaining has been fun, shake the vendor's hand. This is a warm, caring gesture.
- Street vendors often have their family with them. Giving kids a treat is often appreciated, but occasionally turned down.

Shopping Problems

- Never have anything made to order. Your deposit may simply evaporate, or the item finished well after your departure.
- The markets are glutted with cheap imitations of very fine products, especially in regards to precious metals and stones.
- It's not considered deception if an item is vastly overpriced. It's strictly buyer beware!
- Make sure you get what you pay for. Some shopkeepers will switch items while packing them up (this is very rare).
- More common is asking a shop to ship you something and never getting it. Don't ship anything. Carry it home with you.

A Good-Buy Guide

Following are some items which generally cost less in Central America and Mexico. Some prove quite expensive, but the quality of the work can be exceptional, making them unique in their own right.

- Many goods can be imported free of duty. For information on this contact the nearest customs office for a copy of "GSP and the Traveler." At this time there are over 4,000 duty-free items.

• Many credit cards have a guaranteed protection program against loss, theft, and breakage. This added insurance can be quite valuable for more expensive articles. Keep your receipt.

What to Buy

BELIZE

Art, black coral (please do not buy), baskets, beads (hardwood), birds (ziricote), cowhorn carvings, jade, and jewelry. Please do not buy bracelets and combs made from tortoise shells. Note that many items for sale are actually imported from Guatemala and Mexico.

COSTA RICA

Bracelets (wood), Cafe Rica (coffee liqueur), ceramics, clothes, coffee (some of the finest in world), earrings (wood), flower seeds (if packaged), gold (wrought), hammocks (better ones are found in Mexico), jewel boxes (wood), leather products, musical instruments (wood), orchids (if all paperwork is in order from both Costa Rica and Canada or United States), paintings, sandals, and Triple Sec (liqueur). Warning: Do not buy or sell pre-Columbian pottery (most are forgeries anyway). Never buy anything made from a protected species.

GUATEMALA

Baskets (*canasta*), blankets, blouses (*guipil* or *huipil*), ceramics (Totonicapan is a major center), furniture (lovely, but hard to get home), hammocks (better in Mexico), hand-woven fabrics, jade (in Antigua), jewelry (buy for beauty not metal value), incense burners, leather, masks (wooden or painted), mats (*petates*), napkins (*servilletas*), place mats (*individuales*), pottery, sandals (*caites*), sculptures, shirts (*camisas*), tortilla cooking pans (*comales*), tunics for men (*capixayo*), water jars, and weavings (in any style and color).

HONDURAS

Ceramics, cigars, coffee, leather goods, necklaces (made from seeds), paintings (the primitive art is superb—Antonio Velasquez is famous), purses, straw products, and wood products.

MEXICO

Abalone shell items, antiques, art, artifacts (no pre-Columbian), bark drawings, baskets, blankets, blouses (beaded and embroidered), brass, bronze, candles, ceramics, charms (silver), chess sets, clothes, copper, coral (black—please don't buy), embroidery, furniture, glass, gold, guitars, hammocks, hats (panama and straw), Indian art, jewelry, Kahlua, lacquerware, leather, masks, mats, onyx, opals, painting on tin, paper flowers, paper mache items (fanciful animals), pewter picture frames, piñatas, ponchos, pottery, sandals, serapes, shawls, shirts, silver, table clothes, tin, toys, watches, weaving, wood animals, wood bird cages, wood bowls, wrought iron, and yarn paintings.

Tips on foreign purchases

On some purchases you have to be cautious. Following are a few tips when shopping:

- *Alcohol*: The better tequilas are aged (*anejo*) and turn yellow. Here's the normal progression: *joven* (aged three months), *extra* (aged roughly a year), *hornitos* (aged longer), and *commemorativo* (aged six or seven years).
- The most famous are José Cuervo and Sauza. Naturally, you pay the most for older tequilas from name-brand companies.
- Bootlegged tequila is quite common. Real tequila comes from Jalisco, Nayarit, or Tamaulipas. Look for DGN on the label.
- Mezcal is less popular than tequila but made from the same kind of plant—the agave. Some bottles contain a worm which Mexican machos eat with a flourish (rumors are that these unfortunate worms are quickly and quietly disappearing).
- Triple Sec, a popular liqueur, is bottled in San José, Costa Rica.
- *Ceramics*: Unless a vessel is certified lead-free, do not use it for cooking or serving acidic foods. Glazed pottery, especially green-colored, should be used with caution. Highly decorative or brightly colored pottery is usually not suitable for cooking or serving food. Mexico is notorious for having ceramics with high lead content.
- *Clothes*: Most clothes will shrink, so buy them on the large side and wash in cold water (let them drip dry). Some people say that adding salt and vinegar to cold water during the wash helps. Many fabrics bleed badly no matter what you do.
- Many clothes fall apart unless the seams are sewed when you get home. Mexicans assume you'll do this for yourself. Guatemalans are more careful.
- Glossy ribbons will shrink, yarn embroidery will bleed, and some colors are not colorfast (*firme*).
- Clothes are more expensive when handmade (*hecho al mano*). The cotton thread for embroidery often does not bleed.
- Cotton (*algodón*) tends to be pure, while wool (*lana*) is often a blend. Polyester gives off a shine in the sun. To find out if something is 100 percent wool, say in Spanish: "*¿Cien por ciento lana?*" Who knows whether the answer will be truthful.
- *Hammocks*: Get hammocks made for two people (*matrimonial*). They really only fit one person comfortably. The weave should be tight and the loops at the end taut. Best hammocks are made in Tixcocob. Good hammocks can be found in Mérida at La Poblana, Calle 65.492 between Calles 58 and 60.

- *Jade*: Study jade before going abroad. Talk to dealers about what to look for. Real jade is expensive. Unfortunately, imitation jade abounds. Antigua (Guatemala) is known for quality jade products. Ask locally about reputable stores. Jade comes from the Montagua Valley. Some Costa Ricans claim that it washes up on the beaches there occasionally.
- *Leather*: Make sure you're getting leather and not strips of leather glued to cardboard.
- *Rugs*: Rugs made in Teotitlan about 20 miles from Oaxaca are valuable. The best rugs are heavy, 100 percent wool, tightly woven (note puckering at ends), colored with natural dyes (green is one of the loveliest), and often have many color changes in one row—difficult weaving. Synthetic dyes are bright and sparkle in the sun. Authentic rugs fade in sun and will lose color unless washed in cool water.
- *Sandals* (*huaraches*): Try both sandals on to make sure they fit. Buy them a little on the snug side because they'll stretch.
- Some people suggest soaking them in fresh water and then putting them on—this will make them shape to your feet.
- Don't expect sandals to be comfortable from the start. They take time to work in.
- *Silver*: Buy silver from a reputable shop, since most of the silver in the street is really alpaca, a very cheap imitation.
- Mexican silver should be stamped sterling, or have a spread eagle mark, or bear the number .925 (92.5 percent pure). If it doesn't, buy the piece only for its beauty, not its silver content.

Take Purchases with You
- Contrary to what many guides tell you, most shops are *not* experienced at handling shipping.
- Take any purchase with you *if* you have the ability to hand carry the item to the United States or Canada. In short, is it small enough to take on a bus, plane, or train, or to fit into a car or RV?
- If you ship an item that's worth more than $50 to the United States or more than $40 to Canada, you'll have to pay duty on it. It won't fall under your personal exemption which requires all goods to accompany you across the border.

Thank-you Gifts
- Never send a thank-you gift through the mail.
- It probably won't get there.
- If it does, it is hell for your friend to retrieve it.
- The person will not be told who the package is from.
- The person will have to pay a stiff duty on whatever is sent in.

- And finally, the whole process takes so much time and is so frustrating that no matter what the gift is, it isn't it.
- If you want to thank someone, do it on the spot.

Sightseeing

As mentioned earlier, there are thousands of travel agents throughout Canada and the United States capable of setting up sightseeing excursions throughout Central America and Mexico. However, the following are a few which do quite a bit of work in this area. Some work primarily with prearranged tours, others with setting up more individual itineraries, and many with both. Compare their offerings to those of a local company to make an intelligent choice.

Companies Offering General Sightseeing Tours

AIB
2500 Northwest 79th Avenue
    Suite 211
Miami, FL 33122
Tel: (800) 242-8687
    (305) 715-0056
Costa Rica, Guatemala.

Americas Tours and Travel
1402 Third Avenue North,
    Suite 1019
Seattle, WA 98101
Tel: (800) 553-2513
    (206) 623-8850
Costa Rica, Honduras.

Belize Tradewinds
8715 West North Avenue
Wauwatosa, WI 53226
Tel: (800) 451-7776
    (414) 258-6687
Will handle just about any kind of trip to Belize.

Bentley Tours
1649 Colorado Boulevard
Los Angeles, CA 90041
Tel: (800) 821-9726
    (213) 258-8451

Belize, Costa Rica, Guatemala, Honduras.

Best of Belize
31 F Commercial Boulevard
Novato, CA 94949
Tel: (800) 735-9520
    (415) 884-2325
Can set up just about any kind of trip to Belize. Also, does trips to Costa Rica, Guatemela, and Honduras.

Brendan Tours
15137 Califa Street
Van Nuys, CA 91411
Tel: (818) 785-9696
Belize, Costa Rica, Guatemala, Honduras.

Clark Tours of Guatemala
9 Boston Street, Suite 9
Lynn, MA 01904
Tel: (800) 223-6764
    (617) 581-0844
The oldest company specializing in all aspects of travel to Guatemala.

Costa Rica Connection
975 Osos Street
San Luis Obispo, CA 93001
Tel: (800) 345-7422
      (805) 543-8823
Belize, Costa Rica, Guatemala,
Mexico.

Elegant Vacations
1975 North Park Place,
   Suite 200
Atlanta, GA 30339
Tel: (800) 451-4398
      (404) 850-6891
Belize, Costa Rica (primarily),
Guatemala, Honduras.

Explore Belize Tours
718 Washington B Avenue
Detroit Lakes, MN 56501
Tel: (218) 847-3012
Will set up almost any type of
tour in Belize.

Globus & Cosmos Tourama
5301 South Federal Circle
Littleton, CO 80123
Tel: (800) 221-0090
Costa Rica, Mexico.

Hotel Cacts Travel
Apartado 379-1005
Calles 28/30, Avenida 3a
   bis No. 2845
San José, Costa Rica
Central America
Tel: 011 (506) 21 65 46 or
      21 29 28
Costa Rica only. Owned by
Costa Ricans who know the
country well. Aimed at young
or highly independent types.

Magnatours
410 New York Avenue

Huntington, NY 11743
Tel: (800) 856-2462
      (516) 424-2000
Costa Rica, Mexico.

Mexico Tourism Consultants
246 South Roberton Boulevard
Beverly Hills, CA 90211
Tel: (800) 252-0100
      (310) 854-8500
Mexico.

Mila
100 South Greenleaf
Gurnee, IL 60031
Tel: (800) 367-7378
      (708) 249-2111
Belize, Costa Rica, Guatemala,
Honduras, Mexico.

Ocean Connection
211 East Parkwood,
   Suite 108
Freindswood, TX 77546
Tel: (800) 331-2458
      (713) 996-7800
Belize, Costa Rica, Guatemala,
Honduras, Mexico.

Paradise Tours
P.O. Box 42809-400
Houston, TX 77242
Tel: (800) 537-1431
      (713) 850-1664
Belize, Costa Rica, Guatemala,
Honduras.

Path Tours
25050 Peachland Avenue,
   Suite 201
Newhall, CA 91321
Tel: (800) 843-0400
      (805) 255-2740
Belize, Costa Rica, Guatemala,
Honduras, Mexico.

Pinto Basto Tours
40 Prince Street
New York, NY 10012
Tel: (800) 526-8539
     (212) 226-9056
Belize, Costa Rica, Guatemala,
Honduras, Mexico.

Roatan Charters
P.O. Box 877
12251 Curley Road
Antonio, FL 33576
Tel: (800) 282-8932
     (904) 588-4131
Honduras.

Sea and Explore
1809 Carol Sue Avenue,
  Suite E
Gretna, LA 70056
Tel: (800) 345-9786
     (504) 366-9985
Will set up almost any type of
tour in Belize.

Solar Tours
1629 K Street, Suite 502
Washington, DC 20006
Tel: (800) 388-7652
     (202) 861-5864
Belize, Costa Rica, Guatemala,
Honduras, Mexico.

South American Fiesta
910 West Mercury Boulevard
Hampton, VA 23666
Tel: (800) 334-3782
     (804) 825-9000
Belize, Costa Rica, Guatemala,
Honduras.

Special Expeditions
720 Fifth Avenue
New York, NY 10019

Tel: (800) 762-0003
     (212) 765-7740
Belize, Costa Rica, Guatemala,
Honduras.

Swiss Travel Service
P.O. Box 7-1970
Corobici Hotel
1000 San José, Costa Rica
Central America
Tel: 011 (506) 31 40 55
Costa Rica.

Travel Belize, Ltd.
637 B South Broadway
Boulder, CO 80303
Tel: (800) 626-3483
     (303) 494-7797
Will set up almost any type of
tour to Belize.

Travel Plus, Inc.
N87 W16453 Appleton Avenue
Menomonee Falls, WI 53051
Tel: (800) 255-4359
     (414) 255-6461
Belize, Mexico.

Triton Tours
1111 Veterans Boulevard,
Suite 5
Kenner, LA 70062
Tel: (800) 426-0226
     (504) 464-7964
Will set up almost any type of
tour in Belize.

Tropical Travel
5 Grogans Park, Suite 102
The Woodlands, TX 77380
Tel: (800) 451-8017
     (713) 367-3386
Belize, Costa Rica, Guatemela,
Honduras, Mexico.

Local Tour Companies

- In every city or tourist town you'll find companies offering tours of the most popular sights. Such tours are well organized, but usually expensive.
- A long list of local tour companies is usually free for the asking from the local tourist office.
- Prices for equivalent tours vary greatly, so comparison shop.
- Many hotels have a travel agency (*agencia de viaje*) to set up tours. Each time an agency is involved, the price rises.
- Sometimes, these agencies corner the market on tickets to popular events. You may be forced to use them.

Putting Together Your Own Local Tour

- Sometimes, you can put together an equivalent tour for yourself, using local transportation, for a fraction of the cost of more organized tours. It takes time and energy to do this, and it doesn't always work. Some local tours are really good buys.
- Many local companies discourage this by telling you that there is no way to get to the local sights without a tour. This is usually false. For example, you can get to all of the major sights in Mexico City using public transportation. You can get to the ruins of Monte Albán on a bus from the Hotel Meson del Angel. Getting this information can be tough, but persistence pays off.
- Cost is not the only big advantage of using public transportation. The other is freedom. You get to stay or leave an area when you feel like it, not at the command of a tour guide.
- For free information on suggested sights and routes, pick up brochures, maps, and detailed commentary from local tourist offices, from hotels, and from travel agencies.
- Good sightseeing suggestions are often listed in the yellow pages of local phone books. Free and detailed guides are often given away at better hotels and from tourist offices if you'll ask for them. Don't settle for a two-page pamphlet that tells you less than you already know.
- Allow plenty of time for an individual tour. Public transportation is slow. So you do trade time and energy for money.

Special Sightseeing

- If you're a romantic and want to try a buggy ride, expect to pay in spades, not hearts.
- Whenever you're bargaining for a price for that "special" ride, get the price in writing or pay upfront.

Walking Tours
- In Mexico City free walking tours are arranged. Call 512-6879.
- Walking is the only practical way to get to know many popular tourist towns or sights.
- Always pick up booklets, pamphlets, and special maps designed for walking tours in the places you visit. These can point out places you might otherwise miss.

Hiring Guides
- Guides give you new perspectives on tourist attractions. Bargaining on fees is common.
- Get a guide who can speak English fluently.
- At some sights you can join a group for a set price—usually just pennies. These arranged tours leave at a specific time.
- Or hire a private guide, either for a couple of hours or for a couple of days. For the latter arrangement you pay for all meals and lodgings.
- Don't "pick up" guides in the street or at tourist sights unless they can prove that they are licensed. A bonded, licensed guide carries a special permit with a photo.
- Many guides get kickbacks from factory outlets and shops. Don't feel forced to buy things in shops they recommend. In fact, if you're not into shopping, make this clear from the start.
- With any guide set the price firmly upfront.
- A tip related to performance is always in order.

Sound and Light Shows
- At major archaeological sites in Mexico, attend sound and light shows from mid-October to late May (sometimes into June). Ask locally about these. Some of them are really memorable.

When to Go
- Before making a special trip to any tourist sight, find out the hours and days the sight is open.
- If you're traveling a long distance, call ahead to make sure it's open. Strikes and other "natural calamities" can shut sights down.
- Most museums and galleries close at odd times. If a particular museum is important to you, get full information before traveling abroad.
- Most sights offer reduced admission on Sunday, a day which is usually very crowded.
- Holidays are also very crowded.
- Mid-week is usually the best and most relaxed time to visit most

sights. Get to ruins at the earliest possible hour to avoid crowds and to get the best photos.
- The seasons may affect the beauty of natural sights. Some can be disappointing at the wrong time of year.
- The time of day can be important. For instance, the Sumidero Canyon is best visited in the early morning.
- The day itself can be crucial. Certain markets are best on certain days. Some are only open one day a week. Bullfights take place only on Sundays. *So plan sightseeing accordingly.*

Other Sightseeing Tips
- Always wear comfortable shoes. Leave high heels at home and settle for a snappy pair of tennis shoes or buy walking shoes.
- If someone opens up a secret little box or remote little room in a church or museum, that someone expects a nice little tip.
- There's always someone telling you that there are just *no* tickets for such and such. Show up to such and such and buy a ticket. They've got scalpers too.
- If you're traveling by car, note that many sights have parking fees—even in the most remote areas.
- Hang onto your tickets when visiting tourist sights. They may be required for entry to a sight within a sight, or they may be necessary for spot inspections.

Snorkeling

Going to Central America or Mexico without snorkeling is like going to the movies and not eating candy or popcorn. Many of the natural history and whale watching trips include snorkeling. Look for tour companies under those sections.

Where to Go

BELIZE
Belize has the second largest barrier reef in the world. It extends along the entire coast for approximately 175 miles. Plus, there's even more reef around the atolls.
- Ambergris is one of the larger cayes or islands. It is very popular and easily accessible from Belize City. Off its southern end is the Hol Chan Marine Reserve. Go with a group to this area to keep costs down and for safety reasons.
- There are a number of smaller cayes with excellent snorkeling. Whenever you choose one of these, the main question to ask is how close is the reef to the island. A few islands are right on the reef. This makes snorkeling easy and safe.

- Snorkeling is best in Belize during the dry season. This is when the water is clear. In theory, the dry season extends from November through May, but there are frequent windy periods in the Caribbean which are totally unpredictable and make snorkeling less fun.

COSTA RICA

While you would think that this would be a great country for snorkeling, the waters are often murky or agitated. In theory, Cahuita National Park on the Caribbean coast is said to be one of the finer snorkeling areas. It's supposed to be clear from February through April. I would not make a special trip to this area without calling ahead to find out local conditions. However, if the water is clear, there is abundant coral formations—easily accessible from shore. Other snorkeling areas are Isla del Caño (off the southern coast); and Tortuga Island near Puntarenas. In most cases you'll need to get a boat to get out to the good areas, some off nearby islands. Waters can be quite dangerous, so only go out with other people on calm days.

HONDURAS

Here you can find fabulous snorkeling if the weather is good. If it's raining, the runoff reddens and pollutes the water for several days. Best time to go to the Bay Islands is in late spring and early summer. This is also the best diving time.

MEXICO

Akumal (fabulous), Cancún (good), Cozumel with its Chancanab Lagoon (tops), Isla Mujeres at Garrafon (beautiful), the water off the ruins at Tulúm (drift lazily like a sea otter in the current), and the National Park at Xelha—this is Mexican snorkeling at its best. All of these areas are in the Yucatán.
- Visibility in the Caribbean can reach 250 feet in ideal conditions.
- Snorkeling in the Sea of Cortez off the Baja or along small islands can be just as great as in the Yucatán.

What to Bring

- Bring a mask (*visor*), snorkel, and fins (*aletas*) if you can. If you can't, skip the fins (bulky and heavy).
- The mask should cover both your eyes and nose. Get a high-quality silicone mask. It is highly resistant to chlorine, ozone, and sun. It is also hypoallergenic. The mask should fit snugly against your face. Try it out in water before going abroad. Exchange it if it doesn't fit properly.
- Snorkelers with poor vision can have masks made with prescription lenses built in.

- When you put on a mask, avoid catching any hair which will cause a leak. The strap goes almost on top of your head, not directly behind it.
- Shoe fins, the kind you step into, are most commonly used for snorkeling. The heel-strap fins are actually better for deep diving, but you need special socks or neoprene booties for them to be comfortable.
- If you're an avid snorkeler, consider getting a snorkeling jacket or a wet suit.
- You can often rent equipment. But you can snorkel almost any-where with just a mask and snorkel, and you want to have good equipment—so bring your own. Fins help you explore caves and push against strong currents. Rent these, if necessary.
- Consider wearing a leather glove on your strongest hand (golf gloves work great). You need to be able to push off from coral in emergencies. However, never deliberately touch coral. You'll kill it if you do. And, some corals can hurt you.

Safety
- Cover yourself with a water-resistant sunscreen on initial outings. You simply forget time when snorkeling. Wear something over your back. If you're bald, wear a swim cap.
- Never drink alcohol before snorkeling.
- Do not swim alone. This is a fundamental rule worldwide.
- Never go into water without asking locals about its safety. Ask anywhere, in little restaurants, at the hotel, in local shops—but ask. Don't accept one person's version. Get confirmation from two or more people in two or more places.
- Some areas have strong currents, riptides, and deadly under-tows—and you often cannot detect these, even on calm days.
- Watch for warning flags in areas where these are posted. And if the sea looks rough, it probably is.
- Never swim at night. This is the time sharks like to feed.
- Never dive into water. Slide in gently.
- Never swim if a storm is approaching. If you hear any thunder, get out immediately.
- Never swim after a storm in silty or muddy water. Waters are often highly polluted at this time from the runoff.
- Never snorkel where fishing is going on. When a fish is caught, it gives off distress signals. This attracts sharks.
- Take one deep breath before each dive. Do not inhale more than once, since this can cause hyperventilation.
- When trying to dive deep, flip over and dive straight down—not at an angle.

- Look at but do not touch coral. Unless you're an expert, you cannot tell which varieties sting. Touching coral is a conservationist's nightmare, since coral dies where it's been touched.
- Shy away from sea urchins (*erizos*). Don't touch them, not even lightly. They'll sting you with their sharp spines.
- After swimming, wash off with fresh water. Dry yourself well.
- Clean your ears with rubbing alcohol mixed with vinegar. Let the solution sit in your ear for a few seconds, then lean to one side and let it drain out. Ear infections are quite common.
- Disinfect your mask and snorkel with a bleach solution.
- Avoid swimming in fresh water lakes or rivers. These bodies are often polluted or contain disease-causing organisms.

Special Tips
- If you're in a boat looking for a good place to snorkel, watch for dark blotches under the water. These are often rocks or coral, places where fish congregate.
- You'll get very thirsty snorkeling. Pack something to drink—a large bottle of water or a six-pack of Coke.
- If your mask fogs up repeatedly, spit on the glass and rub saliva over the surface with your fingers. Rinse it off, and, presto, you have a no-fog solution.

Preserving Coral and Marine Life
- Never stand on a reef. This will kill the coral. People do this all the time, destroying entire sections of a living reef.
- If you're a beginning snorkeler, wear a bouyant vest so that you won't feel the need to stand up when you get tired.
- Avoid touching coral with your hands or any other object, such as the tips of your fins.
- Never remove coral, dead or alive, from a snorkeling area.
- If spear fishing, aim carefully to avoid hitting coral.
- When swimming in a shallow area, move slowly. Move your fins as gently as possible to avoid stirring up sand from the bottom. This sand can settle on coral and kill it.
- Never throw any debris into the water, such as leftover beer or soft drinks, food, or anything else.
- Never hand feed fish.
- Avoid dropping anchors onto coral. If buoys are available, use them. Or, tie onto another boat if necessary.
- Don't drive your boat over coral. A prop can do enormous damage in seconds. Skirt good areas and anchor in sand.

Spas

Write to the nearest Mexican Government Tourist Office for information on the many spas in Mexico. A detailed list will fill a book, or at least a long brochure.

- Hot water springs are common in the countryside and a good place to relax and clean up.
- The following company deals with a spa in Belize and two in Mexico:

Custom Spa Vacations
1318 Beacon Street, Suite 5
Brookline, MA 02146
Tel: (800) 443-7727
    (617) 566-5144

Spectacles

Two of the most famous are the high divers at La Quebrada in Acapulco (go to Hotel Mirador) and the Flying Indians of Papantla. If you can't go to Papantla (really El Tajin), see them in Acapulco.

Study

Both short- and long-term study holds great appeal for many people who want to learn Spanish or get to know the region well.

Visas

You are allowed to enter each country for a specific time period. After that, you must leave. If you intend to study for a longer period than that allowed on your entry document, check into visas (see p. 3).

Information

The following organizations have information aimed at student travelers.

Council on International
   Educational Exchange
205 East 42nd Street
New York, NY 10017
Tel: (212) 661-1450

Institute of International
   Education
809 United Nations Plaza
New York, NY 10017
Tel: (212) 883-8200

STA
6560 North Scottsdale Road,
 Suite F-100
Scottsdale, AZ 85253
Tel: (800) 777-0112
 (602) 596-5151

Travel Cuts
187 College Street
Toronto, ON M5T 1P7
Canada
Tel: (416) 979-2406

Tips for Studying Spanish

- There are numerous Spanish schools throughout Central America and Mexico. Dozens exist in Antigua (Guatemala) and San José (Costa Rica). But, there are schools throughout the entire region, even in little towns.
- You cannot learn a language if you're speaking English each day. Live with a foreign family and don't speak English at all until you have reached the level of proficiency you're aiming at.
- Listen to the radio and watch television in the foreign language. When you begin to understand both, you're becoming fluent.
- If you're a serious language student, pick up the book *501 Verbs*. It's bulky and heavy, but the essence of the language.
- If you're given a room you really don't like, don't grin and bear it. Ask the administration to find a new place to stay for you.
- Many times you'll just find a room on your own.
- Carry a good pocket dictionary, but note that these rarely have the kind of detailed listings that a serious student will need after more than an introductory course in the language.
- Little calculator-like dictionaries are now on the market and contain nearly 50,000 words. These are much lighter and easier to carry, but more expensive.
- No one learns a language in a few weeks—no one! Patience, practice, and time—these are essential to master any language.
- Don't be timid about making mistakes. You can only learn to speak by speaking.
- In some areas Spanish is a dialect or not spoken at all. So don't overreact to your inability to get the point across. Just smile and move on.

Sun

For many people a vacation to Central America is most enjoyable if it's sunny. However, sun is not really what Central America is all about. On the other hand Mexico is world-famous for winter sun, lots of it and for long periods of time.

BELIZE

Your best chance for sun is in the dry period. This supposedly starts in mid-December or so and runs to late spring or early summer.

COSTA RICA

If you have to choose an area, go to the northern portion of the Pacific, especially the Nicoya Peninsula. Its got great beaches and the best chance for winter sun.

GUATEMALA

The dry season runs from early December to late spring or early summer. It's often sunny at this time.

HONDURAS

Mid to late spring into early summer is your best bet.

MEXICO

Mexico has the most reliable winter sun of any country in the world—and that says it all. In Puerto Vallarta I met a woman who had experienced 7 months straight of winter sun with only a few semi-cloudy days in late December. The lower part of the Pacific Coast and the southern tip of the Baja are excellent choices for winter sun. The Caribbean can also be good, but often experiences windy periods and occasional storms.

Surfing

Surfing has been popular in Mexico for years. It's now catching on in Costa Rica as well. It's a long way to go, but surfers don't mind.

COSTA RICA

The reason that surfers go to Costa Rica is that the water is warm, and you don't have to fight for waves. Going from north to south on the Pacific, the recommended beaches are Playa Naranjo, Playa Tamarindo, Boca de Barranca, Playa Jacó, Playa Hermosa, Playa Dominical, and Pavones (longest wave in the world). On the Caribbean side the recommended areas are Playa Bonita and Puerto Viejo.

- Since travel this far is expensive, talk to people who have already surfed to find out best times. The northern and central Pacific beaches are supposed to be best from early December through April, but I met many surfers who had come down earlier and found good waves. The southern Pacific is supposed to be good year-round. On the Caribbean waves are supposed to be best from December through February and from June through August. These "supposed to be's" are someone suspect and about as difficult to predict as the weather itself.

- Since surfing depends on wind, you may have to be patient—not a problem with surfers who roam for months at a time.
- Ask locally about conditions. Jacó Beach is relatively close to San José. Begin the networking process there.
- When renting a 4-wheel drive, don't tell car rental companies that you're surfers. They detest you.

MEXICO

Surfers guard their spots, but most say that surfing is best in the Baja in the "Ensenada area" and good in the "Playa Blanca area" and the "Puerto Escondido area" on the Mainland. Getting a pinpoint definition is like asking a fisherman where he catches his biggest trout.

Tennis (*tenis*)

COSTA RICA

The three most elegant places to play tennis are Cariari, Costa Rica (in Escazu), and Los Reyes (in La Guacima) country clubs. Other courts are scattered throughout the country at major resorts.

MEXICO

There are three great, and equally expensive, places to play tennis in Mexico: the Villa Vera in Acapulco, the Cuernavaca Racquet Club in Cuernavaca, and the Guadalajara Racquet Club in Guadalajara. But there are dozens of other resorts throughout the country which offer fine facilities at a wide range of prices.

- Bring your own equipment, including extra balls.
- Early morning and evening are the best times to play. For this reason it's often easiest to rent a court in the middle of the day.
- Some private complexes open their courts at offhours—ask to be sure.

A Highly Touted Train Ride

There used to be a number of great train rides in Central America and Mexico. Now only one is left. It's the trip from Los Mochis to Chihuahua on the Chihuahua al Pacifico Railway in Mexico. The trip is often called the Copper Canyon (*Barranca del Cobre*) train ride because it passes by six canyons which are deeper and longer than the Grand Canyon. The train passes over 39-48 bridges (number varies by source) and runs through 86 tunnels. The total trip is 406 miles long. It generally takes about 13 hours. You get the best views by starting your trip from Los Mochis. Many people get off at the halfway point at Bahuichivo or Divisadero and return to Los Mochis. From Divisadero you can see three canyons (Cobre, Tararecua, and

Urique). The town has several nice places to stay (make reservations in advance during peak seasons). From Bahuichivo you can go down to Cerocahui and stay at the Hotel Misión. If you want to set up a trip on your own, stay at the Hotel Santa Anita in Los Mochis. The staff there are most helpful. You can also get information and book a tour directly from the railway:

Mexico By Train P.O. Box 2782 Laredo, TX 78044 Tel: (800) 321-1699 (210) 725-3659	Ferrocaril de Chihuahua al Pacifico Apartamento 46 Chihuahua Chihuahua, Mexico

- Always go from south (Los Mochis) to north (Chihuahua) to see the most spectacular areas in the day.
- The best time to make the trip is in spring and fall. The two best months are April (lots of birds) and mid-September (wildflowers by the millions).
- If arranging your own trip, eat well before getting on board. Carry food and something to drink with you.
- Buy your tickets at the station. Get there early, because trains sometimes take off far ahead of schedule.
- The railroad runs on central time while Los Mochis is on mountain time—be at the station on the train's, not local, time.
- The heated cars are not so heated in the winter, and both mud slides and avalanches may close down the train or catch you for several days in a shivering situation. Bring warm clothes. Summer can be a season of violent storms.
- The train can carry cars and RVs, but it might be easier just to make a round-trip. The fare is quite reasonable.
- The cars are sometimes advertised as vista domes. They are not. The train uses older French, Italian, and Japanese cars.
- Make reservations in advance for hotels in the canyon area. You can call ahead from Los Mochis in off-peak periods. Otherwise, make reservations far in advance.
- Find out whether hotels have their own septic systems as a way of promoting business to those which do—this area is threatened environmentally.
- If you prefer to go with a tour, contact any of the following companies which offer extremely diverse types of travel, varying from birding and trekking to luxury travel in deluxe cars with gourmet food:

Baja Discovery
P.O. Box 15252
San Diego, CA 92195
Tel: (800) 829-2252
        (619) 425-4456

Betchart Expeditions
17050 Montebello Road
Cupertino, CA 95014
Tel: (800) 252-4910
        (408) 252-1444

Borderland Productions
2550 West Calle Padilla
Tucson, AZ 85745
Tel: (800) 525-7753
        (602) 882-7650
Tours the canyon with an
emphasis on birding. Trips
often sell out far in advance.

Brennan Tours
1402 Third Avenue, Suite 717
Seattle, WA 98101
Tel: (800) 237-7249
        (206) 622-9155
Tours to bottom of canyon.

Collette Travel Service, Inc,
162 Middle Street
Pawtucket, RI 02860
Tel: (401) 728-3805

Columbus Travel
Route 12, Box 382B
New Braunfels, TX 78132
Tel: (800) 843-1060
        (210) 885-2000
Operates the greatest number
of tours through the area and is
working to protect the local
environment.

DRC Rail Tours
1600 Smith, Suite 1650
Houston, TX 77002
Tel: (800) 659-6702
        (713) 659-7602

Mountain Travel
6420 Farmount Avenue
El Cerrito, CA 94530
Tel: (800) 227-2384
        (510) 527-8100

Nature Expeditions
    International
P.O. Box 11496
Eugene, OR 97440
Tel: (800) 869-0639

Remarkable Journeys
P.O. Box 31855
5231 Arboles
Houston, TX 77231
Tel: (800) 856-1993
        (713) 721-2517
Tours to bottom of canyon.

Safari International
3201 North Sepulveda
    Boulevard
Manhattan Beach, CA 90266
Tel: (800) 223-6046 (Canada
    and U.S.)
        (310) 546-4411

Sanborn Tours, Inc.
1007 Main Street
Bastrop, TX 78602
Tel: (800) 531-5440
        (512) 321-1131

Sierra Madre Express
P.O. Box 26381
Tucson, AZ 85726
Tel: (800) 666-0346
     (602) 747-0346

Wildland Adventures
3516 Northeast 155th Street
Seattle, WA 98155
Tel: (800) 345-4453
     (206) 365-0686

Turtle Watching

Seeing a 700-pound leatherback lay her eggs on a deserted shore in the middle of the night is an unforgettable experience. Timing is critical, since turtles only nest at specific times of year.

- In many areas poaching is common. You may be required to go to nesting grounds with a guide.
- The collecting of eggs is permitted by some countries during the earliest part of the season. The eggs are sold locally as an aphrodisiac. The rationale behind allowing some collection is that the turtles arrive up to 5 times and will scoop up the eggs anyway in laying new batches.
- Groups are sometimes limited in number.
- You often go out at night because nesting is related to tides.
- Never shine a flashlight onto a turtle. This blinds the animal and may cause it to move inland. Turtles can only stay out of water for a few hours. If they go in the wrong direction, they die. Guides have special lights which shine red, not white.
- Never take a flash photo for the same reason.
- Never stand between the turtle and the sea once she has laid her eggs. This may cause her to turn inland and die.
- Note that a few male turtles sometimes come on shore and pretend to lay eggs.
- Never touch eggs as they are deposited in the nest. This will kill them.

COSTA RICA
- Playa Grande (Nicoya Peninsula) is the nesting ground for approximately 30 leatherbacks (*Dermochelys coriacea*) from late summer to late fall.
- Playas Nancite and Naranja (Nicoya Peninsula) attract up to 75,000 turtles from August to November. Some of the prime areas may be closed in October for scientific research.
- Ostional (Nicoya Peninsula) attracts the olive ridley sea turtle to its beaches in late summer and early fall.
- Tortuguero National Park (northeastern Caribbean region) is the main breeding ground for green sea turtles in that area. Turtles come in from July to late September. The prime viewing time is

late July to early August. Some enormous leatherbacks come in primarily in April and May, although a few may come in through July. Hawksbill turtles (*Eretmochelys imbricata*) also nest from July to October in small numbers. Loggerheads (*Caretta caretta*) come in from April to July.

MEXICO
There are 9 miles of protected beach on Costa Careyes (Turtle Coast) between Puerto Vallarta and Manzanillo. Turtles come March to May:

Caribbean Conservation Corporation
P.O. Box 2866
4424 Northwest 13th Street, Suite A1
Gainesville, FL 32602
Tel: (800) 678-7853
      (904) 373-6441
An organization trying to protect endangered sea turtles: Australian flatback, green, hawksbill, Kemp's ridley, leatherback, loggerhead, and olive ridley. Please do not eat turtle (*tortuga*) or buy any products made from their shells (illegal).

Volcanoes

COSTA RICA
This is a good country for people who want to see or climb volcanoes. The most popular volcano is Poás (about 20 miles north of Alajuela). You can easily reach the crater by car or bus. The volcano is multi-colored, partially active, and quite impressive. Not quite as popular, but easily accessible up a winding mountain road is Irazú. The Arenal Volcano near Fortuna has been very active recently. During peak activity it's a major tourist attraction. The red glow is most impressive at night. Rincón de la Vieja National Park is well worth seeing. Turrialba can be visited by horseback (see Riding). Note that cloud cover is often a problem in seeing volcanoes, especially Arenal. The dry season is most highly recommended, but if you're patient, the off-season is fine.

GUATEMALA
There are many volcanoes in Guatemala. Climbing these is a popular sport. Presently, I do not recommend this. Although many people continue to climb without incident, the number of murders, rapes, and robberies is frightening.

MEXICO (SEE CLIMBING).

Waterfalls

There are many lovely waterfalls throughout the region. In Costa Rica you'll see them as you drive around the country or take long horseback rides into the mountains. However, the best is in Belize. It's called Hidden Valley Falls and drops approximately 1,000 feet. You'll find it in the Pine Ridge Mountain Area. This area is one of the prettiest in the country. It is probably best to go with a local guide or tour.

Whale Watching

Whale watching in the lagoons along Mexico's Baja is superb during the winter as they migrate south. In February and March nearly 18,000 whales congregate in the San Ignacio Lagoon. The following companies offer diverse whale watching expeditions, some short, others long. Many also include other activities from birding to trekking.

American Cetacean Society
P.O. Box 2639
San Pedro, CA 90731
Tel: (310) 548-6279
Trips to spot gray whales, snorkle, and enjoy wildlife.

Baja Expeditions, Inc.
2625 Garnet Avenue
San Diego, CA 92109
Tel: (800) 843-6967
     (619) 581-3311
Whale watching either on cruises or from land camps.

Betchart Expeditions
17050 Montebello Road
Cupertino, CA 95014
Tel: (800) 252-4910
     (408) 252-1444

Biological Journeys
1696 Ocean Drive
McKinleyville, CA 95521
Tel: (800) 548-7555
     (707) 839-0178
Cruises for whale watching,

natural history, snorkeling, hiking, and bird watching.

Fisherman's Landing
2838 Garrison Street
San Diego, CA 92106
Tel: (619) 221-8500
Whale watching on varied boats as well as deep-sea fishing.

Great Whale Trips
P.O. Box 4045
Palos Verdes, CA 90274
Tel: (310) 541-9010
Whale watching on same ship as that used by the American Cetacean Society.

Green Tortoise
P.O. Box 24459
1667 Jerrold Avenue
San Francisco, CA 94124
Tel: (800) 227-4766
     (415) 821-0803
Casual bus tours into the Baja (includes whale watching), Mexico, and Central America.

National Audubon Society
700 Broadway
New York, NY 10003
Tel: (800) 765-1228
    (212) 979-3066
Combines whale watching with birding and wildlife trips to the Baja.

Oceanic Society Expeditions
Fort Mason Center, Building E
San Francisco, CA 94123
Tel: (800) 326-7481
    (415) 441-1106
Varied whale watching tours.

Pacific Sea Fari Tours
2803 Emerson Street
San Diego, CA 92106

Tel: (619) 222-1144
Both short and long whale watching trips.

San Diego Natural History
    Museum
P.O. Box 1390
San Diego, CA 92112
Tel: (619) 232-3821 ext. 203
Both short and long whale watching trips.

Special Expeditions, Inc.
720 Fifth Avenue
New York, NY 10019
Tel: (800) 762-0003
    (212) 765-7740
Luxury and highly professional whale watching trips.

White-Water Rafting

White water rafting and river kayaking are extremely popular in Costa Rica, Honduras, and Mexico.

- Go to the library and read about white water rafting in some of the magazines, such as "American Whitewater." Many have ads for the equipment you may have to buy if you're a first-timer.
- Write or call the various companies to get an idea of what kind of trips they offer and when.
- You can also use foreign outfitters. The National Tourist Offices will provide you with the names of local agencies.
- Expect to pay more for quality tours with expert guides, qualified not only for white water but also for medical emergencies. Ask about this before booking a tour. People do get hurt.
- The better tour operators also have better equipment. Always ask about the kayaks or rafts to be used.
- Each outfitter will require you to bring varying gear. They'll provide you with a list of exact requirements.
- If you are required to bring your own paddle, put it in a ski bag. Airlines are used to ski bags, but often charge for paddles.
- You're going to get wet. Your gear will get wet too unless it's properly protected. Sporting goods stores aimed at kayakers and white water rafters will give you good advice on gear.

- Some people cannot do this sport without motion sickness. If you're prone to this, medicate before getting on the river.
- Cameras should be waterproof and protected in a bag which won't be lost if you capsize.
- Some trips are more relaxed than others. When you're traveling to view birds and wildlife, bring binoculars.
- Always bring a flashlight.
- Never dress in any camouflage outfits or carry army gear. This is inviting trouble, particularly in border areas.
- You may get Swimmer's Ear, a generic term meaning that your ear gets infected because the acidity is lowered by water and encourages bacterial growth there. Prevent the problem by dropping a few drops of vinegar in your ear after each run. If the ear gets badly infected, use antibiotics as you would for other bacterial problems.

Far-Flung Adventures
P.O. Box 377
Terlingua, TX 79852
Tel: (800) 359-4138
     (915) 371-2489
Offers trips to Mexico.

Mariah Wilderness
   Expeditions
P.O. Box 248
Point Richmond, CA 94807
Tel: (800) 233-2303
     (510) 462-7424
Costa Rica.

Mountain Travel
6420 Fairmount Avenue
El Cerrito, CA 94530
Tel: (800) 227-2384
     (510) 527-8100
Offers trips to Costa Rica.

Nantahala Outdoor Center
13077 Hwy 19 West
Bryson City, NC 28713
Tel: (704) 488-2175
One of the premiere white-

water rafting companies with trips to Costa Rica and Mexico.

Ocean Connection
211 East Parkland, Suite 108
Friendswood, TX 77546
Tel: (713) 996-7800
Offers rafting in Costa Rica and Honduras.

Riós Honduras
10281 Highway 50
Howard, CO 81233
Tel: (800) 255-5784
     (719) 942-3214
The main company exploring and expanding river trips into Honduras. It may be adding some remote rivers to its repertoire in the near future.

Slickrock Adventures, Inc.
P.O. Box 1400
76 South Main No. 1
Moab, Utah 84532
Tel: (801) 259-6996
Offers rafting in Mexico.

White Magic Unlimited
P.O. Box 5506
Mill Valley, CA 94942
Tel: (800) 869-9874
 (415) 381-8889
Costa Rica, Mexico.

COSTA RICA

Costa Rica has roughly 480 miles of white water with a wide range of difficulty. The rainy season offers best waters and lasts from June to late October or mid-November. Water is generally quite warm.

- The *Chirripo* trip is not as well known as some of the others, but it has over 100 rapids in the first 38 miles.
- A trip on the *Río General* starts in San Isidro and ends 50 miles later in El Brujo. The river starts out as a stream, ends as a torrent with waves up to 15 feet high in what is nicknamed the "Chachaloca" rapid.
- The *Río Pacuare* flows through a narrow, jungle canyon starting at San Martin and ending at Siquirres. Rapids vary from intermediate to difficult. A very scenic trip. Note that this trip may be obsolete if a proposed dam is built.
- The *Río Reventazon* is often broken into segments according to skill levels. From the Cachi powerplant to Tucurrique you'll be in Class IV rapids. From there to Angostura things are calmer. Then the river squeezes into a narrow canyon and from here on to Siquirres you'll encounter varying rapids, some rated Class V. Much of the trip is through agricultural areas, so if you want a jungle trip, go to the Pacuare.

HONDURAS

Rafting and kayaking in Honduras are just catching on. The best season for these two sports is the rainy season, equivalent to winters in the United States and Canada. This is the worst season for diving in the Bay Islands or traveling to Copan. During the rainy season the waters are high and rapid. Rafting is intense. Rivers would be rated quite high in difficulty and fall into the pool-drop category (calm waters followed by steep drops which require lots of skill).

- The *Río Congregal*, a pool drop river, falls into the Class IV-VI range. It's a spectacular trip through jungle with high ridges.
- The *Río Mame* offers continuous rapids in the Class III-IV category. The river glides by villages along the way.
- The *Cuero y Salado* is a relaxed trip, good for families, and best viewed as a wildlife rafting experience. You'll see birds, caymans (like alligators), manatees (occasionally), and monkeys.

MEXICO
- The *Río Antigua* trip is through jungle terrain and includes white water in the Class III-IV ranges.
- The *Río Chancala* falls in the class II-III category.
- The *Río Jatate* is similar to the Antigua with Class III-IV rapids and a jungle atmosphere. There are some nice waterfalls.
- Probably the most famous river trip is along the *Río Usamacinta* near the Guatemalan border. This is less of a white water trip than one oriented to archaeology, birding, and wildlife. It takes you past some minor, but fascinating Mayan ruins. Note that guerrila activity has occurred in this area, and you should ask about this before signing up for a trip.

Wildlife

The chance of seeing animals in the wild varies with the species. Some you're almost certain to see (monkeys), others are almost impossible to find (jaguars). Having a guide on a tour often helps. Here are a few organizations which really are geared to people interested in wildlife:

Friends of the National Zoo
National Zoological Park
Washington, DC 20008
Tel: (202) 673-4961
Belize, Costa Rica (trips change annually).

Imagine Travel Alternatives
P.O. Box 27023
Seattle, WA 98125
Tel: (800) 777-3975
    (206) 624-7112
Belize, Costa Rica, Guatemala, Honduras.

International Zoological
    Expeditions
210 Washington Street
Sherborn, MA 01770

Tel: (800) 548-5843
    (508) 655-1461
Belize (owns part of Southwater Caye and 200 acres of rain forest at Blue Creek), Guatemala. Works with many colleges and universities.

Nature Expeditions
    International
P.O. Box 11496
474 Willamette
Eugene, OR 97440
Tel: (800) 869-0639
    (503) 484-6529
Belize, Costa Rica, Guatemala, Mexico.

BELIZE
The Cockscombe Basin Wildlife Preserve has been established to protect habitat for the Jaguar. Whether it's a large enough area to do the job remains to be seen. Jaguars are present, but they come out at

night—not a time to be out yourself. Chances of seeing a jaguar are minimal. The Community Baboon Sanctuary is noted for the black howler monkey. These monkeys are found in other areas of Belize as well. Your chances of seeing them are very good. When the monkeys howl, it sounds almost like a giant cat roaring on your heels.

COSTA RICA
Jaguars are present in the northeastern part of the country, but you're unlikely to see one. Most wildlife is spotted in jungle treks through national parks or on boats going through preserves. The Tortuguero area is recommended but expensive to get to.

GUATEMALA
The best place for the average tourist to see wildlife is at Tikal, which also is the finest archaeological site in Central America. You'll see and hear howler monkeys as well as one other variety of monkey.

Windsurfing

COSTA RICA
Lake Arenal is well-known for its excellent winds. It's a huge, beautiful lake. The sport has really caught on here as well as along the Pacific (Jacó Beach, for example). One company specializes in this activity:

Caradonna Caribbean Tours
P.O. Box 3299
Longwood, FL 32779
Tel: (800) 328-2288
    (407) 774-9000

MEXICO
Beginning to catch on in a number of resorts and already running with the wind in the Loreto area and at the Rancho Buena Vista near La Paz.

Work

Work permits are difficult to get in Central America. However, if you are interested in staying for an extended period with a combination of low pay and volunteer spirit, consider joining the Peace Corps. It's open to people of all ages. The Oceanic Society Expeditions can give you leads on finding research-oriented work abroad.

Oceanic Society Expeditions
Fort Mason Center, Building E
San Francisco, CA 94123
Tel: (800) 326-7491
    (415) 474-3395

Peace Corps
1990 K Street Northwest
Washington, DC 20526
Tel: (800) 424-8580

Special Tips on Working Abroad

- You may be required to have an AIDS test if you plan to stay in a country for 6 months or more.
- Some countries allow you to bring in a recent test. Others require you to have one done locally. Make sure that blood is drawn with a new, just unwrapped needle.
- Often needed in Central America and Mexico are reporters (for local English newspapers) and teachers.

Yachting

If you would like to try this out, contact:

Baja Expeditions
2625 Garnet Avenue
San Diego, CA 92109
Tel: (800) 843-6967
    (619) 581-3311
Mexico's Sea of Cortez.

Ocean Voyages
1709 Bridgeway
Sausalito, CA 94965
Tel: (415) 332-4681
Belize, Costa Rica, Guatemela,
Honduras, and Mexico.

Fraser Charters, Inc.
3471 Via Lido
Newport Beach, CA 92663
Tel: (714) 675-6960
For Mexico.

Zoos

BELIZE

The Belize Zoo is just a short drive from the International Airport outside Belize City. Although small, it has a number of animals native to the area. It is very unlikely that you will see a number of these in the wild. At least, you'll know what to look for and what you've seen in the jungle if you're extremely lucky.

Trouble-Shooting

Even in the best-planned trips, something could go awry. Read the chapters on Personal Safety (p. 178) and Protecting Property (p. 173) to avoid many of the more common problems.

Arrests

If you're arrested, your rights are defined by local, not U.S. or Canadian law. These laws are quite different from ours, and your government is powerless to do much about controversial cases. For example, here's an outline of the Mexican judicial system:

- The Mexican judicial system is based on Napoleonic law. You are presumed *guilty* until proven innocent.
- There is no trial by jury. A judge decides your fate based on documents presented to him. Never admit responsibility for anything.
- You can be detained for 72 hours without being charged.
- Although bail exists, it rarely is allowed—they assume (often quite rightly) that you'll split the minute you're free.
- There is presently an agreement for prisoner exchange.

Car Accidents

Yes, accidents do happen. Even minor ones can be serious.

Minor Accidents

If you have a minor accident (*accidente*) and no other car is involved, take off. Running off the road, nailing a wandering goat or burro, missing a corner and hitting a sign—these qualify as minor accidents. If the police get involved, you've got trouble.

- If you have a fender-bender, follow the local resident's lead. If he wants to exchange information, fine. If he splits, do the same. Remain totally polite and calm—never get into an argument. Try to avoid any police involvement.

Serious Accidents

If you're involved in a serious accident and if you're at fault, you can be open to criminal charges.

- Be prepared for lengthy questions and a detailed report. These reports are used in court. Admit to nothing.
- The language and cultural barriers put you at a disadvantage.
- You're assumed to be wealthy. By local standards, you are.
- All people involved are detained while police determine responsibility, which in turn determines your fate.

- In practice the police often split responsibility for an accident so that both insurance companies have to pay up.
- Contact your insurance company as soon as possible after an accident. Good insurance will keep your stay with the police short and sweet (or a little less bitter).

If You See An Accident...
- If you see an accident, don't stop unless you feel you can give first aid *before* police arrive on the scene.
- Residents advise tourists not to stop since they can be blamed for an accident in which they were not even involved.
- This is a very difficult decision, but you can get into deep trouble, including a suit for medical malpractice.

Drunken Driving
If you get arrested for drunk driving, you are in trouble.
- If you have been drinking, you're liable for criminal charges. Since "drinking" is a vague term meaning anything from a glass of wine to a total stupor, don't drink at all before driving.
- In short, take a taxi if you've had any alcohol to drink.

Traffic Violations
- In Belize the roads are so bad that violations are rare.
- In Costa Rica speeds are occasionally posted. Most roads are so poor that you couldn't possibly go faster than the speed limits. If you are pulled over, do not pay for the ticket. If the police tell you that you have to pay on the spot or return to the capital immediately, they are lying. You will have to pay for the ticket at the appropriate office. The process can be long and frustrating. But payment is not to the cop. Nor does it have to be made immediately in San José.
- In Mexico the police generally leave traffic to the survival of the fittest. Mexicans routinely disobey signs and speed laws.
- If you're pulled over for a traffic ticket, you're in a situation where the police are milking the tourists and the cows. When requested for a certain amount, hand the cop less than what was asked for—that will often do the trick.

Documents
- Always carry appropriate identification with you. If you don't have your passport or a photocopy or are not carrying the local tourist card (or its equivalent), you can be arrested.

Drug Dealing
- Do not use drugs—it's not worth the risk, even though you can't help smelling the stuff frequently. It's especially common in Belize, Costa Rica, and Mexico.
- If you're jailed for dealing in drugs, God help you. Sentences served in foreign jails are best described as *intolerable*. The present sentence for drug dealing in Honduras is 20 years.
- The same people who sell drugs often play a double role as police informant. It's a bad scene. Skip it.

Homosexuality
- It is not considered unusual for people of the same sex to share a room. It won't raise an eyebrow. Any open display of homosexuality or lesbianism can easily get you into trouble.

Illegally Exporting Artifacts
Although it's legal to take antiques out of many countries, it is illegal to take out any genuine Pre-Columbian artifacts.

Nudity is Illegal
Extreme modesty is the norm. Nudity requires extreme discretion and caution.
- As far as local residents are concerned, it's never hot enough to take it all off.
- In the most popular beach areas appealing primarily to tourists you can get away with the barest of essentials. Women can even go topless and nearly bottomless *if* they're surrounded by other foreigners doing the same thing (mostly in Mexico).
- On a few beaches nudity is more or less tolerated, as at El Mirador, roughly a mile south of the ruins of Tulúm in Mexico. But keep clothes handy, just in case.
- Inland, it's extremely offensive to be caught nude. If you're hiking and want to clean up, keep something on. And men and women should never wash together in the altogether.
- Remember, too, inland waters are often polluted.
- Women should note that nude bathing may attract admiring machos. The situation can turn hot, especially if they've been drinking. Nudity implies sexual promiscuity.

Soliciting Sex
While nudity is provocative, prostitution is either legal or tolerated. It doesn't have to make sense, it's just the way it is. Sex between consenting adults for pleasure or pay is just plain okay.

Pornographic Material

Don't bring in magazines or materials which could be considered obscene even by prudish standards. Movies, for example, are heavily censored in Costa Rica even though the red light district flourishes.

If You're Arrested

Getting arrested abroad is extremely serious.

- Call the nearest embassy or consulate immediately. This call is guaranteed by international law.
- Although the consulate has no power to get you released, it can provide many vital services.
- Once in jail, don't pay anyone for a "quick release"—a con.
- Don't hire a lawyer or pay out any "bribes," until you've talked to the embassy or consulate. They have detailed information on local scams. They also know who, how, and when to bribe people—not that they would ever admit it.
- You are entitled to have an oral translation of any document you sign.
- Don't have money sent to you in jail. Checks and money orders are commonly cashed—fraudulently. Have the consulate or embassy help you with transfer of funds.

Lost or Stolen Items

Report losses to the police. Keep a copy of the report for insurance. Also, report all thefts and problems to U.S. and Canadian consulates, since they keep statistics on such incidents. Do not expect to retrieve stolen goods. It is considered your responsibility to protect them.

Lost Passports

- If you lose your passport in the United States, report the loss immediately to the local branch of the Justice Department.
- If you lose your passport in Canada, report its loss to the nearest passport office. There is one in each province.
- If you lose your passport abroad, contact the nearest U.S. or Canadian consulate or embassy.
- As a precaution, carry two spare passport photos, a notarized copy of your birth certificate, and a photocopy of the information in your passport. This will speed up the process of getting a new one if the original is lost.

Lost Entry Permits
- Guard any entry permit as if it were a passport.
- Make a photocopy (*fotocopia*) of any entry permit and use that for identification. Leave the *original* in a safe place.
- If you lose the original, report it to the police and consulate.
- A photocopy will be invaluable in getting a new permit.

Lost Traveler's Checks
- Report the loss immediately to the appropriate company. You'll need the numbers of all checks lost.
- If a company tries to reimburse you in local currency, simply refuse. Say that you want new checks.
- Have your passport with you when filing a claim.
- Before traveling, get a list of offices abroad and a toll-free number for problem resolution.

Lost Credit Cards
- The faster you report a lost credit card, the better. If you report a card before it's used fraudulently, you're not liable for any charges. In any event, your liability is usually limited to $50.
- Before traveling, ask for a toll-free number which you can call in the case of such a loss.

Lost Luggage
If you've followed the advice of never packing irreplaceable items in checked bags, you'll be relatively calm (if frustrated).
- Report the loss to the airline representative. Be polite but vocal about the loss and note the representative's name.
- If the airline can't find your bags, file a written notice. You'll need a detailed list of the bag's contents. It helps if you've already made one out.
- Get a copy of the claim and do not surrender your claim checks, the only proof that the airline has indeed lost your bags. If the airline insists on keeping a claim check, get a written receipt for it and the name of the person who takes it from you.
- Ask the airline to deliver your bags to your hotel in town if they are recovered shortly.
- You can also ask for emergency funds to handle necessities. In the United States you'll be given an overnight kit and enough money to buy odds and ends. Don't count on this abroad, but you can always ask.
- If the airline loses your bags permanently, you'll be paid a set

amount by the airline. This is just a token amount abroad. In the United States and Canada the limit is higher.

- You may have to prove the value of lost items with *receipts*. Who can do that? And then each item will be depreciated.
- If you're concerned about this, take out baggage insurance.

Dealing with Damaged Luggage

- If bags are damaged, check the contents immediately.
- If you find damaged goods, file a claim on the spot—not later. Corner an airline representative and get a copy of the claim form. You may be reimbursed for damage done to the bag and its contents.
- To collect money the airline has the right to collect your bag and its contents in return.
- A claim for *any* bag that is overpacked will be disqualified.

Lost Cars or RVs

- If you have a rental car or truck stolen, report it immediately to the company. Your responsibility is often limited to a set deductible if you've taken out insurance (see p. 95).
- If your own car or RV gets stolen (not just parts of it), report the theft to the police, your insurance company, and the consulate nearest you.
- The consulate is especially helpful in advising you how to handle this *delicate* situation, since there is always the suspicion that you sold the car.
- Furthermore, your entry documentation has been stamped *con automóvil* which means you cannot leave the country without it—that is, without paying duty.
- If the hassle becomes overwhelming in Mexico, here's the solution: Go to a border town and walk across the border with day visitors (tourist cards are not required for short stays within 14 miles of the border).
- Okay, the solution is *not* what you want to do, and it's definitely *not* what the Mexicans want you to do—this is a case of both sides not getting what they want. It's also illegal.
- The same approach may apply to a car crippled in a serious accident. But check on the insurance ramifications before abandoning a wrecked car in Mexico!

Problems With Police and Military

- Military and police inspections are routine and rarely include body searches. They're most common along the coasts and borders.

- Always stop at checkpoints. If you don't, you may be shot.
- Mexico does have secret police.
- Never take photos of police or military personnel.
- Never become hostile or angry with police.
- Never wear camouflage clothing in Central America or Mexico.
- Never wear any military gear whatsoever, including army boots.

Bribes
- Bribes (*mordidas*) are also a fact of life, but most tourists rarely find themselves in a bribe situation.
- If you are asked for a bribe, the best thing is to ignore the request. If the person turns nasty, pay the "tip".
- Don't go abroad expecting to pay bribes. You can cover yourself in most situations so that you don't have to.
- However, if you're in a tight spot, use a bribe to get out of it.

Police Rip-offs
Police like to confiscate all knives, even if they're just for filleting fish. Don't make a scene over the loss of a knife. Electronic equipment is also a favorite item to be taken—without any real reason. Here I would make a stand, unless I felt physically threatened. If you think that the police have ripped you off, *write* a formal complaint to:

Dirección de Supervision
Departamento de Quejas
Secretarío de Turismo
Presidente Mazaryk 172
Colonia Polanco
México 5, D.F.

- If you think you're being ripped off in Mexico City, call 250-8555. Ask for extension 223. Or Call 250-0123. Don't be afraid to call this office if you're right in the midst of a ripoff.

Problems With Customs

If you have registered valuable items before traveling abroad, if you declare all of the items purchased abroad, and if you don't try to bring in any illegal item, you should have no problems with customs.

Oral Declarations
- You must declare the total value of purchases. If under $400 per person, make an oral declaration.
- A head of household makes a declaration for the whole family.

- Note that many items are duty-free if purchased from developing countries (see p. 311).

Written Declarations
- If over your $400 personal exemption, you have to fill out a written declaration.
- Anything related to business must be declared.
- You are required to make a written declaration if asked by a customs inspector to do so.

Possible Snags in Customs
- Things for sale abroad may not be allowed into the United States. Call your local customs office for up-to-date regulations. Most problems occur with archaeological artifacts, birds, bullion or gold coins, plant materials (especially orchids without special permits), products made from endangered species, products made in Cuba or North Korea, products made in prisons, and trademarked items (scrape off the trademark).
- If drugs contain controlled substances, have a prescription with you.
- If you've got more than $10,000, you must fill out a form with customs.
- If an official catches you bringing in something that you haven't declared, admit the mistake immediately. Just say that you forgot about it. Avoid confrontations and arguments.
- If an official breaks an item while searching bags, file a U.S. Government form SF9-5 with the regional customs office in the state where the damage takes place. You'll be reimbursed.

Custom Inspection Tips
- Have your registration slip at hand for valuable articles that you took from the United States, or you'll have to pay duty on them if you're over the $400 personal exemption.
- Have all your sales receipts handy to prove cost. Customs officials know values almost to the cent. Don't use doctored sales receipts.
- Put all purchased items in one spot, so that it's easy to check them over. The official may feel the corners of your bags, but often he'll take your statement at face value.
- *Never* carry bags or items for someone else through customs— you don't know what's in them. What would you do if they found something illegal?
- A customs official may ask you to empty your pockets, and very rarely may ask for a body search.

- You're expected to be slightly nervous going through an inspection. But don't make jokes, jabber, or volunteer information. Answer all questions as politely and briefly as possible.
- It is common for dogs to inspect all bags for drugs as you wait in line to clear customs.

Problems with Customs
If you have a problem with customs or think that a duty seems unreasonable, take up your complaint with the following person:

Assistant Commissioner
Office of Inspection and Control
U.S. Customs Service
Washington, DC 20229
Tel: (202) 566-8195

U.S. State Liquor Regulations
- Each state in the United States has its own regulations on the amount of liquor which can be imported from abroad. This ranges from no restrictions to no liquor at all. If you intend to import liquor, write for the pamphlet summarizing local liquor laws published by the following organization:

Distilled Spirits Council of the United States, Inc.
1250 I Street Northwest, Suite 900
Washington, DC 20005
Tel: (202) 628-3544

Canadian Customs

- Canada allows a personal exemption on goods purchased abroad. Once each year, you're allowed to bring in $300 worth of goods duty-free *if* you stayed abroad for a week or longer.
- Smaller exemptions are allowed for shorter stays.
- After a one-week stay you're also allowed to import 40 ounces of alcohol, 50 cigars, 200 cigarettes, and 2 pounds of tobacco.
- Register all valuables with customs before going abroad. You'll fill out form Y-38 which applies to items with serial numbers.
- If an item has no serial number, have a bill of sale or an appraisal with photo (signed and dated) to prove that the product was of Canadian origin. It's easier to leave valuables at home!
- You're not allowed to import alligators, cacti, cats (wild), crocodiles, falcons, ivory, monkeys, orchids, otters, and sea turtles—or the products made from these endangered species.

- You're allowed to send gifts to friends and relatives as long as the value is less than $40. Check locally for current restrictions and regulations since they change frequently.

Problems with Local Residents

There are a few things worth noting about cultural differences. They can cause some bitterness, anger, and resentment.

Bureaucracy
The bureaucracy in this region has been described as stifling, rigid, and illogical. It is so time-consuming that local residents actually hire people to handle bureaucratic paperwork on a fee basis. A simple trip to a large bank to cash a few dollars will give you an inkling about just how frustrating a transaction can be. Imagine if it were something more complex.

Con Games
Most con games involve the sale of land. Always check with the local branch of the American Chamber of Commerce for information on competent organizations and lawyers who will help you through an intricate maze of local regulations.

Corruption
Just as do many of our cities, so does much of Central America and Mexico work on a bribe system. No one pretends it doesn't exist. For the average traveler bribes (*mordidas*) are rarely a problem, especially if you stay out of trouble.

Good Intentions
Many local residents appreciate our attempt to help save tropical rain forests and endangered species. However, any lectures or bullying attitude are highly resented. Our record has not exactly been spotless. The fact is that the rain forests are being destroyed as are many birds, mammals, and sea creatures. But, where are the buffalo?

Indians
Indians are abused locally as they have been in Canada and the United States. Many of them cannot speak Spanish. The word *indio* (Indian) is considered abusive. The word *indígena* is preferred.

Lying
You will be lied to. You're considered fare game. The purpose of lying is usually to separate you from your money—nothing else. In a

few instances, lying is considered a polite thing to do. For example, when you ask someone a direction, they want to be helpful even if they don't have the faintest idea what to tell you. So you learn to ask twice or even three times to reconfirm what the first person tells you.

Machismo
The Latin sense of manliness occasionally borders on insanity. Avoid all confrontations while driving. Men should not get into drinking matches or similar male games. Women should not flirt or accept drinks or gifts from any man unless they intend to send out a sexual message. Obviously, if you're staying with a family or are introduced to someone, having dinner or drinks does not matter.

Time
You're entering into cultures where time has a different meaning. If you're spinning at 45, slow down to 33. Offices may be closed at odd times or for no reason at all. People may be gone from an office at odd times or for no reason at all. We're considered overly compulsive. They're considered inconsiderate. In reality, we're different.

Using the Word American
From the time we're born we call ourselves Americans. Canadians, Mexicans, Central Americans, and South Americans are also Americans. It may seem like a minor point, but when asked where you're from, say the United States (*los Estados Unidos*), not America.

Index